From Pantry to Table

From Pantry to Table

Creative Cooking from the Well-stocked Kitchen

MARLENA SPIELER

ARIS BOOKS

▲
▼▼

ADDISON-WESLEY PUBLISHING COMPANY, INC.

READING, MASSACHUSETTS   MENLO PARK, CALIFORNIA   NEW YORK

DON MILLS, ONTARIO   WOKINGHAM, ENGLAND   AMSTERDAM   BONN

SYDNEY   SINGAPORE   TOKYO   MADRID   SAN JUAN

PARIS   SEOUL   MILAN   MEXICO CITY   TAIPEI

Many of the designations used by manufacturers and sellers to distinguish their products are claimed as trademarks. Where those designations appear in this book and Addison-Wesley was aware of a trademark claim, the designations have been printed in initial capital letters (e.g., Tabasco).

Library of Congress Cataloging-in-Publication Data

Spieler, Marlena.
    From pantry to table : creative cooking from the well-stocked kitchen / Marlena Spieler.
      p. cm.
    Includes index.
    ISBN 0-201-56795-4
    ISBN 0-201-57072-6 (pbk.)
    1. Cookery, American. I. Title. II. Series.
TX715.S756 1991
641.5973—dc20   91-2645
                                        CIP

Text design by Helene Berinsky
Cover design by Diana Coe
Cover and text illustrations by Andrea Brooks
Set in 10-1/2 point Palatino by G&S Typesetters, Inc.

1 2 3 4 5 6 7 8 9-VB-9594939291
First printing, August 1991

To Leah, with love and appreciation

CONTENTS

ACKNOWLEDGMENTS

Deepest thanks to:
Teresa Chris, agent and friend

◆◆◆◆◆◆

John Harris, esteemed editor, for his focus on the pantry; Amanda Hamilton for her friendship and Macintosh; Joyce Goldstein for her excellent suggestions and enthusiasm; the following publications in which I first published versions of many of the recipes in this book: *Cook's Magazine*, *Bon Appétit*, *Taste* (Britain), and the *San Francisco Chronicle*; also to Leslie Forbes and Paul Richardson, sources of fun and inspiration.

◆◆◆◆◆◆

Josephine and India Aspin, Alex Bratell, Fred and Mary Barclay, Lena Ruth Gilbert, Paula Levine, David Lane and Rebecca Urwitz-Lane, Jo McAllister, Gretchen Spieler, Wayne Strei, and Dinah and Noah Stroe, for testing, tasting, and enthusiasm. To my cat Freud, for eating his way through the recipe testing and for warming up the computer by sleeping on it.

◆◆◆◆◆◆

◆◆◆

My grandmother, Sophia Dubowsky, for her love of cooking and feeding those dear to her; and for her own appreciation of good food.

◆◆◆◆◆◆◆

My parents, Caroline and Izzy Smith, and my Aunt Estelle and Uncle Sy Opper.

◆◆◆◆◆◆◆

Alan McLaughlan, for making everything taste wonderful.

◆◆◆◆◆◆◆

Leah Spieler, for her patience and understanding, as well as her endless tasting.

LIST OF RECIPES

Appetizers

Salads

Soups

Pastas and Grains

Main Courses: Meat, Fish, Poultry and Vegetarian Plates

Vegetable Side Dishes

Cheese and Egg Dishes

Sandwiches, Tacos, etc.

Breakfast and Supper Dishes

Beverages

Baked Things

Barbecue, Grilled, and Picnic Foods

Sweets

Spice Mixtures and Seasonings

Condiments, Relishes, Pickles, Dressings, and Sauces

INTRODUCTION

F_resh, fresh, fresh_ has long been the dictum of contemporary American cuisine. And well it should be, blessed as we are with an abundance of fruits and vegetables, poultry, meats, and fish. But while the freshness of ingredients forms the basis of our way of eating, it is the flavoring ingredients and oils, as well as dried foods such as beans, rice, pasta, and so on that make our cooking distinctive.

For instance, add any of the bright flavors that have become part of the American palate, to fresh zucchini, and the possibilities for wonderful dishes are endless: zucchini sautéed with olive oil and garlic, stir-fried with soy and sesame, steamed and marinated with sun-dried tomatoes in balsamic vinaigrette, simmered in a curry-scented soup, and on and on. This often spontaneous combination of fresh food with stored ingredients yields a wealth of varied and enticing meals full of strong, delicious flavors yet quick and simple to prepare.

While some of the ingredients may be quintessentially contemporary, there is nothing new about this kind of cooking. Nor is it difficult or time-consuming. It is the way great cooks work. And here in America, we have a wide variety of exciting condiments, spices, pickles, oils, legumes, and grains from all over the world as well as from our own backyard. I think it's fair to say that yesterday's foreign exotics are to-day's local staples.

Our contemporary pantry thus reflects the foreign shores that have become so accessible to our travel; the exceptional restaurants we have grown to expect in the last decade or so; the wonderful array of cook-books available to us that yield often-exotic foods to our tables and also make enticing bedside reading; our indigenous foodstuffs and Native American food heritage; and finally, the waves of ethnic cultures that have formed and continue to form and enrich the culture of America.

Keeping a pantry full of exciting ingredients gives us an opportunity for creativity and expression, too, for what we keep in the pantry is what flavors our entire cuisine. Just as a glance through someone's bookshelf reveals the tastes and outlook of the reader, so too does the contents of his or her pantry.

In this book I had hoped to create a thorough compendium of ingre-dients and how to use them. The more I worked, however, the more ingredients and possibilities I discovered, and the larger the project be-came. Even a ten-volume set would likely be inadequate to catalogue it all. So, please accept my apologies for any omissions that scream out to you, and enjoy and share the discoveries that you make on your own.

Our Traditions of Pantry

The concept of pantry and civilization go hand in hand, dividing primi-tive hunters and foragers from those who plant and reap. Though no doubt the hunter-gatherers stored any extra foodstuffs, cultivation produced a larger yield of storable products, i.e. grains and legumes. Producing surplus foodstuffs to store for following seasons and for trading created the free time needed to take the first steps toward civilization.

What the ancients kept in their pantries tells us about the texture of their everyday life. The Aztecs, as early as 6,000 years ago, had devel-oped a sophisticated cuisine based on dried and preserved food: corn, beans, and chilies. These were combined with whatever fresh foods were available. Similarly, native North Americans kept stores of corn and grains, smoked fish, and dried vegetables.

The Romans and Greeks stocked their pantries with some sophisti-cated foods: in addition to grains, they kept dried figs and salted olives, jugs of honeyed wine, and an array of spices culled from their empire's extended territories. Perhaps the most interesting ingredient in the ancient Roman pantry, however, was garum. A pungent-smelling seasoning sauce based on fermented fish, garum was kept in large ceramic jugs and was splashed with abandon onto nearly every food.

By the Middle Ages, European architecture became specialized, and the interiors of private homes were separated into rooms devoted to specific tasks. Pantry rooms were often built next to the kitchen. In them were hung slabs of salted meat and fish, crocks of pickled vegetables, baskets of nuts, dried fruits, and jars of fragrant spices.

With the discovery of the "New World" began the most remarkable exchange of ingredients history had ever seen. Within an amazingly short period of time American foods such as potatoes, tomatoes, paprika, chilies, coffee, and chocolate transformed the eating habits of the rest of the world. From Europe to the Americas came cooking oils and fats, domesticated animals, and a wealth of spices from Asia as well as rice and tea. It is remarkable to think of the extent to which the world's cuisines were altered: imagine Hungarian food without paprika, Italian without tomatoes, Thai or Indian food without chilies.

Before the Industrial Revolution, foods were preserved with salt, smoke, brine, or by drying and pickling. Many of these foods, such as sauerkraut, bacon, kimchee, dried mushrooms, and fruit preserves, originated out of necessity but are now eaten for flavor rather than because of their keeping qualities. With the industrial age came canning, a revolutionary food-preservation method, and later, freezing, which has the advantage of retaining more flavor, texture, color, and nutritional value than does canning.

In America we have a strong tradition of keeping a pantry, dating back to the early settlers. Because of the huge distances between the farms, towns, and cities, along with harsh winters that made transport difficult, a pantry was necessary to sustain a family through the blustery winter. Usually a room set aside from the kitchen (though sometimes a cellar was used), the pantry could be filled to bursting with the basic foods needed to survive the coming year: shelf after shelf of home-canned vegetables, fruit preserves, jars of pickles, crocks of sugar, bags of flour, sacks of grains and beans, hanging slabs of bacon, baskets of root vegetables, and so forth.

The tradition continued until the Second World War, even in urban areas. The typical pantry at that time was a small storage room set off from the kitchen, often containing a cupboard that opened onto the outside, protected by thick screens of wire mesh. In the winter this cool cupboard acted as a simple refrigerator, keeping milk and prepared foods cool and relatively safe to eat.

With the advent of our modern urban lifestyle, the entire concept of pantry almost disappeared. Women working outside the home during World War Two returned to the role of homemaker as the men returned from abroad. Yet traditional home cooking did not return to the family table. Indeed, the "modern" fifties culinary scene was dominated by packaged foods, sold to the American public as better than old-fashioned dishes made from scratch. These foods were available in the corner grocery or supermarket, and did not need many added ingredients. To make a cake, one bought a cake mix; ditto for pizza. Frozen meals, beginning with the TV dinner, appeared, and the whole concept of cooking fresh foods along with savory flavoring ingredients began to disappear. Note, too, that the dominant dietary advice of the day emphasized meat and vegetables, and overcooking was seen as the way to rid food of frightening germs. Ethnic flavors were forgotten in deference to the all-American hamburger, broiled steak, baked potato, and roast chicken.

The natural foods movement of the sixties and seventies returned fresh foods to our tables and perked up our interest in exotic and ethnic cuisines. At the same time our cultural horizons were expanding, and travel, courtesy of the jumbo jet, was suddenly available to much of the population. Americans were beginning to appreciate the new flavors they found, and waves of immigration brought unfamiliar cultures and foods to our shores. Our appetites were rapidly becoming global.

The eighties honed our taste for sophisticated restaurant food, culminating in the chef-as-celebrity phenomenon and in an unabashed enthusiasm for the pleasures of the table. Today, fickle food trends are being replaced by a return to real food: hearty but healthy, sophisticated yet homey and rustic, with big, robust flavors.

It is true that Americans are cooking less, and that family mealtime isn't the everyday occurrence it once was; many of us are simply too busy to spend much time preparing complicated meals from scratch. Maintaining a well-stocked pantry allows us to cook exciting everyday food with a minimum of fuss, even for the busiest of us.

Against this changing backdrop, American cuisine is flourishing. Our interest in good food has never been keener, and while we may be cooking less often, we are enjoying the process of preparation more because we are learning how to do it quickly, healthfully, and intelligently. The pantry today is like an in-home supermarket, with a wide variety of flavoring ingredients on hand to enliven and enrich the fresh foods we pick up at the market or gather from the garden.

Regional Cuisines

Enthusiasm for America's regional cuisines has reached the level once reserved for foreign ones. Each region of our nation has a way of eating that reflects not only its geography, but its ethnic structure, history, and heritage. Along with specialty dishes, each region has its own pantry foods. California, with its Mediterranean climate, innovative attitude, and varied population, dotes on olive oil, garlic, hot peppers, pastas, and Asian and Latin ingredients. Louisiana simmers exuberant chilies and spices into its Cajun and Creole fare: andouille sausages, red beans, hot pepper sauce, ham hocks, and gumbo filé. The Southwest enjoys a diet built on chilies and tortillas. The Northwest focuses on foresty things such as mushrooms and wild berries, and foods from the sea, such as the superb smoke-dried salmon found at roadside shops (virtually the same food local Native Americans have always kept in their larder). On the East Coast you'll find a breakfast cornmeal sausage called scrapple in Philadelphia, along with the sweet and hot peppers served with cheese-steak sandwiches; Vermont pantries feature maple syrup and sweets made from that distinctively scented sweet. In New York, most pantries will have good kosher dills, maybe a garlicky salami, some smoked mozzarella, and a selection of pasta and herbs from the local deli; in Florida, Cuban foods are joining the ethnic lineup. A pantry in the Southeast might have a preserved ham, a box of hominy grits, and a bottle of bourbon. Midwestern food, the mention of which until recent years brought only an indulgent smile to the lips of sophisticates, now commands culinary attention for its meats, grains, baked goods—even good ol' mashed potatoes. Especially mashed potatoes. All of these are basic, good American foods.

A Return to the Pleasures of the Home Table

Our interest in good food has reached an unprecedented intensity. Some call it a return to home cooking, since the focus has shifted from the restaurant to the home. (Glance through an architectural journal or home-decor magazine, and you will see homes designed with the kitchen as the central room so that all can partake in the preparation of the meal as well as the eating. Pantries are increasingly prominent in these open-kitchen designs, whether as separate rooms or as specialized shelving and storage systems.) The food we are enjoying, however, is quite different from what we grew up eating. To be sure, there are the heirloom dishes: Granny's baked apples, Mamma's Irish stew, Uncle Ned's killer chili con carne and so on. Yet we are also borrowing what everyone else grew up eating. Bagels and cream cheese, enchiladas, stir-fried vegetables, and *pasta con pomidori* no longer necessarily reflect the ethnic heritage of those who eat it, because we all do. With our new, extended-boundary cuisine, keeping a large pantry once again makes consummate sense. Our diets boast a heretofore unimaginable range of foods and flavorings, most of which would not long ago have been considered exotic. Having them on hand in the pantry (including the freezer) gives us a "palette" for flavoring the fresh foods that form the basis of our contemporary diet.

Confessions of a Pantry Fanatic

My first experience with the possibilities that a good pantry provides involved larceny. I was stranded along with friends in a farmhouse in the Dutch countryside. It was a long holiday weekend, with all the shops closed for three days. I was completely unprepared, with no food stocked except for a few pantry items. The first morning was fun; we nibbled at various crackers and jams accompanied by pots of good strong tea. Then the serious hunger pangs set in. Across the street was a farm with the largest mountain of potatoes I had ever seen, and the farmer was conveniently gone for the weekend.

Over the next several days I visited and revisited that pile of potatoes, returning for the makings of each meal. My pantry contained hot pepper sauce, eggs, vegetable oil and olive oil, lemons, garlic, onions, canned tomatoes, and anchovies, among other ingredients. Along with the potatoes, it fed us well: thick potato soup, vinaigrette-dressed potato salad with silky anchovies, a hearty casserole of sliced potatoes and lots of chopped herbs I gathered from the field. We enjoyed a platter of crisp golden fries sprinkled with a bit of vinegar and hot pepper sauce; chunks of potatoes simmered in tomato-and-herb ragú; a bowl of freshly boiled potatoes with aïoli for dipping. No two meals were alike, thanks to the pantry.

Another time I was snowed in with a group of friends during a fierce Oregon winter. We had brown rice, olive oil, dried herbs, garlic, lemons, a vast quantity of sesame seeds, a few cans of tomatoes, a cabbage, a handful of potatoes, and, for some inexplicable reason, in the middle of a snowstorm our pantry yielded two gleaming purple eggplants. We soon tired of each others' company, but never of the meals: sesame seeds ground into tahini one day, toasted and crushed into sesame salt the next, made into a halva-like sweet another day. Tomatoes were combined with dried chilies into savory salsas and spooned over brown rice, or used as a dressing for cabbage and potato salads. By the time the snow let up I had once again realized the importance of keeping a good pantry.

In practical terms, a well-stocked pantry gives you the ability to come home at the end of a long day and, with the addition of a few fresh vegetables and perhaps a little meat or fish, put together a satisfying and pleasurable meal. At times, you can eat exclusively from the pantry, and at other times, when you have the luxury of an entire afternoon to devote to cooking, your pantry gives you the potential for creativity and lets you enjoy the process rather than wasting time searching in the shops for this or that hard-to-locate ingredient.

With an abundant pantry I often find myself indulging in a bit of what I call "forage cooking." Traditionally this means seeking and culling food from the wilds, but to me it is based on perusing the pantry shelves, then flinging open the refrigerator door and seeing what bits and pieces can be assembled into a delicious meal. Bottled green olives can be warmed with chopped garlic, rosemary, hot peppers, and a splash of vinegar for an appetizer; canned chick peas or butter beans are brilliant simmered with a garlicky tomato sauce for a pasta topping. Sardines can be mashed with refried beans and used as a spread for crispy tostadas; lentils can be stewed with carrots and spicy sausages; pasta can be tossed with ginger, hot peppers, garlic, and olive oil or with strips of olives and prosciutto, or with red beans, peppers, and tomatoes. Even a cheese sandwich can be transformed by bottled salsa, or chopped green olives, or *giardiniera* (that wonderful Italian mix of pickled vegetables).

With a well-stocked pantry our eating enjoyment is limited only by our imagination. I hope you will enjoy preparing and eating the following collection of dishes based on the contents of my own pantry as much as I have enjoyed gathering and creating them.

I ◆ Creating a Pantry

GETTING STARTED: THE BASIC, INTERMEDIATE, AND ADVANCED PANTRY

The contemporary kitchen offers much potential in the way of food storage space. The pantry can be no more than several shelves set aside, or a whole cupboard. It can also encompass an entire room dedicated to the purpose.

The organization of a pantry depends on individual preference. Common sense is your best ally in organizing your pantry since no hard and fast rules apply. Keep oils and vinegars together, unless you use any of them primarily as condiments rather than for cooking or for dressings (such as Asian sesame oil, for example); similarly, ethnic ingredients such as soy sauce, curry pastes and chutneys, olive oil and anchovies, etc., seem to work best grouped together. Grains and legumes go together; and mustards make a nice grouping, as do jars of condiments: sun-dried tomatoes, pesto, olive paste, capers, etc. Practicality and your own taste will dictate what works best. The important thing is to keep the ingredients out of direct sunlight and away from heat sources. Specifics on storage are covered in individual sections to follow.

Where to Put Your Pantry

Like individual tastes, each person's pantry reflects his or her esthetics. And you don't need a designer kitchen to assemble a good pantry. Limitations of space should be seen as challenges to be overcome rather than roadblocks. Even the tiniest kitchen has space for a few shelves to house your selection of well-chosen ingredients.

Since some of the delight of many ingredients is visual—from the foreign-language labels with their striking graphics to distinctive and unusually shaped bottles and cans—try not to shut them behind a closed door. Think of your pantry as a still life, an ever-changing arrangement of intriguing foods that make your surroundings all the more attractive to be in. Though a closed door does keep foods cooler and darker, thereby adding to their storage life, their charm also is hidden from view. And in terms of practicality, you are less likely to use pantry foods if they are not visible.

One of the most beautiful pantries I have seen was at a cooking school: a long and airy room with light pine shelves lining the walls, and at the far end a large window overlooking a field of herbs and fruit trees, and a hillside dotted with sheep. Along the shelves were assorted oils, vinegars, liqueurs, flours, grains, and bunches of dried herbs. Work counters lined the walls, and underneath were baskets filled with onions, potatoes, shallots, and garlic. Students came and left the pantry, gathering ingredients, occasionally gazing out the window as they went about their tasks.

A more unusual pantry, belonging to a cookbook-author friend, leads into a cave that tunnels into the hillside outside her kitchen. The insulation of the earth keeps the cave-room cool in summer as well as winter. The most attractive bottles, jars, and containers are kept on shelves in the kitchen.

A closet with its door removed from the hinges also makes a wonderful pantry, as does a freestanding bookcase or a metal shelf system.

A pantry can be organized around the dining area as well. A wall lined with narrow shelves can hold a huge amount of pantry ingredients: add a sliding door, either a folding or Japanese paper-type one, and the room can be either formal or informal, depending on whether or not the door is opened. One friend of mine kept her pantry and extensive wine collection on shelves lining her rather formal dining room. The mixture of classical paintings, bottles of wines and containers of exotic ingredients made it an exciting room to sit in. The dining table sat regally in the middle of the room, and the only drawback was the constant cool temperature needed for the well-being of the wine. Dinner at that house meant wearing several sweaters, but I never minded.

Country pantries have their own special appeal. I remember one with long wooden boards running along its length, heavy with rows of big unmatched jars, each holding a different legume, grain, herb, pickle, and so on. Arranged randomly, it was terribly appealing. The dining table sat in the center of the room; I think fondly of meals eaten there, with good friends around the table and a variety of colors, shapes, and patterns lining the pantry shelves.

My current pantry consists of floor-to-ceiling metal shelving fitted into an alcove in a brick wall in my converted-warehouse flat. Inevitably guests are drawn into conversations by the ever-changing items that line the shelves. The graphics and charmingly busy quality of the labels and tins is particularly attractive next to the starkly modern brick, the high ceilings, and the huge leaded windows. The shelves, in addition to having a pleasingly high-tech look, can be moved around the apartment or disassembled for moving. And due to the lack of solid wooden shelves and sides, the ingredients are more visible.

For a more classic display, I collect flea market and antique cupboards and bookshelves. Several of these, placed in various parts of my kitchen and dining room, show off pantry foods elegantly; I especially like small glass-doored cupboards for spices. In Brittany, it is a tradition to use an old armoire, the type used for hanging clothing in, for storing homemade liqueurs and fruit preserves. Closed, it looks graceful and elegant; open, it is a veritable treasure trove.

Storing spices is often a problem because no commercial spice shelf offers enough room for the modern cook. Besides the above-mentioned glass-doored cupboards, my solution is to build a stack of narrow wall-anchored shelves, adding another shelf as needed to accommodate a growing spice collection. Remember not to store spices above the stove, however. That is the warmest spot in the kitchen, and spices kept there will deteriorate rapidly.

The walls and ceiling beams of the kitchen, dining room, and pantry are excellent for hanging garlic, dried chilies, bunches of herbs, and edible flowers. Turn them upside down and hang them on a nail; not only does this give your kitchen a rustic look, it is extremely handy. Break off hanging garlic and herbs, pluck several bay leaves, pull off a handful of the dried flower petals and crumble them into a sauce, soup, stew. Really use your hanging foods so that nothing becomes stale and flavorless; as such they become mere decor. (Note: While I adore the idea of keeping a salami or two hanging from the rafters, along with a slab of bacon and leg of prosciutto, it is not terribly practical for most homes. These meats do need a certain amount of temperature control. They also should be refrigerated as soon as they are cut into.)

The freezer is one of the more important elements of our contemporary pantry. For real benefit however, you need a freestanding freezer rather than the one that is part of a refrigerator; it is too small and inefficient. The freestanding freezer may not be attractive, but it is useful. Beware, though; freezing can rapidly turn from being a good tool to being the ruination of good food. Do not use it as a holding place for prepared foods. Outside of ice cream, I can think of no prepared dish that is improved by the deep freeze. Flavor pales, texture goes from crisp to soggy, and general oomph is dissipated. On the plus side, however, the freezer is a superb way to keep certain foods in a state of suspended animation. Fruits and vegetables by and large respond well; frozen homemade pesto is much better than bottled; soup stock (such as pork, duck, fish, etc.) is worth devoting an entire freezer to; and salsa, though not as crisp and fiery as when freshly made, supplies a nearly instant taste of sunshine when kept on hand in the freezer.

Stocking Your Pantry

Part of assembling a pantry is discovering the delight of a new ingredient. Perhaps you buy a spice for one recipe, then think: "It might be good with chicken . . ." You try it; it's delicious. Next you sprinkle some onto a vegetable salad, love it, then simmer a whiff of it into your next savory sauce. Soon you have a full portrait of the flavor aspects of this new spice or condiment, and it has a secure space in your pantry. Try buying something new regularly; ask the shopkeeper for advice on what it tastes like and how to use it, then take it home to your pantry shelves and wait for the right moment.

Ethnic groceries and farmers' markets are good sources for many uncommon ingredients, as are the better-stocked supermarkets.

The Basic, Intermediate, and Advanced Pantry

◆◆

Your pantry may be as basic or extravagant as you like. For simplicity's sake, I have created basic, intermediate, and advanced pantry categories. Each recipe is marked to indicate its category to give at a glance a general sense of the recipe's sophistication. A recipe marked "Advanced" is not necessarily difficult; but it does contain ingredients not found in a basic pantry. The Basic Pantry contains the essentials: oils, spices, chutneys, legumes, rices, seasonings. The Intermediate Pantry adds some more unusual ingredients, and the Advanced Pantry includes delicacies and exotic tastes, as well as lesser-known and harder-to-find foods. The lists are, by their nature, incomplete, as the variety of ingredients available these days is nearly endless and each person's taste distinctively his or her own. While hazelnut oil or dried codfish might be in some people's Advanced Pantry, to others these foods are everyday basics. Also, there are few prepared foods in the following lists; I think of these as belonging in the "comfort pantry," which holds foods that only need reheating. We all have our favorites; mine is corned beef hash and canned tamales—I'm no food snob. However, since we already know what we love in this realm of ready-made "comfort" foods, they are not included below.

Most of the items in the following lists are discussed in detail and are used in this book. Use the index to locate the items listed for descriptions and suggested uses.

The Basic Pantry

◆◆◆◆◆◆◆

◆ **OILS AND VINEGARS**

bland vegetable oil such as canola

olive oil (extra virgin for everything, or extra virgin for salads and a pure olive oil for cooking)

sesame oil (Asian toasted)

wine vinegar (red and/or white)

cider vinegar

◆◆◆◆◆◆◆

◆ **SPICES, CONDIMENTS, AND SEASONING INGREDIENTS**

A basic spice and herb collection to suit your taste

anchovies

barbecue sauce

capers

chutney

Note on Pantry Levels

◆◆◆◆◆◆

Dividing the world's pantry ingredients into categories–Basic, Intermediate, and Advanced— is an exercise that I hope will help cooks at every level to be creative in the kitchen. My goal in creating this structure is to give organization to these ingredients and to supplement the descriptions and recipes: to be a help rather than dictatorial hindrance. The creative, experienced cook may find the designations useful or regard them as unnecessary. You are free to ignore or modify the system to suit your own culinary style.

I am the first to admit that my categories are subjective. Ingredients such as salt cod, canned chestnuts, or dried morel mushrooms might be one cook's once-a-year flourish, yet serve as everyday fare for another cook. Ditto for caviar, smoked salmon, achiote, or coconut milk.

Each recipe also has been given a pantry level designation. When a recipe or variation doesn't have a designation, the previous pantry level applies. This designation refers only to the complexity of the pantry

(cont.)

involved rather than to the difficulty of the recipe itself. For example, a recipe with a "Basic Pantry" label may be technically demanding, but its ingredients fall into the Basic category. Likewise, a recipe marked "Advanced Pantry" may be a very simply prepared dish, but with unusual ingredients.

Italian pickled vegetables (giardiniera) and/or peppers (pepperoncini)
hot sauce such as Tabasco
pickled chilies with/without vegetables (pickled jalapeños)
jams and jellies (strawberry, apricot, etc.)
honey
maple syrup
mayonnaise (including seasoned mayonnaise such as delectable Creole mayonnaise)

mustards (1 coarse, 1 sweet-hot, 1 herbed)
Greek olives
green pimiento-stuffed olives
pungent garlicky kosher dills
tangy sweet bread-and-butter pickles
salsa (red and/or green)
soy sauce (all purpose)
sun-dried tomatoes
sea salt
whole peppercorns for crushing and grinding as needed

◆ GRAINS AND LEGUMES

barley
bulgur wheat
rices (long grain and/or short grain in both brown and white)
cornmeal
oats

muesli-type cereals
dried beans (lima, red kidney, white, pinto, chick-peas, brown lentils, split peas)
soup mixtures that contain grains, legumes, and pasta

◆ NUTS, DRIED FRUITS AND SEEDS

almonds
peanuts
walnuts
prunes

raisins
pumpkin seeds
sunflower seeds
sesame seeds

◆ THE PASTA PANTRY

long thin pasta: spaghetti, capellini, fettuccine
short macaroni: elbows, seashells, farfalle (bow-ties)
tiny pastina such as alphabets
lasagne (plain and/or spinach)

ramen-type quick-cooking Asian noodles
tricolor vegetable pastas (spaghetti is especially delightful)

◆ THE ROOT CELLAR

apples, carrots, citrus fruit (lemons, grapefruit, and oranges)

garlic, fresh ginger, onions
potatoes (1 boiling type and 1 all-purpose baking type)

◆ THE DRY GOODS PANTRY

baking ingredients such as yeast, baking soda, powder, etc.

bread, dried for crumbs and croutons
breadsticks (grissini)

hard candies (peppermint sticks,
lemon drops, etc.)
coconut (dried)
cookies such as oatmeal or
gingersnaps
crackers (simple water biscuits or
saltless saltines)

flours (white, whole wheat,
masa harina, instant)
popcorn
sugar (white, brown, powdered)
tortilla chips

◆ THE FROZEN PANTRY

homemade broths and stocks
(chicken, beef, pork, vegetable,
fish)
chopped chives
chunks of hard cheese for grating
pie crust dough or ready-made
tart shells
frozen breads such as Jewish
seeded rye

bagels
sourdough
herbed focaccia
bread dough
vegetables, fruits, meats/
chicken/fish, as desired
tortillas (flour, corn, blue, etc.)

◆ CANNED AND BOTTLED GOODS

artichoke hearts in marinade or
vinaigrette
bamboo shoots
hominy
peanut butter
sardines

sauerkraut
tomatoes (diced, sauce, pastes,
etc.)
tahini
tuna fish
water chestnuts

◆ BACON, SAUSAGE, HAM, SMOKED AND CURED MEATS, AND FISH

bacon, ham, simple smoked sausages (of beef, pork, and/or
turkey), salami such as Kosher
garlic-scented or

San Francisco Italian air-dried
sausage
pastrami or corned beef

◆ COFFEE, TEA, CHOCOLATE, WINES, AND SPIRITS

black tea such as Darjeeling
green tea
herbed tea
fresh-roast coffee (whole beans
keep best)
chocolate (dark, milk, and white
in whichever form you adore
most)
cocoa (powdered, sweetened,
and/or unsweetened)

good drinkable wines for
sauces, braises, stews, and
the cook
a selection of beers (one light
lager, one heartier ale, one
dark and heady bitter or
stout)
brandy
several liqueurs of choice
dry sherry

Intermediate Pantry

◆◆◆◆◆◆◆

In addition to Basic Pantry ingredients:

◆ OILS AND VINEGARS

chili oil
hazelnut oil
additional olive oils of varying
    flavors and strengths

balsamic vinegar
fruit vinegar
rice vinegar (mild)

◆◆◆◆◆◆◆

◆ SPICES, CONDIMENTS, AND SEASONING INGREDIENTS

black beans (salted, Chinese)
chili-garlic paste
cloud ears (Chinese black
    fungus)
coconut milk
cornichons
dried mushrooms (shiitakes, por-
    cini, cèpes, cremini)
canned chipotle chilies in
    marinade
chilies (mild dried red ones)
    such as ancho, pasilla, New
    Mexican, California, mulato,
    etc.)
flower waters (rose and orange
    flower)
green peppercorns (preserved)
herbs for hanging in bunches to
    dry: sage, oregano, bay leaves,
    etc.

hoisin sauce
hot sauces (such as Mexican
    Habanero sauces)
Indian spices and spice mixtures
    (such as tikka and tandoori)
mustards such as Creole, horse-
    radish, whole seed, or mixed
    peppercorn
olive paste
soy sauce (both light and dark)
spices (additional ones such as
    Chinese five-spice, Hungarian
    paprika, herbes de Provence,
    dried mint, saffron, Szechuan
    peppercorns, achiote seeds,
    mole powder, gumbo filé, plus
    whole-seed spices such as
    mustard seeds, cumin, and
    fennel)

◆◆◆◆◆◆◆

◆ GRAINS AND LEGUMES

buckwheat groats (kasha)
couscous
millet
rice: Arborio, basmati, wild and
    brown rice–exotic rice
    combinations

black beans
flageolets
Indian red lentils
mixed grains and legumes for
    soup
grits

◆ NUTS, DRIED FRUITS, AND SEEDS

almond paste
cashews
hazelnuts
pine nuts
pistachios

apricots
figs
golden raisins
candied citrus or mixed glacéed
   fruit

◆◆◆◆◆◆

◆ THE PASTA PANTRY

buckwheat soba
fusilli (twists)
gnocchi (dried, vacuum-packed,
   or frozen)
Italian whole-wheat pasta
mung bean noodles

papardelle
orzo
orecchiette
rice noodles
stuffed pasta such as tortellini
   raviolini, etc.

◆◆◆◆◆◆

◆ THE ROOT CELLAR

celery root
elephant garlic
Jerusalem artichoke

limes
red onion
shallots

◆◆◆◆◆◆

◆ THE DRY GOODS PANTRY

candies such as English toffee
chicharróns (Mexican crisp-fried
   pork rind)
cookies such as amaretti and
   biscotti
corn husks
falafel mix
flour (soy, bread [high gluten],
   whole-wheat pastry, cake,

chick-pea, buckwheat, masa
   harina [blue])
lime syrup
matzo and matzo meal
molasses
soy meat substitutes
sugar (rustic French cubes, vanilla sugar, raw sugar)
tortilla chips (blue corn, black
   bean, etc.)

◆◆◆◆◆◆

◆ THE FROZEN PANTRY

butter (seasoned and flavored)
chopped fresh herbs (parsley,
   cilantro, rosemary, etc.)
combinations such as chopped
   fresh rosemary, basil, and
   grated lemon or orange zest
and more exotic fresh herbs as
   they are available, such as Thai
   or cinnamon basil, rose gera-
   nium, etc.

filo dough
lemon grass
pasta (fresh, stuffed, etc.)
pesto
salsa (homemade)
stock (duck, turkey, seafood,
   etc.)

◆ CANNED AND BOTTLED GOODS

nopales
roasted red peppers
hominy

salmon
tomatillos
vine leaves

◆◆◆◆◆◆◆

◆ BACON, SAUSAGE, HAM, SMOKED AND CURED MEATS, AND FISH

bacon (thick cut) or salt pork
cured cooked meats (coppa, mortadella, etc.)
pancetta
prosciutto

sausages (American regional,
ethnic, and imported) such as
apple-curry, spicy turkey, bratwurst, chorizo, etc.
smoked salmon (lox)

◆◆◆◆◆◆◆

◆ COFFEE, TEA, CHOCOLATE, WINES, AND SPIRITS

dark-roast coffee
a smoked tea such as gunpowder
or lapsang souchong
oolong tea or jasmine tea
an aperitif wine of choice
Calvados or applejack
Cointreau or other orange
liqueur
fruit brandies, or eaux-de-vie
gin
Marsala, port, or Madeira

ouzo
tequila
vermouth (dry for cooking; semisweet for aperitif)
vodka
whiskey
rice wine (Chinese, Japanese
[sake])
sparkling wine (Champagne,
Asti, regional American ones)

Advanced Pantry

◆◆◆◆◆◆◆

In addition to Basic and Intermediate Pantry ingredients:

◆ OILS AND VINEGARS

mustard oil
walnut oil
flavored oils
malt vinegar

rice vinegar (such as strong Chinese "black" vinegar)
sherry vinegar
truffle oil

◆ SPICES, CONDIMENTS, AND SEASONING INGREDIENTS

Chinese bean sauces (brown, hot
   bean, yellow)
cardamom (whole pods)
curry paste (Indian or Thai)
dried morel mushrooms
duck or goose fat
fish sauce (Thai or Vietnamese)
green olive paste
Indian lime pickle or other oil-
   and-chili-based Indian
   condiments

jams and preserves (exotic
   ones such as rose petal,
   quince, etc.)
kaffir lime leaves
lavender buds
pickled ginger
Bransten pickle (British brown
   chutney-like relish)
sumac
truffle paste (black and/or white)
za'atar

◆◆◆◆◆◆◆

◆ GRAINS AND LEGUMES

brown ful beans
French lentils
quinoa

exotic rices (Thai, jasmine,
   black, glutinous)

◆◆◆◆◆◆◆

◆ NUTS, DRIED FRUITS, AND SEEDS

angelica
dried cherries

macadamia nuts

◆◆◆◆◆◆◆

◆ THE PASTA PANTRY

acini di pepe
anellini
tiny squares
flavored pastas: saffron,
   mushroom, etc.

radiatore
cavatelli
exotic stuffed pastas

◆◆◆◆◆◆◆

◆ THE DRY GOODS PANTRY

candled flowers
dried codfish
flours (barley flour, rye flour, rice
   flour, oat flour)
fruit syrups (Italian and/or
   French)

rice paper
seaweed
sugar (crystalized amber chunks,
   maple sugar, date sugar)

◆◆◆◆◆◆◆

◆ THE FROZEN PANTRY

banana leaves
unusual broths (pigeon, smoky
   ham stock, shrimp, lobster
   stock, etc.)

less-common stuffed pastas (pelmeni, seafood-stuffed ravioli,
   etc.)

◆ CANNED AND BOTTLED GOODS

caviar (red, yellow, and black, Greek tarama)
chestnuts (plain, pureed, and/or sweetened and pureed)
confit (duck, pork, or goose)

◆ BACON, SAUSAGE, HAM, SMOKED AND CURED MEATS, AND FISH

bacon (lean British or Irish)
bresaola (Italian air-dried beef)
barbecued pork (Chinese style)
ham (Serrano, Westfalian)
sausages: Chinese, North African (merguez)

◆ COFFEE, TEA, CHOCOLATE, WINES, AND SPIRITS

a wider selection of beer
a more ambitious wine collection/cellar
several more exotic teas
Campari
additional liqueurs such as fraises du bois and Frangelico

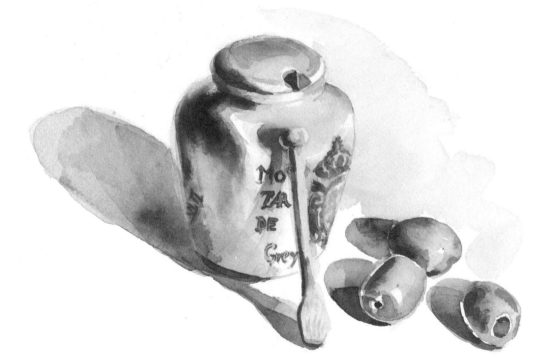

FORAGE COOKING
FROM THE PANTRY

◆·◆

The creativity that a bounteous pantry offers you is endless. Having a selection of excellent ingredients on hand is one way professional chefs add their personal signature to simple foods. Many chefs make their own seasoning pastes, condiments, oils, etc.; others use good-quality store-bought ones. You have the same choice. By having these ingredients readily available, you can prepare a delicious variety of dishes easily.

For instance: Glance along your pantry shelves. You see a jar of dried spaghettini, a bottle of olive oil, and a head of garlic. This is a meal. Further along the shelf you notice a tin of anchovies and a jar of capers; this is a slightly more ambitious meal. Then you think of the chopped herbs you have in the freezer: more possibilities. The world of leftovers is also given creative dimension with a good pantry. You might have a bowl of olive oil-and-balsamic-marinated tomatoes left-over from last night's dinner: their freshness will add a new dimension to your pantry pasta. And so it goes. You could eat this way forever, or at least as long as your pantry holds out.

Dishes from the Pantry Only

Following is a selection of dishes, or ideas for dishes, to prepare using ingredients from your pantry. The dishes depend on the pantry entirely, with variations that take them from basic pantry level to the advanced. I assume that you have a few basics in the kitchen such as eggs, some potatoes or onions, and milk. I have used an abbreviated, narrative style for these recipes to emphasize their informal, spontaneous nature. Feel free to alter these recipe ideas to match what your pantry actually contains.

Rustic Springtime Muesli

◆ BASIC PANTRY

Serves 2, generously

One morning, in County Cork, Ireland, I awoke to a beautiful sight: outside the window lay a lush green field, and beyond it a hillside with a ramshackle farmhouse. I enjoyed the view, tucked into my warm, cozy bed with a breakfast tray perched atop my knees. The coffee was strong; I held it next to my face and inhaled its warm fragrant vapors. A basket of breads beckoned, and they were good, but it was the simple muesli that captured my attention: so fresh and pure, made with excellent oats, and lightened with shredded fresh apple.

◆◆◆◆◆◆

TO PREPARE Moisten 1 cup **oatmeal** with an equal amount of water; cover and let stand 15 minutes or so. Pour off any excess liquid and add 1 cup of your favorite **toasted granola-type cereal,** 1 to 2 teaspoons **sugar or honey,** and 1 coarsely shredded **apple** (including peel). Serve immediately, accompanied with spoonfuls of **rich milk or cream.**

◆◆ INTERMEDIATE PANTRY

Apple-Hazelnut Muesli

To the **above recipe** add 1 ounce coarsely chopped **toasted hazelnuts.**

Fragrant Apple-Almond Muesli

To the **basic recipe** add 1 tablespoon **almond paste** that has been mashed or softened in a little **milk**, several tablespoons (1/2 ounce) of chopped **almonds**, and a dash of **almond extract**.

Bulgarian Breakfast Barley

◆ BASIC PANTRY

Serves 2, with leftovers

The simplicity and slight surprise of the following barley dish is delightful: the sweetness and spice are an unexpected pleasure to those of us who are used to eating barley with savory flavors or only in soup. I first tasted this in Bulgaria, less out of gastronomy than necessity, when food shortages were curtailing the usual breakfast foods available. It has been a staple at my table since.

✦✦✦✦✦✦

TO PREPARE Cook 1 cup **pearl barley** in water to cover over medium heat for about 40 minutes, or according to package directions (barley brands vary as to cooking time). Add enough water to keep it liquid but not swimming. When tender, let cool; it will thicken as it stands. Season with **sugar or honey** and a generous amount of **ground cinnamon.** Enjoy warm, at room temperature, or cool.

Red Bean and Peanut Voodoo Soup

◆ BASIC PANTRY

Serves 4

This smooth Caribbean bisque conjures up images of the hot and sultry South, and the mysterious powers that lie beneath life's mundane surface. The woman who first fed me this soup claimed that eating it gave good luck; the truth is that anyone eating it is lucky indeed. It is sustaining and deeply flavored, vibrant yet light.

And whoever chooses to cook it is lucky, too: all of the ingredients are readily available in the basic pantry.

✦✦✦✦✦✦

TO PREPARE Lightly sauté **1 chopped onion** and 4 coarsely chopped **garlic cloves** in **1 tablespoon vegetable oil.** When they begin to turn golden, stir in **1 tablespoon flour** and cook a minute or two to rid the flour of its rawness. Add 1 cup cooked and drained **red kidney beans,** cook a few minutes through, then add 1 quart **broth** of choice, 1/2 to

1 teaspoon **curry powder,** and **2 bay leaves.** Bring to a boil, then reduce heat and simmer for 10 minutes, or until soup has thickened somewhat and smells enticing.

Remove bay leaves and puree bean mixture in a food processor or blender, adding enough liquid for a smooth mixture. Return puree to broth, then stir in 3 tablespoons **peanut butter,** letting it melt into soup. Serve immediately, each portion seasoned with a generous dash of **hot pepper sauce** such as Tabasco and a sprinkling of chopped fresh **chives.**

Mexican Hominy Soup

[POZOLE]

◆◆ INTERMEDIATE PANTRY

Serves 4

Nuggets of hominy awash in a bowl of clear broth, brought alive by enough salsa to make things interesting, and the crunch of shredded cabbage as well as bits of crisp chicharróns (Mexican pork rind). Pozole is the sort of homey folk food that becomes legendary, with each region having its version of the dish. Some may serve it with a drizzle of thin salsa made from combining broth and pasilla chili powder; others might serve it enriched with a spoonful of pumpkin seed paste (see page 257). The broth you choose will dictate the flavor of the pozole: I lean toward one based on both pork and turkey, simmered with whole garlic heads and bay leaves, though duck broth makes a suave and elegant pozole.

Traditionally, pozole is served as a restorative after a night of overindulging.

◆◆◆◆◆◆

TO PREPARE Simmer 2 cups cooked and drained **hominy** and several cloves coarsely cut-up **garlic** in 1 quart flavorful **broth** for 10 minutes, or long enough to heat through and cook the garlic to softness. Season with mild **chili powder** to taste (such as pasilla) and serve with a bit of **Cilantro-Lime Paste** (page 360) and a little shredded **cabbage.** Accompany with wedges of **lime** and a sprinkling of broken-up **chicharróns.**

Rag-Tag Bean and Legume Soup-Stew

Inevitably, at some point as you cook your way though the beans and lentils in your pantry, you will have small amounts not yet used in recipes. Save them in a jar, adding to them until you have a rich and

Serves 4 to 6

varied mixture. Butter beans, black beans, kidney beans, flageolets, pinto beans, chick-peas and any other beans you can find will give a meaty substance to the dish; lentils, split peas, and barley thicken the soup deliciously. It is the variety of ingredients that gives this simple soup its complex flavor. That, and the whole garlic cloves. It's wonderful.

◆◆◆◆◆◆

TO PREPARE Place 2 cups **mixed beans and legumes** as described above into a large, heavy pot and cover with water. Bring to a boil, then reduce heat and simmer for about an hour, or until beans are almost tender. Use enough water so that the beans don't burn, but not enough to make them soupy. When beans are tender, add enough **broth** (about 3 cups) to thin it down to a soupy consistency. (The lentils and barley will have thickened the mixture, and some of the beans will also fall apart a bit, further thickening it into a soupy stew consistency.) Add 6 to 8 whole **garlic cloves,** 2 **bay leaves,** 2 or 3 **carrots** cut into chunks, and 1 **potato,** peeled and diced. Continue simmering until vegetables are cooked through and tender and beans are equally so; stir and add water or broth as soup cooks, so that it does not burn. Add **salt** and **pepper** to taste, and serve sprinkled with a bit of chopped fresh **parsley** if desired.

Pasta in Hot and Tangy Orange-scented Broth

Serves 2

Cook a handful of broken **spaghetti strands** or small **soup pasta** in 3 cups **broth** (chicken, beef, or vegetable). When just tender, add a squeeze of **orange** (about 1/2 orange) and a bit of finely grated **zest.** Serve with a dash each of **wine vinegar** and **hot pepper sauce,** and sprinkle generously with grated **Parmesan.**

Baked White Cheese with Green Salsa

[QUESO AL HORNO CON SALSA VERDE]

Creamy, mild fresh cheese is delicious broiled to bubbling and served with a tangy and piquant green salsa. Warm flour tortillas make perfect scoops; tear off pieces and roll up bits of the warm, melted cheese and salsa. Any mild white cheese will do nicely: fresh mozzarella or pecorino, jack, Mexican queso fresco, etc.

◆ BASIC PANTRY

Serves 4

TO PREPARE Slice 10 to 12 ounces of **mild white cheese** and arrange in a flat baking pan. Top with several spoonfuls of **green salsa,** then bake or broil in a hot oven until melty and bubbly around the edges. Serve immediately with warm soft **flour tortillas.** (Note: *Immediately* is the operative word with mozzarella, since it strings unpleasantly as it cools, making eating more a battle than a pleasure.)

Melted Cheddar and Red Salsa

Substitute a good flavorful **Cheddar** for the mild white cheese, and a zesty **red salsa** for the green.

◆◆ INTERMEDIATE PANTRY

Baked Cheese with Bits of Browned Chorizo
[QUESO FLAMEADO]

To either of the **above dishes** add 1 to 2 crumbled and browned **chorizo** sausages.

Apple-poached Sausages

◆◆ INTERMEDIATE PANTRY

Serves 4

A mixture of half apple juice and half white wine makes a delicious poaching liquid for sausages, especially any sausage that already has a whiff of apple, such as apple-chicken sausages. Be sure to reserve the poaching liquid in your frozen pantry for another use, such as braising pork, deglazing a roast duck, or simmering a chicken.

◆◆◆◆◆◆◆

TO PREPARE Place 8 to 12 **apple-chicken or -pork sausages** in a pan and cover with a mixture of half **apple juice,** half **white wine.** Simmer until cooked through, then remove from liquid and serve with **Honey-Herb Mustard** (page 39).

Bratwurst in Port or Madeira

Substitute **bratwurst** or any delicate white pork sausage for apple-chicken ones, and **port** for juice and wine. Serve at room temperature as an appetizer, cut into bite-sized pieces and accompanied with **Honey-Herb Mustard,** page 39.

Duck-and-Green-Peppercorn or Spicy Italian Sausage

Substitute **duck-and-green-peppercorn or spicy Italian sausage** for apple-chicken sausage in basic recipe, using **white grape juice** in place of apple juice. When nearly cooked through, pour off most of juice and let remaining juice cook into a glaze as sausage browns.

Cactus with Chili Salsa

[NOPALES CON SALSA]

◆◆ INTERMEDIATE PANTRY

Serves 4, as a side dish

Makes 1-1/2 to 2 cups

This pantry salad-relish makes a spunky opening or accompaniment to any Mexican or California/Southwestern meal.

◆◆◆◆◆◆

TO PREPARE: Drain 1 bottle (approximately 6 ounces) **nopales** and arrange on a plate. Season with **green salsa** to taste.

Nopales Salsa

Decrease the amount of **nopales** by half, dice, and combine with 1 cup **salsa** (either red or green). Serve with grilled meats, seafood, or Black Bean Chili with Pozole (Hominy) (page 37).

Sun-dried Tomato and Anchovy Toasts

◆◆ INTERMEDIATE PANTRY

Serves 4 to 6

Crisp and crusty toasts sizzling with a savory spread of sun-dried tomatoes and garlic, with either a bit of anchovy or olive. A dash of red wine vinegar adds a slight tang, and with leftover stale bread, the whole dish is pantry perfect.

◆◆◆◆◆◆

TO PREPARE Combine 5 chopped **garlic cloves** with 15 coarsely chopped **sun-dried tomatoes** and whirl in a blender or food processor to puree, adding about 1/4 cup **olive oil** and 2 teaspoons **red wine vinegar** as you puree. Season with 1 teaspoon **herbes de Provence** and spread mixture over slices of **dry baguette.** Broil until sizzling, and garnish each toast with several slices of pitted **Mediterranean-type black olives** or **anchovy fillets.** Serve immediately.

Citrus-scented Sweet Peppers and Olives

◆◆ INTERMEDIATE PANTRY

Serves 4 to 6

Roasted red peppers dressed with a whiff of orange zest and enough mild chili to intrigue but not to inflict pain. Enjoy as a Mediterranean-style appetizer or as an accompaniment to a robust meaty meal; excellent picnic fare.

◆◆◆◆◆◆

TO PREPARE Drain one 10-ounce jar of **roasted red peppers** and arrange peppers on platter. Toss with 1 teaspoon **finely grated orange zest,** 1/4 teaspoon **cumin seeds,** 1-1/2 teaspoons **ancho or other mild chili powder,** 1 chopped **garlic clove,** 10 to 15 **green olives** halved or coarsely chopped, 3 tablespoons **white wine vinegar,** 2 tablespoons **extra-virgin olive oil, salt,** and **black or red pepper** to taste. Chill and serve as desired.

Marinated Kidney Beans, Three-Continents Style

◆◆ INTERMEDIATE PANTRY

Serves 4

The flavors—sweet, tangy, olive- and garlic-scented, and touched with a bit of earthy mild chili—hail from disparate continents and cultures (Mexico, Soviet Georgia, U.S.A., Mediterranean), but they blend harmoniously. Heating the garlic in oil and tossing the beans in this fragrant mixture helps set the dish apart from other marinated bean dishes that have similar ingredients.

◆◆◆◆◆◆

TO PREPARE Heat 3 chopped **garlic cloves** in 2 tablespoons **olive oil** until fragrant but not browned, then add 2 cups drained **cooked kidney beans** and warm through together. Season with a pinch each of **sugar, salt,** and **pepper;** 1/2 teaspoon or so **mild chili powder** such as ancho or pasilla; a pinch of **thyme;** and 1 tablespoon **red wine vinegar.** Remove from heat and add a tablespoon or two of chopped fresh **cilantro.** Serve at room temperature.

White Beans with Olive Oil, Garlic, Lemon, and Parsley

[CANNELLINI ITALIANI]

Serves 4

White beans dressed with lots of garlic, olive oil, lemon, and parsley are typical of the deliciously simple food of the Mediterranean.

◆◆◆◆◆◆

TO PREPARE Toss 1-1/2 cups cooked and drained **white kidney beans** (cannellini) with 3 tablespoons **olive oil**, 1 chopped **garlic clove**, a squeeze of **lemon,** and sprinkling of chopped fresh **parsley.** Add **salt** and **pepper** to taste.

Mediterranean White Bean Pâté

Smooth and creamy, this cousin of hummus is essentially the same dish as above, but pureed into a smooth and pungent spread.

◆◆◆◆◆◆

TO PREPARE Proceed with the above ingredients, but whirl it all in the processor or blender and increase the amount of lemon juice dramatically: 2 to 3 tablespoons, or to taste (the juice of 1 to 1-1/2 lemons). Season with salt and pepper, sprinkle with **paprika,** and garnish with a scattering of **pickled pepperoncini.** Accompany with warm **pita or French bread.**

Cannellini Beans with Red and/or Black Caviar

Garnish **either of above dishes** with a spoonful or two of **red or black caviar.** Do not use artificially dyed lumpfish caviar, or dish will become gray and unattractive.

Tuna Fish Plate with Chili Salsa

[TUNA CON SALSA]

Rich and meaty tuna fish transcends its lunch-counter image when enlivened with a splash of chili salsa. Green salsa is especially good, particularly one with a pronounced cilantro flavor.

◆ BASIC PANTRY

Serves 2 to 3

TO PREPARE Arrange 6 ounces well-drained **tuna chunks** on a bed of **greens** and dress with Cilantro-Lime Paste, page 357. Garnish with crisp **tortilla chips.**

◆◆ INTERMEDIATE PANTRY

Tuna with the Flavors of Vera Cruz

Garnish **basic dish** with 1/4 cup or so **roasted red peppers** cut into strips and a handful of **green pimiento-stuffed olives,** sliced or halved.

◆◆◆ ADVANCED PANTRY

Tuna with Salsa and Blue Tortilla Chips

Prepare **basic recipe** and garnish with spiced Sicilian- or Moroccan-style **black oil-cured olives;** garnish with **blue tortilla chips.**

Broth-cooked Spaghetti, Tossed with Olives and Parsley

[SPAGHETTI OLIVETTI]

◆ BASIC PANTRY

Serves 4 to 6

Cooking dried pasta in broth, then draining it and tossing with simple seasonings is a technique I first came upon in Venice, Italy. There, it was seafood broth, and the dish was sprinkled with toasty browned bread crumbs. The pasta becomes suffused with a brothy flavor, which contributes distinctively to the simple, straightforward dish.

And whatever you do, don't throw away the broth when you drain the pasta; save it for soups, sauces, etc.

◆◆◆◆◆◆

TO PREPARE Cook 1 pound **spaghetti** in 1 to 2 quarts **chicken or vegetable broth** until just al dente. Drain, reserving broth, and toss pasta in 3 to 4 tablespoons **extra-virgin olive oil** along with 3/4 to 1 cup pitted and halved **Kalamata olives** and 1/2 cup chopped fresh **parsley.** Serve immediately.

Spaghetti Tossed with a Caribbean-inspired Fiery Lime-Chili-Tomato Sauce

[RASTA PASTA]

◆ BASIC PANTRY

Serves 4

This simple dish of pasta tossed with tomato-lime salsa sings of the Caribbean; a bowlful makes me want to listen to reggae music and consider taking mambo lessons. That's a very powerful pasta.

◆◆◆◆◆◆

TO PREPARE Combine 2 cups diced **canned tomatoes,** lightly drained of all except for about 1/2 cup of canning liquid, with 6 or more chopped **garlic cloves,** juice of 3 to 4 **limes,** finely grated **zest** of 1 lime, and **hot pepper sauce** such as Tabasco to taste. Serve spooned over 3/4 pound hot al dente **spaghetti** that you've tossed with 1/3 cup **extra-virgin olive oil;** season with **salt and black pepper** to taste.

Fennel-scented Seashell Pasta with Peas in Tomato Sauce

◆◆ INTERMEDIATE PANTRY

Serves 4 to 6

Whole fennel seeds give a sweetness to this simple garlic-tomato sauce. Serve as an accompaniment to herb-redolent meatballs braised with spinach for a homey Sunday-night supper.

◆◆◆◆◆◆

TO PREPARE Cook 1 pound small **seashell pasta** until al dente, then add 2 cups fresh or frozen **peas.** Drain pasta and peas and keep warm. Make a sauce by heating 4 chopped **garlic cloves** in 2 tablespoons **olive oil** along with 1/4 to 1/2 teaspoon **fennel seeds** and a pinch of dried **oregano.** When garlic is lightly gilded, add 3 cups **tomato sauce,** cook over high heat a few minutes, then season with **salt and pepper.** Serve over drained pasta and peas, and pass **Parmesan.**

Pasta con Pesto

Serve with a spoonful of **pesto,** page 364, atop **sauced pasta,** like a condiment.

Baked Fennel-sauced Pasta with Soft Cheeses

[PASTA CON FORMAGGIO AL FORNO]

Make a rustic casserole by layering **leftover pasta** with slices of **jack or mozzarella** cheese, and spoonfuls of **ricotta or mild fresh goat cheese.**

Bake in a preheated 400° oven until cheese melts and turns bubbly and lightly browned on top, about 20 minutes. Serve immediately.

Asian Pasta

Serves 4

Asian groceries offer a wide range of noodles and pastas: choose thin or wide Vietnamese noodles made from rice, delicate and nearly translucent; or try fat Japanese udon, or flat Korean buckwheat vermicelli-type dried pasta; even ordinary spaghetti is delicious served dressed with soy sauce and Asian sesame oil.

◆◆◆◆◆◆

TO PREPARE Toss al dente cooked **noodles** with **soy sauce** and Asian (toasted) **sesame oil** to taste.

Asian Peanut and Chive Pasta

Serve **Asian pasta,** above, garnished with coarsely chopped **peanuts** and chopped fresh **chives.**

Don-Don–style Chinese-Flavor Noodles

Add several spoonfuls **hoisin sauce** to **Asian pasta** along with **soy sauce** and **sesame oil.** Serve as a bed for a crunchy raw vegetable salad: **mung bean sprouts,** shredded **carrots,** diced **cucumber,** and bits of **grilled or roast pork.**

Pasta with Tomato-Red Chili Pepper Sauce

[PASTA ARRABBIATA]

Arrabbiata means "enraged," and the name is given to a simple dish of pasta in a hot pepper–seasoned tomato sauce. Anything else can go in it as long as it is *piccante* enough to raise a warm glow across the face.

◆◆◆◆◆◆

TO PREPARE Lightly sauté 3 or 4 coarsely chopped **garlic cloves** in several tablespoons of **olive oil or olive oil combined with butter.** Add

◆ BASIC PANTRY

Serves 4

2 cups **tomato sauce,** simmer a few minutes, then season with **red pepper flakes** to taste. Serve with al dente **spaghetti** or **penne,** and accompany with grated **Parmesan.**

◆◆ INTERMEDIATE PANTRY

Pasta Arrabbiatta with Sun-dried Tomatoes

To **above recipe** add 10 or so **marinated sun-dried tomatoes,** cut into halves or strips. Simply toss into hot sauced pasta, and garnish with a sprinkling of fresh **parsley** if desired.

Sun-dried Tomato Pasta Arrabbiatta with Pesto

To **sun-dried tomato pasta,** above, add a spoonful of **pesto.**

Pasta with Chick-pea and Tomato Sauce
[PASTA AL CECI]

◆ BASIC PANTRY

Serves 4 to 6

Robust and full of lusty flavors, *pasta al ceci* (pasta with chick-pea and tomato sauce) typifies the flavors of Italy's South. The *mezzogiorno,* as it is affectionately called, simmers in the midday sun; its food tastes vividly of tomatoes, olive oil, and garlic, as in the following dish.

◆◆◆◆◆◆

TO PREPARE Sauté 1 chopped **onion** and 6 coarsely chopped **garlic cloves** in 2 tablespoons **olive oil.** When softened, add 2 cups **cooked and drained chick-peas,** 3 cups diced **canned peeled tomatoes,** 1/2 teaspoon **dried thyme,** and 1 **bay leaf.** Cook over medium-high heat until thick and sauce-like. If too acidic, add a pinch of **sugar.** Season with **salt** and **pepper** and serve over 3/4 pound al dente pasta; sprinkle with grated **Parmesan.**

Chick-Pea and Tomato Antipasto

Make a double batch of **sauce,** above, and serve at room temperature as an antipasto. May be kept in freezer.

Mediterranean Vegetable Stew

Use any **leftover chick-peas in tomato sauce** to add to sautéed chunks of **eggplant and/or zucchini** for a ratatouille-like vegetable stew. Or add to simmered **lamb** for an instant Greek flavor.

Pasta with Hazelnut Pesto

◆◆ INTERMEDIATE PANTRY

Serves 4

In the streets of Genoa, vendors sell hazelnuts tied up distinctively in long strings. This dish is inspired by those hazelnuts as well as by the herb pestos of the region. It makes a delicious and simple pasta during the winter when basil isn't in season, or anytime you want a meal straight from the pantry.

◆◆◆◆◆◆

TO PREPARE Toast 1 cup shelled **hazelnuts** in an ungreased skillet over medium-high heat, tossing and turning them to keep them from burning. Remove skins by rubbing hazelnuts against each other inside a clean towel. In a blender or food processor, puree 4 to 5 **garlic cloves** with toasted hazelnuts until it becomes a coarse meal. Add 1/4 cup **olive oil** or more if needed, and mix until it is a thinnish paste. Season with **thyme** and **black pepper,** and serve tossed with 3/4 pound hot al dente **spaghetti,** generously showered with grated **Parmesan.**

Hazelnut Pesto Focaccia

Spread **hazelnut pesto** from above recipe over flattened rounds of **raw bread dough,** then sprinkle with **olive oil,** grated **Parmesan, thyme,** and **olives.** Bake in a hot oven until crusty brown, about 30 minutes. *Al bacio!*

Cupboard Couscous

◆◆ INTERMEDIATE PANTRY

Serves 4 to 6

Couscous prepared with a strong-flavored curry-scented broth is quickly prepared yet makes an out-of-the-ordinary dish. Serve as an accompaniment to spiced kabobs, meatballs, or felafel balls, along with curried vegetables and yogurt.

TO PREPARE Make a broth by sautéing 2 **garlic cloves** and 1 chopped **onion** in 2 tablespoons **olive oil** until softened, then add 1 teaspoon **curry powder** and a generous pinch *each* of ground **ginger,** ground **cinnamon, lavender, paprika,** ground **turmeric,** and ground **cumin.** Add 1 cup chopped **tomatoes,** a tablespoon or two of **Cilantro-Lime Paste** (page 360), and 3 cups **broth.** Simmer for 10 minutes, or until flavorful.

Pour hot broth over 1-1/2 cups **couscous** mixed with 1/4 to 1/2 cup **raisins.** Let sit, covered, for a few minutes, then toss with several tablespoons unsalted **butter or olive oil.** Sprinkle with a judicious whiff of ground **cinnamon** and a few generous drops of **orange flower or rose water.**

LEFTOVERS Use to stuff **poussins or game hens** for roasting, or as a filling for **stuffed cabbage leaves,** simmered in a cinnamon-scented **tomato sauce.**

Black Bean Chili with Pozole (Hominy)

◆◆ INTERMEDIATE PANTRY

Serves 4

There was only a small amount of black bean chili in the saucepan when my neighbor came by for a surprise visit, so I added a can (drained) of bland, chewy hominy to the inky, strongly flavored beans. Both pairings were delicious, the black beans and hominy as well suited to each other as my neighbor to myself. Somehow, I've always known that my fate in love was tied up with my recipe for black bean chili.

◆◆◆◆◆◆

TO PREPARE Warm 3 coarsely chopped **garlic cloves** in a tablespoon of **olive or vegetable oil,** then sprinkle in 1/2 teaspoon ground **cumin** and 1 to 2 teaspoons mild **chili** (ancho, pasilla, or a chili-spice combination) **powder.** Let spices and garlic lightly cook but not brown, then add 2 cups **cooked black beans** plus about 1 cup cooking liquid. Simmer for 5 to 10 minutes, then season with **salt** and **hot pepper sauce** to taste. Add 1 cup cooked and drained **hominy,** warm through, and serve immediately. Garnish with **tortilla chips,** wedges of **lime,** and a sprinkling of chopped **cilantro.**

Tomato-sauced Butter Beans with the Flavor of Greece

[FASSOULIA]

◆ BASIC PANTRY

Serves 4

Butter beans combine good-naturedly with the simple, strong flavors of the Mediterranean, where similar bean dishes are enjoyed as staple foods. The following dish is delicious served at room temperature as an appetizer, or warmed and mounded onto a platter as a bed for rosemary- and garlic-studded roast lamb.

◆◆◆◆◆◆◆

TO PREPARE Heat 2 to 3 chopped **garlic cloves** in a tablespoon or two of **olive oil;** when softened add 1-1/2 to 2 cups cooked and drained **butter beans** and continue cooking a few minutes so that garlic oil permeates beans. Add 1 cup **tomato sauce** along with a generous pinch or two of dried **thyme** and simmer a few minutes, just long enough to meld flavors. Season with **salt, pepper,** and a squeeze of **lemon,** and enjoy at room temperature.

◆◆ INTERMEDIATE PANTRY

Fassoulia with Olive Paste

Serve **basic recipe** warm, each portion garnished with a nugget of **olive paste.**

French Beans with Garlic-Parsley Butter

[FLAGEOLETS AU BUERRE]

◆◆ INTERMEDIATE PANTRY

Serves 4

The lamb was an exotic breed raised on a bucolic hillside in Devon, roasted to rosy tenderness; next to each slice nestled a delicate mound of French flageolets, voluptuous in their cloak of garlicky butter. "Such good beans," I murmured, nearly drunk from sheer pleasure as well as from the bottle of St-Emilion we had just polished off. "Thank you," replied my host, "the beans are canned."

I later prepared flageolets this way, cooking one pot from scratch and one from a can. They were both very good.

◆◆◆◆◆◆◆

TO PREPARE Take a generous nugget, say 3 to 4 tablespoons, of **Garlic-Parsley Butter** (page 350) and gently warm in a saucepan. Add 3 cups cooked and drained **flageolets,** stirring and mashing as you gently cook them for several minutes. Add 1/2 cup water to make a somewhat creamy sauce, and season with **salt** and **pepper.** Serve warm. If beans sit and thicken, add a bit more water when reheating.

LEFTOVERS Serve **leftover flageolets** warmed and spooned over thick slices of toasted and buttered **rye bread** that you have rubbed with a cut slice of raw **garlic.** Garlicky **flageolets** make a delicious bed for meat or cheese **ravioli** or **tortellini.** Top the **pasta** and **beans** with a spoonful or two of a garlic-scented, herb-seasoned **tomato sauce** and gild it all with a nugget of melting **butter** and a sprinkle of fresh **rosemary.**

San Luis Potosí Cactus Tacos

◆◆ INTERMEDIATE PANTRY

Serves 4

Strips of juicy nopales combine well with rich refried beans to roll up into warm corn tortillas, along with whatever else might be languishing in your kitchen: shredded meat, browned hamburger, diced potato chunks mixed with a soy-based meat substitute, chili-seasoned seafood, or humble sardines.

◆◆◆◆◆◆

TO PREPARE Drain 1 jar (about 6 ounces) **nopales** and cut into bite-sized pieces; set aside. Heat about 2 cups **refried beans;** keep warm. Do the same for 8 **corn tortillas,** and 1 cup whichever **filling** you're using (browned ground beef or chorizo, sautéed shrimp, mashed sardines, diced browned potatoes, etc.). Cut several canned **chipotle chilies** into strips. Spread beans over tortillas, then place a little of nopales, filling of choice, and chipotles on top. Roll up into plump tacos and enjoy immediately.

Honey-Herb Mustard

◆◆ BASIC PANTRY

Makes 1/2 cup

Enjoy with thyme-and-garlic-studded roast pork, juicy sausages, sweet-savory ham, and so forth; or coat fillets of firm-fleshed fish with a bit of mustard, then broil.

◆◆◆◆◆◆

TO PREPARE Mix 1/3 cup **Dijon mustard** with 3 tablespoons full-flavored **honey** and a pinch of dried **marjoram or thyme.** Mix well; lasts about 2 weeks, tightly covered, in refrigerator.

◆◆ INTERMEDIATE PANTRY

Raspberry–Whole Seed Mustard

Use **raspberry jam** in place of honey and **whole-seed mustard** in place of Dijon mustard.

Mango-Marmalade Dipping Sauce

◆◆ INTERMEDIATE PANTRY

Makes 1-1/2 cups

Serve with fried wontons, crunchy macadamia-nut-coated fish fillets, skewers of grilled chicken breast, or coconut-marinated turkey fillets. Chef Phillipe La Mancusa gave me this recipe; he serves it with seafood-stuffed wontons or coconut-coated fried shrimp.

◆◆◆◆◆◆

TO PREPARE Mix 1/2 cup **mango chutney** (the large bits coarsely chopped) with 3/4 cup **orange marmalade,** 1/4 cup **Creole mustard (or whole-seed mustard),** and 1 tablespoon bottled **horseradish.** Lasts at least 2 weeks tightly covered in refrigerator.

Pureed Artichoke Mayonnaise

◆ BASIC PANTRY

Makes about 1-1/4 cups

Tangy marinated artichokes, pureed into a sauce with creamy mayonnaise, is delicious spooned over cold poached fish, mixed seafood salad, or chicken on a bed of crisp romaine lettuce.

◆◆◆◆◆◆

TO PREPARE Puree 1 small jar (about 6 ounces) drained **marinated artichoke hearts** (reserve marinade for another use); add 1/2 cup **mayonnaise** and whirl to a smooth sauce. Chill before serving to firm it and meld flavors.

Sesame-Ginger Mayonnaise

◆ BASIC PANTRY

Makes about 1/3 cup

So good slathered onto a French bread sandwich of soy-brushed and grilled sole fillets, sprinkled with thinly sliced green onions. Or enjoy on a salmon fillet sandwiched between slices of whole wheat with lots of peppery watercress.

◆◆◆◆◆◆

TO PREPARE Combine 1/4 cup **mayonnaise** with 4 teaspoons Asian (toasted) **sesame oil** and 1/4 to 1/2 teaspoon **ground ginger** and chill; lasts about 2 weeks, tightly covered, in refrigerator.

Garlic-Mustard Vinaigrette

Makes 1/2 to 3/4 cup

Delightfully unsubtle, this garlic-mustard vinaigrette reeks deliciously and makes a wonderful cloak for crunchy lettuce greens such as romaine; it's also a good dressing for hearty salads with smoked sausage or herring, and for boiled potatoes.

◆◆◆◆◆◆

TO PREPARE Combine 1 to 2 chopped **garlic cloves** with 2 tablespoons **mustard** of choice: Dijon, green herbed, herbes de Provence, whole seed, Creole, etc., with 1 tablespoon **red wine vinegar.** Whisk in 6 tablespoons **extra-virgin olive oil** until creamy, then add **salt** and **pepper** to taste.

Red Wine–Mustard Vinaigrette

Use a full-flavored **red wine** in place of vinegar in **basic recipe.**

Raspberry-Mustard Vinaigrette

Use **raspberry vinegar** in place of wine vinegar in **basic recipe.**

Anchovy Vinaigrette

Makes 3/4 cup

Enjoy on boiled potatoes, or on slices of rare garlicky roasted lamb resting on a bed of spring greens.

◆◆◆◆◆◆

TO PREPARE Crush 4 **anchovies** (or use anchovy paste to taste) and combine with 3 tablespoons **red wine vinegar;** mix in 1/2 cup **extra-virgin olive oil** and 2 chopped **garlic cloves.** May be stored in refrigerator for up to 2 weeks.

Serves 4 to 6

Anchovy Roast Potatoes

Use vinaigrette as a seasoning mixture for oven-roasted potatoes: Parboil 8 to 10 medium somewhat **waxy potatoes;** drain and toss with about 1/4 cup **anchovy vinaigrette,** along with a generous amount of **herbes** de **Provence** and as much chopped **garlic** as you can bear. Roast in a preheated 400° oven until golden, about 40 minutes. Serve sprinkled with chopped fresh **parsely.**

Saffron Vinaigrette

◆◆ INTERMEDIATE PANTRY

Makes 1 to 1-1/4 cups

A bright yellow vinaigrette that is at its best atop mesclun-type greens, especially when topped with a selection of seafood.

◆◆◆◆◆◆

TO PREPARE Combine 1/4 teaspoon **saffron** threads with 1/4 cup **red wine vinegar,** 1/4 cup **fish stock or chicken broth,** 1/2 to 3/4 cup **vegetable oil,** 1 **shallot,** and 1 tablespoon **Dijon mustard.** Whirl in a blender or food processor to combine well; store in refrigerator for not longer than 3 days (since it has broth in it).

Chutney Vinaigrette and Two Salads to Enjoy with It

◆ BASIC PANTRY

Makes about 1 cup

Sweet and spicy, chutney adds a new dimension to vinaigrettes, making a bright change from more usual ingredients.

◆◆◆◆◆◆

TO PREPARE Combine 1/3 cup **mango chutney** (larger pieces finely chopped) with 1/3 cup **vegetable oil** and 2 tablespoons **white wine vinegar.** Mix well.

Salad No. One: Taj Chef's Salad

Top mixed greens with cubes of **ham, smoked turkey, sharp Cheddar** and bits of **red bell pepper.** Toss with **Chutney Vinaigrette,** above. Sprinkle with **cilantro** and chopped **green onions,** with a scattering of **toasted sunflower seeds** for a nutty crunch.

Salad No. Two: Tandoori Chicken Salad

Coat boneless **chicken breasts** with an **Indian spice paste** such as tikka or tandoori. Sauté or broil until just cooked through. Place the warm sliced chicken breasts atop a salad of **mixed greens, cucumbers, onions.** Dress with **Chutney Vinaigrette** and sprinkle with chopped fresh **cilantro** and coarsely chopped **peanuts.**

Dried Hot Chili and Vinegar Salsa

[SALSA DE CHILE ARBOL]

◆ **BASIC PANTRY**

Makes about 1/3 cup

This simple salsa adds a bracing welcome to nearly anything it touches.

◆◆◆◆◆◆

TO PREPARE Whirl 4 to 6 crumbled small **hot dried chilies** (preferably arbol) in a blender with 1/2 cup **white vinegar or white wine vinegar** and 1/2 teaspoon **salt.** Store in a bottle in refrigerator for up to 1 month.

Vietnamese Five-Spice Marinade for Grilled Poultry

◆◆◆ **ADVANCED PANTRY**

Makes 1/2 cup

Use to marinate poultry or pork before grilling over charcoal; traditionally served with steamed rice and shredded cabbage, carrots, and other crisp and crunchy vegetables.

◆◆◆◆◆◆

TO PREPARE Combine 6 chopped **garlic cloves** with 2 chopped **green onions** or 1 chopped **shallot,** 1-1/2 tablespoons *each* **sugar, salt,** and **black pepper,** 1/2 to 3/4 teaspoon **five-spice powder,** and 1-1/2 teaspoons *each* **Vietnamese fish sauce, light soy sauce,** and **dry sherry** (or omit fish sauce and substitute soy sauce). Pour over chicken and let marinate for 2 hours to overnight, then grill over charcoal.

Drunken Dried Fruit

◆ **BASIC TO**
◆◆ **ADVANCED PANTRY**

When dried fruits soak luxuriously in spirits they plump up into succulent sweet morsels. Serve a small amount with coffee as an after-dinner sweet, or spoon them over ice cream.

◆◆◆◆◆◆

TO PREPARE Choose **golden raisins** in **grappa, figs** in **brandy, prunes** in **Armagnac, apricots** in **Sauternes, cherries** in **brandy, dark raisins** in **rum,** and so on. Whichever fruits you choose, place them in a jar with **spirits** to cover, and let them sit, covered, for 2 weeks. Store in refrigerator and use as desired. I keep them for about 3 months this way, though I suspect they keep much longer.

Coffee Syrup

◆ BASIC PANTRY

Makes about 1 cup

Boiling leftover brewed coffee with sugar for a syrup is not for the fainthearted: the syrup is strong and intensely coffee flavored, good to spoon judiciously onto ice cream or to flavor soaked cakes such as rum babas and the like.

◆◆◆◆◆◆

TO PREPARE Mix 1 cup strong-brewed **coffee** with 1 cup firmly packed **dark brown sugar.** Heat gently to dissolve sugar, then raise heat and boil, uncovered, for about 10 minutes. Let cool, then add 1/2 teaspoon **vanilla extract** and 1 tablespoon **whiskey or brandy.**

Mocha Syrup

Combine equal parts basic **coffee syrup** with a strong **chocolate syrup.**

◆◆ INTERMEDIATE PANTRY

Coffee Syrup alla Roma

Add a bit of **Sambuca or ouzo** to basic **coffee syrup.**

Gelato with Whiskey and a Sprinkling of Ground Espresso Beans

[GELATO SPAZZACAMINO]

◆ BASIC PANTRY

Serves 1

Loosely translated, the Italian name means "chimney sweep ice cream," because the powdered espresso sprinkled on top looks like soot. The combination of bitter coffee and sweet ice cream with a heady dash of whiskey or brandy makes a nice finish to a brightly flavored meal, or a decadent lone pick-me-up.

◆◆◆◆◆◆

TO PREPARE Sprinkle bowls of rich **vanilla or chocolate ice cream** with a bit of **finely ground espresso coffee** beans, then drizzle **Scotch or Irish whiskey, or brandy,** over each bowlful.

◆◆ INTERMEDIATE PANTRY

Gelato alla Via Veneto

Choose **coffee ice cream** instead of vanilla, and drizzle with **Sambuca, Pernod, or ouzo** in place of whiskey or brandy.

Ice Cream with Drunken Figs, Rose Petal Sauce, and Pistachios

◆◆◆ ADVANCED PANTRY

Serves 4

Here is a grown-up ice cream sundae, with brandy-plumped figs strewn over creamy vanilla ice cream along with a fragrant spoonful of rose petal sauce, and a scattering of pistachios.

◆◆◆◆◆◆

TO PREPARE Cut stems from 8 to 10 dried **figs,** cut figs into halves, and place in a bowl with **brandy** to cover. Let sit, covered, for at least 2 hours, or until figs plump up. Meanwhile make rose petal sauce: Heat 1/3 cup **rose petal jam** with 3 tablespoons water until it melts together. Let cool and stir in a generous dash of **rose water.**

Serve bowls of **vanilla ice cream,** each portion topped with several pieces of figs, a spoonful of rose petal sauce, and a scattering of shelled **unsalted, untoasted pistachio nuts.**

Basic Dishes with Pantry Accents

◆◆

Pantry ingredients flavor and give body, texture, and visual appeal to food. The dishes that follow are rather basic: soups, roast poultry, meat stews, broiled fish fillets, green salads, chicken and rice casseroles, and so on. But these may be transformed into distinctive personal dishes, depending on the pantry ingredients used. Here, then, are some basic, universally appealing dishes with suggestions for varying their flavors. Feel free to use these recipes as a guide, adapting them to suit your pantry.

Garlic Soup

◆ BASIC PANTRY

Serves 4

This may be the only cookbook listing garlic soup as a basic dish. Indeed, this fragrant broth of simmered garlic lends itself to a myriad of variations. In Provence it is made with water, and considered an all-purpose cure, much like our Jewish chicken soup. I tend to make it using broth or a combination of broth and water for added flavor.

◆◆◆◆◆◆

TO PREPARE Combine 1 to 2 heads **garlic,** the cloves peeled and separated, in 1 quart **water, broth,** or combination; add any of the following flavorings. Bring to boil, then reduce heat and simmer for 20 minutes or until the garlic is soft and tender.

Garlic Soup with Sage

Add 1/2 to 1 teaspoon coarsely crumbled dry **sage leaves** or 5–7 fresh chopped leaves to basic recipe, along with a tiny pinch of **cayenne.** When broth is fragrant and garlic cloves soft, remove from heat. Beat 2 **eggs** with 1/4 cup grated **Parmesan cheese** and add a bit of broth to thin out. Pour egg-cheese mixture into hot soup, stirring vigorously to mix eggs and broth.

Garlic Soup with Cheese-topped Croûte

Melt a slab of **creamy jack cheese** on 1 crunchy **garlic-rubbed croûte** of dry baguette per serving; float croûte atop each bowl.

Garlic Broth with Pastina Provençal

To **basic garlic broth** add a handful of tiny **soup pasta** (pastina) or spaghetti broken into small bits. Add pasta when garlic is about half cooked through (10 minutes). A sprinkling of **diced ripe tomatoes** and chopped **fresh thyme** adds a rustic South of France flavor.

Cold Garlic-Barley Soup with Yogurt and Herbs

Add several tablespoons of half-cooked **barley** to simmering **broth.** When barley is tender, remove from heat and cool. Beat in 2 cups plain **yogurt,** 2 chopped raw **garlic cloves,** and 2 tablespoons *each* chopped fresh **dill** and **mint,** and **green onion** or chopped fresh **chives.** Enjoy chilled for a summer supper.

"Scotch" Eggs

◆ BASIC PANTRY

Serves 4

Hard-cooked eggs coated with a layer of spiced sausage meat, then browned to a golden crispness, are known as Scotch eggs, named for their land of invention. You see them there in pubs and delis, eaten as snacks along with a glass of good strong beer.

The idea lends itself brilliantly to a wide variety of seasoning ingredients and sausage meat, and while they look rather lumpen and dull brown just lying there whole, once you cut into them to expose their yellow and white centers they are quite attractive, especially when served hot on a bed of greens, with sautéed tomatoes and chilies, or grilled eggplant.

◆◆◆◆◆◆

TO PREPARE Hard-cook 4 **eggs** until just tender, about 6 minutes. Run under cold water. When cool enough to handle, peel and set aside. Mix 1 to 1-1/2 pounds **chopped meat or sausage meat** with seasonings, then divide mixture into 4 balls. Flatten each one, then wrap one around each egg. Dredge in **flour,** then **beaten egg,** then **bread crumbs,** and brown in hot **oil** in a heavy skillet. Traditionally these are fried in a not insubstantial amount of oil; I find that roasting them in a hot (425°–450°) oven for about 20 minutes, or until browned and cooked through, is just as good.

◆ BASIC PANTRY

Traditional Herbed Scotch Eggs

Use **pork sausage** meat that has a strong flavor of **herbs,** or add a handful of your own: sage, parsley, thyme, etc. Serve on a bed of **watercress leaves,** accompanied with a **mayonnaise** seasoned generously with **Dijon mustard,** or with **aïoli.**

Indonesian Eggs on a Bed of Spinach

Use **ground pork** and season with 1 tablespoon chopped **fresh cilantro,** 2 chopped **garlic cloves,** a teaspoon or two chopped **fresh ginger,** and 1 tablespoon **soy sauce.** Mix and add a little **cornstarch** if too soft.

Coat **egg** with this mixture and cook, then serve cut into halves atop a bed of raw **spinach leaves,** accompanied with **Spicy Asian Peanut Dip** (page 178).

Moroccan Kofta with Grilled Eggplant

Combine **ground lamb** with 4 chopped **garlic cloves,** 1/2 to 1 teaspoon **curry powder,** 1/4 cup plain **yogurt,** 2 tablespoons minced **fresh cilantro,** and 1/4 cup **whole-wheat bread crumbs;** add **salt** and **pepper** to taste. Use this mixture to coat **eggs.** Cook, cut into halves, and serve on a bed of browned sliced **eggplant,** the whole thing sprinkled with ground **cumin** and **salt.**

Stuffed Pasta in Broth

**◆ BASIC TO
◆◆◆ ADVANCED PANTRY**

Serves 4

Stuffed pasta comes in an endless variety of ethnic, traditional, and nouvelle versions: ravioli filled with meat, fish, cheese, or vegetables; pelmeni; wontons; pirogi; etc. Mix and match the pastas with the broth you choose, and season accordingly: Cajun-spiced seafood ravioli in a crawfish or shrimp broth, porcini pasta in turkey or duck broth, chicken-and-sorrel-filled wontons in chicken broth, eggplant tortellini in vegetable-studded broth. Or choose a combination of pastas and let each bowlful offer the delight and variety of a treasure hunt.

A bowl of steaming hot broth and stuffed pasta makes a delicious yet simple dish: elegant enough for beginning a company meal, comforting enough for a solitary supper. It is perhaps the only dish I know of that seems to transcend generations and tastes; from infants to elders, few eaters are not delighted by its straightforward savor.

◆◆◆◆◆◆

TO PREPARE Cook about 1/2 pound **stuffed pasta** of choice in boiling salted water until barely tender. Drain carefully and set aside. Heat 1 quart **broth** to boiling point, then add pasta and heat through for only a moment or two. Serve each bowlful of hot broth with a handful of plump pasta.

Wontons in Hot and Sour Broth

Choose seafood, pork, or chicken-filled **wontons** and chicken- or dried-mushroom-flavored **broth.** Season pasta and broth with **soy sauce,** Asian (toasted) **sesame oil, vinegar,** and a **hot chili seasoning** such as chili paste. Sprinkle with chopped fresh **chives or cilantro.**

Goat Cheese Ravioli in Broth, with Chives

Choose **goat-cheese-filled ravioli,** or make your own using wonton noodles. Serve in **mushroom or chicken broth,** along with a sprinkling of **Parmesan cheese** if desired.

◆◆ INTERMEDIATE PANTRY

Pelmeni in Broth

Choose either beef-, chicken-, potato-, or cabbage-filled **pelmeni,** and serve in **chicken or beef broth.** Garnish with a generous sprinkling of chopped fresh **chives** and/or a dollop of **sour cream.**

Ravioli in Herbed Broth

Choose **meat ravioli and beef broth;** stir in a spoonful of chopped **fresh herbs,** along with a fine grating of **lemon zest,** and serve drizzled with a touch of **extra-virgin olive oil.**

◆◆◆ ADVANCED PANTRY

Meat and Spinach Ravioli in Duck Broth with Shreds of Wild Mushrooms

Choose **meat-and-spinach-filled ravioli** and serve in hot **duck broth,** adding several **dried mushrooms,** reconstituted and cut into strips to broth when you add cooked pasta. Also add strained soaking liquid from mushrooms.

Seafood Ravioli in Lemon Grass–scented Broth

Choose **seafood-stuffed ravioli,** preferably one with Asian flavors. Serve in hot **seafood or chicken broth** to which you've added 1 trimmed and sliced stalk of **lemon grass,** as well as a spoonful of **Cilantro-Lime Paste,** page 360.

Garlic Pasta, Pantry Style

◆ BASIC TO
◆◆◆ ADVANCED PANTRY

Serves 4

Al dente pasta tossed with garlic-scented oil is surpassed by few other dishes; it tastes like a walk down the Via Veneto but is much cheaper. The sort of thing to throw together regularly, it can be varied at whim. The pantry yields a nearly endless variety of ingredients for flavoring this simple dish.

◆◆◆◆◆◆

TO PREPARE Gently heat about 8 coarsely chopped **garlic cloves** in 1/4 cup **olive oil** for a few moments; remove from heat. Add about 1/4 cup coarsely chopped fresh **parsley** and set aside. Boil 1 pound **spaghetti** until al dente, drain, then toss with garlic-parsley oil. Season with **salt,** freshly ground **pepper,** and/or **red pepper flakes.**

Tuna-Caper Pasta

Add 3 ounces or so **tuna** chunks plus 1 to 2 teaspoons drained **capers** to **garlicky oil.** Toss as described previously, seasoning dish with a gentle squeeze of **lemon.**

Lemon-Pepper Pasta

Add finely **grated zest of 1/2 lemon** to **basic recipe,** and season with **black pepper.**

Garlic-Ginger Pasta

Add a pinch of **ground ginger** to **garlic oil** in basic dish, and use **red pepper flakes** in place of black pepper.

◆◆ INTERMEDIATE PANTRY

Pesto and Peppers Pasta

To **basic garlic pasta recipe,** add strips of **roasted red peppers,** as well as a spoonful of **pesto** and handful of **pine nuts.**

Field of Fresh Herbs Pasta

Add several tablespoons **chopped fresh herbs** such as chives, marjoram, thyme, basil, sage, etc. to **basic pasta dish.** Season with **salt** and **black pepper.**

Whole-Wheat Spaghetti with Potatoes, Pesto, and Olive Paste
[SPAGHETTI INTEGRALE ALLA GENOVESE]

Choose **whole-wheat spaghetti,** preferably a good firm type imported from Italy. When pasta is softened, add 2 to 3 medium **waxy potatoes** to boiling water and cook together until both are al dente. Drain.

To **garlic, olive oil, and parsley** add 2 diced seeded **tomatoes,** then toss hot pasta in seasoned oil. Serve immediately, each portion garnished with a nugget of **pesto** and **olive paste,** with a handful of **olive-oil-and-vinegar-dressed lettuce** strewn around edge of pasta.

◆◆◆ ADVANCED PANTRY

Pasta with Prosciutto or Pancetta, Rosemary or Sage, and Parmesan

Omit parsley from **basic recipe** and add several teaspoons chopped **fresh sage or rosemary.** Add 3 to 4 ounces cut-up **prosciutto** or browned diced **pancetta** to garlicky oil, and serve hot pasta tossed with coarsely grated **Parmesan cheese.**

Rich Pasta with Truffles
[PASTA AL TARTUFO]

Omit parsley from **basic recipe** and add as much **truffle paste or truffle bits** as you desire or can afford (1 ounce would give a delicious flavor; a 2-ounce tube is delicious excessiveness).

Broiled Fish Fillets

◆ BASIC TO
◆◆◆ ADVANCED PANTRY

Serves 4

TO PREPARE Coat 1 pound fish fillets with a savory seasoning paste; brush with oil and broil.

◆ BASIC PANTRY

Mustard-Paprika Fillets

Coat fish with a mixture of 1 chopped **garlic clove,** a tablespoon or two of a mild but tangy **mustard,** a teaspoon or two of **paprika,** and **salt** and **pepper** to taste. Or choose tangy-sweet **Honey-Herb Mustard** (page 39), seasoned with a bit of **thyme.** Brush with **oil** of choice, then broil. The mustard-coated fillets could also be dusted with **flour** and pan-fried to a golden brown.

Red Chili–seasoned Fish
[PESCADO ENCHILADO]

Coat fish fillets with **Red Chili-Citrus Paste** (page 128); brush with **olive oil** and broil until just tender; serve with wedges of **lime** and **Cilantro-Lime Paste** (page 360).

◆◆◆ ADVANCED PANTRY

Asian-flavor Fish Fillets

Coat **fish fillets** with a mixture of 1 tablespoon **soy sauce,** 1 teaspoon Asian (toasted) **sesame oil,** 1 teaspoon grated **fresh ginger,** 1/2 to 1 teaspoon **sugar,** and 2 teaspoons **dry sherry.** Broil until just tender, then serve on a bed of briefly stir-fried greens tossed with a little **Chinese black bean sauce or mesclun** dressed in **black bean vinaigrette.**

Sausages and Lentils

◆ BASIC PANTRY

Serves 4

A quintessential peasant dish, hearty and robust. The legumes absorb the flavors from the sausage, so the dish will taste of whichever sausage you choose. This dish can accommodate almost any vegetable and/or meat, which only adds to its vibrant flavor.

◆◆◆◆◆◆

TO PREPARE Lightly sauté 1 pound **sausage** of choice (about 2 per person), adding 1 to 2 chopped **carrots** and 4 to 6 coarsely chopped **gar-**

lic cloves as sausage is sautéing. Remove sausage from pan and set aside, then add 1-1/2 cups **dried lentils,** along with 3 cups **liquid of choice,** and a **bay leaf** or two. Bring to a boil and cook until legumes are cooked halfway through, about 30 minutes. Return sausage to pot and simmer until sausage is cooked through and lentils are tender.

Kielbasa with Split Peas

Add several chunks of diced **celery root or turnip** to carrot mixture, as well as 1 chopped **onion.** Choose either **green or yellow split peas,** use **beef or vegetable broth** as cooking liquid, and season with 1/2 teaspoon ground **cumin** as well as a good pinch of dried **marjoram.**

◆◆◆ ADVANCED PANTRY

Merguez with Red Lentils

Choose North African **spicy lamb sausage** (merguez) and **red lentils,** and **lamb or beef broth** to cook the mélange in, sautéing carrots and garlic with a sprinkling of ground **cumin** and **curry.** When you return sausages to pan, add a cup or so thinly sliced **spinach,** and season finished dish as needed with **lemon juice** to taste.

Seafood Sausage with Brown Lentils

Choose a full-flavored **seafood sausage** and take care not to overcook; unlike meat sausages, seafood ones take only about 10 minutes to cook through. Use chopped **shallots** in place of garlic, and simmer **brown lentils** in a mixture of half **white wine** and half **fish stock** or **shellfish broth.**

Italian or French Garlic Sausage with French Lentils

Choose spicy, garlicky **Italian or French sausages** and **French green lentils;** for cooking liquid, use a mixture of half **red wine** and half **beef**

broth. Season generously with **thyme,** and a pinch of both ground **cumin** and **cayenne** (if sausages are not spicy).

Sausages Simmered with Beans

Other legumes are equally delicious prepared this way. Use beans that have been cooked or nearly so. Pair **chorizo** with **pinto beans,** roasted mild **green chilies,** and whole **cumin seeds; seafood sausage** with **white beans; andouille** with **red kidney beans; kielbasa** with **black beans** and **cumin**-seasoned sautéed **red and green bell peppers.**

Chicken (or Turkey) Paillards

♦ BASIC TO
♦♦ INTERMEDIATE PANTRY

Serves 4

Boned chicken breasts, pounded and enthusiastically seasoned, then quickly browned or grilled, make an exquisitely simple dish. They take readily to a wide variety of flavors, making them a perfect food to take to your pantry in search of the right seasonings.

♦♦♦♦♦♦

TO PREPARE Remove skin from 4 boned **chicken breast halves** (or use turkey fillets cut into individual portions) and with a mallet (I use a clean wine bottle), lightly pound breasts into an even thickness (turkey fillets are usually cut into thin slices and will probably not need pounding; use your judgment). Rub flat cutlets with whichever **seasoning paste** you choose, then cook quickly in a hot pan or over an open fire, only a minute or so on each side, to keep them from overcooking. Alternatively, breasts may be left as is, with skin intact and of an irregular thickness. Marinate same way but allow a slightly longer cooking time to compensate for thickness. Remember that even the loveliest seasoned chicken breasts taste dry and unappetizing when overcooked.

♦ BASIC PANTRY

Garlic and Rosemary Paillards

Use **Olive Oil–Rosemary Marinade** (page 86). Serve grilled chicken breasts with **Olive Aïoli** (page 158).

LEFTOVERS Juicy room-temperature **rosemary-garlic-grilled paillards** are sublime stuffed into **rosemary rolls** and slathered with **aïoli.**

◆◆ INTERMEDIATE PANTRY

Southwestern Chilied Chicken Breasts

Use **Red Chili-Citrus Paste** (page 128) to coat **chicken breasts;** serve grilled paillards each with a nugget of **Green Chili–Cilantro Butter** (page 350).

Southeast Asian Paillards

Coat **chicken breasts** with several tablespoons of **coconut milk,** a good sprinkling of **curry powder,** a squeeze of **lime,** and dash of **soy sauce.** Serve grilled paillards as is, or with **Spicy Asian Peanut Dip** (page 178).

Tandoori Paillards

Coat **chicken breasts** with **Indian spice paste** that you've thinned with a little **yogurt** and let marinate for 30 minutes or so. Serve grilled or pan-browned breasts accompanied with **Double-Onion Nan** (page 347) or other thin flat bread such as **flour tortillas.**

◆◆ INTERMEDIATE PANTRY

Middle Eastern Chicken Sandwich

Slice and stuff **chicken breasts** into **whole-wheat pita breads,** and dress with **yogurt,** diced **cucumber,** chopped **fresh mint and/or cilantro,** and **green onions.**

Red Beans and Rice

◆ BASIC TO
◆◆ INTERMEDIATE PANTRY

Serves 4

Throughout much of Latin America, beans and rice keep the population alive and healthy. The combination is also delicious, with enough variations that you could eat it nearly every night.

◆◆◆◆◆◆

TO PREPARE Begin with 2 cups **dried beans** (red, black, or pinto) cooked until just tender, then add a chopped **onion** and several chopped **garlic cloves,** along with distinctive flavorings of your pantry. Simmer together for about 10 minutes, until it forms a saucy, savory mélange. Serve ladled over rice, garnished with pungent seasonings.

Tex-Mex Red Beans and Brown Rice

Use **olive oil** for sautéing onion and garlic, then season with 1/2 teaspoon *each* ground **cumin** and **chili powder.** Add **red kidney beans,** 1/2 cup chopped **tomatoes,** and 1 grated **carrot.** Season with **pickled jalapeños or Cilantro-Lime Paste** (page 360), and serve ladled over **brown rice.** While not a pantry item, a garnish of cool **sour cream** is lovely.

◆◆ INTERMEDIATE PANTRY

Caribbean Coconut-spiced Red Beans

To **sautéed onion and garlic** add 1/2 cup **coconut milk,** 1/2 teaspoon ground **cumin,** and **salsa or chopped chilies** to taste. Simmer with **red kidney beans,** as in basic recipe. Serve ladled over **white rice,** with a **vinegar-based hot sauce** on the side. For a more elaborate dish, garnish with bits of browned **smoked sausage** and sliced **banana.**

New Orleans Red Beans and Rice

Add chopped **celery** (1/2 stalk) and several ounces chopped **smoked ham** along with **onion and garlic.** Serve ladled over **white rice,** and sprinkle with chopped **fresh chives or green onions.**

Savory Simmered Chicken

◆ BASIC TO
◆◆ INTERMEDIATE PANTRY

Serves 4

Sauté 1 cut-up **chicken** in a tablespoon or two of **oil;** cook until golden-tinged. Sprinkle with **seasonings** (spices, garlic, onion, etc.); cook a few minutes longer, then add a flavorful **liquid to cover** (about 2 cups). Bring to a boil, reduce heat, cover, and simmer until chicken is tender, about 45 minutes.

Chicken with Olives

[COQ AUX OLIVES]

Season sautéing **chicken** with 3 to 4 chopped **garlic cloves** and a generous pinch of dried **thyme or herbes de Provence,** along with a **bay leaf** or two. For the liquid use a combination of half **wine (red or white)** and half **broth.** When chicken is nearly cooked, add 1/2 to 3/4 cup halved **pimiento-stuffed green olives.** If sauce is too thin when chicken is cooked through, pour it off and boil down to condense and intensify.

Burmese Curried Chicken and Noodles

Season the sautéing **chicken** with 1 teaspoon **curry powder,** or to taste, along with several chopped **shallots;** for the liquid use 1 cup *each* **coconut milk** and **chicken broth.** Simmer until tender, then serve ladled over boiled **thin egg or rice noodles,** with an optional sprinkling of chopped fresh **chives, cilantro,** and coarsely chopped **dry-roasted peanuts.**

Chicken in Tomatillo Sauce

[POLLO EN MOLE VERDE]

Add 1 chopped **onion** and 3 **garlic cloves** to the sautéing **chicken;** sprinkle with 1/2 teaspoon ground **cumin.** For the liquid use mashed **tomatillos** thinned with a little **broth,** and a bit of **Cilantro-Lime Paste** (page 360) or **Basic Salsa** (page 368). Serve with **rice** or warmed **corn tortillas.**

Robust Tomatoey Meat Braises

Serves 4

Enjoy a goulash over spaetzle, a cinnamon-scented Greek stifado with orzo, or an African beef curry, depending on the pantry ingredients you choose.

◆◆◆◆◆◆

TO PREPARE Sauté 1 or 2 **onions** and a clove or two of **garlic;** when softened and somewhat translucent remove them and brown 1-1/2 to 2 pounds **stewing meat,** cut into chunks. Add **aromatics** of choice, then a mixture of **broth** and chopped **tomatoes** to cover. Simmer, covered, until very tender, about 2 hours. If sauce is too thin, pour out, skim off fat, and boil down to condense flavors.

◆ BASIC PANTRY

African Beef Curry

Choose **beef** and sprinkle sautéed meat, onions, and garlic with 1/2 teaspoon **curry powder** and a pinch of ground **cinnamon.** Add 1 **sweet potato,** cut into chunks, and 2 tablespoons **golden raisins,** along with **tomatoes and broth,** then simmer until very tender.

◆◆ INTERMEDIATE PANTRY

Hungarian Paprika Beef with Spaetzle

Choose either **beef or pork.** Add a tablespoon or two of **Hungarian paprika** to the meat just as it has browned, and cook together a few minutes to remove any raw flavor. Add 1/2 cup chopped **roasted red peppers,** 1 **bay leaf,** and 1 cup chopped **tomatoes,** along with **broth** to cover. Serve over **Saffron Spaetzle** (page 323) with a dollop of **sour cream** as a garnish.

Greek Stew with Orzo

Choose **beef or lamb;** season sautéed **onion, garlic,** and meat with 1/4 teaspoon ground **cinnamon,** and a generous pinch *each* ground **cumin,** ground **cloves,** and **oregano.** Add chopped **tomatoes** and **broth** to cover and simmer. When meat is tender, take several spoonfuls of sauce and toss with nearly tender cooked **orzo.** Continue cooking orzo a minute or two until al dente, then serve orzo with stew, the pasta sprinkled with **Parmesan cheese.**

Roast Duck

◆ BASIC TO
◆◆◆ ADVANCED PANTRY

Serves 2

Crisp-skinned and succulent-fleshed roast duck gives itself to nearly any sort of seasoning: from gentle fruity flavors to fiery chilies and tomatoes, from red wine and olives to hoisin sauce and stir-fried greens.

◆◆◆◆◆

TO PREPARE **Salt** and **pepper** the **duck,** place something aromatic in its cavity, then roast it in a preheated 450° oven for 20 minutes. Reduce the heat and continue cooking in a gentler 325° oven for another 60 minutes, or until thermometer reads 180° in the thigh. Halfway through roasting, baste or coat with whatever seasonings you've chosen.

◆ BASIC PANTRY

Mexican Chilied Orange Duck

[PATO EN NARANJA]

Place a halved **orange** inside the **duck** before roasting, and coat the inside of the duck with **Red Chili-Citrus Paste** (page 128). When duck is half roasted, spread with more of the citrus-chili paste and continue cooking. Serve with a salsa of chopped **onions, cilantro,** and **serrano chilies** seasoned with **salt, pepper,** and **lime, grapefruit, and orange juices** and accompany the duck with **rice and black beans.**

◆◆ INTERMEDIATE PANTRY

Red-Wine-and-Herb-roasted Duck with Gnocchi

[ANITRA CON GNOCCHI]

Stuff the **duck** with 1 whole **head of garlic** separated into cloves before roasting. When duck is halfway cooked, pour off fat and add 1 cup *each* **beef broth, red wine,** and chopped **tomatoes,** along with 1 teaspoon chopped fresh **rosemary** and several cloves of **chopped garlic.** Return duck to oven to finish roasting, then serve the duck carved into individual portions, accompanied with al dente **gnocchi** with some of the pan juices poured over.

◆◆ INTERMEDIATE PANTRY

Hoisin Duck

Stuff the **duck** with several **green onions** before roasting. When duck is halfway cooked, glaze it with **hoisin sauce,** basting it every so often.

Chinese Duck with Black Beans

Stuff the basic **duck** with **green onions** and a knob of **fresh ginger;** rub with **soy sauce,** Asian (toasted) **sesame oil,** and **five-spice powder** to taste. Roast according to the basic recipe; when half cooked pour off fat and add 3/4 cup *each* **dry sherry** and **chicken broth** as well as a few spoonfuls of **Chinese black bean sauce.** Finish cooking, adding water to keep pan juices from burning. Serve sprinkled with chopped fresh **cilantro and/or chives.**

Choose-Your-Own-Flavor Roast Chicken

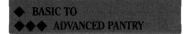

◆   **BASIC TO**
◆◆◆ **ADVANCED PANTRY**

Serves 4

Whichever pantry ingredient you choose, the basics are the same: stick a fragrant, moist **vegetable and/or fruit** inside the **chicken,** then season and roast it in a 325° oven until the bird is golden brown and the juices run clear when the thigh is pricked with a fork. This should take about 45 minutes for a medium chicken. Lately I've been roasting the bird in a very high—450°—oven for 20 minutes, then reducing the heat to 325° to finish it. Both ways result in a brown-skinned, juicy bird.

To truss or not to truss is the next question. Trussing protects the inside from losing moisture, and the legs do tie up nicely into neat parcels, but I seldom bother. The birds will still emerge from the oven golden and juicy.

Italian Lemon-Herb Chicken

[POLLO ARROSTO]

Chop several **garlic cloves** and mix with 2 tablespoons **olive oil.** Coat the **chicken** with this oil, then stuff it with **1/2 lemon,** half a head of garlic broken into cloves, and an herb sprig; **rosemary or thyme** work best. Add **salt** and **pepper,** then roast as in basic recipe. Other flavorings such as **tarragon, crushed fennel, or herbes de Provence** could be added to oil as well. For a Greek flavor, rub chicken with lots of dried **oregano** mixed into the garlic olive oil, and roast as in basic recipe. When chicken is golden and nearly cooked, squeeze one **lemon** over roasting bird, then return to oven for 10 minutes.

Egyptian Cinnamon-Garlic Chicken or Poussin

Follow **basic recipe,** rubbing bird with several teaspoons ground **cinnamon** and a sprinkling of **garlic powder** (actually good in this dish). Stuff with several **garlic cloves,** sprinkle with **salt** and **pepper,** and roast. Serve tender bird accompanied with a **brown rice pilaf** and bowl of cooling **yogurt,** chopped **cucumbers,** and chopped fresh **mint.**

Indian-flavor Chicken

Rub **chicken** inside and out with a **tikka or tandoori paste** thinned down with a little **lemon juice.** Place a knob of **fresh ginger** and a few **garlic cloves** in cavity of chicken and roast as above.

Aromatic Glazed Chinese Chicken

Rub **chicken** with **five-spice powder** to taste; mix 1 tablespoon *each* **plum sauce** and **dry sherry** with 2 tablespoons *each* **bean sauce** (also known as **brown bean sauce**) and **hoisin sauce.** Rub chicken inside and out with this mixture. If possible, let sit and marinate overnight in refrigerator; if not, leave for 1 hour. Mix 1/4 cup **soy sauce** with an equal amount of **maple or golden syrup** and rub onto marinated chicken. Roast as in basic recipe.

Casseroled Chicken and Rice

Serves 6

This savory ethnic dish of chicken and rice is enjoyed by cultures throughout the world, varied by the seasonings chosen.

◆◆◆◆◆◆

TO PREPARE Brown 1 cut-up **chicken** in several tablespoons **oil** of choice until cooked halfway through, about 10–15 minutes (chicken could be roasted to this stage instead). Pour off fat, then add a little oil **or butter** and sauté 1 cup raw **rice** and several chopped **garlic cloves or shallots,** taking care that crusty bits of chicken remaining in pan do not burn. Add 2 cups **broth,** cover, and simmer for 20 minutes, or until both rice and chicken are cooked through.

Garlic Chicken and Rice

Increase number of **garlic cloves** to 10 or even more. Delicious accompanied with **black bean chili.**

Middle Eastern Chicken and Rice

Season the sautéing **chicken** with 1/2 teaspoon ground **turmeric,** adding a pinch of **cardamom, ginger,** and **curry** to rice, substituting 1 cup chopped **tomatoes** for half the broth. Serve accompanied with a bowl of **yogurt** seasoned with chopped fresh **dill, cilantro, and mint.**

◆◆ INTERMEDIATE PANTRY

Curried Chicken and Rice Biriani

Season **chicken** with a generous amount of **curry powder** and a few pinches of ground **cumin** and **turmeric.** Use **basmati rice,** and shortly before rice and chicken are cooked through add 1 cup diced **broccoli** or chopped and squeezed blanched **spinach,** and fold in 1 cup or so of **yogurt.** Heat through and serve accompanied with a selection of several chutneys and a simple salad of sliced **cucumbers, onions, tomatoes,** and **peppers.**

Spanish/Mexican Rice with Chicken, Vegetables, and Chorizo
[ARROZ CON POLLO]

Use 1 chopped **onion** in addition to garlic, and add 1/2 *each* **green and red bell peppers,** diced, to sautéing **rice,** along with 2 spicy Mexican **chorizo** sausages, crumbled. Use 1 cup chopped **tomatoes** for half of broth, and season dish with ground **cumin,** chopped **oregano,** and ground **coriander,** adding 1/2 cup **green pimiento-stuffed olives or marinated artichoke hearts** when dish is nearly finished.

Spanish Rice with Duck

[ARROZ CON PATO]

Use 1 cut-up **roast duck** in place of chicken in preceding recipe and serve finished dish mounded onto a platter, garnished with fresh **cilantro** and wedges of **oranges** and **limes**.

◆◆◆ ADVANCED PANTRY

Persian-style Garlic Chicken and Rice

Prepare basic garlic chicken and rice, serving the finished dish sprinkled generously with tangy **red sumac spice**.

II • A Cook's Guide to the Pantry's Bounty

OILS AND VINEGARS

◆◆

In our contemporary pantry, oils and vinegars provide a broad palette of flavors culled from all over the world. They can be used for cooking, seasoning, dressing, or marinating.

The essential character of a cuisine is based on the fat it is cooked in. We can choose Mediterranean olive oils that range from subtly perfumed to frankly olive, the colors a veritable landscape of greens and yellows. Nut oils such as hazelnut or walnut taste lyrically of the nuts they are pressed from and are evocative of country food from the regions of France and Switzerland. Asian sesame oil, with its dark, deep toasted flavor, adds a Pacific Rim accent to anything it touches.

Vinegar is surprisingly versatile, good for much besides salads: deglazing a skillet and making piquant pan sauces, sparking rich braises, marinating nearly anything, and serving as the basis for buttery beurre blanc. Its versatility lies not only in what the cook can do with it, but in the range of flavors it comes in: sherry vinegar from Spain, its tang accented with sherry's distinctive nuttiness; English malt vinegar, all assertive sourness, but perfect for the classic pairing of fish and chips; rice wine from Japan and China, subtle and slightly sweet-tangy, to dress cold vegetable salads and rice dishes with an Asian savor. Italy and France offer up a wide range of vinegars, usually made from wine and sometimes flavored with herbs or fruits, and aged in various woods. As well as the wealth of flavors that oils and vinegars bring to our table, the packaging of these flavoring ingredients brings visual excitement to our pantry shelves: tall, thin, graceful bottles, round-bottomed chemistry lab beakers, endearingly clumsy square bottles made from thick glass, or gleaming tins with long pouring spouts. Then there are the labels, marked in foreign languages, often elaborate, and usually brightly colored.

A changing selection of oils and vinegars on your pantry shelf is almost a revolving gallery exhibition, and is essential to good pantry cooking.

About Oils

Though often they seem to be working in the background, oils are perhaps the most important ingredient in cooking. Oils and fats meld the flavors of other ingredients and give character to an entire cuisine. For example, olive oil gives the distinct flavor of the Mediterranean, while sesame oil conjures up Asian lands. Bland vegetable oils are neutral and let the other flavors of a dish shine through. Butter and poultry fat such as goose, duck, or chicken, and lard add regional European flavors, but animal fats are less a part of our contemporary cuisine than flavorful vegetable oils. A little butter, however, is inimitable and has a place in my home cooking, while margarine, with its fake buttery pose, does not. (I do, however, occasionally use the low-fat spreads made from butter mixed with oils and buttermilk solids.)

Oils with a high ratio of mono- and polyunsaturated fats to saturated fatty acids are considered healthier; those with a high saturated fat level, such as the "tropical oils" (coconut, palm, and palm kernel) are thought to raise "bad" cholesterol levels in the blood. Until we know more about the latter, we should avoid them. Besides, they add little in the way of flavor.

STORAGE TIP Oils should be stored in a cool place, though there is no need to refrigerate them. Olive oil, especially, should not be refrigerated, as it becomes solid and cloudy and difficult to pour. (No problem if it does; simply warm it at room temperature until it is pourable once again.) Most unrefined oils last around 6 months; periodically taste your oils for freshness, and don't use any that have the slightest whisper of rancidity—they will ruin an entire dish.

Pantry List: Oils

◆◆◆◆◆◆

Almond oil	**Grapeseed oil**	**Olive oil**
Bland vegetable,	**Hazelnut oil**	**Sesame oil**
seed, or nut oils	**Mustard oil**	**Walnut oil**
Chinese chili oil		

Asian (Toasted) Sesame Oil is amber-colored and tastes of the essence of toasted sesame seeds. It has a low smoking temperature so should not be used for cooking, but rather for seasoning. A drizzle of Asian sesame oil combined with a splash of soy sauce defines classic Chinese flavor. Try it on steamed chicken and/or broccoli, or any stir-fry, or use it to season plain rice, topped with a sprinkling of green onions.

Bland Vegetable Oils Corn, canola, safflower, sunflower, and soybean oils are all polyunsaturated, with canola reputed to have anti-cancer benefits. Grapeseed oil is another neutral oil with an exceedingly high smoking temperature that makes for nearly smokeless frying. All of these mild oils harmonize with stronger flavoring ingredients, and are excellent for frying or sautéing when flavors other than the oil are meant to shine through.

Mustard Oil is similar to Asian sesame oil in that it is used mostly for flavoring rather than frying, though many Asian cuisines do use it for cooking. Try mustard oil in a dill-seasoned vinaigrette.

Nut Oils such as walnut and hazelnut taste as woodsy as the nuts they are crushed from, with strong flavors that usually need to be diluted by an equal or larger amount of a blander oil. Peanut oil is more neutral and often used for Chinese stir-fries because of its high smoking temperature, while almond oil is so delicate I cannot decide what to do with it besides using it to make a light vinaigrette. Avocado oil is another very delicate, very expensive oil.

Olive Oil Our word for oil is derived from the Greek *elaia,* and since the dawn of civilized humankind olive oil has influenced the rituals, gastronomy, and even languages of the Mediterranean people. First cultivated around 6000 B.C.E. in Syria and southern Iran, olive trees and their resulting olives and oil were brought to central and western Mediterranean countries by the Phoenician traders and, later by the Greeks and Romans. There are numerous references to the oil of the olive in the literature of these ancient peoples, including prominent mentions of it in the Bible and the Koran.

Much later, the Spaniards brought olives from the Mediterranean to the New World, and today much of California cuisine is decidedly olive oil based.

Olive oil is mono-unsaturated. Recent research has shown that unlike polyunsaturated oils, mono-unsaturated oils have the potential to lower the amounts of LDL (low-density lipoprotein), the "bad cholesterol" while leaving the beneficial HDL (high-density lipoprotein) cholesterol untouched. Polyunsaturated oils reduce both, which may be less beneficial. Olive oil is so delicious I am grateful that discoveries now show it to be healthful; but I must confess that while everyone else was busy pouring on the polyunsaturates in the name of fitness, I was clinging to my olive oil and would have continued to eat it regardless of the consequences.

Olive oils are graded "pure," "virgin," and "extra-virgin." "Pure" olive oil tends to be more refined, contains more impurities, and is blended with a bit of virgin oil for flavor. "Virgin" and "extra-virgin" oils are graded on their percentage of oleic acid. The maximum of "extra-virgin" is 1 percent, while the maximum allowed "virgin" is 3.3 percent. "Extra-virgin" must also pass higher standards of taste, flavor, aroma, and color.

As fine wines vary according to the type of grape, and the location and makeup of the soil it is grown on, so too do olive oils reflect their varietal source and home. Their colors range from deep green to the color of sun-bleached hay, with flavors that can be smoky, fruity, or nutty. Tuscan olive oil has a peppery kick that assaults the throat of the unprepared but is in fact a prized component of the oils of that region.

There is such a wide range of olive oils available you will have to taste your way through to find your favorites. Ask advice where you buy oil, and purchase small bottles for sampling. As with wine vinegar, many specialty shops have a house brand.

A fun thing to do is hold an olive oil tasting, much like a wine tasting, by buying a selection of oils. Fill small bowls or saucers with a wide range of oils, offer crusty bread and raw vegetable sticks for dipping. It's interesting to see how each oil compares with others and how tasters' opinions differ.

Many experts advise keeping a "pure" or mildly flavored olive oil for cooking and a "virgin" or "extra-virgin" for salads, but I disagree. Excellent olive oil with robust flavor is my weakness and I could not do without it. Since cooking does alter the delicate flavor of olive oil, use more subtle, finer-flavored oils for salads. Use cost, too, as a guide. There's no sense in using an expensive oil to cook with if its flavors will be overwhelmed. However, I do use "pure" olive oils that have a good "olivey" flavor. Without that distinctive olive character, what's the point? I am fondest of several local California olive oils.

About Vinegar

The English word *vinegar* is derived from the French, *vin aigre,* which means simply "**sour wine.**" Though wine vinegar is most common and versatile, vinegar can be made from anything that ferments: wine, cider, beer, grain, and fruit or sugar syrups such as molasses or maple (I remember a strongly acidic vinegar in Greece made from fermented grapefruitlike citron fruit).

American homesteaders on the Great Plains made vinegar by combining molasses, yeast, and rainwater, and some Germans still make vinegar from potatoes.

Deliciously sour, vinegar can have an acidity count of anywhere between 2 and 9 percent, though American law requires a minimum acetic acid content of 4 percent for distilled and 6 percent for wine vinegars.

Vinegar has been around since Biblical times and was no doubt discovered accidentally when a batch of wine picked up a renegade bacteria that then converted the alcohol into acetic acid. The Babylonians used vinegar as a preservative along with salt brine, and as a condiment flavored with herbs. Ancient Greeks and Romans sprinkled it onto bread, while Roman soldiers carried it with them to drink diluted as a beverage. In 13th-century Paris, street vendors sold it from barrels. By the 14th century vinegar-making was prospering in Orléans, a city on the Loire that was the destination for ships traveling along that river. Often, by the time the wine carried in the ships had arrived, an amount of it had turned to vinegar. In England vinegar produced from beer or ale was already popular. In 17th-century France, vinegar was most popular not only for culinary uses, but as a means for the aristocracy to endure the stench of the smelly peasants: they carried around tiny boxes called *vinaigrettes* that contained small sponges soaked with vinegar, which they sniffed as the aroma of the unwashed grew too much to bear. (The aristocrats were also unwashed, but they doused themselves with perfumes, etc.)

Though there are three methods to making vinegar, it is generally agreed that the smoothest, loveliest result is produced from the Orléans method, named after the French city. It begins by placing the wine—and the quality must be good, for a wine vinegar is only as good as the wine it is made from—into oak barrels. The wine is then helped along its journey to vinegar by the addition of bacteria starters that convert its alcohol to vinegar. Chemicals and heat are both forbidden, and the result is a vinegar that is rich in flavor and aroma. There is no quick fix to this method; it requires four to eight months of aging. Wines may be turned into vinegar by quicker and more artificial means, which produce a harsh, aggressive product. All is not lost, however, as proper aging can mellow its puckery shock.

These days, the choice of vinegars is staggering, and we can taste our way through a variety of vinegars, building a pantryful of their invigorating flavors as we decide which we love and want at our table.

STORAGE TIP Vinegar, by its nature a preserving agent, lasts nearly indefinitely, though it should be discarded if it develops an unpleasant odor. Store away from direct sunlight to retain its flavor; if, however, you'd like the vinegar to absorb other flavors, add such flavoring agents as sprigs of herbs to the bottle, set it in a sunny window for 2 weeks or so, then return the bottle to a cool cupboard or shelf.

Pantry List: Vinegars

◆◆◆◆◆◆◆

Balsamic	Herbed vinegars: tarragon, basil, rosemary, thyme, combinations	Seasoned vinegars: garlic, chili, peppercorn
Cider vinegar		
Distilled vinegar		
Fruit vinegars: blueberry, blackberry, raspberry, pear	Malt vinegar	Wine vinegars: red, white, champagne, sherry
	Rice vinegars: Chinese, Japanese, Thai	

Balsamic Vinegar With its subtle sweetness and rich depth of flavor, balsamic vinegar transcends the realm of mere vinegar. It is a full-flavored liquid that can add sparkle to pan sauces, marinades, grilled fish, soups and stocks, braised vegetables, boiled potatoes, and, obviously, vinaigrettes. Balsamic vinegar, or *aceto balsamico*, is classically sprinkled on lightly sugared strawberries to intensify the "berriness" of the fruit. The fruity quality of this vinegar also adds a lovely note to tomato sauces and peperonata, or any dish that calls for a zesty edge without the citrus flavor of lemon. I am fond of a dash of balsamic vinegar added to pasta that has been dressed in olive oil and garlic. It makes a delicious bed for grilled vegetables and fresh herbs.

Balsamic vinegar is made only in the Modena commune of Italy's Emilia-Romagna region. It is made from the juice of the sweet white Trebbiano grape and aged first in a wooden barrel placed in sunlight instead of the more usual dark cellar. The sunlight quickens evaporation. After a period of up to two years the liquid is poured into a smaller barrel, where it continues its evaporation and aging. This is repeated every two years, with each move to a smaller barrel resulting in a more concentrated liquid. By law, it is aged a minimum of 10 years, but basalmic vinegar can be aged as long as 40 years for a product as complex and exhilarating as a fine wine. One winemaker I know is fond of a balsamic that has been aged 70 years.

The wood of the barrels themselves, made of juniper, mulberry, oak, or chestnut, contributes to the flavor, and families often hand down barrels from generation to generation.

Like all products of excellence, balsamic vinegar reflects the care and attention given to it in its price. And unfortunately, the best balsamic vinegar is usually the more expensive one. The times I've tried to save money when buying balsamic vinegar I was sorely disappointed.

Cider Vinegar Made from fermented apple cider, its flavor can be coarsely acidic. It's better for deglazing pans, for adding punch to savory stews of rich meats, for pickling and making chutneys, and for making strongly seasoned dressings rather than for simple vinaigrettes (though combined with apple juice and whisked with hazelnut oil it makes a delectable vinaigrette for sturdy greens). Classic American pickled vegetables such as piccalilli, chowchow, spiced peaches, and catsups are made from cider vinegar, which also gives a tang to Pennsylvania Dutch vinegar pie. Cider vinegar was once promoted as a health elixir, along with a dash of honey. A big glass drunk first thing every morning was supposed to "cure whatever ails you" and prevent overweight (though I am living proof of its failure to do the latter).

Distilled White Vinegar Strongly acidic, it is good for canning and pickling but not for salads. It's worth keeping a bottle in your pantry, however, because nothing cleans windows like newspaper and vinegar, and a periodic bath of strong vinegar keeps sink drains running smoothly. It's also good for making certain pickles and condiments.

Fruit Vinegars Though they came into current celebrity under the reign of the nouvelle chefs, fruit vinegars were popular in France and Italy during the 19th century, when they were diluted with water and drunk as hot-weather refreshment.

They are delicious in vinaigrette: raspberry vinegar, with its fruity nose and playful flavor, makes a delightful vinaigrette with mustard, garlic, and olive oil, while soft and fragrant pear vinegar makes a lyrical combination with hazelnut or walnut oil. And while warm beets may not sound terribly exciting, they are delicious dressed with olive oil and raspberry vinegar.

Herbed Vinegars are made by infusing wine vinegar with sprigs of herbs: oregano, thyme, rosemary, garlic, or tarragon.

When I was first learning to cook I discovered the joy of making my own herbed vinegars. The previous tenant in my apartment had been a gardener, and glass shelves lined the kitchen window. I soon filled them with my growing assortment of herbal vinegars in their varied bottles, with all sorts of herb combinations macerating in their acidic baths. Tarragon, rosemary, oregano, thyme, garlic, dill, basil—all went into this bottle or that one, often along with whatever wine was leftover from the last dinner party. Sometimes I would simply flit between bottles, opening them one at a time and thoroughly indulging myself in a nose-tingling orgy of sniffing.

Making your own herbed vinegars is simple: Clean an old wine bottle, fill with wine vinegar, and add whichever herbs you like. Steep for about 2 weeks. Strain, pressing the herbs to extract all of the flavor you can, then pour into a clean bottle. It should keep up to a year. I am particularly fond of tarragon-scented vinegar, especially on a warm lamb salad, and garlic vinegar with nearly anything. Around the Caribbean and in America's Deep South, fresh chilies are steeped in vinegar (distilled, cider, or sherry) for a peppery table condiment.

Malt Vinegar Best known as the condiment of choice for fish and chips, this has been a must for the British table since the 16th century. Made from malted barley, it is colored with caramel and has a harshness that limits its use, though it is good for pickling onions when you want a tangy jolt.

Rice Vinegars Made throughout Asia; the rice wine from which they are distilled gives them a slight sweetness. Chinese black rice vinegar is rich and deeply colored, dark red to nearly black. It is much like balsamic vinegar, which, in fact, can be substituted for black rice vinegar. The best Chinese rice vinegars come from Chinkiang. Besides black, Chinese vinegars also come in red and clear. Japanese rice vinegars are lighter in body and clear in color, though there is a red vinegar flavored with bonito, and a black *aji-pon* flavored with citrus and soy, as well as *ponza* vinegar made from a citrus fruit much like a lime.

White Chinese vinegar is used in sweet-sour dishes or in sharp pickles, while the black is used as a dip or condiment with spring rolls, pot stickers, and the like.

Japanese vinegar is used in *sunomono*, those lightly pickled vegetables that are so sprightly and appetizing, and in making sushi rice.

Asian vinegars are generally milder and less acidic than American vinegars, with Chinese the strongest, Japanese milder, and Thai vinegars even milder than the Japanese.

Sometimes rice vinegars, especially Japanese ones, are sweetened slightly.

Seasoned Vinegars Usually based on a mild wine vinegar, they are infused with strong aromatics such as garlic, dried chilies, or peppercorns.

Wine Vinegars are available in red, white, Champagne, sherry, and occasionally rosé. Some are labeled as varietals. The best have been aged in wooden casks, and their labels will so state. A good wine vinegar is made from a good wine, pure and simple; the frailties of a wine will be exposed in the resulting vinegar. The acidity will generally be 6 to 7 percent unless otherwise noted.

Sherry vinegar should be well aged in wood. The best are aged up to 25 years. While the finest sherry vinegars I've tasted have been from Spain, no doubt there are good ones from California and other regions.

With its full body and sweet aftertaste, sherry vinegar brightens salads made from cheese, fruits, and nuts, and greens such as arugula and mâche, and is delicious combined with walnut oil over tiny green beans.

Since a good wine vinegar is one of the most indispensable ingredients in any kitchen, shop around until you find one you absolutely love. Many delicatessens or specialty food shops have a house brand that is reasonable in price and often sensational in taste.

Homemade Flavored Oils and Vinegars

In addition to the wide range of fruit and herb vinegars and herbed oils available in the stores, all sorts of homemade flavoring oils and vinegars can be made. They add an out-of-the-ordinary touch to simple foods and are easy to put together.

Chili Oil

◆ **BASIC PANTRY**

Makes 1 cup

Crumbled dried red chilies such as tepin, péquin, and árbol, etc., add heat and flavor to oil. Chinese cuisine uses peanut or a bland oil, while a Mediterranean flavor requires olive oil.

In Tuscany, chili oil is used, along with a generous handful of strong herbs such as thyme or marjoram, to sauté shrimp used to top hot pasta. Chili oil made with olive oil is delicious on pizza, steamed vegetables, and seafood, and mixed with lemon juice and chopped parsley or cilantro it is used to baste grilling fish. Chinese chili oil, based on vegetable or peanut oil, is dribbled onto pot stickers and other plump dumpling dishes, along with soy sauce and a strong, sour vinegar.

◆◆◆◆◆◆

TO PREPARE Pour 1 cup **oil** over 2 tablespoons crumbled small hot **dried chili peppers or red pepper flakes,** depending on heat of peppers and your own taste. Some chilies (such as bird's eye) are incendiary, and need to be used more sparingly.

For a more pronounced flavor, gently heat with chili oil. A **bay leaf** or two may be added for an herbal note.

◆◆ **INTERMEDIATE PANTRY**

New Mexico Chilied Oil

Use a mild **New Mexico chili powder** or a combination powder in place of the crumbled hot chilies above.

Curry Oil

◆ **BASIC PANTRY**

Makes 1/2 cup

This strongly scented oil is a lovely component in vinaigrettes and dressings, with a flavor that varies according to the spice mixture you use.

◆◆◆◆◆◆

TO PREPARE Mix 2 teaspoons **curry powder** with enough water to form a paste, then slowly mix in 1/2 cup **mild vegetable oil.** Let sit for 1 to 2 days, or long enough for it to develop a good aroma, then pour off scented oil, leaving behind solids.

Ginger Oil

Use 1 teaspoon **ground ginger** in place of curry powder, above.

Garlic Oil

◆ **BASIC PANTRY**

Makes 1 cup

I first tasted this mixture of garlic and olive oil in a little trattoria in Florence, when the proprietor with a great flourish brought out a little bowl to accompany a selection of summer-fresh vegetables. Barely cooked spinach, roasted peeled peppers, strips of grilled eggplant, boiled white beans—it was all simple until he spooned on the garlic oil. Then it was still simple, but spectacular. Truly there is little that garlic oil is not delicious on: drizzle it over salad leaves, pizza or crusty breads, toss with pasta, or dress lightly cooked vegetables; and when no one is looking dip your finger into it and lick up the glorious oil.

◆◆◆◆◆◆

TO PREPARE Chop up lots of **garlic**—4 to 10 cloves—and add to a cup of **olive oil.** You can do it in a food processor but be careful not to totally puree garlic or it will be quite strong, and garlic and oil will emulsify. Store in refrigerator. Though it will cloud, leaving at room temperature to warm for a few minutes will solve the problem. Note: It is very important to remember that chopped garlic in olive oil can provide an unfortunately hospitable environment for botulism. Do not keep for more than 2 weeks.

When this garlic-scented oil is used for cooking, some of the garlic flavor dissipates and becomes subtle. At times I find a bit of extra garlic added to the dish gives several layers of garlicness, balancing subtlety with passion. Lovely.

Green Onion Oil

◆ BASIC PANTRY

Makes 1-1/2 to 2 cups

This simple-to-prepare Vietnamese condiment is strikingly good. Spoon it into clear broths and onto crisp vegetable salads, dab it onto rice and ginger-seasoned fish or chicken, and use it to stir-fry mushrooms, chicken, Napa cabbage, etc.

◆◆◆◆◆◆

TO PREPARE Gently heat 1 cup **mild vegetable oil** just until hot but not smoking, then pour over 1 bunch thinly sliced **green onions** and let cool. Kept tightly covered in refrigerator, it should last 4 to 5 days.

Olive-Olive Oil

◆◆ INTERMEDIATE PANTRY

Makes 1 to 1-1/2 cups

Oil-cured olives soaking in olive oil does double duty: the oil flavors the olives and the olives return the compliment, making the oil taste even more like the fruit it is pressed from.

Use to slather onto a crusty roll along with herbal vinegar, a clove of chopped garlic, and sliced tomatoes and peppers. Chunks of tuna and hard-cooked egg would make the classic niçoise sandwich, *pan bagnat*.

◆◆◆◆◆◆

TO PREPARE Place 1/2 cup or so **oil- or salt-cured black olives** in a 1-cup glass jar along with a sprig of **rosemary,** and fill it up with **olive oil.** Let sit for several days, then use as desired. Over a period of about 2 weeks, the oil will improve, taking on the flavorful essence of the fruit.

Old South Hot Pepper Vinegar

Hot pepper seasonings based on vinegar are indispensable to the Southern table, adding a tart piquancy to simple, hearty fare such as wilted greens and pan-fried catfish.

Makes 1 cup

You may use chilies with or without their seeds: the seeds will give a more intense heat, and without them you will likely need a larger number of chilies.

◆◆◆◆◆◆

TO PREPARE Scald 3 to 5 diced **fresh chilies** such as jalapeños or serranos by pouring boiling water over them. Drain, then add 1 cup **cider vinegar.** Let sit a day or two to ripen, then use at will.

New Mexico Hot Pepper Vinegar

Increase the amount of **jalapeños or serranos,** above, to 6 to 10, adding 10 or so **black peppercorns** to underline the heat as well as a good pinch of **salt.** In many Southwestern homes the pickled chilies are kept on the table, and more vinegar is added as the liquid is used up. The pickled peppers may be dug out and eaten as a relish.

Caribbean Sherry Peppers

In Bermuda and parts of the Caribbean, hot-pepper condiments are based on **sherry vinegar or wine vinegar. Tiny hot fresh chilies** are best for this.

Double Berry Vinegar

Makes 1/2 cup

Tangy, fruity raspberry vinegar is amplified by an infusion of crushed fresh blackberries. The resulting vinegar is lush and fragrant: perfect for saucing a roast duck or for combining with olive oil as a vinaigrette over butter lettuce with thin shreds of fresh mint.

◆◆◆◆◆◆

TO PREPARE Crush several spoonfuls of ripe **blackberries** in 1/2 cup **raspberry vinegar;** the amount of berries should be adjusted according to taste and seasonal quality of berries.

Mixed Herb Vinegar

This is more a description than a recipe, since no exact measurements are needed.

◆◆◆◆◆◆

TO PREPARE Into each clean bottle place **dried herbs** of choice, preferably in sprigs (1 or 2) or crumbled leaves (1 to 2 tablespoons), along with several whole **garlic cloves** and a pinch of **salt.** Tarragon, basil, rosemary, thyme—are all delicious; whichever you add will give its essential character and fragrance to the vinegar. Pour **red wine vinegar** into bottle and seal, then place in a window to mellow for 2 weeks. Remove to a cool pantry shelf and use as desired. An excellent and frugal variation of this is to add the small amounts of **leftover wine** from dinner parties to the bottle, letting each turn into vinegar and add its individual flavor to the brew.

Vinaigrettes

In addition to enlivening salad greens, vinaigrettes can also be splashed, sauce-like, onto steamed vegetables, meats, and fish. The Italian *bollito misto,* a simmering pot of assorted meats, vegetables, and sausages, is traditionally served with *salsa verde,* a vinaigrette thick with chopped parsley. The tanginess of the sauce cuts the richness of the dish. And simple boiled white beans are a Tuscan delicacy when anointed with olive oil and lemon or vinegar.

Vinaigrettes are delicious to use as a marinade, not only for food that is to be grilled, but for food that is to be baked. Toss a vinaigrette-marinade onto a full-flavored fish or meat, let sit in the refrigerator overnight, then bake in the marinade on low heat until the foods fall into tender morsels.

Vinaigrettes can perk up leftovers, too. Fried fish is delicious sparked with a bath of oil and vinegar or lemon, thinly sliced onion, and a few thin slices of chili, then marinated until the next day's lunch.

In addition to the following vinaigrettes, refer to "Forage Cooking" (page 23) and "Condiments" (page 117) for such dressings as Garlic-Mustard, Raspberry-Mustard, Chutney Vinaigrette, Sun-dried Tomato Vinaigrette, Saffron Vinaigrette, among others.

Basic Vinaigrette

◆ BASIC PANTRY

Makes 1/2 cup

The classic ratio of oil to vinegar is 3 or 4 parts oil to 1 part vinegar, but many prefer a tarter dressing with less oil and more vinegar, or dilute the vinegar with a little fruit juice. Red wine or slightly warm broth can add depth to a dressing, and flavorings such as mustard, garlic, chopped onion and herbs, chutney, cream, and the like all give varying flavor dimensions.

◆◆◆◆◆◆◆

TO PREPARE Combine 6 tablespoons **oil** (or a combination of oils) of choice with 2 tablespoons **vinegar; ** add **salt** and **pepper** to taste. Seasonings such as **shallots, garlic, mustard, chutney,** etc., usually combine best if mixed first with vinegar.

Spicy Moroccan Vinaigrette

Makes about 1/2 cup

Particularly good as a sauce for grilled eggplant slices, kebabs, swordfish, etc.

◆◆◆◆◆◆◆

TO PREPARE To 1/2 cup **basic vinaigrette** prepared with olive oil and white wine vinegar and/or lemon juice, mix in 1 tablespoon pureed **fresh cilantro,** or **Cilantro-Lime Paste** (page 360), as well as a good pinch of ground **cumin.**

Vinaigrette al Zeitoon

To **Spicy Moroccan Vinaigrette,** above, add 2 tablespoons minced **pimiento-stuffed green olives.**

Mediterranean Olive Vinaigrette

◆◆ INTERMEDIATE PANTRY

Makes 1/2 cup

Serve this spunky sauce as a dressing for tomato salad, roasted peppers, steamed chicken or fish, or for crusty French bread sandwiches.

◆◆◆◆◆◆◆

TO PREPARE Add a heaping tablespoon or two of **olive paste** to the **Basic Vinaigrette** recipe. A little chopped **garlic and/or herbes de Provence** makes a delicious variation.

Salsa Basilica

This is an invigorating sauce for a selection of spoon-tender simmered meats and vegetables, or for whole-wheat pasta with diced tomatoes.

◆◆◆◆◆◆

TO PREPARE Add 1 tablespoon **pesto** to the basic **Mediterranean Olive Vinaigrette.**

Salsa Verde

◆◆ INTERMEDIATE PANTRY

Makes 2/3 cup

The classic sauce to accompany a *bollito misto,* an Italian *pot au feu* of simmered poultry, meats, sausage, and vegetables.

◆◆◆◆◆◆

TO PREPARE To 1/2 cup **Basic Vinaigrette** made with olive oil and red wine, add 1/4 cup chopped **Italian parsley,** 2 teaspoons chopped drained **capers,** 1/2 to 1 teaspoon **anchovy paste or chopped anchovies,** and a clove of minced **garlic.**

Hazelnut and Cider Vinaigrette

◆◆ INTERMEDIATE PANTRY

Makes 1/3 cup

Delicious with a classic American wilted spinach and bacon salad, or as a dressing for sliced smoked turkey, sliced apples, walnuts, crumbled Gorgonzola, and Belgian endive, all on a bed of watercress.

Enjoy this vinaigrette on an autumnal warm salad of toasted hazelnuts, sautéed bits of smoky ham or lean Canadian or Irish-style bacon, quick-sautéed sliced mushrooms, and julienned apples, all on a bed of mesclun. Warm the dressing and pour it over the greens after everything is arranged on the plate.

◆◆◆◆◆◆

TO PREPARE Combine 2 tablespoons **mild vegetable oil** with 2 tablespoons **hazelnut oil,** then mix in 1 tablespoon *each* **cider vinegar** and **apple juice.**

Pear-Hazelnut Vinaigrette

Use **pear vinegar** in place of cider vinegar and **pear juice** for apple juice.

Sesame Rice Vinaigrette

Makes 1/2 cup

Mild and delicate, without the deep soy sauce flavor of so many rice vinaigrettes. I particularly like this dressing splashed onto a salad of arugula leaves, topped with sweet-tangy mango slices and salty, pungent prosciutto.

◆◆◆◆◆◆◆

PREPARE as for **Basic Vinaigrette,** page 81, using a combination of half **vegetable oil** and half Asian (toasted) **sesame oil** and a **sweet rice vinegar.**

Vinaigrette Chinoise

Makes 1/2 cup

Slightly sweet and scented with sesame, this soy-seasoned vinaigrette adds a distinctively Asian flavor to any salad: thinly sliced lettuce or Napa cabbage, cucumbers, lightly steamed spinach or asparagus, sliced tofu or cold poached fish chunks.

◆◆◆◆◆◆◆

TO PREPARE Follow **Basic Vinaigrette** recipe, page 81, using half **vegetable oil** and half **sesame oil**, and adding 1 to 2 tablespoons **soy sauce** along with **vinegar.** Season with 1/2 teaspoon grated **fresh ginger,** 1 chopped **garlic clove,** and 1 tablespoon **sugar.**

Southwestern Chili and Thyme Vinaigrette

Makes 1/2 cup

Warm and earthy, this vinaigrette makes a good dressing for a Southwestern-style Caesar salad using crisp fried tortillas in place of croutons. Good, too, on grilled or sautéed pumpkin slices.

◆◆◆◆◆◆◆

TO PREPARE Follow the **Basic Vinaigrette** recipe, page 81, using a mixture of half **vegetable or olive oil** and half mild **New Mexican chili oil;** season with 1/2 teaspoon dried **thyme,** or to taste.

Ginger-Cilantro Vinaigrette with Asian Flavors

Soy sauce, sesame oil, fresh ginger, and lots of cilantro make this vinaigrette far from ordinary. Besides using on salads, splash it onto a broccoli-and-wide-noodle stir-fry, or serve it as a dip for roast chicken or steamed dumplings.

Makes about 1-1/2 cups

1-1/2 tablespoons chopped
   fresh ginger
1 cup fresh cilantro leaves,
   loosely packed
2 green onions, thinly sliced
1/4 cup Asian (toasted)
   sesame oil

1/4 cup soy sauce
1/4 cup rice wine vinegar
2 teaspoons sugar
Tabasco sauce or other hot
   sauce to taste

1. Puree ginger in a food processor or blender, then add remaining ingredients and combine well.

2. Taste for seasoning. If it seems sharp, thin with a small amount of a mild vegetable oil such as corn or safflower, or with cool brewed tea.

3. Serve on a bed of greens scattered with strips of chicken or duck, a handful of mung bean sprouts, julienned cucumber, green onions, chopped fresh mint, and coarsely chopped peanuts.

Recipes Featuring Oils and Vinegars

Ten Appetizers Based on Extra-Virgin Olive Oil

◆◆◆◆◆◆

◆ Fresh creamy mozzarella cheese splashed with olive oil and sprinkled with coarse black pepper.

◆ Feta cheese topped with olive oil and sprinkled with chopped green onions and chopped fresh herbs such as mint and oregano. Sliced cucumbers optional.

◆ Garlic- or herb-flavored fresh goat cheese, studded with green olives, sprinkled with chopped fresh thyme and splashed with olive oil.

◆ Boiled potatoes, still slightly warm, dressed with olive oil and topped with salty pungent anchovies or smoked herring fillets.

◆ TOMATO BRUSCHETTA Broiled or grilled French or Italian bread, rubbed with garlic, then drizzled with olive oil and sliced tomatoes or roasted peppers.

- **ORANGE, ONION, AND POMEGRANATE SALAD** Thin slices of peeled orange and red onion, studded with pomegranate seeds, sprinkled with a few drops of balsamic vinegar, and drizzled generously with extra-virgin olive oil.

- Air-dried beef (bresaola) drizzled with olive oil. Ditto for prosciutto or thinly sliced and pounded raw beef or salmon (carpaccio). Serve with a baguette or other country bread.

- Diced tomatoes combined with thinly sliced arugula, garlic, crushed dried pepper flakes, and a generous amount of olive oil.

- Thinly sliced fennel and red bell peppers, bathed in olive oil with wedges of lemon on the side.

- Smoked tofu (or smoked chicken or white-fleshed fish), drizzled with olive oil and a grinding of black pepper.

Two Olive Oil and Balsamic Dipping Salsas

◆ BASIC PANTRY   Makes about 1-1/4 cups

Both crisp-textured, brightly flavored salsas are particularly good spooned over crusty bread or grilled fish.

◆◆◆◆◆◆◆

TO PREPARE Combine 3 tablespoons **olive oil** with 1 tablespoon **balsamic vinegar** and add **chopped vegetables** and/or aromatics as desired.

Parsley, Tomato, and Garlic Salsa

To basic recipe, add 1/2 cup coarsely chopped fresh **parsley,** 1/2 cup diced fresh **tomatoes,** and 3 minced **garlic cloves.**

Fennel and Black Olive Salsa

To basic recipe, add 3/4 cup diced or coarsely chopped fresh **fennel** and 1/4 cup coarsely chopped pitted **black Mediterranean olives** such as Kalamata.

Olive Oil–Rosemary Marinade for Grilling

◆ BASIC PANTRY

Makes enough to marinate 4 chicken breasts or fish fillets

This exquisitely simple marinade brings out a tender succulence in grilled chicken breasts.

The recipe may be multiplied indefinitely; I've used it to prepare chicken breasts for 200 guests and it was marvelous.

◆◆◆◆◆◆

TO PREPARE Combine 4 coarsely chopped large **garlic cloves** with 2 tablespoons minced **fresh rosemary** leaves, 2 tablespoons **olive oil,** and 2 teaspoons **white wine vinegar or lemon juice.** Pour over boned **chicken breasts or fish fillets** and let marinate from 15 minutes to overnight in the refrigerator.

Garlic Oil–marinated Sea Bass alla Siciliana

◆ BASIC PANTRY

Serves 4

Homemade flavored garlic oil is a delicious basis for marinades, especially for sea bass fillets.

◆◆◆◆◆◆

TO PREPARE Combine 1/4 cup **Garlic Oil** (page 77) with a generous squirt of **lemon juice or balsamic vinegar;** add a shake of **red pepper flakes** if you like, plus **salt** and **pepper,** then pour over 1 pound **sea bass fillets** and marinate for 30 minutes. Broil and serve sprinkled with chopped fresh **parsley or rosemary.**

Garlic Oil–marinated Shrimp

Prepare **above recipe,** using **shrimp** in place of sea bass.

Frittata with the Flavors of Tuscan Springtime

I usually prepare this omelet with leftover broccoli, but it's good with any green vegetable. Homemade garlic oil adds a more delicate fragrance than does adding garlic directly to the dish.

◆ BASIC PANTRY

Serves 3 to 4

2 cups diced al dente broccoli
  or other green vegetable
1 tablespoon Garlic Oil, page
  77, or combine 1 chopped
  garlic clove with 1 tablespoon
  olive oil

4 to 6 eggs, lightly beaten
4 ounces diced white cheese
  such as asiago, dry Jack,
  Italian fontina, or sharp
  Cheddar (about 1/2 cup)
Salt, pepper, and thyme to taste

1. Quickly heat broccoli in garlic oil.

2. Add remaining ingredients. Let cook a minute or two until eggs cook around edges, then lift up edges and let runny eggs flow under, stirring lightly until you have a scrambled mixture of soft fragrant curds of eggs and cheese encasing nuggets of bright green broccoli or whichever vegetable you have chosen. (For a less messy classic frittata rather than a stirred one, pour egg and cheese into greens. Cook on bottom for about 2 minutes, then pop under a hot broiler and continue cooking by browning top under broiler.)

Asparagus Scramble

In Spain, on the La Mancha Plain, I was served a similar dish. Prepare as above, using young tender **asparagus** as the green vegetable.

Spanish Tortilla, or Flat Omelet, of Red and Green Peppers, Onions, and Potatoes

◆ BASIC PANTRY

Serves 2 to 3 for a hearty breakfast, 4 to 6 as an appetizer

It sounds so simple, a flat omelet of red and green peppers interspersed with diced potatoes and sweet melting onions, but there are two secrets that make this a memorable dish: using enough olive oil and cooking slowly and gently to melt the potatoes and onions into tenderness.

Enjoy for brunch, along with glasses of orange juice whirled into an icy frenzy along with strawberries; or serve small squares at room temperature as an appetizer, accompanied with chilled very dry sherry or crisp white wine.

1 medium to large baking potato, unpeeled and cut into
  small dice

1/2 onion, coarsely chopped
3 garlic cloves, coarsely
  chopped

(continued)

2 to 4 tablespoons olive oil
1/2 red bell pepper, diced
1/2 green bell pepper, diced
1 medium to large tomato,
    sliced

3 eggs, beaten lightly and
    mixed with 1 tablespoon
    water
Salt and pepper to taste
Generous pinch of a chopped
    fresh herb such as thyme,
    optional

1. In a heavy skillet over medium heat, place potato, onion, garlic, and 2 tablespoons olive oil. Let cook a few minutes, then cover and let simmer for about 10 minutes, or until potatoes and onions are tender. Every so often, use a spatula to loosen and toss pieces of potato and onion.

2. Adding more oil if needed, add peppers and tomato, then cover again and let cook another 5 to 10 minutes.

3. Pour egg over mixture, pulling up edges to let egg flow underneath and cook evenly. (Another, more traditional method is to remove sautéed vegetables from pan, mix with egg in a bowl, then pour mixture into hot pan, to which you've added a bit more olive oil.) Season with salt and pepper.

4. Cook on bottom, then place under a hot broiler to brown top. Serve immediately, or later at room temperature. An optional sprinkling of fresh thyme is lovely.

Warm Broccoli Salad with Roasted Red Peppers and Olives

◆◆ INTERMEDIATE PANTRY

Serves 4

Broccoli, stir-fried simply with garlic and served with roasted red peppers, olives, and a splash of balsamic vinegar, makes a delicious warm salad, joyously colored green and red and dotted with tiny black olives, good for either a first course or a vegetarian main course. Serve with crusty bread.

2 bunches broccoli, cut into
    florets, stalks peeled and cut
    into bite-sized pieces
3 tablespoons Garlic Oil, page
    77, or 3 tablespoons olive oil
    mixed with 1 to 2 chopped
    garlic cloves

2/3 cup roasted red peppers,
    cut into bite-sized pieces
16 to 20 niçoise olives
1 tablespoon balsamic vinegar
    or to taste
Salt and pepper to taste
1 tablespoon chopped fresh
    parsley and/or basil

1. Stir-fry broccoli in garlic oil until crunchy-tender; add a spoonful or two of water and red peppers, cover, and let steam a minute.

2. Serve on a platter, garnished with olives and sprinkled with balsamic vinegar, salt, pepper, parsley and/or basil.

Inner City Eggplant and Peppers

◆◆ INTERMEDIATE PANTRY

Serves 6 to 8 as a side dish or appetizer

The first time I tasted this marinated eggplant was at a delicatessen in an inner city neighborhood that had seen better days. I became a staunch devotee of these tangy strips of eggplant and peppers awash in a garlicky marinade and visited the deli as often as I could. Frankly, the neighborhood scared me to death, so I always went when it was light, parked close by, and scurried into the shop, peeking over my shoulders, alert to danger. One day as I left the shop I was followed. Faster and faster I walked, and just when I thought I had reached the safety of my car the man caught up with me. I was prepared to give up my handbag and scream for my life when in menacing tones he demanded, "Do you have any of those marinated eggplants?" I did. Soon he did. I decided in the future to make them at home.

This is an emphatically garlic-scented dish, tart with vinegar and rich with olive oil, then freshened with lots of chopped parsley. Broiling the eggplant slices instead of frying them lightens the dish up considerably. Frankly, you could probably even cut down further on the amount of olive oil called for in my recipe. It is a bright dish that is a good accompaniment to any informal zesty meal, or can serve as a Mediterranean-style appetizer along with several other savory marinated morsels. I particularly like to make sandwiches with it, on rolls with or without salami, cold roasted meat, or grilled fish.

Covered, it will last 2 weeks in the refrigerator.

1 medium to large eggplant, sliced into 1/2-inch-thick slices
1/2 cup extra-virgin olive oil
1/2 to 2/3 cup roasted red peppers, cut into strips or bite-sized pieces

4 to 6 chopped garlic cloves
1/4 to 1/2 cup white wine vinegar
Salt and pepper to taste
1/4 cup coarsely chopped fresh parsley

1. Preheat broiler, then place eggplant slices on a baking sheet, preferably a nonstick one.

2. Brush or drizzle with olive oil, then broil on highest heat until browned in spots. Turn over and cook on other side. Repeat until all eggplant slices are just tender.

3. Place cooked eggplant slices in a bowl, and while they are still warm mix with peppers, garlic, vinegar, salt, and pepper. Let cool.

4. Add parsley and serve at room temperature.

Eggplant with the Flavors of North Africa

[AUBERGINE MOROCCAINE]

◆◆ INTERMEDIATE PANTRY

Serves 4 to 6

The technique is inspired by Paula Wolfert, from her *World of Cooking:* first the eggplant is sautéed, then slowly simmered in a sauce to evaporate the liquid and concentrate the sauce.

The spicing of the dish, emphatically my own, dances through the Mediterranean, picking up marvelous flavors that balance themselves in a most delicious concoction. When this dish comes to the table, to be eaten as an appetizer or scooped onto chunks of bread as party food, it is a fragrant mixture of eggplant, tomatoes, onion, and garlic, all bound up with an exotic landscape of spices and the tartness of yogurt and lemon.

1 medium eggplant, diced or cut into bite-sized pieces
About 1/4 cup extra-virgin olive oil, as needed for browning eggplant (plus extra if needed for sautéing other ingredients)
1 onion, coarsely chopped
2 garlic cloves, chopped
1/4 to 1/2 fresh green chili such as jalapeño, chopped or thinly sliced
1/2 teaspoon ground cumin
1/4 teaspoon ground turmeric
1/4 teaspoon ground coriander
1/8 teaspoon ground ginger
1 tablespoon paprika
1 cup diced fresh or canned tomatoes
Juice of 1/2 lemon or lime
2 tablespoons plain yogurt
2 tablespoons chopped fresh cilantro or parsley
Salt to taste
Cilantro or parsley sprigs and black olives for garnish

1. Lightly brown eggplant in olive oil. Remove from pan and let cool.

2. Pour off all but 1 tablespoon of olive oil (add fresh if none is left in pan) and lightly sauté onion, half of garlic, and chili for a minute or two.

3. Sprinkle in spices and continue cooking, then add tomatoes and cook until saucelike, about 5 minutes.

4. Add reserved sautéed eggplant to tomato sauce, turning heat to low and mashing eggplant a bit with a fork or spatula as it cooks.

5. Let mixture cook over a low, low heat for 10 to 15 minutes longer, or to a jamlike consistency, with oil exuding from solids around edge of pan.

6. Pour off any excess oil (or blot with absorbent paper if you like, taking care not to let any paper stick to vegetables). Remove from heat.

7. Stir in remaining garlic, lemon or lime juice, yogurt, cilantro, and salt.

8. Let cool to room temperature and serve accompanied with chunks of bread, sprigs of cilantro or parsley, and black olives.

Artichokes and Peppers, Baked with Olive Oil and Balsamic Vinegar, Served with Caper Mayonnaise

BASIC PANTRY

Serves 4

Steamed artichokes, baked with sweet peppers, olive oil, and balsamic vinegar make a spunky first course. Served with a simple caper mayonnaise, it couldn't be easier. Follow with a grilled burger made of duck or turkey, or a roasted chicken scented with lemon, garlic, and rosemary.

4 medium artichokes
1/2 lemon (optional)
1 red bell pepper, thinly sliced or coarsely chopped
1 yellow bell pepper, thinly sliced or coarsely chopped
2 garlic cloves, coarsely chopped

3 to 4 tablespoons olive oil
1 to 2 tablespoons balsamic vinegar
Salt and pepper to taste
2/3 cup mayonnaise
About 3 tablespoons capers, slightly mashed with a tiny bit of their marinade

1. Preheat oven to 400°. Cut artichokes in half. With a knife, remove their chokes and cook by either boiling them quickly with lemon half or steaming them until almost tender yet not completely cooked through. Allow 15 minutes for small artichokes, 20–25 minutes for large ones. Drain and place cut side down in a baking dish.

2. Toss with peppers and garlic, then drizzle with olive oil and balsamic vinegar, and sprinkle with salt and pepper.

3. Bake until peppers are cooked through, about 15 minutes.

4. Meanwhile, prepare sauce: Mix mayonnaise with mashed capers and marinade.

5. Serve artichokes hot or tepid, accompanied with mayonnaise sauce.

Angel Hair Pasta, with an Uncooked Sauce of Tomatoes, Arugula, and Basil

[CAPPELLINI MEZZOGIORNO]

◆◆ INTERMEDIATE PANTRY

Serves 4 to 6

As fresh as a summer day, this pasta dish is gilded with olive oil and balsamic vinegar and forcefully scented with garlic before it is tossed with sweet ripe tomatoes, arugula, and basil. It is at its best at room temperature, and is just as good made from leftover pasta as from freshly cooked.

1 pound capellini, spaghettini, or other very thin pasta
3 tablespoons extra-virgin olive oil, or as desired
4 garlic cloves, chopped
Coarse salt and pepper to taste
1 teaspoon balsamic vinegar, or as desired

4 to 6 sweet ripe tomatoes, diced (choose a combination of yellow, red, orange, and green if available)
1 bunch baby arugula leaves
5 to 10 basil leaves, torn or cut coarsely

1. Cook capellini in rapidly boiling salted water until just al dente. Drain well.

2. Toss with olive oil, garlic, salt, and pepper.

3. When ready to serve, top each portion of pasta with a shake of balsamic vinegar and some tomatoes, arugula, and basil.

"On the Verge of a Nervous Breakdown" Gazpacho

After seeing the strange and delightful film *Women on the Verge of a Nervous Breakdown,* all I could think of was gazpacho. The combination of the soup and the movie, in fact, led me to take a gazpacho-soaked pilgrimage through Spain.

By the way, this is spicier than most Spanish gazpachos, with decidedly Mexican overtones. There is none of the usually included bread to get in the way of the refreshing salady quality of the soup. The vegetables in this mixture are all finely chopped, then half of them are pureed with the liquid. The result is a great balance of textures as well as tastes.

3 garlic cloves, chopped
1 quart tomato juice, or 2 cups
    tomato juice plus 2 cups
    chicken broth
2 cucumbers, peeled and diced
2 green bell peppers, diced
3 tomatoes, diced

1 tablespoon medium-hot salsa,
    or to taste
1/4 cup extra-virgin olive oil
2 tablespoons red wine vinegar
1 tablespoon ground cumin
Salt, pepper, and thyme or
    oregano to taste

1. Combine chopped garlic with 1 cup tomato juice, then whirl in a blender or food processor with half of all vegetables.

2. Add salsa, olive oil, wine vinegar, cumin, salt, pepper, and thyme or oregano, and remaining vegetables and tomato juice (including chicken broth if using).

3. Chill before serving and adjust seasonings, as cold food demands more salt and other flavors than does warm.

4. Serve each portion ladled into a bowl over 1 or 2 small ice cubes.

Nopales Gazpacho

In place of green peppers use **nopales,** and use half **tomatillos** for half of tomatoes. Do not blend or process mixture; simply combine and have chopped vegetables swimming in a brothy mixture.

Baked Cumin and Garlic Eggplant Appetizer

First steamed to tenderness, then doused with garlic, spices, and olive oil and baked, this is one of the most delicious and easiest of eggplant dishes. Steaming the eggplant before baking it with the olive oil lets the oil act as a flavoring ingredient and sauce rather than being soaked up by the thirsty eggplant.

This eggplant salad is wonderful as part of a selection of appetizers, Middle Eastern style, or as picnic fare for a hot-weather supper along with grilled lamb or fish kabobs.

2 whole large eggplants,
   stemmed
6 garlic cloves, coarsely
   chopped
1/4 cup extra-virgin olive oil
1-1/2 teaspoons paprika

1-1/2 tablespoons ground cumin
Pinch of cayenne
Salt to taste
Juice of 1/2 lemon
2 tablespoons chopped fresh
   cilantro

1. Preheat oven to 425°. Cut several gashes in eggplants. Place them in a pot with a tiny bit of water. Cover and steam until tender, about 15 minutes, adding more water if needed to keep eggplants from burning.

2. Cut cooked eggplants lengthwise into thirds or quarters. Place them in baking dish, then sprinkle with garlic, olive oil, paprika, cumin, cayenne, and salt.

3. Bake for 10 minutes, or until eggplant has heated through and flavors have permeated its flesh.

4. Remove from oven and let cool. Drizzle with lemon juice, sprinkle with cilantro, and serve at room temperature.

◆ BASIC OR
◆◆◆ ADVANCED PANTRY

Asian-flavor Eggplant Appetizer

Omit garlic, olive oil, and spices in above recipe and instead season eggplant with **Ginger-Cilantro Vinaigrette with Asian Flavors** (page 83) or a mixture of Asian **sesame oil, vegetable oil,** grated **fresh ginger,** and **Chinese black bean sauce.**

Italian Quickly Cooked Garlic-scented Greens
[VERDURI ITALIANI]

Any vegetable is delicious and healthy too when briefly steamed, then swirled through a tiny bit of hot garlic-scented oil. A squeeze of lemon or a splotch of balsamic vinegar gives a bright touch. Try chard, broccoli, spinach, summer squashes, green and yellow beans, waxy new potatoes, or whatever your garden or greengrocer offers, and serve as part of a vegetable feast for a summer supper.

3 zucchini or yellow summer squash, cut into bite-sized chunks
1 bunch broccoli, florets broken into bite-sized pieces and stems peeled and cut into same size, or 2 cups sugar snap peas
About 2 cups chard, cut into strips

1 to 2 tablespoons extra-virgin olive oil
3 garlic cloves, coarsely chopped
Several fresh basil leaves, thinly sliced (optional)
Salt and pepper to taste
Lemon wedges

1. Steam or boil zucchini or summer squash for a minute or two. Remove from heat and drain, then set aside. Repeat with other vegetables.

2. Heat olive oil and garlic together for a moment or two, just long enough to smell enticing, then toss drained vegetables in hot garlic oil.

3. Remove from heat and season with fresh basil, salt, and pepper.

4. Serve hot or at room temperature, accompanied with wedges of lemon.

Quick Pan-cooked Greens and Vegetables with Pancetta

Add diced **pancetta** to warming olive oil before you add vegetables. Omit salt and pepper, as pancetta is both salty and peppery.

VARIATION For Southwestern flavors, season oil and garlic with a teaspoon or two of **mild chili powder,** then sprinkle cooked vegetables with chopped fresh **cilantro** instead of basil.

Fresh Tomato and Ginger Chutney

Makes about 1 cup

Stewing tomatoes in mustard oil along with fresh ginger and chilies gives them a strong, hot, and delicious flavor. Serve alongside turmeric-tinted rice and grilled chopped lamb or Indian-spiced baked fish.

2 teaspoons mustard oil
1/2 medium onion, coarsely
   chopped
2 teaspoons chopped fresh
   ginger
1/2 jalapeño chili, seeded and
   chopped

1/2 teaspoon ground turmeric
1/2 teaspoon ground coriander
2 cups chopped fresh tomatoes
1/2 teaspoon sugar or to taste
Salt to taste

1. In mustard oil, gently sauté onion, ginger, and jalapeño until onion is softened. Sprinkle in turmeric and coriander, and cook a minute longer.

2. Add tomatoes, sugar, and salt to taste. Cook over medium heat until mixture thickens and is no longer watery, about 10 minutes. Let cool.

Berries with Vinegar

◆ **BASIC OR**
◆◆ **INTERMEDIATE PANTRY**

Serves 4

A few drops of raspberry vinegar or red wine vinegar adds a sassy edge to strawberries, bringing out their tangy berry quality.

◆◆◆◆◆◆

TO PREPARE Divide 2 cups or so sweet ripe **strawberries** among 4 bowls and sprinkle with a few drops of **raspberry or red wine vinegar** and a sprinkling of **sugar** to taste. In Italy, a few grindings of **black pepper** are added.

Fragrant Fresh Berry Coulis

Follow **above recipe** but puree berries into a thick sauce; season to taste with vinegar and sugar. Raspberries and strawberries combined make a nice sauce, especially served over blackberries or mixed summer fruits.

Oregon Summer Zucchini Bread-and-Butter Pickles

That Oregon summer when I planted zucchini for the first time I had no idea what I was getting into. No one tells you when you innocently buy the seeds that if you plant zucchini you had better have homes lined up for them, and that they keep coming mercilessly, tiny unassuming creatures in the morning, medium-sized squashes by mid-day, huge green-striped monsters by evening.

That was the summer I learned to pickle, after I had exhausted my repertoire of zucchini breads and muffins, salads and soups, omelets and pastas. I discovered all sorts of pickles by substituting zucchini for cucumbers; piccalilli was good, and I vaguely remember a chutney. (There were kosher dills, too, but they are better left forgotten.)

These pickles are sensational, a wonderful twist on the usual cucumber ones, and they were delicious the following winter, little jars full of tangy sunshine.

4 pounds sliced zucchini or zucchini and other summer squash	1/3 cup kosher or other pickling salt
	Coarsely crushed ice
6 medium white or yellow onions, peeled and sliced	5 packed cups dark brown sugar
1 green bell pepper, diced	2 teaspoons ground turmeric
1 red bell pepper, diced	2 teaspoons celery seeds
4 garlic cloves, peeled and cut into halves	3 tablespoons mustard seeds
	3 cups cider vinegar

1. In a large bowl, combine zucchini, onions, peppers, garlic, and salt. Cover with ice and mix thoroughly. Let stand at room temperature for 3 hours. Drain.

2. In a separate bowl, combine brown sugar, turmeric, celery seeds, mustard seeds, and vinegar. Pour over drained vegetables, then transfer to a large saucepan and bring to a boil.

3. Pour mixture into 8 to 10 sterilized 1-pint canning jars, leaving at least 1/4-inch head space.

4. Seal, following directions on canning jars.

5. Process in a boiling water bath for 20 minutes, then remove from bath and cool, or keep tightly sealed and refrigerated for up to 2 months. Processed pickles will keep unopened in a dark place for 6 to 8 months. Once opened, jars should be refrigerated.

SPICES, HERBS, CONDIMENTS, AND FLAVORING INGREDIENTS

Spices and Herbs

Learning about spices and herbs is what got me hooked on the pleasures of the table and cooking. Each time I found a recipe that contained a new herb or spice, I bought the seasoning and made the recipe. If I liked it I experimented further, flinging it into dishes with a certain abandonment and enthusiasm (no doubt too much enthusiasm at times). But I was happily oblivious, and soon had a collection of spices and herbs and the knowledge of how to use them.

There are guidelines, to be sure; certain flavors just seem to "go" with other ones. Many of these combinations are based in ethnic tradition and work best in that tried-and-true way. But the most exciting discoveries are always made when two or more flavors that have no business in the same dish end up falling in love. And the cook makes these discoveries either by using good, well-crafted recipes or by experimentation.

The terms *herbs* and *spices* are not interchangeable. *Spices* generally refers to fragrant seasoning seeds, roots, and barks, while *herbs* describes the leaves and occasionally the stems. Usually (but by no means always) herbs are best fresh, growing in a little pot by the window or purchased in the market.

STORAGE TIPS Spices keep their fragrance best when purchased and kept whole, then ground for use as desired. This is not always practical, however, and I don't always do it.

Storing your spices and herbs presents a challenge. Never keep them above your stove, since the heat will quickly dissipate their aroma and turn them into little more than dusty bits. Keeping them in a cupboard or on a revolving round shelf adds protection, but makes the spices more inaccessible than I like. The best storage system is a large shelf (or a collection of smaller shelves) filled with spices and herbs on a wall in the kitchen that has easy access but is not in direct sunlight or near cooking heat.

Buy your spices loose if possible, and keep them in jars with tight-fitting lids. Most spices keep their fragrance well for about 6 months, then begin their downhill slide. Generally they should be replenished every 12 months or so, but the more delicate herbs, such as tarragon, need to be replaced more often. Let your nose be your guide. When buying spices and herbs, purchase only as much as you think you'll use within 6 months to a year.

Pantry List: Spices and Herbs

◆◆◆◆◆◆

Allspice	Fennel seeds	Oregano
Aniseed	Fenugreek	Paprika
Annatto (achiote)	Filé powder	Peppercorns
Basil	Fines herbes	Quatre épices
Bay leaves	Five-spice powder	Rosemary
Cajun spice mixtures	Garlic	Saffron
Camomile	Garlic powder	Sage
Caraway seeds	Ginger: fresh and	Salt
Cardamom	ground	Savory, winter and
Cayenne pepper	Herbes de Provence	summer varieties
Celery seeds	Horseradish	Star anise
Chervil	Juniper berries	Sumac
Chili powder mixtures	Lavender	Szechuan peppercorns
Cinnamon	Mace and nutmeg	Tarragon
Cloves	Marjoram	Thyme
Coriander	Mint	Turmeric
Cumin	Mustard seeds	Vanilla
Curry powder	Onion seeds	Wasabi powder
Dill	Orange and tangerine	
	peels	

Allspice Not, as it sounds, a mixture of spices, allspice is a round berry that looks much like a large peppercorn and tastes of cinnamon, cloves, nutmeg, and juniper. It is used in sweets and bakery goods, and also in Greek, Arabic, and other Mediterranean tomato sauces and meat dishes as well as in French liver pâtés.

Anise With its licorice-like flavor, aniseed is the main flavoring ingredient in ouzo and Pernod. The tiny and strongly flavored seeds are classically added to biscotti.

Annatto Tiny rock-hard seeds from the fruit of the tropical annatto tree, this spice is used for the yellow color it imparts to everything it touches. Nowadays it is used prosaically as the coloring for margarine, butter, smoked fish, cheeses, and candies, but it was once used by Native Americans to color their bodies.

Annatto has a slightly lemony flavor, with a hint of musk and paprika, and is used either by steeping it in water overnight to soften, then grinding it into a paste, or by heating it in oil, then straining it. In the Yucatán, annatto paste is mixed with other spices and used for *recado colorado,* the seasoning paste that gives distinction to *pollo* and *conchita pibil,* spiced pork and chicken dishes wrapped and baked in banana leaves.

Basil originated in India, where it is considered a holy herb and not used for culinary purposes. It is, however, enjoyed a great deal in Southeast Asia, where its sweetness contrasts with the spiciness of the rest of the cuisine. In Provence and Italy basil scents salads, pastas, soups, sandwiches—indeed the entire cuisine. There are numerous types of basil: purple and green leafed, large and tiny leafed, basils with the scent of lemon or cinnamon, peppery or oh-so-sweet. Fresh basil is so good that keeping a pot on the windowsill makes for the best sort of pantry one could hope for. Some use basil dried, and indeed I usually keep a small bottle on my shelf, but it is for emergency use only and is no comparison to the fresh stuff. Better to substitute dried thyme, oregano, or herbes de Provence, which are good and flavorful when dried.

Bay Leaves Grown on the laurel, or bay tree, bay leaves have a particular affinity to tomato dishes, lentil and split pea soups, lamb stews, and curried dishes. Plop one in a jar of olive oil to add a forestry fragrance to the oil, or powder several bay leaves and add them to herbes de Provence or similar mixtures.

Cajun Spice Mixtures Thanks to Paul Prudomme, the whole country, indeed, the whole world, has embraced the spicy Cajun mixtures of chilies and other spices. Use it as a base and build onto it with other spices, much as you would a garum masala in Indian cookery. Try this mixture rubbed onto butter-brushed fish or kabobs before broiling, or to add a jolt to a simmering jambalaya. I seem to remember going through a phase that entailed eating many bowls of buttered popcorn powdered with this mixture.

TO MAKE YOUR OWN CAJUN SPICE MIXTURE Combine 2 tablespoons dried **oregano**, 2 tablespoons **garlic powder**, 2 teaspoons **cayenne pepper**, 1 tablespoon **paprika**, 1 tablespoon ground **cumin**, 1 tablespoon **dried thyme**, 1 tablespoon **onion powder**, 1 teaspoon ground **black pepper**.

Camomile You might recognize the tiny golden flowers and lacy leaves of this useful herb in the wild. It makes a wonderfully calming tea (remember Peter Rabbit and the camomile tea his mother served him after his close encounter with Farmer Brown?) and a hair rinse that brightens the heads of blonds. In Italy it is believed that camomile tea acts as an anti-aphrodisiac. It doesn't have many culinary uses, but a little bit of powdered camomile added to chili powder gives a haunting, subtle Southwestern aroma and flavor; in the same vein, use any leftover cold brewed camomile tea to mix with chili powder for a seasoning paste.

Caraway Seeds Tiny crescent-shaped seeds that give rye bread its characteristic flavor and crunch. They are used in sauerkraut and noodle dishes throughout Eastern Europe.

Cardamom A three-sided pod containing small, dark, and very fragrant seeds. Cardamom is second only to saffron in its high price. It should be purchased in the pod rather than already peeled, since it quickly loses its perfume. Use the tiny seeds whole, or grind in a marble mortar and pestle. (Wooden mortars are too soft to crush the hard seeds.) Already ground cardamom consists of both the ground pod and seeds and has had its strength diluted by the tasteless pod. Cardamom is used in Arabic sweets or thick syrupy Greek-style coffee, and is quite delicious in curry powders and stews. The Swedish use it a good deal in their sweet cakes and breads.

Cayenne Pepper Ground cayenne pepper is pure fire. Use in Mexican, Indian, North African, some Chinese and other Southeast Asian sauces with a generous hand, and very discreetly in buttery bland sauces such as hollandaise. Cayenne may be used interchangeably with Tabasco sauce.

Celery Seeds Used in pickles and spice mixtures. I find this a rather boring spice, but I like to use celery leaves as an herb, cut up and tossed into soups. Celery root is a delicious flavoring ingredient, especially good as a base for lentil or mushroom soup, or added to curry or Cajun spice mixtures.

Chervil Delicate and lacy-leafed, chervil has a strange, tarragony, slightly anise flavor. It is one of the *fines herbes*, the classic seasoning of the French kitchen. Nice added to salads when fresh, but not much when dried. I wouldn't include it on my spice shelf, but I do keep a pot on the windowsill.

Chili Powder Usually refers to a mild, richly flavored chili powder. Most commonly sold mixed with other spices such as cumin, oregano, coriander, etc., chili powder is increasingly available in unadulterated forms such as ancho, New Mexico, pasilla, California, and mulatto, among others.

For further information, including how to prepare your own chili powder, see the listing for chili peppers on page 125.

Cinnamon is the fragrant bark from a tree that originated in Ceylon. Sold rolled into scroll-like sticks, cinnamon is always ready to stir its sweet fragrance into a cup of hot chocolate or coffee, to add zest to a curry or Middle Eastern tomatoey stew, to enrich a chocolatey Mexican *mole*. And cinnamon toast is perhaps the most comforting dish I know.

Cloves Tiny nail-shaped buds with a distinctive aroma and flavor. Use very generously to stud a glazed ham (any glaze, as long as you use lots of cloves), or poke cloves all over an onion to be used in a smooth and subtle sauce or simmer. Take a bay leaf and anchor it to a garlic clove using a clove as a nail, then add as a flavor enhancer to any robust braise that catches your fancy. Cloves are ground and used in curries, sweets, and marinades, and the oil is used as a balm for an aching tooth, dabbed gently around the offending area.

Coriander is one of those amazements: the seed is a spice with a sweet and gentle flavor, and is used in curries and hot dogs, to name two things. But plant the little seeds, which look like white peppercorns, and in about two weeks you will have cilantro, an herb that has taken American cuisine by storm, having already conquered Mexico, the Middle East, India, China, Southeast Asia, North Africa and Portugal. Cilantro evokes passion in most people: they usually love it or hate it. However, even those who fall into the latter category can grow to love it, and I think it is a taste worth acquiring for the way it brilliantly balances chili-based cuisines.

Cumin Sold as seeds or ground into a powder, cumin is dusky and musky and an indispensable part of Mexican and Indian food, as well as being prominently featured in certain North African dishes. The whole seeds are used in Holland and Denmark to flavor cheese, breads, and the liquors aquavit and schnapps.

Cumin seeds benefit by a good toasting in an ungreased skillet. About 5 minutes should do it. You want them to slightly darken in color and smell very fragrant; take care not to let them burn. These toasted seeds, either added to a dish whole or ground into a powder, are cumin intensified and are very good.

Moroccan Cumin-baked Fish

◆ **BASIC PANTRY**

Makes enough for 1 pound of fish fillets

A potent paste of cumin, garlic, and cilantro gives tender fish a distinctive allure. This dish is more subtle and complex than would be expected from such a brash little recipe.

◆◆◆◆◆◆

TO PREPARE Combine 5 minced **garlic cloves** with 2 tablespoons ground **cumin,** 3 tablespoons **olive oil,** 1 teaspoon **red pepper flakes** or more, 2 tablespoons chopped **fresh cilantro or parsley,** and the juice of half a **lemon;** add **salt** to taste. Spread over **fish fillets** of choice and roast or steam them until just tenderly firm to the touch. Particularly good on fish wrapped in parchment or aluminum foil, then baked.

Curry Powder I use curry powders as bases and build on them with individual spices for complex flavors and aromas. Usually at the end of cooking, I sprinkle a fresh shower of spice into the dish, as the cooked and raw are quite different in flavor. I do buy curry powders since some are excellent, but the following do-it-yourself mixture is wonderful and worth making. Roasting the whole spices before grinding them produces the best results, but using ground spices (you may then eliminate the roasting) is good too.

TO MAKE YOUR OWN CURRY POWDER Combine and mix well 3 tablespoons ground **coriander,** 1 tablespoon ground **cumin,** 2 teaspoons ground **cloves,** 2 teaspoons ground **cardamom,** 1/2 teaspoon **cayenne pepper,** 1 teaspoon ground **fenugreek,** 1/2 teaspoon ground **ginger,** and 1 tablespoon ground **tumeric.**

All the spices, except for ginger, fenugreek, and turmeric, may be roasted whole in a baking dish in a preheated 200° oven for about 30 minutes. Grind in a coffee grinder, along with the ginger, fenugreek, and turmeric.

Chinese Curry Tomato Beef

◆◆ **INTERMEDIATE PANTRY**

Serves 2 to 3

The curry-soy seasoning makes an excellent flavoring mixture to add to other dishes; I recently added several tablespoons to a hot-and-sour chicken-and-water-chestnut stir-fry and it was brilliant. Whichever curry powder you use will give its own character to the sauce.

CURRY SAUCE
3 tablespoons curry powder
1/4 teaspoon five-spice seasoning

2 tablespoons soy sauce
1/2 cup beef broth

STIR-FRY
8 ounces lean tender beef, cut into thin strips
1 tablespoon cornstarch
2 bacon slices, diced
2 garlic cloves, chopped
One 2/3-inch piece fresh ginger, chopped

2 teaspoons vegetable oil, or as needed
1 green bell pepper, cut into strips
2 large tomatoes
2 teaspoons sugar, or to taste
2 teaspoons Asian (toasted) sesame oil

1. Mix sauce ingredients together. Set aside.

2. Mix meat with cornstarch and 3 tablespoons curry sauce. Set aside.

3. Stir-fry bacon with garlic and ginger, then remove from wok or frying pan.

4. Using a little vegetable oil, stir-fry pepper and tomatoes, then set aside. Remove meat from its marinade (reserving marinade for sauce), and stir-fry in a wok or skillet, adding more oil as needed.

5. Return other stir-fried ingredients to pan, along with marinade from meat. Heat until it thickens, then season with sugar and sesame oil and add remaining curry sauce. Cook until mixture is thickened, then serve immediately, accompanied with steamed rice.

◆◆◆◆◆◆

Dill Both the small flat seeds and the long feathery leaves of dill are classic ingredients in potato dishes, marinated cucumbers, hearty root vegetable soups, and sour cream sauces. Fresh young dill is lovely chopped and added to salads or sprinkled over boiled potatoes. The older stems of the herb are what makes dill pickles dill pickles (that plus a lot of garlic).

Fennel Seeds share the same licorice-like flavor as aniseeds but are milder in taste and larger in dimension. They are delicious in sausages, tomato sauces, breads, and other Italian and Italian-American dishes. Good in meatballs with spinach or chard, as well as on sausage-topped pizza.

Fennel branches are not often sold in America, though they may be found growing wild in empty lots and along freeways in areas that once housed a large Italian population, since fennel is quite hardy and after the first crop rapidly goes wild. Take care when picking, though, as fennel branches resemble hemlock, a plant you most certainly do not want to use. Fennel branches are occasionally sold in imported-food shops and add a particular savor when tossed onto the flames of an open fire, the seeds falling onto the fire below and creating a fragrant smoke that permeates the food that cooks over it.

Fenugreek Tiny hard flat seeds, ground and used in curry powders. I seldom use it on its own, but mix it with other Indian spices. The seeds may be planted and grown into a leafy Indian green known as *methi*. In an old Indian recipe book I came across the advice to eat much fenugreek if one wanted to grow "beautifully fat." How times change.

Filé Powder Also known as gumbo filé, this is a Creole mixture of herbs usually including sassafras leaves along with sage, thyme, allspice, and coriander. It gives a distinctive flavor to gumbo that comes with a warning: Do not use in conjunction with okra since okra thickens a mixture, and so does gumbo filé. Add both and you have a gluey gloppy potful.

Fines Herbes A mixture of fresh herbs favored in French food, fines herbes are at their best fresh. Fresh chervil, tarragon, and chives are not always available, but combining fresh parsley with dried herbs rehydrates the herbs and gives the same basic flavor. Green onions or garlic chives can substitute for the chives, a little lemon zest can stand in for the chervil, and dried tarragon can replace the fresh.

TO MAKE YOUR OWN FINES HERBES MIXTURE Combine 1/2 cup chopped fresh **parsley** with 2 tablespoons chopped fresh **chervil (or 1 tablespoon dried, or a bit of grated lemon zest)**, 2 tablespoons chopped fresh **chives (or scallions or garlic chives),** and 1-1/2 teaspoons dried **tarragon.** This keeps, refrigerated for up to 2 days, and stores well in the freezer, as long as you don't expect it to be other than limp when defrosted. Fines herbes are wonderful tossed into green salads, sprinkled onto delicate chicken or fish sautées, or simmered into creamy pureed soups.

Five-Spice Powder From Northern Chinese cooking, this all-purpose mixture of cinnamon, fennel, ginger, cloves, star anise, and pepper is as useful in the kitchen as the European spice blends.

TO MAKE YOUR OWN FIVE SPICE POWDER Combine 1 tablespoon **Szechuan peppercorns,** 8 **star anise,** 6 **whole cloves,** and 1 tablespoon **fennel seeds.** Toast in a dry pan in a 300° oven for 20 minutes. Let cool to room temperature, then pulverize in a coffee or spice grinder along with 1 tablespoon ground **cinnamon** and a generous pinch of **ground ginger.** Use to shake onto a roasting chicken or piece of meat, or add a pinch to hoisin-sauced dishes and barbecued duck or pork.

Garlic This member of the lily family (along with its relatives, onions, leeks, shallots, and chives) won my undying devotion the first time I smelled it. I must have been eight or nine years old, and the aroma and intense flavor seemed to transform my world from black and white to Technicolor, as in the Wizard of Oz. No doubt about it, life with garlic was much more interesting than it had been without.

When it comes to garlic, prudery has no place in my kitchen. A discreet whiff cannot compare to voluptuous abandon. Cooking with garlic often seems like cheating, because adding garlic improves nearly everything. My favorite meal is raw garlic sliced onto a piece of bread. I sometimes try to go a day or two without eating any garlic at all for the sheer pleasure of having it returned to me.

Garlic is at its best when young, when its fragrance is fresh and sprightly. Older garlic has a heavier, more concentrated, flavor, and when older still its flesh dries up inside its papery skin, or it goes moldy, with its once-aromatic oils growing rancid.

Garlic has flavoring properties that vary wildly and in inverse proportion to how much you do to it and how long you cook it. Left whole and cooked slowly for a long time, it is sweet and gentle, delicious spread on bread or used as the basis for a smooth sauce or soup. Chopped coarsely, then sautéed, it adds punch; chopped finely it is pungency itself. Added to a dish at the last minute, it will add its fine and potent impact.

There are a number of Mediterranean sauces whose main flavor ingredient is garlic: Provençal aïoli, Italian bagna cauda, Greek skordhalia, and the Spanish alioli, all similar emulsions of garlic and olive oil and little else, and enjoyed especially with seafood and vegetables.

Probably no other food evokes the amount of folklore that garlic does. It is said to ward off evil spirits when worn in an amulet around the neck, and it doubles as an anti-vampire agent. Before antibiotics, mothers would place a little packet of garlic in a necklace for their children to wear as a preventative. Medical folklore and fact points to any number of ailments that garlic is good for. Some claim that garlic should be eaten before travel to a country where one is apt to pick up some nasty intestinal ailment. I find that a pimple can be cleared up quickly by rubbing a cut slice of garlic on it. And modern medical research points to garlic as an anti-hypertensive. Veterinary medicine in England prescribes garlic to dogs as an anti-worm tonic. (For a fascinating read on garlic, consult *The Book of Garlic,* authored by my editor, John Harris.)

Most shops have a supply of reasonably fresh garlic for much of the year.

STORAGE TIPS As for storing garlic, a cool dark place is best. Do not refrigerate, as it seems to change the flavor, it makes it more prone to mold, and, frankly, the garlic doesn't last any longer than the two months or so it does at a cool room temperature. The same holds true for freezing: why on earth would anyone freeze garlic, when it does not prolong its life (and may in fact shorten it), and when the process of freezing destroys the fresh garlic flavor, giving it a definite frozen flavor and texture. Kitchen shops sometimes sell ceramic containers with holes in them to let air circulate while keeping the garlic cool and in the dark.

I find that a kitchen drawer or a basket on a pantry shelf keeps garlic dry and cool. And I always have a small bowl of several cloves next to the stove for immediate use. The braid I keep on the wall not only looks good, but is there when I need garlic right away and my bowl is empty. The best way to always have fresh garlic on hand is to buy only as much as you will be needing in the next month or two, then replace as you run low.

As for the anti-social effects of garlic: If everyone would eat garlic, no one would notice any unpleasant aroma. And remember the New York Yiddish saying: "A nickel gets you onto the subway, but garlic gets you a seat." Try that on your next transcontinental flight.

Spanish Browned Sliced Garlic Topping for Grilled or Fried Whole Fish

◆ BASIC PANTRY

Slice lots and lots of peeled whole **garlic cloves,** then fry quickly in **olive oil.** Serve the golden sliced garlic spooned over **baked, grilled, or pan-fried fish** with some of its fragrant oil, a sprinkling of chopped fresh **parsley,** and a little chopped **roasted red pepper.**

◆◆◆◆◆◆

ROASTED GARLIC In addition to fresh garlic, gentle, nearly sweet roasted garlic makes a delicious seasoning ingredient.

When you roast a chicken, toss in several heads of garlic, broken into cloves but left unpeeled, to roast to tenderness in the juices of the baking bird. If no bird is roasting, place the garlic in a shallow baking dish, toss with a little oil, and bake in a preheated 350° oven for 40 minutes or so. Keep roasted garlic in the refrigerator, covered, for up to a week (unless it has been roasted with a chicken, in which case keep only up to 3 days). To use, peel and add to sauces for lamb, vegetables, chicken, turkey, fish, or pasta. The cloves can remain somewhat whole, or be mashed into a flavoring paste. A particularly delicious dish is sautéed chicken or turkey simmered in broth, cranberry juice, and roasted garlic, the sauce thickened with cream and whole-seed mustard. Roasted garlic is delectable with swordfish, lemons, artichokes, and sun-dried tomatoes.

GARLIC POWDER AND DEHYDRATED GARLIC No substitute for the real thing, nonetheless it is good in Cajun-type mixtures. I think granulated garlic is awful, but there is a dried sliced garlic from Asia that is interesting. I have experimented with it, adding it to breads and rustic potato casseroles, and while I haven't come up with the definitive recipe for it, I enjoy having it on my pantry shelf.

◆◆◆◆◆◆

Ginger: Fresh and Ground This golden-colored rhizome with its distinctive aroma and flavor seasons many of the savory dishes of the Eastern world while adding a peppery fillip to sweets in the Western world. Use fresh in a stir-fry or braise, simply chopped (I never bother to peel it). Grated, it is delicious added at the last minute, especially combined with a bit of vinegar for a tangy condiment. Ground, it shows up as part of the mélange of North African spices that flavor their *tajines,* or rich braises, and many Sicilian fish dishes. Ginger is also sold preserved in sugar syrups, and that sweet spicy syrup makes a good addition to Asian-style vinaigrettes. Young tender ginger is sold preserved in a vinegary solution, and used as a condiment with rice and rich dishes.

An excellent resource book on ginger is *Ginger: East to West* by Bruce Cost (Aris Books).

Herbes de Provence: A mixture of dried herbs from the Provence region of France. I always buy the kind that comes in a little ceramic tub with a handwritten label. Unfortunately, the tops of these charming containers don't fit terribly tightly, and if I don't use the herbs quickly enough I end up transplanting them into a jar with a tighter seal to retain their aroma. The sweet little ceramic pot can then be made into a candle by pouring melted wax into it and suspending a string down its center.

TO MAKE YOUR OWN HERBES DE PROVENCE Combine 1/4 cup **dried basil,** 2 tablespoons **dried savory,** 2 tablespoons **dried thyme,** 1 tablespoon **dried rosemary,** 2 tablespoons **fennel seed,** and 1 teaspoon **dried**

lavender flowers. Optional additions include crumbled **dried bay leaves,** a pinch of **ground nutmeg** and/or **ginger.**

Horseradish This plant has huge roots that grow into the earth to a depth of 6 feet. Sold fresh in chunks, it needs only to be grated and combined with a little vinegar for a spicy condiment powerful enough to unblock any sinus. Horseradish is the classic accompaniment for the Eastern European Jewish gefilte fish.

Grating the horseradish is a problem, however, as the fumes send even the most stouthearted of us fleeing the room with tears streaming. You can use a food processor for grating if you like; just protect your face when you release the cover.

For the cowardly, horseradish is available in jars already grated and mixed with vinegar and/or beet juice. The combination of horseradish with sour cream or unsweetened whipped cream makes a delectable sauce for rare roast beef or, less traditionally, for smoked salmon. When added to mustard, horseradish emphasizes its sharp edge and is a much-appreciated flavoring for Creole mustard. Try thickening the pan gravy from a pot roast with roasted garlic cloves and hotting it up with a dash of horseradish, fresh if possible.

Juniper Berries The flavoring ingredient for gin and choucroute garnie, juniper has an affinity for the flesh of wild and domestic game. I usually keep a bottle of gin on my shelf rather than juniper berries, since it doubles for the occasional martini.

Lavender The fragrant little buds that form the basis of numerous perfumes, sachets, and soaps also make a lyrical flavoring ingredient. In North Africa lavender is added to *ras al hanout*, a currylike mixture of spices. In Provence it is used in herbes de Provence, along with ground bay leaves, rosemary, thyme, basil, savory, white pepper, nutmeg, and cloves. On its own, lavender may be steeped with honey and used to flavor a most delicate milk ice, or ground with sugar and used with fruit to make Provençal-tasting desserts.

Mace and Nutmeg Mace is the outer husk, nutmeg the inner nut. Both have a sweet aroma and are good in curries, eggnogs, fruit dishes, puddings and custards, and cream and cheese sauces.

Marjoram With a sweet, herby flavor, it is similar to oregano and may be used interchangeably in tomatoes and meaty sauces, vinaigrettes, etc.

Mint The mint family is a big one, with flavors and fragrances ranging from sweet to spicy, fruit scented to peppery. There is apple mint, pineapple mint, orange mint, peppermint, and spearmint. Catmint, otherwise known as catnip, drives cats wild, though I have found that any patch of mint I have growing seems to attract more than its share of feline attention.

Mint is one of my favorite herbs. Dried it is delicious in a variety of Middle Eastern dishes as well as a tea, and fresh it is springtime itself tossed into salads, pasta dishes, vegetables such as peas or marinated eggplant, stews, and even crusty savory sandwiches.

Keep a jar of dried mint on your shelf and a pot of mint growing on your windowsill.

Mustard Seeds The two most common mustard seeds are the black and yellow, though brown is increasingly seen on the American market. As a condiment, mustard is described on page 160. The seeds are the basis of the condiment, but they also may be used as flavoring ingredients. They are delicious in pickling and in curries, as well as cooked with rice, Indian style (squeeze fresh lemon juice over the rice at the end of cooking). Mustard seeds are good added to a simmering pork roast or to a marinade. In early spring, mustard flowers cover the hillsides in many areas; the pungent wild greens taste much like sharp broccoli and occasionally can be purchased in a farmer's market. Try them added to rustic vegetable soups or blanched and eaten with olive oil as a salad.

Onion Seeds Tiny hard black seeds that are mostly used to sprinkle onto Indian tandoori flatbreads.

Orange and Tangerine Peels Dried orange peel adds a delicious citrus flavor to savory dishes such as tomato-braised meats and fish soups, and to many of the heartier Chinese dishes. Wash well and peel an orange or tangerine each time you enjoy the fruit, taking care to remove only the colored part where all of the flavorful essential oils are located. The white pith won't hurt you, in fact it is full of vitamins such as bioflavinoids, but it doesn't add much flavor. Dry the peels on a wire rack in a slow oven, then keep for use as desired. Or, more esthetically, peel the orange, keeping it intact in one long curled piece. String with a needle and thread, then hang it where it can get sun and dryness. Let hang until it is dry enough to be stored in the pantry or until you use it up. Less esthetically, but more practically, I often don't bother drying orange peel, but stash a small supply in the refrigerator (where it will keep for up to 1-1/2 weeks) or the freezer (for up to 2 months).

Oregano Available in Mexican and Greek varieties, each with a differing yet pungent herbal aroma and flavor. The Greek definitely has a more forceful presence, and I strongly recommend searching for it. Use in tomatoey sauces and stews, crumble to release its captivating fragrance, and sprinkle it over an omelet or salad, or a piece of hot roasted lamb. Oregano is delicious added to vinaigrettes and Mexican chilied dishes.

Paprika Ground from sweet red pimientos, paprika was not a part of Hungarian food until the discovery of the New World. *Rose paprika* is sweet, with the strongest flavor, and best for using in generous quantity in goulashes and other Hungarian dishes. *Hot paprika* has a wallop of heat along with the sweet richness of paprika. It is worth keeping both on your pantry shelves—I especially like hot paprika jazzing up good ol' American macaroni and cheese, along with a jolt of mustard. A sprinkle of paprika adds color to roasts and adds depth to any sauce based on sweet peppers. Imported Hungarian paprika is best, needless to say.

Peppercorns I often get so bound up in other flavor possibilities that I forget about the simplest and most basic: pepper. There is as wide a variety of peppercorns as there is of other spices, with each type offering its own warmth and perfume. Kept whole, they retain their pungency for a remarkably long time; preground, they add little but heat.

Peppercorns are at their best crushed in a mortar to a coarse powder, but I confess that I often buy coarsely ground pepper just so that it is readily available if I am not in the mood to crush by hand.

Black peppercorns make black pepper. Beneath the black coating of the peppercorn, however, the seed is white. These defrocked peppercorns are referred to as white peppercorns and ground into white pepper. Green peppercorns are the immature version of the black, and as such have their own peppery flavor. They are often pickled in brine, tasting somewhat like a peppery caper, and are very good in sauces, especially those for sautéed steaks. Pink peppercorns, which look like little red polka dots when used in pale creamy sauces, were for a while the darlings of the nouvelle set. They are actually not pepper at all, but a similar berry, one that unfortunately is rather allergenic. Some specialty shops and spice companies package a combination of the five types of peppercorns, and they make a happy change of pace when used in dishes that usually highlight black peppercorns. I like them crushed and sprinkled onto a buttered baked potato or added to mustard. Another good pepper mixture is Cajun pepper: Mix equal amounts of ground black, white, and cayenne pepper and use as desired.

Quatre Épices is a mixture of peppercorns and spices used in French cooking to season pâtés, sausages, and the occasional sauce.

TO MAKE YOUR OWN QUATRE ÉPICES Mix 1 tablespoon ground **white pepper** with 1 tablespoon freshly **grated nutmeg,** 2 teaspoons **ground cloves,** and 1 teaspoon **ground ginger.**

Rosemary I really hate dried rosemary leaves. They are sharp, get stuck in the throat, and don't add that much flavor or aroma. Fresh rosemary is a perennial, it grows nearly anywhere and everywhere, and it is often sold in markets as well. I do, however, keep a jar of dried rosemary for emergency use only, and crush it well in a mortar before using.

Saffron The delicate red-colored stigma of the autumn crocus adds a distinctive bright yellow color and sweet, yet deep and rich flavor. No wonder it is the most expensive spice on earth: it takes 225,000 flowers to make one pound of saffron. Much of it is grown on the Tunisian island of Djerba, and in Spain and India. Mexican saffron is apt to be diluted with marigold leaves, as is any saffron that is already powdered. If saffron is too reasonably priced, you can be sure it has been diluted.

Bouillabaise, paella, risotto milanese, curries and rice dishes, and many European sweets all owe their individuality to this spice. Saffron pairs perfectly with many seafood dishes, vinaigrettes, and buerre blancs.

Sage A classic of the American kitchen, sage comes into its own at Thanksgiving, when it flavors turkeys and bread stuffings. Breakfast sausages are seasoned rather forcefully with sage. In Greece, cafes exude the aroma of *faskomila*, a tea brewed from sage leaves. Sage is good in pasta dishes, in chowders and stews, and with tomatoes and poultry.

Again, since it is a perennial and grows through even pretty harsh winters (at least on a windowsill), I prefer it fresh.

Salt Most of us just sprinkle a bit on, trying to avoid its perils, but how many of us really give attention to how it tastes? Or how it affects our lives?

Salt, the first preservative, was extremely important during the time when refrigeration did not exist. Salt figures in many rituals, such as the Jewish tradition of dipping bread into salt after the blessing over the food. Our word *salad* comes from *sel*, the French word for "salt," because a salad originally was a collection of fresh leaves dipped in salt. The word *salary* has the same root, since at one time salt was the most valuable of commodities, and was used as payment for services and debts.

Salt has a place in nearly every pantry, but don't limit yourself to the fine-milled salt routinely sold. Try kosher salt, which is somewhat coarse and has a good strong flavor, or sea salt, which is made from evaporated unrefined sea salt and has a faint whiff of minerals.

Savory, Winter and Summer Varieties The winter variety is stronger, the summer one sweeter. Both are best fresh, though dried they are good powdered and combined with other herbs, then shaken onto grilling meats, etc.

Star Anise A large brown star-shaped anise-scented seed pod used in Chinese cooking, especially in the rich soy sauce–based braises known as "red-cooking." Shop for star anise in an Asian grocery, and try using it in Western as well as Asian foods: in marinades for fruit, in custards, in tomato sauces, and so on.

Sumac A sour red berry that is ground and used as a spice in the Middle East. Keep a jar on your shelf and shake onto buttered rice, or even rice without butter. It may be combined with other spices and nuts in a mixture called za'atar, and used to dip bread and cheese in. Sumac is marvelous sprinkled onto fresh vegetables and salads, and it gives a lift to tabbouli and to marinades for chicken that is to be grilled.

Szechuan Peppercorns Looking much like regular peppercorns but browner in color and somewhat less tidy in shape, Szechuan peppercorns have an evocative, somewhat minty fragrance and flavor. Among other ways of using them, they are traditionally roasted and crushed with salt as a dipping condiment for poultry, meats, and fish.

Roasted Salt and Szechuan Pepper Seasoning Mixture

Heat 1/2 cup **salt** in an ungreased skillet over medium-high heat for 6 to 8 minutes or until salt goes lightly golden. Cool and combine with 3 tablespoons coarsely ground (in a mortar is best) **Szechuan peppercorns.**

◆◆◆◆◆◆

Tarragon is at its best fresh, but is perfectly good dried as long as it hasn't sat on the shelf too long. It is one of the first herbs to go, and I wouldn't keep it for longer than 6 months. Dried tarragon usually reflects its freshness in its color, so when stale will look the part, veering toward the color of hay. Tarragon is sometimes sold preserved in vinegar and makes a good basis for sauces such as bernaise and buerre blanc. The fresh herb belongs in a pot in your kitchen window.

Thyme comes in a wide array of varieties when fresh, but dried it is generally sold just as thyme. It's good dried, with a strong herbal flavor that doesn't dissipate as easily as those of other herbs. Thyme is used so much in this book, suggestions here seem redundant. Generally, however, fresh and dried thyme are somewhat interchangeable, at a ratio of 4 parts fresh to 1 part dried.

Turmeric is ground from a tuber that looks much like a smaller ginger root. Its coloring, however, is shockingly yellow, and its flavor distinctively warm, with a bitter edge. Large quantities are used in the manufacture of mustards to oomph up the yellow color, and in curries, while tiny amounts are used to color packaged soups and pickles.

Vanilla This New World native, botanically known as *Vanilla planifolia*, is a member of the orchid family. Grown on high, often precariously steep mountainsides, it blooms only one day a year. The long pods that result from this blooming are the vanilla beans. A vanilla bean may be simmered in milk for a custard or ice cream, then removed from the liquid, dried, and reused. This can go on for months; to extract the remainder of its flavor, open the pod and scrape its aromatic seeds into whatever you like.

For homemade vanilla essence, keep a vanilla bean in a bottle of vodka or brandy for a month or so, letting the spirits absorb the sweet vanilla fragrance; use droplets as you would vanilla extract. Do not keep in a window or in sunlight, as the mixture will lose its essential character.

For vanilla sugar, place a vanilla bean into a canister of sugar. Scrape the inside of the bean and mix it with the sugar for maximum effect.

Wasabi is the powdered Japanese horseradish most commonly used as a condiment to accompany sushi. I find a tiny bit added to mayonnaise gives it a lilt, especially spread on salmon, or bacon-lettuce-tomato sandwiches.

Drying and Preserving Fresh Herbs

Bay leaves, dill, marjoram, mint, oregano, sage, savory, thyme, and tarragon all make delightful decorations when hung about the kitchen or pantry along with other rustic things: baskets, chilies, garlic, etc.

If you don't grow fresh herbs, anytime you buy a bunch and can't use it, simply hang it up on a kitchen or dining room wall. Not only is it an instant country look for your home, you can pinch off bits of the fragrant herbs as you need them. Use dried branches of fennel, rosemary, thyme, etc., especially the woodier branches, to throw on the flames of a barbecue to perfume the cooking foods with their herbal scent. Remember to hang herbs upside down so that the flavorful oils will migrate to the leaves rather than getting clogged in the stems.

Cilantro freezes well for up to a month, but don't expect garden-crisp freshness. It will be limp, though it will taste perfectly fine.

Chives, chervil, rosemary, dill, taragon, and sage can all be mixed with unsalted butter and a squeeze of lemon, then frozen into little pats or ice cube trays, as can other, more exotic herbs: lemon thyme, chive flowers, etc. Basil pureed into pesto keeps beautifully, letting the scent of Genoa and the Italian Riviera seep into your kitchen each time you take out a little parcel of the green basil-garlic sauce.

Condiments and Flavoring Ingredients

When I was growing up the array of spices in our shelf was limited to cinnamon, paprika, cloves, and ginger (for gingerbread). The condiments strayed no further than yellow mustard (inexplicably, catsup was frowned on with an almost religious fervor), kosher pickles, soy sauce, and taco sauce. And our cupboard might have been considered daring for the times.

These days it is a different story. A walk down the aisle of a modern urban American supermarket offers such a wide range of condiments and flavoring ingredients that a recent visitor from Europe asked me, as we gazed at the colorful packed market shelves: "Do people really know what all of these things are?"

That is how varied and extensive our choice is these days; with such an array of seasoning ingredients, you could serve the same basic food every day of the year and still season it differently.

Pantry List: Condiments and Flavoring Ingredients

Anchovies
Barbecue sauce
Black bean sauce
Capers
Catsup
Chilies
Chili paste (Garlic, Chinese or Vietnamese)
Chinese fermented black beans
Chipotle chilies
Chutney
Coconut milk
Corn husks, banana leaves
Cranberry sauce
Dried mushrooms (cèpes, porcini, cremoni, morels, etc.)
Flower waters (rose, orange flower)

Giardiniera
Hoisin sauce
Hot bean sauce (Chinese)
Indian spice pastes (tandoori, tikka, etc.)
Jamaican fruit sauces
Jalapeño jelly
Kaffir lime leaves
Kimchee
Lemon grass
Limes (dried)
Maple syrup
Mayonnaise
Mustards
Olives (black and green)
Olive paste (black and green)

Peanut butter
Pickled jalapeños
Pickle relish
Pickles (cornichons, kosher dill, bread and butter)
Plum sauce
Salsa (green and red)
Salted turnips
Soy sauce (both light and dark or an all-purpose one)
Sun-dried tomatoes (dried or oil-marinated)
Tabasco sauce
Tahini
Truffles or truffle paste
Vine leaf Kopanisti

Anchovies "Hold the anchovies" is probably the most-often-repeated phrase in a pizza parlor. But visit Provence or Italy and you're likely to change your mind. You might not even know that you're eating anchovies; you'll just notice that the dish tastes particularly savory, with a salty seaside quality. Soon you might find that the silky anchovies are your favorite bits in the crusty sandwiches you tote down to the beach, or on the chewy focaccia breads you munch walking along the old cobbled streets.

Once you fall under their influence, try adding them to vinaigrettes and mayonnaises, chopping them and eating them with boiled potatoes, or inserting them into a leg of lamb and letting them melt into the rosy flesh.

Seafood and Fennel Risotto with Anchovy Butter

[RISOTTO AL MARE]

◆◆ INTERMEDIATE PANTRY

Serves 4 to 6

Anchovy paste, beaten with unsalted butter, makes a delicious addition to a recipe. Try the following risotto, filled with juicy shrimp, bites of chewy squid, briny black mussels, and bits of sweet fennel, all enlivened by melting nuggets of anchovy butter.

This is an elegant dish, at its best when prepared with homemade fish stock—a good excuse for keeping some on hand in your freezer.

1/2 pound unsalted butter, at
   room temperature
1 tablespoon anchovy paste, or
   2 tablespoons chopped
   anchovies, mashed
1/2 onion, chopped
1-1/2 cups coarsely chopped
   or thinly sliced fresh fennel
   (1 small to medium bulb)
1 garlic clove, chopped
1/4 teaspoon fennel seeds
1-1/2 cups Arborio rice
1/2 pound squid, cleaned and
   cut into 1/2-inch rings

1 cup dry white wine
4 to 5 cups Fish Stock, page
   343, hot but not boiling
1/2 pound mussels, scrubbed
   and debearded, then soaked
   in cool water for 20 minutes
   to rid them of any grit
1/4 pound shrimp, shelled
Black pepper to taste (you will
   most likely not need salt as
   the anchovy butter and seafood are salty)
2 tablespoons chopped fresh
   basil or Italian parsley

1. Combine 2 tablespoons butter with anchovy paste or anchovies. Set aside.

2. Lightly sauté onion, fennel, garlic, and fennel seeds in remaining butter until vegetables are softened. Add rice and squid, and coat in mixture, lightly cooking.

3. Slowly stir in white wine and cook over medium heat until wine is absorbed, then slowly add hot stock, 1/2 cup at a time, then increasing amount to 1 cup. Add more whenever rice has absorbed its last addition. Continue for about 15 minutes, or until rice is somewhat plump but still too chewy to eat.

4. Add mussels and cook 10 minutes, or until mussels are just beginning to open, continuing to add liquid as needed. Add shrimp and cook a minute or two.

5. Risotto is ready when rice is al dente, sauce fairly soupy, and seafood just tender. Add black pepper.

6. Serve immediately, each portion garnished with a nugget of anchovy butter and a sprinkle of basil or Italian parsley.

NOTE Extra anchovy butter may be used on pasta or sandwiches and may be wrapped tightly in plastic and frozen.

◆◆◆◆◆◆

Barbecue Sauce In recent years barbecue sauce has become gastronomically respectable, with lots of good ones on the market. In truth, some are wonderful, others insipid. As with olive oil and wine vinegars, taste until you find your favorite. These days I'm partial to Kingsford, Lloyd's Rich and Natural, Firehouse, and K-C Masterpiece.

A bottle of zesty barbecue sauce has a place in most pantries and can add a thrill to duller foods. Barbecue sauce is good on hamburgers, especially when jazzed up with ancho chili powder, ground cumin, or a little of the sizzlingly spicy marinade from chipotle chilies. Pantry confession: I have been known to splash some barbecue sauce onto canned pork and beans, along with a little chopped onion and black pepper, then cover and bake them long and slow.

Pantry Barbecue Sauce

Even if you don't have a jar of barbecue sauce in your pantry, the ingredients to make it are probably sitting on your shelf.

This makes a basic barbecue sauce, K-C style (Kansas City, that is); regional variations follow the recipe. I have included liquid smoke in the recipe; it adds that distinctive smoky fragrance. Instead of using it, you could simmer the sauce over the charcoal for an hour or so to absorb the smoky scent of the fire.

Note: Authentic barbecuing is not grilling. It is long, slow, cooking over an open fire (traditionally a pit) yielding meat that is succulent and meltingly tender, infused with the scent of smoke. Barbecue sauce can, however, be used for grilled foods to impart barbecue flavor. Use a classic tomato-based, sweet barbecue sauce at the very end of cooking, or as a table sauce. Basting the roasting meats with it will caramelize, then burn the sugar. Instead, rub meat with a mixture of spices and seasonings such as salt, pepper, paprika, cumin, oregano, cayenne, and garlic powder, then cook slowly over the fire.

1 onion, grated or minced	1 cup water
3 garlic cloves, chopped	1 tablespoon molasses
3 tablespoons butter	1 tablespoon chili powder
1 cup catsup	Pinch cayenne or Tabasco sauce to taste
1/3 cup Worcestershire sauce	
1/2 cup cider vinegar	1/2 to 1 teaspoon *each* salt and ground black pepper
2 tablespoons dark brown sugar	2 teaspoons liquid smoke

1. Combine all ingredients and heat together. Bring to a boil, then reduce heat and simmer for about 30 minutes, or until onion is soft and flavors have melded.

VARIATION Lightly sauté onion and garlic in butter until softened, then add rest of ingredients, simmering until flavors are well combined.

TEXAS BARBECUE SAUCE Substitute **beer** for the water, and add 1 tablespoon **prepared horseradish** and 1 to 2 teaspoons **dry mustard.**

ANOTHER TEXAS SAUCE Substitute half **chili sauce** for half of catsup.

MEXICAN BARBECUE SAUCE Instead of liquid smoke and cayenne or Tabasco, use a bit of **chipotle chili,** including some of the fiery **marinade.**

GEORGIA BARBECUE SAUCE Substitute 1 cup **tomato sauce** for 1/2 cup of catsup; season with a bit of **prepared horseradish, Dijon mustard,** and **paprika.**

CAJUN BARBECUE SAUCE Season with ground **cumin, oregano,** and **Cajun spice mixture.**

SOUTH CAROLINA BARBECUE SAUCE Traditionally, the meat is a whole pig, roasted in a pit (shoulder of pork is more practical for the home cook). Baste the roasting meat with **cider vinegar** seasoned with **cayenne,** then serve with **Pantry Barbecue Sauce,** above, in which you've decreased the amount of catsup to 1/4 cup.

Texas Barbecued Brisket

◆ BASIC PANTRY

Serves 8 to 10

This is classic barbecue beef sandwich filling, of the type that I remember eating on big dipped French rolls in restaurants that had names like Myrtle's Trail, or Chuckwagon, and floors covered with sawdust. The barbecue sauce makes a great marinade for this long-cooking brisket, resulting in a dish that tastes and smells like one you'd eat at a cowboy hoedown, yet it doesn't even need to be in the same neighborhood as fire and hot coals.

Barbecued beef brisket is at its best with baked beans and potato salad with lots of green onions, and a plate of pickled jalapeño chilies on the side.

1 beef brisket, about 5 pounds	2 tablespoons brown sugar
2 onions, chopped	2 teaspoons ground cumin
4 garlic cloves, chopped	1/2 teaspoon ground ginger
2 cups beer	1/4 cup Worcestershire sauce
3 cups good spicy barbecue	Juice of 1 lemon or lime
sauce	Oil for browning

1. Place beef brisket in a large nonaluminum pan and add all remaining ingredients except oil.

2. Cover and marinate in refrigerator for 2 days, turning it in its marinade from time to time.

3. Remove meat from marinade, reserving marinade for cooking. Pat brisket dry, then heat a heavy skillet and brown brisket in a little oil for 5 to 10 minutes on each side or until browned.

4. Place browned meat with its marinade in a large baking pan. Cover tightly with aluminum foil, then bake in a 300° oven for 10 to 12 hours.

5. Slice brisket thinly across grain and serve it dipped into its pan juices.

Cowboy Beans

Serves 6

Barbecue sauce seasons this potful of multicolored flavored beans. The array of different types of beans gives the dish an added dimension, as each offers its own flavor, shape, and texture.

◆◆◆◆◆◆

TO PREPARE Cook a total of 1 to 1-1/2 cups mixed **dried beans** in a variety of types such as pinto, white, black kidney, red kidney, and chick-peas until just tender. You will have 3 to 4 cups cooked beans. (You can also use canned beans.) Drain, place in a large baking pan, and combine with 1 to 2 cups **barbecue sauce**, 1 chopped **onion**, 1 chopped **green pepper**, 3 chopped **garlic cloves**, and 1 cup **beer or broth** of choice. Season with **chili powder**, ground **cumin, oregano, dry mustard,** and **black pepper** (optional: top with slices of **bacon**).

Cover and bake in a low oven or over a slow open fire for 2 hours or so.

◆◆◆◆◆◆

Black Bean Sauce and Chinese Fermented Black Beans With their pungent, salty flavor these are unlike any Occidental seasoning ingredient. A little goes a long way; they are superb not only in traditional Chinese dishes such as steamed spareribs with black bean sauce, or duck and rice noodle chow mein; they lend themselves extremely well to East-West experimentations.

These black beans must not be confused with the Latin American black beans that are simmered into hearty potfuls. These Asian beans are salted and dry, and they must be soaked for a few minutes before being crushed (a fork will do the trick, although traditionally the handle of a cleaver does the honors).

Black bean sauce is an easy and ready-to-go alternative to soaking and crushing. Available in jars, it lasts a good long time (probably up to 3 months) in the refrigerator and may be spooned out judiciously and added to stir-fries, marinades, savory braises, and the like.

To prepare fermented black beans: soak 2 tablespoons **fermented black beans** in 1/4 cup **water** for about 5 minutes. Pour off water, then mash beans with a fork or cleaver handle. Mix with 1 minced **garlic clove,** and 2 tablespoons *each* **dry sherry** and **soy sauce.**

STORAGE TIPS Black bean sauce lasts in the refrigerator for 3 months. When storing dried fermented black beans, keep them in the plastic bag they came in, on your pantry shelf away from heat or sunlight. They will last up to a year if kept dry and cool.

Broccoli and Rice Noodles with Black Bean Vinaigrette

◆◆ INTERMEDIATE OR
◆◆◆ ADVANCED PANTRY

Serves 4

Black bean vinaigrette lasts, refrigerated, up to five days and up to two months in the freezer. This East-West dressing is good on steamed fish and asparagus for a quick spicy supper, or with steamed rice and braised Napa cabbage.

8 ounces rice noodles or rice vermicelli (thin or fat)

1 to 2 bunches broccoli (3 cups florets and peeled stems)

BLACK BEAN VINAIGRETTE
2 to 3 tablespoons Chinese black bean sauce
1 teaspoon finely grated fresh ginger
1 to 2 chopped garlic cloves
1 tablespoon Asian (toasted) sesame oil
1 tablespoon soy sauce
1-1/2 tablespoons dry sherry or rice vinegar of choice
1 tablespoon sugar, preferably brown

1 tablespoon chopped fresh cilantro
2 tablespoons mild vegetable oil
Dash red pepper flakes, Chinese chili oil, or chili paste with garlic

1/2 red bell pepper, thinly sliced
1/4 cup unsalted dry-roasted peanuts

1. Cook rice noodles in boiling salted water, according to directions on package. Time will vary quite a bit depending on size of noodles. Drain well and rinse in cold water. Set aside.
2. Steam or blanch broccoli until just crisp-tender. Set aside.
3. Combine black bean sauce with ginger, garlic, sesame oil, soy

sauce, sherry or vinegar, sugar, cilantro, vegetable oil, and pepper seasoning. Whirl in a blender to mix well.

4. Arrange a bed of cool rice noodles on a platter and top with broccoli.

5. Spoon dressing over, garnish with red peppers, and serve at room temperature sprinkled with peanuts.

◆◆◆◆◆◆

Bean Sauce Also known as brown bean sauce, this is made from the fermented soybean residue left over from making soy sauce. It is thick, medium brown in color, and pleasantly pungent. Use to flavor bland foods such as chicken, fish, or vegetable stir-fries, or in combination with other sauces, such as hoisin and plum.

STORAGE TIP Bean sauce will keep in a jar (transfer from can if it came in one) in refrigerator for about 2 months.

Capers Like anchovies, capers are much maligned in the American kitchen but adored in the Mediterranean one. By themselves they are a bit sharp, but they add a distinctive tang to so many simple dishes it is worth having a jar on the shelf ever-ready.

The buds of the caper bush, pickled in a salty brine, are delicious lightly crushed and added to mayonnaise, then served with artichokes and roast chicken. Capers transform egg salad and raise it above the ordinary, and are delicious in all sorts of pasta dishes. Occasionally nasturtium seeds are sold pickled like capers, with a flavor much like the Mediterranean bud.

STORAGE TIP Once open, capers should be stored in the refrigerator, where they will keep for an indefinite length of time.

Pasta with Marinated Tomatoes, Capers, Olives, Garlic, Chilies, and Herbs

This pasta dish would not be the same without the piquancy it picks up from the capers, and from its Italian name. The dish loosely translates as "bad woman pasta," as several other lusty tomato and garlic and herb pasta dishes do. Legend has it that these dishes are so named because they are very aromatic and lure customers in when other charms fail. Another explanation is that the dishes are so quick they can be prepared between customers.

Regardless, this dish tastes of the essence of summer. Besides the tomatoes and fresh herbs, the rest of the dish is from the pantry.

Enjoy as a summer supper, outdoors, accompanied with the sounds of crickets chirping.

1/4 cup extra-virgin olive oil
20 Kalamata or other black
    Mediterranean-style olives,
    pitted and halved
1 tablespoon capers, plus
    1/2 teaspoon or so of the
    marinade
4 to 5 garlic cloves, chopped

1 cup coarsely chopped ripe
    fresh tomatoes
1/4 cup fresh basil leaves, some
    left whole, others torn in half
Salt to taste
Generous pinch red pepper
    flakes
3/4 pound macaroni pasta such
    as penne

1. Combine olive oil with olives, capers, garlic, tomatoes, basil, salt, and pepper flakes. Let sit and marinate for half hour if possible.
2. Cook penne in rapidly boiling salted water until al dente.
3. Drain and toss with sauce.
4. Serve immediately, or let cool and enjoy as a salad.

◆◆◆◆◆◆◆

Chilies, Dried An entire book could be written about chili peppers. In fact, a number of them have. (I wrote one of them: *Hot & Spicy*, J. P. Tarcher.)

A selection of dried whole and powdered chilies in your cupboard is one of the most exciting and versatile ingredients in your kitchen. They can transform even the most mundane of dishes, such as guacamole, marinated kidney beans, or pureed potato soup.

While there are a multitude of types of mild dried chilies, indeed, an uncatalogable amount, they can be broken down into two basic groups: *smooth-skinned and lighter-red* chilies such as New Mexico, California, and occasionally pasilla, and *thicker, more leathery skinned chilies with a dark, almost-black hue* such as ancho, mulato, or again pasilla (same name, different chili). Within each group the peppers are relatively interchangable. Outside the two groups lie the exotics such as the smallish round cascabel, which sounds like a rattlesnake when you shake it, or the guajillo, which, though it appears much like any other mild dried chili, is quite hot and gives a bright orangish tint to the foods it is cooked with. As you experiment with each chili, note the individual characteristics: ancho with its nearly chocolate scent and flavor, New Mexico with its almost fruity overtones, mulato with its full-yet-dry, non-sweet flavor.

STORAGE TIPS Dried chilies store relatively well. I keep a *ristra*, or string, of them on my kitchen wall, and I use it regularly. When I run out I simply sew up a new one. In the pantry I keep a supply of dried chilies wrapped in plastic, placed in a straw basket in a cool, dry place. They will last well like this for up to 6 months, then begin their decline. The main thing is to keep them from insect infestation and to store them in a dark, cool place.

Dried chilies may be rehydrated into an intense puree or into a sauce, fried into crisp garnishes, or toasted and ground into powder.

Rehydrated Chilies

◆◆ INTERMEDIATE TO
◆◆◆ ADVANCED PANTRY

Either toast **dried chilies** over an open fire, then pour **hot water or broth** over them and let sit, covered, for at least 30 minutes, or steep them without toasting; each method gives a slightly different flavor. You can then either scrape off the tender flesh, or whirl the chilies and their liquid to form a sauce.

TO EXTRACT CHILI FLESH Cut off stem end, then open up each chili and, with a knife, scrape the tender flesh from the papery skins, discarding them. Use this flesh as an intensely flavored ingredient, or combine it with broth for a mild chili sauce.

TO MAKE CHILI SAUCE/PUREE When you want a more liquid puree and a less tedious way of preparing it, break up soaked chilies, discarding stems and seeds, and whirl chilies in a blender with a little of their soaking liquid until they form a smooth puree. Add enough liquid to blend smoothly, then strain to remove the tough indigestible bits of skin.

STORAGE TIP Keep rehydrated chili flesh or sauce in your frozen pantry by freezing it in dollops on a piece of plastic or in ice cube trays, then popping chilisicles into a plastic bag for frozen storage.

Crisp Fried Chili Strands

◆ BASIC PANTRY

Makes about 1/4 cup

Slicing mild dried red chili peppers very thinly, then frying them quickly until crisp makes a delicious snack or a crunchy condiment to sprinkle onto salads, soups, etc. Often, when I have duck or chicken skin and fat and decide to make cracklings, I toss a handful of the thinly sliced chilies into the pot when the cracklings have rendered themselves nearly crispy and cooked. The chilies add a warm flavor hue and depth to the already delicious little tidbits.

Since they keep their flavor quite well for at least two weeks, I prepare the chili strips when I have an extra few minutes and then keep them on hand.

◆◆◆◆◆◆

TO PREPARE Using scissors, rather than a knife, cut 2 large **mild dried red chilies** such as New Mexico, California, pasilla, etc., into very thin strands, each approximately an inch or two long and very thin. Heat 3 teaspoons **olive oil** and fry thinly sliced chilies quickly; they will sizzle, change colors somewhat, and become crisp. Remove from pan with a slotted spoon. Drain on paper towels.

Save oil from cooking chilies, as it will be red in color with a warm, almost sweet chili flavor and is delicious added to salad dressings, or to sauté other foods.

Chili Powder

◆◆ INTERMEDIATE TO
◆◆◆ ADVANCED PANTRY

To prepare your own chili powder toast **mild dried chilies** on an ungreased baking pan in a 400° oven for about 10 minutes, or in an ungreased skillet over moderate heat just long enough to toast but not burn. They will change color as they toast, brightening up somewhat from their rather somber color. Break up, remove seeds if desired, and whirl in a coffee or spice grinder until the chilies turn into a powder. This way you can have a selection of individual types of chili powders on your shelf.

Chili powders begin to fade in flavor within about 3 months.

Thai-inspired Tart-Sweet Red Chili Dressing

Makes about 1-1/2 cups

With not a whisper of fat, this lean dressing brings out the best of hearty meat or seafood salads, especially ones with fruit. Try it on a crunchy romaine lettuce salad topped with clementine segments and slices of roast pork, duck, or beef, or with fresh pineapple and scallops or shrimp.

◆◆◆◆◆◆

TO PREPARE Combine 1 cup **water** with 1/4 cup **mild chili powder** such as pasilla and 1-1/2 tablespoons **honey.** Bring to a boil, then remove from heat and add 1 tablespoon grated **fresh ginger,** 1/3 cup **vinegar** or as desired, and a good shake of **salt.** Let cool. This lasts, in the refrigerator, for up to a week, though it gets quite thick and needs to be thinned with a little water or vinegar.

Red Chili-Citrus Paste

Makes about 1/4 cup

Use this pungent paste to coat chicken breasts, roasting ducks, steaks of lamb or beef pounded flat and grilled, fish fillets, and so on; also delicious as a seasoning paste for tamales and other chili-seasoned dishes.

2 tablespoons ancho chili powder
2 tablespoons pasilla, New Mexico, or California chili powder
3 chopped garlic cloves
2 tablespoons fresh orange
2 tablespoons fresh orange juice (optional but wonderful: a bit of grated orange zest)
1 tablespoon lemon or lime juice
1 teaspoon ground cumin
Pinch oregano

Mix all ingredients. Keeps for up to 2 weeks in the refrigerator or for up to 2 months in freezer.

Simple Chili-Citrus Paste

Instead of ancho and pasilla chili powder, use a **commercial chili powder** mixture.

Grilled Chicken Paillards with Pasilla Guacamole

Combine **Red Chili-Citrus Paste,** page 128, with enough **olive oil** to make a thin marinade. Use to coat boned **chicken breasts,** unflattened, with their skin still attached. Grill over charcoal or sauté quickly; serve accompanied with **lime wedges** and **Pasilla-Lime Guacamole** (page 130).

Poc Chuc

Combine **Red Chili-Citrus Paste**, page 128, with enough **olive oil** to make a thin marinade. Use to coat thin slices of raw **beef, lamb, or pork** that you've pounded to a tender and even thickness. Let marinate at least an hour, then grill or sauté. Serve with warm **flour tortillas,** thinly sliced **cabbage** that you've dressed in lots of **lime juice, black beans, and Salsa,** page 368.

Yucatecan-style Chilied Shrimp with Tropical Fruit

◆◆ INTERMEDIATE PANTRY

Serves 4 to 6

Cool papaya or mango contrasts its sweet fruit flavor with the warmth of **Red Chili-Citrus Paste.** Be sure to use unshelled shrimp in this dish; though it is messy to eat, the shrimp are succulent beyond imagining.

◆◆◆◆◆◆

TO PREPARE Coat 1-1/2 to 2 pounds unshelled **shrimp** with 1 recipe **Red Chili-Citrus Paste,** page 128, combined with 1 teaspoon **salt** and 2 tablespoons **olive oil.** Let marinate at least 30 minutes, then skewer and grill over charcoal fire just long enough to cook through. Serve garnished with chunks of peeled ripe but firm **papaya or mango,** wedges of **lime,** and sprigs of **fresh mint or cilantro.**

Arizona Chilied Chicken Thighs with Roast Potatoes and Green Olives

Red Chili-Citrus Paste coats chicken thighs and gives its savor to the potatoes roasting alongside; green olives add a salty edge. The dish tastes distinctively of the Southwest.

◆◆ INTERMEDIATE PANTRY

Serves 4

TO PREPARE Coat 4 large or 8 small **chicken thighs** with **Red Chili-Citrus Paste,** page 128; place in a baking dish and roast for about 20 minutes in a preheated 325° oven. Add 4 medium **potatoes,** peeled and cut into bite-sized pieces, 10 to 12 **green olives** of choice, 1 tablespoon chopped fresh **cilantro or parsley,** and 1 cup **chicken broth.** Raise heat to 375° and bake until potatoes are cooked through, adding a bit of water if liquid has evaporated and potatoes threaten to burn. Serve the potatoes and chicken with their pan juices.

Pasilla-Lime Guacamole

◆◆ INTERMEDIATE PANTRY

Makes about 2 cups

Mild chili flesh such as that of the pasilla adds a sweet warmth to classic guacamole, making a suave sauce that is especially good on grilled chicken paillards or thin grilled meats.

◆◆◆◆◆◆

TO PREPARE Soak 2 **smooth-skinned dried chilies** (New Mexico, California, or smooth-skinned pasilla) as on page 126. Use as seasoning for 2 medium black-skinned Haas **avocados.** Season with the juice of 1/2 **lime,** 2 teaspoons **green salsa,** and **salt** to taste.

◆◆◆◆◆◆

Chili Paste with Garlic A potent paste of hot hot chili peppers pureed with garlic, usually Chinese or Vietnamese in origin. It adds a palate-tingling presence to any sort of Asian dish, especially seafood stir-fries. A dab is delicious as a condiment added to rice and saucy dishes or to mild soups.

STORAGE TIPS Purchase in Asian grocery shops and keep refrigerated once opened; it should last for a good 2 months.

Stir-fried Clams in Their Shells with Chilies and Black Bean Sauce

2 tablespoons vegetable oil, or as needed
2 green onions, thinly sliced
1 tablespoon finely chopped ginger

3 garlic cloves, chopped
2 teaspoons Chinese fermented black beans, soaked for 5 minutes in water to cover,

(continued)

◆◆◆ ADVANCED PANTRY

Serves 4 as an appetizer or
light meal

then drained and coarsely
mashed, or 1 tablespoon
black bean sauce
2 tablespoons dry sherry or rice
wine
2 tablespoons soy sauce
(preferably light)
1 teaspoon chili paste with
garlic
1 teaspoon sugar
1 teaspoon hoisin sauce
24 clams, scrubbed
1/2 cup clam juice
2 teaspoons cornstarch
2 tablespoons cold water
2 tablespoons chopped fresh
cilantro

1. Heat a wok or skillet over high heat, then add a small amount of
oil and quickly stir-fry green onions and ginger.

2. Add garlic and black beans, then pour in sherry or wine, soy
sauce, chili paste, sugar, hoisin sauce, and clams, then stir-fry for a few
minutes.

3. Pour in 1/2 cup clam juice, cover, and reduce heat, letting clams
simmer until they pop open, about 10 minutes. Add more clam juice if
needed as clams cook.

4. Mix cornstarch with cold water, then stir into clams and sauce,
letting cook a few minutes to thicken.

5. Serve immediately, sprinkled with chopped cilantro.

◆◆◆◆◆◆

Chipotle Chilies are made by drying and smoking ripe jalapeños. While
they are sometimes sold dried, I've more often found them in cans
where the fiery chilies are resting in a spicy brown adobo marinade,
which is good as a spicy condiment as well.

Add a strip of chipotle chili to the top of any tostada, or tuck into a
taco. A dab added to barbecue underlines all of the barbecue's good
attributes of spice and smoke. Use to season black beans, sautéed
shrimp, tomatillo sauces, mayonnaise or aïoli, salsas, soups, meatballs,
hearty braises. Mix a bit of chipotle marinade with some broth and use
it to baste a roasting duck or leg of lamb. The list goes on, but remember
that a little goes a long way: it's smoky and hot!

STORAGE TIPS The tiny tin lasts a long time since the chilies are so
potent. After opening, transfer contents of can into a jar or covered container and keep in refrigerator for up to 2 months.

Sweet, Tangy, and Hot Chipotle Salsa

Makes 1-1/2 cups

This makes a thin, sweet-tangy-spicy salsa to shake onto nearly anything: grilled meats wrapped up in a soft flour tortilla or pita bread, rice with beans and smoked sausages, or a zesty fish taco. This sauce is hot, but not killer strength; increase the number of chilies at your discretion.

1/2 cup tomato or mixed vegetable juice
1/2 cup boiling water
3 canned chipotle chilies, chopped, plus 1 tablespoon marinade from can
1 slightly heaped tablespoon dark brown sugar or honey
2 tablespoons vinegar of choice

Combine everything in a blender or food processor and whirl until smooth. Store in refrigerator for up to about 2 weeks.

Salmon with Chipotle Marinade and Chipotle Mayonnaise

Serves 4

1 to 2 tablespoons olive oil
1 to 2 teaspoons chipotle marinade from can, or to taste
4 salmon steaks, about 6 ounces each
Salt and pepper to taste
Chipotle Mayonnaise, page 157

1. Light a charcoal fire in an open grill, or preheat broiler.
2. Mix olive oil with chipotle marinade to taste.
3. Brush onto salmon steaks, then sprinkle with salt and pepper.
4. Grill or broil until salmon is just cooked through.
5. Serve accompanied with Chipotle Mayonnaise.

Chipotle and Black Bean Quesadillas

Serves 4

1 cup cooked black beans
2 teaspoons chipotle marinade, from the can, or to taste
4 large (12-inch) flour tortillas
10 to 12 ounces jack cheese, shredded coarsely or thinly sliced
1/2 cup sour cream
2 tablespoons coarsely chopped fresh cilantro
Several strips canned chipotle chilies, as desired

1. Puree or coarsely mash black beans (with a little of their cooking liquid for a smoother texture) and season with chipotle marinade. Set aside.

2. Spread black bean puree over tortillas, then top with cheese.

3. Broil until cheese is bubbly.

4. Serve immediately, each quesadilla garnished with a dollop of sour cream, a sprinkling of cilantro, and a strip or two of chipotle chilies.

Tortas de Pavo

◆◆ INTERMEDIATE PANTRY

Serves 4

Walk down the streets of any bustling Mexican town and you'll see signs over food stalls on every street announcing *tortas,* or sandwiches, filled with anything and everything. Basically they are crusty rolls, or *bolillos,* spread with a paste of mashed beans and layered with sliced turkey or roasted meat, melted cheese, salsa, pickled chilies, a splotch of sour cream, a handful of shredded lettuce, and there you are.

In the streets of America's Latin American neighborhoods you will find tortas advertised on bright and garish signs on the sides of storefronts.

4 crusty rolls, sliced lengthwise
Vegetable oil for brushing bread
2 cups cooked black beans, page 225
4 teaspoons chipotle marinade from the can, or to taste
12 ounces warm roast chicken or turkey, cut into strips or shredded

1 avocado, peeled and cut into slices and splashed with lime juice
1/4 cup sour cream
2 green onions, thinly sliced, or 2 tablespoons chopped fresh cilantro
1-1/2 cups thinly shredded lettuce

1. Preheat oven to 400°. Pull some doughy insides from roll, then brush with oil. Bake about 10 minutes, or until rolls crisp a bit.

2. Meanwhile, puree or coarsely mash black beans with a little of their cooking liquid and season with chipotle marinade.

3. Remove hot rolls from oven and spread one side of each roll with mashed beans. Top with a layer of chicken or turkey, then avocado and sour cream. Sprinkle with green onions and/or cilantro, then top with other side of roll.

4. Enjoy immediately. Turn the heat up even further with a dose of pickled jalapeños or strips of canned chipotle chili.

Chipotle and Citrus Pot Roast

INTERMEDIATE PANTRY

Serves 8 to 10

1 pork or lamb roast, about 4 to 5 pounds
10 to 15 garlic cloves, about 8 cloves cut into slivers
1 canned chipotle chili, cut into strips, plus several teaspoons marinade from can
3 oranges
Steamed rice, black beans, and salsa of choice as accompaniment

1. Preheat oven to 325°. Make small gashes all over roast and insert slivers of garlic and bits of chipotle chili.
2. Chop remaining garlic and combine with several teaspoons of chipotle marinade and juice of 1/2 orange. Rub all over roast and coat well.
3. Slice remaining oranges (with peel) and layer on bottom of baking pan.
4. Top with roast, then cover tightly with aluminum foil.
5. Bake until meat is meltingly tender, about 3 hours.
6. Remove foil, turn up oven to 450°, and return meat to oven to brown for 20 minutes.
7. Serve immediately, accompanied with rice and black beans, and a salsa of choice. (Since it's a pot roast, you do not have to wait for juices to settle.)

Spicy and Smoky Shredded Meat

INTERMEDIATE PANTRY

Add a bit of **chipotle marinade** to any **leftover fork-tender meat.** Shred with two forks and sauté with **onions** and **garlic.** Season with a little **chipotle chili and/or marinade,** add some diced **tomatoes** (canned are fine), and serve garnished with **sour cream,** chopped fresh **cilantro,** chopped **green onions,** and sliced **avocados** if desired.

◆◆◆◆◆◆◆

Coconut Milk is prepared by squeezing the grated flesh of the fresh coconut. You can make it yourself, or you can buy it in a can and keep it in your pantry for use whenever you need it. Sometimes coconut milk or cream is sold in block form, ready to be reconstituted. Coconut milk may be added to the liquid for cooking rice, or sloshed into a spicy curry to smooth out its rough edges. It may be used in sweets and puddings, ice creams and custards, and tropical fruit drinks with or without the alcohol. Whole cuisines such as Thai, Indonesian, Indian, and Pacific Islands are based on the sweet, creamy coconut, much as Mediterranean cuisine is flavor-based on olive oil.

When buying coconut milk in cans, choose a brand that is not sweetened. That way you can use it for savory dishes, or by adding your own sugar, for sweet ones as well. Sometimes the milk is frozen.

You may also make your own milk using fresh coconut. This is a demanding, time-consuming process, but here is how you do it.

Homemade Coconut Milk First, choose a coconut that makes a noise when you shake it. The noise indicates that there is liquid inside and is also a sign of freshness. Do not choose coconuts that have moldy "eyes," as this usually means that the coconut is over the hill.

To open a coconut you need a hammer and an ice pick (or a screwdriver). Puncture two of the eyes with the ice pick and drive the ice pick in with the hammer. Drain the liquid into a container. This thin, slightly sweet-and-sour liquid is not the coconut milk, but it is a good addition to fresh or frozen tropical drinks.

After draining the liquid, hit the coconut with the hammer about a third of the way down from the top. Rotate the coconut and continue hitting. There is a fault line (something like an equator) that runs around the shell. When you hit this line the right way, a crack will form and the coconut will open right up.

Peel the shell away from the coconut and break the coconut flesh into 1 or 2 inch size chunks. Place the chunks in the food processor and puree, slowly adding almost-boiling water until your quantity of water equals about half the quantity of coconut flesh. When the mixture is thick and chunky, you are ready to extract the coconut milk. Set a strainer over a large bowl and line the strainer with cheesecloth. Pour as much of the mixture into the cloth-lined strainer as possible and press hard with a large spoon to remove the liquid. Twist the cloth and squeeze the coconut as hard as you can to extract as much of the coconut's essence as possible. Repeat until all the coconut mixture is gone. As it sets, the mixture will separate; the bottom will eventually become thin, like skim milk, while the top will thicken and become cream-like. You may keep these separated or stir them together before using.

STORAGE TIPS Transfer any leftover coconut milk to a container, cover, and refrigerate. It will last several days. It freezes well.

Turkey Fillets with the Flavors of Southeast Asia

◆◆ INTERMEDIATE PANTRY

Serves 4 to 6

Coconut milk is good added to a spicy marinade such as this one for turkey.

2 teaspoons to 1 tablespoon
  curry powder
2 tablespoons soy sauce, light
  soy sauce, or fish sauce
1/2 cup coconut milk
1-1/2 tablespoons fresh lime
  juice
1 tablespoon plus 1 teaspoon
  apricot jam

Juice of 1/2 lime
Generous shake hot pepper
  sauce of choice
1 pound thinly sliced turkey fillets, approximately 1/8 to 1/4
  inch thick

1. Combine curry powder with one tablespoon soy or fish sauce, coconut milk, and lime juice.
2. Spread mixture onto turkey fillets and let marinate in refrigerator for at least an hour.
3. Meanwhile, make a sauce by mixing jam and remaining tablespoon soy or fish sauce, then adding lime juice and hot pepper sauce.
4. When ready to serve, sauté turkey fillets in an ungreased hot skillet briefly on each side.
5. Serve with a few dabs of soy or fish sauce.

South Seas Marinade with Fish

Substitute **sea bass or rock cod** for turkey and marinate for 1 to 2 hours. Grill instead of sautéing and serve with **lime** wedges, sliced **papaya**, and **hot pepper seasoning.**

◆◆◆◆◆

Chutney In India, fresh chutneys are purees of various spices, herbs, chilies, and nuts prepared daily. Pickles of fruits and vegetables in sugar syrups, oil marinades, and spicy brines also are common additions to the table. The condiment most Westerners associate with curries is cooked, preserved chutney, that sweet, spicy, and vinegary concoction of mangos, peaches, apples, limes or other fruits. The English embraced it during their reign of the Raj, as the balance of sweet and spicy was reminiscent of their pickles back home.

Chutney is delicious accompanying a curry, but it is also good in Western dishes. Try spreading a little onto a sandwich of Cheddar on whole wheat and top with sprigs of cilantro, or onto a smoked turkey sandwich. Puree a dab of chutney with lentils and yogurt (page 237) for a hauntingly flavored Sauce Indienne that tastes of richness but is in fact as lean as you could want. Chutney is good added to a sauté of leftover lamb, and a dash added to yogurt along with a shake of turmeric or saffron and a little finely chopped garlic is yummy alongside a mound of crisp fried popadums and a selection of condiments (page 117). Chutney is delicious mixed with roast chicken and used to fill samosa-like filo triangles. Or add chutney to a vinaigrette and splash onto Taj chef's salad (page 42).

Corn Husks and Banana Leaves act as flavorful wrappings for foods, giving them a distinctive aroma and savor. Buy corn husks dry in Latino markets or order them by mail. Banana leaves are usually sold frozen in Asian grocery shops. Corn husks need to be soaked for 30 minutes or so to become pliable, while banana leaves need to be heated over a flame or in an ungreased skillet to soften them enough for handling. Once malleable, both corn husks and banana leaves may be wrapped around spicy cornmeal and masa preparations for tamales. Corn husks make delicious wrappers for chili-spiced fish or diced vegetables, while banana leaves are the traditional wrapper for spice-coated and marinated chicken or pork, Yucatán style. Whichever wrapper you choose, it is then folded to enclose the filling and steamed.

STORAGE TIPS Store dry corn husks in a dark, dry place. Kept free of mold and insects, they will last a good year. Drying your own corn husks doesn't work well since the sweet corn we find in our markets does not have husks large enough to be of use.

Since banana leaves are frozen, store them in the freezer. If you can find fresh, unsprayed banana leaves, use them as plates for a dinner party, Indian style, and serve a variety of curries and rice dishes on the lovely green leaves.

Chili-seasoned Corn Husk–wrapped Fish

◆◆ INTERMEDIATE PANTRY

Serves 4

Soak 12 to 16 **corn husks** in warm water and cover for about 30 minutes. Meanwhile, mix 1 recipe **Red Chili-Citrus Paste,** page 128, with 1 pound firm-fleshed **white fish** cut into bite-sized chunks. When corn husks have become pliable, place two husks on a work surface next to each other, overlapping by about 1/2 inch. Seal corn husks together with a paste made from **masa harina** and **water,** then place with several table-spoons or so of the chili-seasoned fish in the center of the doubled husks. Fold the long sides over, making a narrow oblong, then fold over the top and bottom to form a neat parcel. Stack parcels in a steamer and steam for 10 minutes. Serve immediately, accompanied with warm **corn tortillas, avocado** slices, and **pickled jalapeños or salsa** of choice.

Sea Bass Tamales

◆◆ INTERMEDIATE PANTRY

Serves 8 to 10

2/3 cup unsalted butter, at room temperature
2 cups masa harina
1 teaspoon baking powder
1/2 teaspoon salt
1-1/3 cups warm fish or chicken broth

16 or so corn husks
1 pound sea bass fillets, cut into bite-sized pieces
Red Chili-Citrus Paste, page 128
1 tablespoon chopped fresh cilantro

1. Whip butter until fluffy.

2. Mix masa harina with baking powder, salt, and warm broth, then add to butter and beat all together. Chill until ready to use.

3. Meanwhile, soak corn husks in warm water to cover for about 30 minutes.

4. Combine sea bass with chili paste and cilantro.

5. Remove corn husks from soaking liquid and dry with clean towel. Lay out 2 corn husks, overlapping them by about 1/2 inch, and gluing the seam with a little of the masa paste. Spread several tablespoons of masa mixture onto the corn husks. Place a tablespoon or two of fish on top of this, then fold and enclose filling.

6. Place parcels in a steamer and cook over a medium-high heat for 40 minutes, adding more water to steamer if needed.

7. Serve hot, accompanied with salsa and lime wedges.

Cranberry Sauce Uniquely and natively American, tart cranberries are used for a holiday-season sauce, an excellent condiment to keep in the pantry all year long rather than just at Thanksgiving.

Cranberry sauce pairs well with mustard. Try the combination lightened with cream, then splashed over Brussels sprouts. Or try the combination in a vinaigrette:

Cranberry-Mustard Vinaigrette

◆ BASIC PANTRY

Makes 1/3 cup

1 tablespoon cranberry sauce
2 tablespoons whole-seed mustard
1 or 2 garlic cloves, chopped

3 tablespoons olive oil
1 tablespoon raspberry vinegar
Salt and pepper to taste

Mix cranberry sauce with mustard and garlic, then slowly whisk in olive oil and vinegar. Season with salt and pepper.

◆◆◆◆◆◆

Dried Mushrooms and Other Edible Fungi Dried mushrooms have a far greater flavor intensity than do fresh. Part of the reason is that dried mushrooms are wild mushrooms, with the flavor of the forest, and their flavors concentrate when dried. Rehydrated, dried mushrooms give a distinctive aroma and flavor to anything they are added to.

Since their flavor is so special, dried mushrooms should be highlighted and not added to dishes where their flavors will compete with others (with the exception of the long-simmered Italian sauces, sugo and ragù).

The flavor of dried mushrooms varies wildly, depending not only on the type of mushroom you choose, but also on the field they were gathered in and several other variables.

Dried mushrooms such as porcini, cèpes, and morels are usually purchased in specialty food shops or delicatessens, while shiitakes and black mushrooms are usually available in Asian food stores.

STORAGE TIPS Keep in a cool, dry, and dark place such as a jar or tin. Though their flavor does deteriorate, they will keep for up to a year and longer.

All dried mushrooms must be soaked, rinsed, and squeezed before using. And never throw away the soaking liquid—it makes a wonderful base for the sauce, and if you don't need a sauce, save it for soup, risotto, or stew.

CÈPES, PORCINI, AND STEINPILZE are different names for the same delectable mushroom, known formally by its Latin name *Boletus edulis*. Porcini, however, are more intensely flavored and woodsy-scented than their French and German cousins.

The rich brown mushrooms have a particular affinity for artichokes, asparagus, chicken and chicken livers, and pasta sauced with tomatoes or cream. Anytime you sauté fresh domestic mushrooms, a handful of porcini adds a voluptuous mushroom flavor to the dish.

The Simplest Dish of Chicken and Dried Mushrooms

◆◆ INTERMEDIATE PANTRY

Serves 4

*P*etti di pollo ai funghi is Italian for "chicken breasts with porcini," a dish that lets the fresh flavor of the poultry and the extravagant flavor of the mushrooms shine through.

1 ounce dried porcini
   mushrooms
1 cup hot but not boiling
   chicken broth

2 whole chicken breasts,
   skinned, boned, and halved
Salt and pepper to taste
Flour for dredging
2 tablespoons unsalted butter

1. Dust any bits of sand off dried mushrooms, then place them in a bowl and add hot broth. Cover and let sit for at least 30 minutes.

2. Remove mushrooms from soaking liquid and squeeze them into the soaking liquid. Then strain soaking liquid through cheesecloth or pour clear liquid off from sediment at bottom.

3. Rinse mushrooms in cold water, then squeeze dry (discard this water). Coarsely chop mushrooms and set aside.

4. Sprinkle chicken breasts with salt and pepper, then dredge in flour. Shake off excess flour, then lightly sauté in butter for about 2 or 3 minutes on each side, or until chicken is almost but not quite cooked through. Remove from pan.

5. Into pan pour soaking liquid, cook over high heat until reduced by half, then add mushrooms and sautéed chicken breasts. Cook a few minutes longer for flavors to permeate chicken. Serve immediately.

Chicken Breasts with Porcini, Asparagus, and Fontina

◆◆ INTERMEDIATE PANTRY

Serves 4

When the first shoots of asparagus appear I've usually abandoned all hope of winter's end. My coat and boots, which by the end of the season are pretty scruffy, feel like parts of my body. But then I walk down the produce aisle and there they are: graceful green shoots of asparagus, harbingers of the tender vegetables to follow.

1 recipe The Simplest Dish of Chicken and Dried Mushrooms, page 140
2/3 pound asparagus, trimmed of tough stems and cut into

3-inch lengths and briefly steamed until crisp-tender
1/2 pound Italian fontina cheese, cut into thin slices
3 tablespoons freshly grated Parmesan

1. Prepare chicken and mushroom recipe.
2. Place chicken breasts in a shallow baking pan, then arrange asparagus around it.
3. Top with porcini sauce, then with sliced fontina.
4. Sprinkle with Parmesan and broil until cheese melts and lightly browns.
5. Serve immediately.

Frittata of Wild Mushrooms and Peas

◆◆ INTERMEDIATE PANTRY

Serves 4 to 6

2 ounces dried porcini or cèpes
3 tablespoons unsalted butter
1-1/2 cups sliced fresh mushrooms
1 cup tiny tender peas, fresh or frozen

4 to 5 green onions or shallots, chopped
6 eggs, lightly beaten
1/4 cup freshly grated Parmesan cheese

1. Preheat broiler.
2. Pour hot but not boiling water over dried mushrooms, cover, and let steep for 30 minutes. Drain, squeeze, and cut up as in preceding recipe, saving soaking liquid for another dish (though you might like to add a bit to eggs as you beat them).
3. Heat butter in a heavy skillet with a heatproof handle. Add sliced fresh mushrooms and sauté until lightly browned, then add peas, reduce heat, and continue to cook another 5 minutes or so until peas are tender. Add green onions or shallots and stir to meld flavors.

4. Stir together eggs and Parmesan, adding a tablespoon or two of mushroom soaking liquid.

5. Pour egg and cheese mixture into sautéing mushrooms and peas, cooking as for an omelet, lifting edges and letting liquid egg roll underneath every so often.

6. When you have a flat pancake-like mixture, firm on bottom but still mostly raw on top, place under a hot broiler until puffed and lightly browned.

7. Serve immediately, cut into wedges.

◆◆◆◆◆◆

MORELS How wonderful morels are, with their distinctive, almost smoky scent! Certain flavors enhance the morel, Marsala and cream especially.

They appear distinctive too, with their elongated, very wrinkled cap and dark, almost black-gray color.

Turkey or Veal with Marsala, Morels, and Cream

◆◆◆ ADVANCED PANTRY

Serves 4

1 cup hot but not boiling chicken broth
1 package dried morel mushrooms (about 2 ounces)
12 to 16 ounces turkey fillets or thinly sliced veal fillets
Flour for dredging

3 garlic cloves and/or 3 shallots, chopped
2 tablespoons unsalted butter
2/3 cup dry Marsala or port
1 cup heavy cream or half and half

1. Pour hot broth over dried mushrooms. Cover and let soak for 30 minutes.

2. Remove mushrooms, squeeze liquid back into bowl, and reserve. Then rinse rehydrated mushrooms in cold water and squeeze, discarding that liquid. Coarsely chop the rehydrated mushrooms and set aside.

3. Strain mushroom soaking liquid and set aside.

4. Lightly coat turkey fillets in flour. Shake off excess.

5. Gently sauté garlic and/or shallots in butter, then add mushrooms and toss in butter mixture. Add turkey, cooking 2 to 3 minutes on each side until almost cooked through, then remove from pan.

6. Deglaze pan by pouring in Marsala or port and strained soaking liquid. Bring to boil and cook down to reduce quantity to about 1/2 cup.

7. Stir in cream and return chicken and mushroom mixture to sauce, warm through together, and serve immediately.

SHIITAKE MUSHROOMS are rich brown Oriental mushrooms with a woodsy flavor that lend themselves to both Asian and Western dishes. Soak dried shiitakes in warm water or broth as with other dried mushrooms, and cut out the stem, which is usually too tough to chew.

Shiitake mushrooms, once rehydrated, may be sliced and sautéed or stir-fried as desired. Try them paired with fresh mushrooms in a cream sauce ladled over brown rice. Or cut into thin strips and stir-fry with cabbage, carrots, sprouts, and tofu and stuff into a warm hoisin-slathered pita bread.

Shiitakes are often paired with tree fungus or cloud ears. Folklore maintains that cloud ears possess an elixir of health and that eating them leads to long life. Their consistency is strangely chewy, rubbery, and crunchy at the same time, but don't let those adjectives mislead you: they're almost addictively good. Add them to nearly any stir-fry, cut into thin strips or bite-sized pieces, or coarsely chopped. My favorite cloud-ear stir-fry includes bean curd, chili-garlic paste, scallions, fresh ginger, and sesame oil. Cloud ears come in two basic sizes, small and big. I think the smaller cloud ears are more delicate both in flavor and texture. Purchase them in plastic or cellophane bags in Asian grocery shops.

Many Treasure Vegetable Stir-Fry Stuffed into Pita Breads

◆◆◆ ADVANCED PANTRY

Serves 4 to 6

4 or 5 dried shiitake mushrooms
10 or so small cloud ears or tree fungus
1 garlic clove, chopped
One 1-inch piece ginger, chopped
2 tablespoons vegetable oil
1 carrot, cut into julienne
1/2 cabbage, thinly sliced
1 celery stalk, cut into diagonal slices

Six 2-inch pieces tofu, or a 3-by-5 inch chunk tofu, cut into julienne, plain or fried
2 tablespoons chicken or vegetable broth
2 teaspoons soy sauce
2 teaspoons cornstarch
2 teaspoons Asian (toasted) sesame oil
4 to 6 pita breads
Hoisin sauce
Whole green onions
Fresh cilantro sprigs

1. In separate bowls, pour hot water over shiitake mushrooms and cloud ears. Cover and let soak 20 minutes or so. Remove from soaking liquid, rinse, and squeeze dry. Trim shiitake mushrooms of their tough stems, then cut mushrooms into strips. Cut soaked cloud ears into thin slices. Set aside.

2. In a wok or skillet, stir-fry garlic and ginger in oil for a minute. Add carrot, then remove from pan.

3. Next, adding a tiny bit more oil if needed, stir-fry cabbage and celery for just a minute, then remove from pan.

4. Quickly stir-fry tofu, adding more oil if needed, then place tofu with rest of reserved vegatables and stir-fry shiitakes and cloud ears.

5. Mix broth with soy sauce and cornstarch. Combine all vegetables in wok or skillet over medium-high heat, then add broth mixture and cook together for a minute or two, long enough to make a small amount of lightly thickened sauce. Drizzle with sesame oil and set aside.

6. Gently warm pitas in an ungreased or lightly greased skillet. Serve vegetable mixture piled into pita pockets that have been slathered with hoisin sauce (use green onions as paintbrushes, then toss an onion into each pita sandwich). Garnish with cilantro.

Broccoli with Shiitake Mushrooms and Serrano Ham in Garlic Cream with Chilies

◆◆ INTERMEDIATE PANTRY

Serves 4

Shiitake mushrooms add a rich, meaty East-West flavor to the following dish of broccoli sauced with garlicky cream and bits of savory, salty ham. The tiny pieces of slightly *picante* chilies add a warm, peppery accent. This makes a delightful first course followed by thin slices of very lean beef paillards or fish fillets, quickly grilled and served with a spicy salsa, or as a main dish, accompanied with crusty French bread to sop up the saucy pieces of broccoli. To confess, I usually eat this dish with my hands and a piece of bread rather than cutlery.

10 to 15 dried shiitake mushrooms	2 tablespoons olive oil
Hot water or broth, for rehydrating	2 to 3 ounces Serrano ham or prosciutto, diced
1 tablespoon unsalted butter	2 to 3 cups broccoli florets, in-cluding peeled and cut-up stalks
2 to 3 garlic cloves, chopped coarsely	1 cup heavy (whipping) cream
1 mild dried pasilla, New Mex-ico, or California-type chili (smooth skinned)	Salt and pepper to taste

1. Rehydrate mushrooms by pouring hot water or broth over them in bowl, then cover and let sit to soak and soften for 15 to 20 minutes. Remove from liquid (reserving liquid for sauce), squeeze, rinse mushrooms to rid them of grit, and squeeze mushrooms dry. Cut off tough stems and cut mushrooms into bite-sized pieces.

2. In a heavy skillet, sauté mushrooms in butter with 1 garlic clove. Remove from pan and set aside.

3. Using scissors, cut chili into very thin strips. In same pan, quickly fry in 1 tablespoon olive oil, then remove chilies and cooking oil from pan and set aside.

4. Adding remaining tablespoon oil to pan, stir-fry diced Serrano ham or prosciutto, broccoli, and remaining garlic until broccoli is bright green and still crunchy. Add a few tablespoons of mushroom soaking liquid, cover, and cook a minute or two longer—it should still be crisp-tender.

5. Add cream to pan, cover, and finish cooking, another 5 minutes or so. If sauce is too thin, remove cover and boil a minute or two; if too thick add a little mushroom soaking liquid. Add sautéed mushrooms, then season with salt (you won't need much salt, as the ham will be salty) and pepper.

6. Serve each portion sprinkled with a few crisp thin shreds of fried chili.

◆◆◆◆◆◆

Flower Waters Distilled from oh-so-aromatic flowers: usually rose petals or orange blossoms (though occasionally you'll see lavender or jasmine). Flower waters add a fragile fragrance to a wide variety of dishes, savory as well as sweet. Sprinkle whichever one you choose liberally onto couscous or rice pilafs, spicy North African–style braised meats, and sweet filo pastries. Rose water is particularly good added to almond paste or cakes, and orange flower water scents that classic San Francisco brunch drink, Ramos fizz.

Flower waters may be purchased in imported and specialty food shops as well as in wine and spirit shops since they are sometimes used for mixed drinks. Often they come in blue glass bottles, to protect the delicate essences from evaporation and flavor loss. The dark blue bottles, usually bearing a charmingly illustrated lable, are enchanting to use for dried flowers, storing other fragrances or shampoos, etc., long after the flower water is gone.

STORAGE TIP Flower waters last longer when kept in the refrigerator, but then you don't have the pleasure of gazing at their beautiful bottles. Keep in the refrigerator only if the bottles are not so enticing as to demand space on your pantry shelf.

Rose-scented Yogurt and Strawberries

◆◆ INTERMEDIATE PANTRY

Serves 4

3 cups plain yogurt
1 cup fresh strawberries,
 cut into slices or halves
Sugar or honey to taste

2 teaspoons rose water more
 or less, depending upon its
 strength

Stir yogurt to smooth out any lumps, then add strawberries. Season with sugar (or honey) and rose water.

Oranges with Orange Flower Water and Cinnamon

◆◆ INTERMEDIATE PANTRY

Season sliced peeled **oranges** with **sugar,** ground **cinnamon,** and **orange flower water** to taste. Let chill for at least an hour.

◆◆◆◆◆◆

Giardiniera An Italian assortment of vegetables (cauliflower, peppers, carrots, onions, and celery) pickled in a spiced vinegar brine. Terribly good chopped and sprinkled on rare roast beef (page 147) or diced and added to a *tosta,* a Milanese melted cheese sandwich. Tostas are sold in caffè-bars throughout the city of Milan, with a selection of assorted condiments arranged on the bar for each customer to help him or herself to, spooning them into the grilled cheese sandwich. Besides giardiniera, the condiments might range from capers, mustards, chopped herbs, etc. Some of my favorite transplanted-to-America combinations are roasted red peppers and avocado slices with melted jack on rye; melted Cheddar with red onion and diced pickled jalapeños on whole wheat or French.

Melted Cheese Sandwiches from the Street Cafes of Milano

8 slices bread of choice
Mustard as desired
12 ounces jack cheese

3 to 4 tablespoons diced giardiniera pickles
Butter for browning

Serves 4

1. Spread mustard on 4 slices bread. Top each with a slice of cheese, then a bit of chopped pickles and another slice of bread. (Note: I put thinly sliced garlic in my sandwiches, but a true Milanese would be horrified by such crudeness.)

2. Lightly butter outsides of sandwiches, then brown in a medium-hot skillet until golden in color and cheese is melting.

3. Serve immediately.

Rare Roast Beef Salad with a Relish of Giardiniera Vegetables

[INSALATA DE MANZO CON GIARDINIERA]

◆ BASIC PANTRY

Serves 4 as an appetizer, or 2 for a summer supper

Rare roast beef, cut into thin, rosy slices and dressed with a scattering of chopped giardiniera and a drizzle of olive oil. A perfect appetizer for a summer supper or a picnic dish.

10 ounces rare roast beef, cut into thin slices	**1-1/2 to 2 tablespoons extra-virgin olive oil**
5 to 6 tablespoons giardiniera, diced into small pieces	**Fresh parsley or arugula for garnish (optional)**

1. Arrange roast beef on a platter, scatter giardiniera over it, and drizzle with olive oil.

2. Garnish with fresh greens of choice and serve.

◆◆◆◆◆◆

Hoisin Sauce Sweet and spicy, this thick red Chinese sauce is deliciously versatile, transforming stir-fries into memorable meals; use it to sauce bits of chicken breast, water chestnuts, red and green peppers and peanuts. It's good in braises or used to coat a roasting duck or leg of lamb. Hoisin sauce is also good as a dipping sauce for noodle- or pancake-wrapped foods such as mu shu pork. Add a dash of hoisin to other sauces such as Asian-style barbecue sauces. Try adding a spoonful to Spicy Asian Peanut Dip (page 178).

Purchase in Asian food shops and keep on pantry shelf until opened, then refrigerate. If hoisin sauce comes in a can, once opened, empty contents into a jar and store in refrigerator. Keeps up to 2 months.

Since the cans are usually colorful, with beautiful graphics, don't throw them away. Rinse them out and use as pencil tins or mini-planters for an herb or two.

Hoisin Pork with Steamed Bread and Fresh Herbs

◆◆ INTERMEDIATE PANTRY

Serves 6 to 8

Use hoisin to cloak roast pork for a quickly assembled dish that is special but undemanding. The meat is sliced into small pieces, then wrapped in soft slabs of steamed bread, dabbed with more hoisin and garnished with fresh cilantro, mint, and green onions before being popped into the mouth, sandwich style. The steamed bread is a good way to use up leftover French bread; if you have no stale bread, fresh bread works well, too.

4 pounds boneless pork roast (such as loin, or a fattier cut)	**1 bunch green onions, thinly sliced**
Salt and pepper to taste	**1 bunch cilantro, leaves only**
1-1/2 cups hoisin sauce	**1 bunch mint, leaves only**
1/2 pound French bread, sliced about 3/4-inch thick	

1. Preheat oven to 350°.

2. Place pork roast in a shallow roasting pan and rub with salt and pepper; roast for 1 hour.

3. Remove from oven, pour off any excess fat in bottom of pan, then spoon about half of sauce over roast, making sure it is well coated.

4. Return roast to oven and continue cooking for another 30 to 40 minutes, or until internal temperature registers 140°. The pork will continue cooking somewhat as it sits outside the oven. (Pork should never be served underdone, but it shouldn't be overcooked either, especially since modern pork is very lean and gets tough and dry quickly.)

5. Just before serving, arrange French bread slices in a steamer basket. Steam for 3 minutes, or until bread is moistened and hot.

6. Serve pork cut into strips splashed with its pan juices, and accompanied with steamed bread, green onions, remaining hoisin sauce, and a bowl of fresh herbs for each diner to make his or her own tiny sandwiches.

Chinese Duck

Choose **duck** instead of pork. In place of steamed bread you could serve **rice,** or **boiled rice noodles** tossed with a little **soy sauce** and **Asian sesame oil.**

Southeast Asian Lettuce Sandwiches with Noodles, Lamb, and Peanuts

◆◆ **INTERMEDIATE PANTRY**

Serves 4

Wrapping food up in edible leaves is typical of Vietnamese cuisine. These Southeast Asian–inspired bundles of tender, cool noodles wrapped up in a crisp leaf of lettuce, spread with savory peanut sauce, and then scattered with herbs and vegetables are sublime.

Each bite is slightly different, a contrast of tastes, textures, and colors. In tiny portions, these make an intriguing first course; a larger version makes a great party lunch or informal supper.

For a vegetarian version, simply replace the lamb with diced tofu.

8 ounces thin vermicelli, preferably Chinese
3 garlic cloves, chopped
8 ounces ground lamb, beef, or turkey
2/3 cup hoisin sauce
1/2 cup chicken or vegetable broth
2 tablespoons catsup
2 tablespoons sugar
1 tablespoon soy sauce
1 cup unsalted dry-roast peanuts, coarsely chopped
1 head romaine lettuce, separated into leaves, washed, and dried
1/4 cup fresh mint leaves
1/4 cup fresh cilantro leaves
1/2 cucumber, peeled and diced (seed if desired)
1 carrot, coarsely shredded
2 green onions, thinly sliced

1. Boil noodles until just tender. (If fresh, this will take just a minute or two.) Drain and rinse in cool water.

2. Sauté garlic and meat in a wok or heavy skillet. Pour off excess fat and add hoisin sauce, broth, catsup, sugar, and soy sauce. Simmer until slightly thickened, then add peanuts.

3. Arrange lettuce leaves, herbs, and vegetables on a platter. Place cool cooked noodles in one bowl, hot meat sauce in another.

4. Each person makes his or her own bundles by placing a clump of noodles onto a lettuce leaf, then topping with a spoonful of sauce and a scattering of vegetables and herbs.

◆◆◆◆◆◆

Hot Bean Sauce, Chinese This very hot and pungent brown sauce is based on fermented brown beans and hot chilies. It is delicious added to a stir-fry of vegetables and fish, meat, or chicken, or to any sort of Asian-inspired pasta dish. The following measurement is only a guideline. Add more if it needs it, but go carefully: this sauce is really hot.

I particularly like chewy translucent mung bean noodles here, but the dish also is good with rice or wheat noodles, including ordinary spaghetti.

Hot Bean Noodles

Serves 4 to 6

This recipe is adapted from my book *Hot & Spicy* (J. P. Tarcher).

One 8-ounce package mung bean noodles
1 to 2 tablespoons mild vegetable oil
1 carrot, cut into julienne
2 garlic cloves, chopped
One 2-inch piece fresh ginger, chopped
1/2 cup peas, either fresh or frozen
1 zucchini, cut into julienne
3 tablespoons Chinese hot bean sauce
2 tablespoons chicken or vegetable broth
1 teaspoon soy sauce
1 teaspoon cornstarch
1 teaspoon sugar
1 tablespoon chopped fresh cilantro

1. Soak noodles in cold water for 10 minutes to soften. Drain.
2. Bring a large pot of water to the boil and cook soaked noodles until just tender and transparent, 4 to 5 minutes.
3. Heat 1 tablespoon oil in a wok or heavy skillet. Add carrot, garlic, and ginger and stir-fry a minute, then add zucchini and peas and cook a minute or two longer. Remove and set aside.
4. Mix bean sauce, broth, soy sauce, cornstarch, and sugar. Add remaining oil to wok, then add noodles, broth mixture, and remaining vegetables. Cook a moment or two until sauce thickens. Sprinkle with cilantro.
5. Serve warm or at room temperature.

◆◆◆◆◆◆

Indian Spice Pastes (Tandoori, Tikka, Vindaloo, Etc.) Indian communities are springing up throughout various areas of California, and along with them are Indian restaurants and shops selling their enticing variety of spices and seasonings, including a wide range of prepared spice pastes and cooking sauces.

Tangy and vividly flavored, these pastes add a new dimension to dishes. They contain puckery and refreshing tamarind as well as a wealth of spices, and come in a variety of mixtures such as tandoori, tikka, vindaloo (very hot), and so forth. Tandoori paste is usually shockingly red in color, but the flavor is superb. Tikka paste is a dusty, spicy, brown with the tang of tamarind and the aroma of garlic, while the darker brown vindaloo paste is hot and sour. Try mixing a bit of tikka paste with yogurt and enjoying it as a dip for vegetables, crisp fried popadums, or as a sauce for Curried Bulgur Salad (page 199).

Tandoori Chicken Sandwich

◆◆ INTERMEDIATE PANTRY

Serves 4

Generously rub **tandoori or tikka paste** on 4 boned **chicken breast** halves, then let sit for 30 minutes if possible. Broil, grill, or sauté, then let cool. Cut into bite-sized pieces. Mix 3/4 cup *each* **mayonnaise** and **sour cream,** and season with a generous pinch of **dried mint** and 1 to 2 chopped **garlic cloves.** Spread onto 4 slices **whole-wheat bread,** then top with chicken pieces, a lettuce leaf or two, and 4 more slices of whole wheat. Close and enjoy.

Tikka Potatoes

◆◆ INTERMEDIATE PANTRY

Season 1 pound cold cooked **potatoes** (cut into chunks) with 2 tablespoons **vegetable oil** and 2 tablespoons **tikka paste.** Toss together and roast in a shallow baking pan in a 350° oven for 20 minutes or so, tossing occasionally.

Tandoori Fish

◆◆ INTERMEDIATE PANTRY

Serves 4

Rub **tandoori or tikka paste** generously over a small **whole fish** such as a sea bass. Stuff with a slice or two of **onion** and **lemon,** and a few sprigs of **cilantro.** Wrap in foil and bake in a preheated 350° oven for about 30 minutes, or until fish feels firm to touch; you may also roast it without its foil wrap.

◆◆◆◆◆◆

Jamaican Spicy Fruit Sauces A wild weekend on a tropical island, far away from midwinter blahs. Ahh, heaven—but for someone else, not me. I was stuck at home, babysitting the cat.

So I roasted a nice duck for the two of us, splashed it (the duck, not the cat) with Jamaican spicy fruit sauce, adding cranberries, mango, and green chili. It tasted like North-America-meets-the-Caribbean-over-a-roast-duck, and it was very good. Jamaican spicy fruit sauces are scented with allspice and cloves, fired up with chilies, and baked on sweet/tart tropical fruit. They make a good dipping sauce for grilled foods and a good addition to marinades.

After dinner, the cat and I shared a game of cards and called it a night.

Wild Weekend Duck

◆◆ INTERMEDIATE PANTRY

Serves 2

1 whole duck
5 to 6 garlic cloves, unpeeled
1/3 cup Jamaican spicy fruit sauce
1/2 cup cranberries
2 tablespoons brown sugar

1 cup dry white wine
1 mango
Juice of 1/4 lime
1 fresh green chili such as jalapeño, seeded if desired, and thinly sliced or chopped

1. Preheat oven to 375°. Place duck in a roasting pan, rub with about 1 tablespoon fruit sauce, then stuff with half of garlic cloves, leaving rest scattered on bottom of pan.

2. Prick duck all over with a sharp knife or fork and roast for 45 minutes, or until duck is just browning and juices run light pink to clear when a fork is pricked deeply into its little plump thigh.

3. Meanwhile, bring cranberries, brown sugar, and wine to a boil and cook until berries begin to pop. Remove from heat and strain, setting aside cranberries to add to duck and reserving wine to deglaze pan with.

4. When duck is nearly ready, peel and dice mango, and toss with lime juice and chili. Set aside.

5. When duck is cooked through, after about an hour, remove duck from pan. Pour off fat. Remove garlic cloves and squeeze flesh back into pan juices, mashing cloves with a fork.

6. Pour in wine, and on top of stove bring to boil, stirring to dissolve brown bits from bottom of pan.

7. When sauce has reduced by half, remove from heat and add cranberries, stirring and mashing some to incorporate into sauce. Add remaining fruit sauce, as well as mango and green chili mixture.

8. Serve duck, each portion garnished with a spoonful or two of tropical-fruit-cranberry-mango-and-chili sauce.

9. Accompany with roasted sweet potatoes or yams.

Jalapeño Jelly Tangy and sweet, some brands of jalapeño jelly veer to really quite hot. Jalapeño jelly follows the English, Irish, and Midwest American traditions of spicy jellies as an accompaniment for savory meats and cheeses (such as mint jelly with lamb, cranberry jelly with turkey, and so on) but with the Southwestern influence of hot chili peppers.

There are lots of things to do with jalapeño jelly besides eating it with cream cheese and whole-wheat crackers. Try serving it with roasted duck or using it to glaze a ham or roast lamb. It's good, too, added to a rich meaty stir-fry as a glaze for lamb marinated in an Indian spice paste.

Remember, that these jellies are sometimes brightly colored with artificial colorings which will transfer to any meat you cook it with. Choose red or yellow jellies; though lamb with mint sauce is a classic, green-glazed lamb isn't very appetizing.

Red-glazed Sweet and Spicy Lamb Chops

◆◆ INTERMEDIATE PANTRY

Serves 4

Marinating tender chunks of lamb in either an Indian spice paste or a Chinese-flavored marinade, then stir-frying the lamb with a bit of jalapeño jelly added to the pan for a sweet-spicy glaze, makes a superbly quick and delicious supper meal. Serve the bits of sweet-spicy meat with steamed rice, and offer diced cucumber and coarsely chopped dry-roasted peanuts to sprinkle over it.

4 lamb chops, or about 5 ounces of meat per person
2 tablespoons soy sauce mixed with 2 teaspoons Asian (toasted) sesame oil and 1 chopped garlic clove, or 3 tablespoons tikka or tandoori paste
2 to 3 tablespoons jalapeño jelly
Accompaniments: Steamed rice, peeled and diced cucumber, coarsely chopped dry-roasted peanuts

Cut lamb chops into bite-sized pieces. Marinate for at least 30 minutes in soy sauce mixture or spice paste. Remove from marinade, discarding any marinade left in bowl, and sauté meat quickly in a hot pan for a few minutes. While meat is browning, add jalapeño jelly and toss to glaze meat as it cooks. Serve accompanied with steamed rice and diced cucumbers, all sprinkled with chopped peanuts.

Kaffir Lime Leaves Dried leaves of the Kaffir lime, this Thai seasoning is lyrically fragrant with the scent of lime trees in bloom and has an undercurrent of spicy pepper. Simmer a few leaves in a simple broth or chilied seafood stir-fry.

Kimchee The Korean equivalent of dynamite, made by fermenting cabbage with red peppers and spices. Eaten as a condiment, it is a welcome accent to the steamed rice, grilled meats, soups, and stews of Korean cuisine. Buy it in an Asian grocery and, after opening, store it in the refrigerator, where it will keep for up to 2 months.

Lemon Grass Looking much like a tough, dried green onion, lemon grass has a strong lemon flavor and fragrance. It's used much in Southeast Asian cookery as well as in cosmetics, especially natural ones.

While it may be bought dried, lemon grass is at its best as a spice when fresh. Peel away the hard outer layers and trim away the greenish top. The part you want to use is the white bottom part. Once it's peeled and trimmed, simply chop. Lemon grass freezes well and can be kept in your freezer for up to 2 months.

Lemon grass makes a delicate seasoning for seafood or chicken broth, and is amenable to a good jolt of chili and a sprinkling of fresh chopped cilantro.

Limes (Dried) Hard-skinned, desiccated, brownish spheres with a pungent citrus flavor, dried limes are used mostly in Persian and Middle Eastern dishes. I like to simmer a few in a potful of yellow lentils and lamb. Discard the limes after cooking with them—you only want the flavor they impart, not their tough, indigestible skins.

Maple Syrup As a child I was totally enchanted with the story of how maple sugar was made by gathering the sap from the trees and boiling it down into syrup. But the part I loved best was smearing it onto the fresh snow, making instant candy. It seemed like magic, and I longed to do it. And with that uninhibited greediness peculiar to childhood, I could never understand how anyone could have any syrup leftover to bring back. I was sure I would gobble it all.

The sap "run" lasts from March to early April, or when the first buds appear on the branches. The flavor is released only when the sap is boiled down; as it takes 40 gallons of sap to make 1 gallon of syrup, it's no wonder pure maple syrup bears a stiff price tag.

Maple syrup is quintessential American food, embraced for its distinct flavor throughout the world. It was the condiment of choice for New England's Native Americans, who were baking beans and basting bear with the sweet amber liquid long before Columbus "discovered" the New World. One native specialty was ground corn mixed with chestnuts, beans, berries, and maple syrup.

Since the syrup is so good slathered onto pancakes, waffles, oatmeal, and other sweet foods, it is easy to overlook the savory foods that maple syrup can give its woodsy sweetness and slight bitter edge to. I particularly like seasoning lentil, tomato, and spinach stew with a sweet-sour edge of maple syrup and balsamic vinegar.

Maple has great affinity for citrus; try it to sweeten a citrus compote. Try it also in the following dish of yams, which offers a refreshing change from the butter-heavy yam dishes most often encountered.

Maple-Lime Yams

◆ BASIC PANTRY

Serves 4

Arrange 4 to 6 sliced peeled **yams** (1/4 to 1/2 inch thick) in a glass baking dish. Pour 1/2 cup **maple syrup** and 1/4 cup fresh **lime juice** over yams. Cover with foil and bake in preheated 350° oven until tender, about 40 minutes.

Steamed Yams with Maple-Citrus Sauce

Steam sliced peeled **yams** until crisp-tender. Remove from heat. In a separate pan, heat **syrup** and **citrus juice,** then add the slices and cook over high heat for a few minutes, or until liquid is almost all absorbed. Take care it does not burn.

◆◆◆◆◆◆

Mayonnaise Since there is little that is attractive about the white gloppy stuff that comes out of the jar, we can forget just how great mayonnaise sauce can be. Homemade mayonnaise is the best, of course, made with good oils and fresh eggs, and it is extremely easy to make (with a food processor or even a fork). But with the recent warnings on salmonella bacteria in raw eggs, making your own mayonnaise is not advised, unless you have access to healthy unpolluted eggs.

Down East Deluxe Lobster or Crab Roll

Serves 4

It started out as a lobster sandwich sort of affair, eaten at a roadside stand in Martha's Vineyard. Basically the lobster was moistened with a bit of mayonnaise and shredded onion, given a scattering of celery for crunch, then stuffed into a grilled hot dog bun. It was good—but when I made it at home and added a bit of sour cream to the mayonnaise it was even better. The diced tomatoes came later, as did the shredded lettuce, and the dash of brandy lit it all up. This is messy stuff, and if it doesn't drip it might not taste as good as it should. And if lobster or crab is not available or is not in this week's budget, this sandwich is equally good made with roasted or leftover chicken.

3 to 4 large leaves romaine lettuce	1 teaspoon Dijon mustard
10 to 12 ounces cooked fresh lobster, crab, or chicken	2 small tomatoes, or 1 medium to large tomato, seeded, juiced, and diced
1/4 cup mayonnaise	2 green onions, thinly sliced
2 tablespoons sour cream	Salt and pepper to taste
2 tablespoons brandy	4 hot dog buns

1. Roll up romaine lettuce leaves, lengthwise, into tight rolls, then slice thinly crosswise.

2. Mix lobster, crab, or chicken with mayonnaise, sour cream, brandy, and mustard. Toss with tomatoes, green onions, salt, and pepper, then add lettuce.

3. Stuff into rolls and eat immediately.

◆◆◆◆◆◆

FLAVORED MAYONNAISES Storebought mayonnaise may not be brilliant on its own, but it takes happily to robust flavorings such as garlic, olive paste, chili powder, capers, herbs, etc. As with anything else, use the best quality available—a dismal mayonnaise will ruin your sauce. Store jars of mayonnaise in the refrigerator once opened, and never leave mayonnaise-based sauces in a warm area.

Flavored mayonnaises last about 3 to 5 days in the refrigerator.

Cheater's Aïoli

◆ BASIC PANTRY

Makes 1/4 cup

Don't compare it to the unctuous, blissful garlic sauce made by hand. However, this is a delicious garlicky mayonnaise.

1 minced garlic clove or more
1/4 cup mayonnaise

1 tablespoon olive oil
Dash lemon juice

1. Combine garlic with mayonnaise.
2. Slowly whisk in olive oil, or use a food processor or blender (add a little extra oil if mayonnaise will accept it without breaking). Season with lemon juice.

Ancho Chili Mayonnaise

◆◆ INTERMEDIATE PANTRY

Makes 2/3 cup

Serve on a sandwich of roast, smoked, or barbecued meats or poultry and crusty French- or Italian-style bread, or as a sauce for grilled swordfish or halibut resting on a bed of vinaigrette-dressed or stir-fried greens.

3 teaspoons ancho chili powder
1/4 cup mayonnaise
2 tablespoons olive oil

2 teaspoons chopped fresh cilantro
1/8 to 1/4 teaspoon cumin seeds
Dash lemon or lime juice

1. Mix all ingredients.
2. Let chill to thicken and blend flavors.

NOTE This is a delicious sauce to serve with **shrimp** marinated in 3 tablespoons **olive oil**, 1 tablespoon **green salsa**, 2 tablespoons fresh **lime juice**, 4 chopped **garlic cloves**, and a pinch of chopped fresh **oregano**, then grilled.

Chipotle Mayonnaise

◆◆ INTERMEDIATE PANTRY

Makes 1/3 cup

Smoky and very hot, a tiny amount of chipotle marinade is all you need to flavor a delicate sauce such as mayonnaise. The sauce is brightened with a bit of red bell pepper to balance it all out. Serve with salmon that has been brushed with chipotle-seasoned oil then grilled, or serve it as a sauce to accompany a plate of steamed potatoes, green beans, and plump shrimp.

Crab cakes, too, are delicious with chipotle mayonnaise, as are slices of garlic-studded roast pork on crusty bread with arugula greens.

1/4 cup mayonnaise
2 teaspoons marinade from
canned chipotle chilies

2 tablespoons olive oil
1 tablespoon minced red bell
pepper

1. Stir together mayonnaise and chipotle marinade, then whisk in olive oil.
2. Add chopped pepper.

Olive Aïoli

◆◆ INTERMEDIATE PANTRY

Makes 3/4 cup

A lusty and full-flavored sauce colored a near violet-gray-black by the olives. It is so delicious, keeping it in the refrigerator is dangerous: it beckons each time you open the door looking for something sensible. Use olive aïoli to sauce nearly anything with rambunctious, bright flavors.

2 garlic cloves, minced
3 tablespoons olive paste or
pureed pitted oil-cured black
Mediterranean olives such as
Kalamata
1/2 to 1 teaspoon chopped fresh
rosemary or a pinch of
herbes de Provence

1/2 cup mayonnaise
2 tablespoons extra-virgin olive
oil
1/2 teaspoon fresh lemon juice
or balsamic vinegar

1. In a food processor or blender, puree garlic, then add olive paste, rosemary, and mayonnaise and process or blend until well mixed.
2. Slowly add olive oil and, when combined, add lemon juice. Chill to firm up a bit and serve as desired. Occasionally the sauce will separate. I add a little more mayonnaise and it usually rights itself.

Olive-Pesto Aïoli

Add about 3 tablespoons **pesto** or more in place of rosemary. Use in whatever begs for its fragrant presence.

Rosemary–Olive Oil New Potatoes with Olive Aïoli

◆◆ INTERMEDIATE PANTRY

Serves 6

Wherever I have lived, I have, within days of moving in, discovered a huge rosemary bush growing in the neighborhood. In San Francisco there was a whole yard covered with the fragrant herb. In Berkeley I found patches of rosemary down by the creek that ran through my front yard. In London the building next door had a barrel filled to overflowing with the largest rosemary plant I'd ever seen. In the suburbs where I grew up I could always count on picking a few sprigs to add to my salad. I've gotten so used to having rosemary easily available that it has become a part of my pantry. Keeping some chopped rosemary in the freezer achieves the same results.

Tossing rosemary into warm potatoes in olive oil is one of the most delicious things to do with either the herb or the potatoes, especially when sauced with olive aïoli. I often serve bite-sized potatoes cooked this way to be picked up, dipped, and popped into the mouth. They look especially nice in a rustic ceramic crock and are easy and economical to make for a huge, huge crowd. Little rosemary-scented potatoes also make a delicious accompaniment to rare roast lamb, with the olive-aïoli acting as a sauce for both.

About 20 to 25 tiny new potatoes, unpeeled but well washed
2 tablespoons extra-virgin olive oil
About 1 tablespoon chopped fresh rosemary, plus extra sprigs for garnish
Coarse salt (sea or kosher) for sprinkling
Olive Aïoli, page 158

1. Steam potatoes until just tender. Remove from heat.
2. Gently heat olive oil in a skillet with rosemary; add potatoes, coating them well and letting them heat through and very lightly brown in spots.
3. Let cool, then sprinkle with a small amount of coarse salt.
4. Serve accompanied with a bowl of olive aïoli for dipping, or with olive aïoli spooned over individual portions of potatoes.

Salami Sandwich Portofino, with Sweet Peppers, Mesclun, and Olive Aïoli

◆◆ INTERMEDIATE PANTRY

Serves 4

Olive aïoli, slathered onto crusty bread, stuffed with roasted red peppers, salami, mesclun and fresh basil leaves, makes a heady, fragrant sandwich.

1 double recipe Olive Aïoli, page 158	About 2/3 cup roasted red peppers
1 baguette, large enough for 4 sandwiches, sliced lengthwise	About 12 ounces garlicky air-dried salami, thinly sliced
	Handful of mesclun leaves and fresh basil

1. Spread olive aïoli very generously over both sides of baguette.
2. On one side of the bread layer peppers; on other side salami, mesclun, and basil.
3. Close and enjoy. I actually like this sandwich better after it sits (up to 2 hours only, and not in a warm spot) and melds flavors.

◆◆◆◆◆◆

Mustard Mustard is one of the oldest spices and is second only to black pepper as the world's most widely used spice. The Chinese cultivated it more than 3,000 years ago. Hippocrates, the Greek "father of medicine" praised mustard for its curative powers in 460 B.C.E. The Roman scholar Pliny the Elder wrote that mustard "excited the soul," perked up the appetite, and strengthened the digestion. Apply it externally as a paste, he advised, to cure snakebite.

It was the Romans who introduced mustard to France by planting the seeds in the Burgundy region of Dijon. At first the mustard seeds were ground and pressed into tablets, but in the early 17th century the king granted Dijon mustard makers the right to sell prepared mustard sauces, as long as they were "dressed properly." Mustard has since become one of Dijon's major industries, and today, before you even reach the cobbled streets of that city, your eyes will likely begin to sting from the heady mustard fumes that permeate the air.

The old Moutard Grey Poupon shop is located on Dijon's Rue de la Liberté in case you would like to make a pilgrimage. It's a charming little establishment, part museum and part shop: mustard containers dating back to the 15th century are on display, along with all sorts of crocks you can buy and tote home.

Mustard seeds come in three basic types (and colors): black, brown, and yellow. Each has its own characteristics, and most mustard companies taste their mustard seeds as carefully as a vintner does his or her grapes for wine. The brown mustard seeds (*Brassica juncea*) are the hottest, used mostly in Asian and Indian mustards, while the yellow (*Brassica hirta*) have a sharp taste but less aroma, so are often the choice for mustards that are to be mixed with other flavoring ingredients. Black mustard seed (*Brassica nigra*) is the most aromatic of the three and has the most staying power, fragrantly speaking.

The long history and lore of mustard, however, has nothing to do with my addiction to it—I loved it long before I knew anything at all about it. Mustard was the main flavoring ingredient in my childhood, and even though it was either yellow or brown, I felt very lucky that it was on my sandwich (and with a heavy hand, too). Of course, an introduction to the wide variety of mustards available only sealed my fate, as my pantry shelves will witness. I consider a collection of mustard jars perfect decor for almost any room.

Mustard de Meaux, Dijon, Rouen; mustards smooth and brown or hot and straw-colored; mustards of whole seeds; made from white wine or Champagne, or from vinegar; mustards from California, sweet and tangy; and Chinese/Russian mustard, hot and sweet and fragrant with sesame oil. I have mustard green with tarragon, pureed or mixed herbs, briny and peppery green peppercorn mustard, flecked mustards tasting of herbes de Provence, red mustards made with pureed hot and sweet peppers, and purple mustard made from steeping the mustard seeds in red Burgundy wine. An Italian concoction of mustard and fruit chutney called mostarda is sitting next to a brown Dusseldorf. There are mustard seeds and dry mustard for cooking, and my home/office is housed in a converted warehouse named Colman's Court, after the Colman's mustard that was once prepared here. How appropriate!

Keep a selection of mustards on your pantry shelf. To find the ones you like best, do what you must do with olive oils, vinegars, etc.: taste, taste, taste, until you find the ones you absolutely love. A general guide, however, is that the French mustards are usually smooth (though many are quite hot) and suave, English mustards hot and sharp (occasionally flavored with beer or ale), and German ones go either way. Russian and California mustards are usually sweet and hot, and a recent entry on the market is Creole mustard, very spicy with a hint of horseradish and molasses—fantastic.

STORAGE TIP Store your mustards on a cool pantry shelf away from direct sunlight or in the refrigerator. Unrefrigerated, they do tend to get darker and stronger with age. Though my sources say they last nearly forever, my common sense says that they don't. Use your nose as a guide.

Basic Mustard Types

◆◆◆◆◆◆

AMERICAN BROWN Sharp and vinegary, with a nice pungent flavor and tang.

AMERICAN YELLOW With a sharp, one-dimensional flavor; not recommended for anything other than ball-park hot dogs.

CALIFORNIA SWEET-HOT Often made from local wines, these are delicious and come in a wide range of other seasonings as well: shallots, garlic, herbs, etc.

CREOLE Seasoned with horseradish, and perhaps a bit of molasses, Creole mustard is sublime.

DIJON Sharp and pungent, with a definitive mustard flavor.

ENGLISH MUSTARD Sharp and pungent, used to liven up the traditionally bland British banger.

FRENCH MUSTARDS Mild mustards with great character, usually prepared from white wine or sometimes red wine or Champagne. Moutarde de Meaux is one of the most famous, and with good reason: it is delicious.

GERMAN WHOLE SEED Usually made with horseradish, this is strong and zesty.

RUSSIAN HOT AND STRONG MUSTARD Seasoned with Asian sesame oil, this is hot, strong, and sweet.

SEASONED MUSTARDS A delicious array of herbs: tarragon, herbes de Provence, chilies, and the like season these mustards. Keep an assortment in your pantry; they're marvelous.

WHOLE-SEED MUSTARD This has a lovely texture, with seeds that crunch pleasingly between the teeth.

Sixteen Things to Do with Mustard

◆◆◆◆◆◆

◆ **HAVE A MUSTARD-TASTING PARTY** Assemble a large and varied selection of mustards, along with small pieces of hearty breads. Serve a dish that is traditionally served with mustards, such as choucroute garni (sauerkraut and sausages) or a simple platter of assorted sausages.

◆ **TRICOLOR SWIRL OF THREE MUSTARDS** Place a generous dab of green tarragon mustard, pale yellow Dijon mustard, and red bell pepper mustard (either buy a French import or mixed pureed roasted red peppers with a bit of mustard) next to each other on a plate. Swirl together to achieve a marbling effect. Serve with charcoal-grilled duck burgers (have the butcher grind boneless duck or use your food processor).

◆ **CAULIFLOWER GRATIN** Add a tablespoon or two of whole-seed mustard to a garlic-and-rosemary-scented béchamel sauce, then toss with 1 medium to large head of cauliflower that you've steamed until al dente and 12 ounces to 1 pound shredded sharp Cheddar or Gruyère cheese. Broil to lightly brown on top.

◆ **SOLITARY SNACK** A cold boiled potato, spread generously with Dijon or mustard of choice, topped with a slice of Gruyère and a slice of red onion.

◆ **GRATINEED TOMATOES** Spread ripe halved tomatoes generously with an American brown mustard or a mild French import, top with a thin slice of Fontina or Gruyère, and broil until melted and bubbly.

◆ **CHEESE, MUSHROOM, AND SHALLOT SALAD** Add mustard of choice to a favorite vinaigrette, then serve on a salad of thinly sliced Gruyère or Appenzeller cheese and mushrooms sprinkled with lots of chopped shallots.

◆ **BROTH-COOKED PELMENI WITH SWEET HOT MUSTARD** Cook meat-filled pelmeni in broth until just tender; drain (and reserve broth) and serve dumplings with a bit of sweet-hot Russian mustard for dabbing on.

◆ **BRUSSELS SPROUTS WITH MUSTARD CREAM** Lightly sauté 1 garlic clove in 2 tablespoons unsalted butter; add 2 teaspoons mustard of choice, then pour in 1/4 cup heavy cream, then bring to a boil and cook a few minutes until reduced and concentrated in volume. Toss with steamed just-tender Brussels sprouts. Salt and pepper to taste.

◆ **BRATWURST WITH SWEET-HOT MUSTARD** Serve sweet California-type mustards with port wine–poached bratwurst sausages cut into small pieces for nibbling.

◆ **CABBAGE, CARROT, AND BEET SALAD** Shred 1/2 cabbage and dice 1 carrot and 2 medium cooked beets. Dress with a vinaigrette which you have seasoned with a tablespoon or two of sweet/hot California-type mustard.

◆ **ROAST-ANYTHING WITH MUSTARD-CREAM SAUCE** Deglaze any roasting pan—lamb, rabbit, chicken, duck, veal, turkey, beef—with a dry white wine or a slightly sweet Madeira-type red wine and a bit of broth. When boiled down to a concentrated sauce, add a tablespoon of your favorite mustard (whole seed or herbed for white wine; sweet and hot for Madeira) and 1/4 cup cream. Season with a little (or a lot) of chopped fresh rosemary if desired, and pour sauce over meat.

◆ **MUSTARD GRILLED SHRIMP** Mix 2 tablespoons mustard of choice—tarragon, herbes de Provence, etc.—with 1 tablespoon wine vinegar and 1/4 cup olive oil. Add salt and pepper to taste, along with any chopped fresh herbs as desired. Use as a marinade and basting mixture for shrimp.

◆ **TANGY MUSTARD-SEASONED PASTA SALAD** Season a basic vinaigrette strongly with mustard of choice. Toss with just-tender peas and carrots, strips of roasted red peppers from a jar, chopped garlic, and chopped fresh parsley.

◆ **CHEESE FONDUE WITH A SELECTION OF MUSTARDS** Serve a warm cheese fondue with a selection of mustards; add fresh crisp-cooked vegetables to the dipping lineup.

◆ **LAMB CHOPS WITH A COAT OF SWEET-HOT MUSTARD AND CRUMBS** Spread lamb chops or a rack of lamb with California sweet-hot mustard or with Creole mustard and press on a layer of bread crumbs. Bake or broil until browned on the outside, rosy rare within.

◆ **MUSTARD-CAPER MAYONNAISE (TO SERVE WITH CRISP FRIED SQUID)** Mix 2 to 3 tablespoons mustard of choice (herb-flavored mustards vary this sauce nearly endlessly) with 1 cup mayonnaise, 2 tablespoons capers, 1 to 2 chopped green onions, and a tablespoon or two of chopped fresh parsley. Or use this mustard-caper mayonnaise to make a sunny egg salad, with diced hard-cooked egg. Serve on a bed of watercress.

Some Simple Seasoned Mustards

The wide range of mustards, combined with the array of simple seasonings from the pantry, yields an almost infinite array of spiced mustards. The flavors can be classic, such as chopped shallots, or they might be more nouvelle, say grated fresh ginger or a spoonful of sweet-spicy chili dressing.

Use the mustards to enliven simmered meats, hearty sandwiches on rye or onion rolls, piquant seafood salads, chunks of cheese, and on and on.

TWO-OLIVE MUSTARD Season 1/4 cup mild French **mustard** or American brown mustard, or a combination of mustards, with a tablespoon or two *each* of chopped **green olives** and chopped **black Mediterranean-style olives** such as Kalamata. Serve on grilled sausages stuffed into crusty rolls, or spread onto grilled fish fillets that have been seasoned with olive oil, garlic, and chopped fresh herbs such as thyme.

CHUTNEY MUSTARD Mix equal parts **Dijon mustard** with **mango chutney,** the large pieces cut into small bits. Serve with a baked ham or ham sandwiches.

SWEET-HOT RED CHILI MUSTARD To 2 tablespoons **whole-seed mustard** add 2 teaspoons **Thai-inspired Tart-Sweet Red Chili Dressing** (page 128).

FRESH GINGER MUSTARD To 3 tablespoons **whole-seed mustard** add 1-1/2 to 2 teaspoons grated **fresh ginger.** Enjoy with ham, grilled seafood, etc.

MUSTARD WITH LEMON OR LIME, PROVENCE STYLE To 2 tablespoons mildish **Dijon or Meaux mustard** add 1/4 teaspoon finely grated **lemon or lime zest** and 1/2 to 1 teaspoon fresh **lemon or lime juice.**

MUSTARD WITH A SCENT OF ORANGE To 2 tablespoons mild Dijon **mustard** or a combination of Dijon and Meaux, add 1/4 teaspoon finely grated **orange zest** and 2 teaspoons **orange juice.**

CURRY MUSTARD To 2 tablespoons **mustard** of choice such as Dijon or whole-seed, add 1/2 teaspoon **curry powder.** Serve spread in an Indian-spiced chicken salad sandwich.

MUSTARD WITH SHALLOTS To 3 tablespoons **mustard** of choice (or mixed mustards) add 2 or 3 minced **shallots;** chopped fresh **chives** are a nice addition, as well.

Green-Herb-and-Garlic Mustard

◆ **BASIC PANTRY**

Makes 1/2 cup

Fresh tasting and tangy, this mustard is delicious surrounded by a platter of salami and French bread for do-it-yourself sandwiches. Whichever mustard you choose will change the character of the sauce; so too will the herbs chosen.

1/2 cup mixed mustards of choice (Dijon, whole seed, mild French, brown American, Creole)
1/4 cup minced fresh parsley
2 to 3 minced garlic cloves

2 tablespoons chopped fresh herbs (chervil, tarragon, dill, etc.) or 1/2 to 1 teaspoon dried tarragon leaves
1 teaspoon red or white wine vinegar

Combine all ingredients.

Makes enough for 2 chicken breasts or fish fillets

Paprika-Tarragon-Parsley-Mustard Coating for Fish or Chicken

Mix **Green-Herb-and-Garlic Mustard,** above, with 2 tablespoons **paprika.** Spread generously onto **chicken breasts** (still on the bone) **or fish fillets,** let sit 15 to 30 minutes to absorb the flavors, then broil until cooked through.

Pickled Mustard Onions

◆◆ **INTERMEDIATE PANTRY**

Makes about 1 cup

Tart little morsels of onion-mustard flavor, these make a delicious relish or accompaniment to sandwiches, fish and chips, or a midnight snack.

1 bag (about 2 cups) tiny pickling onions
3 cups white wine vinegar

Salt to taste
1/4 cup whole-seed mustard

1. Plunge unpeeled onions into boiling water and let cook for 3 to 5 minutes. This will loosen skin and partially cook onions, taking their raw edge off.
2. Drain and plunge onions into cold water. When cool enough to handle, remove onion skins. They will slip easily off; use a paring knife to cut them at root end.

3. Combine vinegar, salt, and mustard and bring to a boil. Pour over peeled onions. Let sit to marinate overnight in refrigerator (will last 2 to 3 weeks in refrigerator), or pack in jars with liquid and process in a hot-water bath.

Swedish Mustard Sauce

◆ BASIC PANTRY

Makes 1/2 to 2/3 cup

Serve this dilled sweet-hot-tangy sauce with browned caper-studded meatballs, or with smoked trout on buttered black bread.

2 tablespoons sweet-hot mustard
2 tablespoons Dijon mustard
2 teaspoons sugar

1 tablespoon white wine vinegar or cider vinegar
2 tablespoons vegetable oil
3 tablespoons chopped fresh or 1/2 teaspoon dried dill

Mix mustards, then stir in remaining ingredients. Serve as desired.

Red Snapper with a Mustard Crust

◆◆ INTERMEDIATE PANTRY

Serves 4

3 tablespoons vegetable oil
1/4 cup finely chopped shallots
1/4 cup whole-seed mustard
1 pound red snapper fillets

Flour for dredging
Several tablespoons oil or butter for sautéing

1. Mix vegetable oil with shallots and mustard.
2. Coat fish with mixture, then dredge in flour.
3. Sauté in a little oil or butter until golden. Serve immediately.

Steamed Salmon Steaks with Tarragon-Mustard Hollandaise

Tangy mustard enlivens buttery hollandaise, along with the fragrance and green color of tarragon. The sauce keeps, well covered, in the refrigerator for up to 3 days.

4 salmon steaks, about 8 ounces each

Small amount of melted butter for brushing

Serves 4

TARRAGON-MUSTARD HOLLANDAISE

2 tablespoons tarragon mustard, preferably bright green	1/2 cup unsalted butter, melted
2 egg yolks	2 teaspoons to 1 tablespoon fresh lemon juice
2 tablespoons water	Salt and cayenne to taste
1 teaspoon dried tarragon, or 1 tablespoon chopped fresh	Tarragon, parsley, or dill sprigs for garnish

1. Place salmon steaks in a broiling pan, steamer, or on 4 pieces of buttered parchment paper. Brush salmon with melted butter.

2. To make mustard-hollandaise, whisk together tarragon mustard, egg yolks, water, and tarragon, then cook over a double boiler or directly on very low heat, whisking mixture until it begins to thicken.

3. Moving pan off and on heat so that it doesn't reach too high a temperature and scramble egg yolks or separate sauce, whisk in butter, a little bit at a time, whisking well in between additions so that it is absorbed into an emulsified sauce. Continue until all butter is absorbed. Add lemon juice, salt, and cayenne.

4. Set sauce aside, covered, and keep warm (a good way to keep hollandaise warm is in a thermos, for up to 30 minutes).

5. Cook salmon either by steaming or by wrapping and baking it in parchment on a baking sheet for 6 to 8 minutes in a preheated 425° oven.

6. Serve salmon steaks topped with a dollop of sauce and a garnish of fresh herb sprigs.

Poached Eggs with Double-Mustard Tarragon Hollandaise

Prepare **Tarragon-Mustard Hollandaise,** above, but double amount of **mustard.** Serve spooned over poached eggs and garnished with fresh tarragon.

Crumb-topped Chicken Breasts with Tarragon-Mustard Hollandaise

◆ BASIC PANTRY

Makes 4

Tarragon-Mustard Hollandaise makes a lovely coating for chicken fillets; it gives flavor and seals in the meat's natural succulence.

4 boned chicken breast halves
Double recipe Tarragon-
   Mustard Hollandaise,
   page 168

Fresh bread crumbs
Drizzle of olive oil or melted
   butter

1. Preheat oven to 400°.
2. Place chicken breasts on a baking sheet and spread liberally with sauce.
3. Top with crumbs, patting them on tightly so that they stick well and form a thick layer.
4. Drizzle with olive oil or melted butter and bake until chicken is just cooked through, about 10 minutes.
5. Serve immediately.

◆◆◆◆◆◆

Olives From briny and firm-fleshed Kalamatas to wrinkled black oil-cured ones; from fennel-scented Sicilian green olives to the pimiento-stuffed Spanish ones, olives come in a wide array of flavors, textures, and colors. They add a sprightly Mediterranean touch to anything they share a table with, and transform anything they're cooked with.

The cultivated olive tree, *Olea europaea*, has been in existence in the Mediterranean since biblical times; approximately 600 years before the Christian age, olives were to be found in the Roman pantry. Olives were brought to the New World from Spain; according to a document in Seville's Archive of the Indies, a treasure house of material relating to early dealings with America, captains bound for America were "obligated to take with them at least some plants of olive and wine."

In 1769 two trees were introduced in what was to become California. They took to the soil and thrived, becoming the basis of California's current olive industry. (Though ripe olives have always been the mainstay, today California boasts some excellent brined and spiced olives.)

For an excellent read on the lore of olives, plus a guide to olive types, consult *The Feast of the Olive* by Maggie Blythe Klein (Aris Books).

A selection of olives is an important part of my pantry, and at any given time I have at least one type of black olive and one type of green.

(Note that most black olives can be interchanged with other black olives. The same is true for most green olives.)

STORAGE TIPS Though olives are often kept at room temperature, I recommend keeping them refrigerated once the jar is opened. At room temperature they develop a surface scum which, though my research says is a harmless crystalization of salt, I don't like one bit. And a recent bottle of Spanish black olives, proudly labeled "low salt," grew a nasty mold in a very short time period.

Basic Olive Types

❖❖❖❖❖❖

The variety of olives is never ending, varying subtly and unsubtly from country to country, region to region. No matter which type of tree was originally planted, it absorbs flavors of the environment from which it grows: the air, the earth, the soul of the people who cultivate it.

A lovely illustration of this: once in the Greek village of Matalla, I asked an elderly woman in a shop for some Kalamata olives. "No," she responded somberly, "we do not have them. We have Matalla olives."

In delis and specialty food shops we usually have a choice of between 6 and 8 basic olive types. The basic pantry should keep at least one of the black and one of the green on hand; the intermediate pantry should have several; and the advanced should maintain an interesting selection.

❖❖❖❖❖❖

BLACK OLIVES

KALAMATA Oval and slightly pointed at each end, Kalamata flesh is firm, with a good strong flavor; usually sold in brine.

❖❖❖❖❖❖

GREEK OLIVE A catch-all term for fleshy olives from Greece. Often quite salty, they taste of the Mediterranean.

❖❖❖❖❖❖

GAETA Reddish-hued olives, slightly fleshier than the Kalamata, but less so than the Greek olive.

❖❖❖❖❖❖

GREEK ROYAL OR ATALANTI OLIVE Greenish purplish, with generous flesh and full flavor.

❖❖❖❖❖❖

SEMI-DRY SALT-CURED BLACK OLIVES From Italy and Morocco especially, these olives have been cured in salt and so retain a certain chewy dryness; they are usually sold coated with olive oil and often herbs. They may be seasoned with a hot pepper sauce such as harissa, or with lemon, garlic, and oregano.

◆◆◆◆◆◆

NIÇOISE These tiny olives do not have much flesh on them but they have a lusty big flavor. Sold in brine.

◆◆◆◆◆◆

RIPE OLIVES These are bland and insipid, though they do have a certain nostalgic appeal. Sold in cans, they should be well drained before serving.

◆◆◆◆◆◆

GREEN OLIVES

PIMIENTO-STUFFED OLIVES No less delicious for being available in every supermarket. Sometimes green olives may be stuffed with almonds or anchovies instead of pimientos.

◆◆◆◆◆◆

MANZANILLA OLIVES Grown in Spain and California, these are rather delicate green olives with a medium-bodied flavor.

◆◆◆◆◆◆

QUEEN OR ROYAL Large green or green mottled with black olives, with a generous amount of flesh, these are usually cracked and marinated in a highly seasoned brine that contains whole cloves (or heads) of garlic, hot red peppers, etc. Queen olives can reach the size of small chicken eggs.

◆◆◆◆◆◆

SICILIAN GREEN OLIVES Seasoned with fennel seeds and orange peel, they are large, with a firm, abundant flesh and a slightly bitter edge.

◆◆◆◆◆◆

CRACKED GREEN OLIVES Small, with a slightly bitter flesh that pulls somewhat away from the pit. Usually seasoned with aromatics such as garlic, herbs, etc.

◆◆◆◆◆◆

GREEN HERBED OLIVES Green olives in an olive oil marinade, rich with chopped parsley, etc.

◆◆◆◆◆◆

HOT PEPPER OLIVES Tunisian or North African olives in a marinade redolent of hot peppers.

Rosemary-scented Lamb with Pumpkin, Black Olives, and Red Peppers

◆ BASIC TO
◆◆ INTERMEDIATE PANTRY

Serves 4

This dish of wintery pumpkin and sun-drenched peppers, punctuated by piquant olives and herbal rosemary, is heartily warming but not stodgy.

I like preparing it with peppers that have been brined in a little vinegar, but plain roasted and peeled peppers are fine.

1-1/2 pounds pumpkin or winter squash, peeled and diced
3 tablespoons olive oil
3 garlic cloves chopped
About 20 black olives, such as Kalamata or oil-cured Italian ones, pitted and coarsely diced
1 yellow bell pepper and 1 red bell pepper, roasted, peeled, and lightly brined with a bit of vinegar and salt, or bottled marinated roasted red peppers, cut into large dice
1-1/2 cups dry white wine
2 teaspoons fresh chopped rosemary, or 1/2 teaspoon dried rosemary, ground in a mortar with a little fresh parsley
4 thick lamb slices cut from the leg, about 6 ounces each

1. Lightly brown pumpkin in 1 tablespoon or so olive oil. When nearly tender, add 1 chopped garlic clove, diced olives and peppers, white wine, and half of rosemary, and cook over high heat until pumpkin is just tender and liquid has nearly evaporated, except for a tiny amount. Remove from heat.

2. Press remaining garlic and rosemary into lamb chops. Quickly brown in a pan with remaining olive oil, searing on each side.

3. Pour off oil, add sautéed pumpkin and olives to pan, and simmer together for several minutes. Lamb should be rare or pink, but cooked no longer than that.

4. Serve immediately, the lamb nestled next to a mound of pumpkin, peppers, and olives.

Green Olive and Chèvre Canapés

◆ BASIC PANTRY

Serves 3 to 4 as an appetizer

Green olives pair so well with goat cheese—you can taste the Mediterranean in each piquant bite.

4 ounces soft goat cheese such as California chèvre or Montrachet
2 teaspoons extra-virgin olive oil

2 tablespoons halved pitted
   green olives
Pinch of chopped fresh thyme

1 slightly dry baguette (or other
   rustic country bread such as
   ciambatta, etc.), sliced 1/4 to
   1/8 inch thick

1. Mix goat cheese and olive oil to smooth it out.
2. Add olives and thyme.
3. Spread onto thin slices of bread.

Cheddar and Olive Pâté

◆ BASIC PANTRY

Serves 4 as an appetizer

Sharp Cheddar bound with tangy Boursin or another herbed cream cheese and a dab of yogurt, seasoned with a shot of garlic and studded with bits of green olives. A dash of cayenne enlivens it.

Serve with whole-wheat sunflower-seed bread or millet bread, or spread onto rye flatbread or warm flour tortillas. Leftover cheese may be kept in the refrigerator for up to a week, or frozen for up to a month.

4 ounces sharp Cheddar cheese,
   coarsely grated (about 3/4–
   1 cup)
2 ounces Boursin or similar
   garlic-flavored cream cheese

10 green pimiento-stuffed
   olives, coarsely chopped
1 garlic clove, minced
1 tablespoon plain yogurt

1. Mix Cheddar with cream cheese until well combined.
2. Add remaining ingredients.

Double-Decker Croque Monsieur

◆ BASIC TO
◆◆ INTERMEDIATE PANTRY

Serves 4

8 slices French bread
Mustard of choice (tarragon,
   whole seed, brown, Dijon,
   etc.)

4 or 8 slices good-quality ham
1 recipe Cheddar and Olive
   Pâté, above

1. Arrange 4 slices bread on a baking sheet; spread with mustard and top with ham.
2. Spread cheese mixture on remaining 4 slices of bread.

3. Place cheese-topped bread on top of ham-topped bread, and place under broiler, broiling until cheese melts and turns bubbly and browned. Serve immediately.

Wine Country Zinfandel-braised Shortribs with Olives

◆ BASIC PANTRY

Serves 4 to 6

Even on my most cynical days, a trip to California's Wine Country puts me right. After an hour or so of inhaling the sweet air and scenery with a glass of wine in my hand, I'm hoping heaven is just like this. And that I go there.

This recipe splashes California's own Zinfandel onto a casserole of shortribs and olives, then leaves it in the oven for a good long braise. I've added the Provençal touch of orange zest and leeks, and the dish is as cozy yet sophisticated a dish as you'll ever want to eat.

3 pounds shortribs, cut into
    2- to 3-inch lengths
About 2/3 cup flour for
    dredging
2 to 3 tablespoons olive oil
3 carrots, diced
3 leeks, diced or cut into
    chunks
1 bottle Zinfandel
3 medium to large ripe
    tomatoes, diced
3 tablespoons tomato paste
1 cup beef broth, or more as
    needed

1/2 teaspoon herbes de
    Provence or dried thyme,
    or 3 fresh thyme sprigs
2 to 3 bay leaves
1 garlic head, cloves peeled and
    very coarsely chopped
Zest of 1/4 orange, cut into
    julienne or chopped
2/3 cup black Greek-style olives
2/3 cup green olives (with or
    without pimientos)
Freshly ground black pepper

1. Dredge meat with flour, then, in a heavy skillet or pot, sauté in olive oil until lightly browned. Add carrots and leeks, and cook together several minutes longer.

2. Pour in wine, tomatoes, tomato paste, beef broth, herbes de Provence or thyme, bay leaves, garlic, and orange zest. Bring to a boil, then reduce heat to low.

3. Cover and cook, either on very low heat on top of stove or in a slow (300° to 325°) oven, for 3 hours, or until meat is tender and sauce richly flavored. About 15 minutes before meat is ready, add olives and black pepper.

4. If sauce reduces too much, add a bit more broth or wine; if sauce is too thin, pour liquid off, defat by spooning fat off surface, and boil to reduce and concentrate flavors, then return reduced liquid to meat and vegetables.

Muffaletta

◆◆ INTERMEDIATE PANTRY

Serves 6 to 8

New Orleans street food: French bread filled with olives and peppers, salami, turkey, and ham, the whole gaudy sandwich awash with vinaigrette to drip deliciously out the side and down your chin with each bite. The flavors are as lively as Dixieland jazz on a sultry summer night.

No exact recipe here: as long as you have too much of everything it will be just right. And if there is anything you fancy adding—say, marinated artichoke hearts or eggplant—it will probably make it even better.

Olive oil
Red wine vinegar
1 loaf French bread, cut in half lengthwise and hollowed out a bit to make room for filling
Chopped garlic
Black Greek olives, pitted
Green pimiento-stuffed olives
Roasted red peppers

Crumbled fresh oregano leaves
Chopped fresh parsley
Assorted cured meats and poultry: prosciutto or smoked ham, salami, turkey, mortadella
Thin slices of provolone, mozzarella, and/or jack cheese

1. Drizzle olive oil and vinegar on both sides of bread and sprinkle with chopped garlic.
2. In bottom half layer olives, peppers, a sprinkling of oregano and parsley, meats, and cheeses, sprinkling with olive oil and vinegar as you go along.
3. Close up, wrap well, and eat when you have a big appetite.

◆◆◆◆◆◆

Olive Paste This potent paste of pureed Italian or other Mediterranean olives is a treasure on any pantry shelf. It may be added to mayonnaise (see Olive Aïoli, page 158), or spread onto pizza, hot crusty bread, or a melted cheese sandwich. Try mixing it with unsalted butter (and a little chopped garlic, naturally) and spreading it onto bread, or serving it on grilled trout, along with a sprinkling of fresh herbs such as thyme.

Purchase in specialty food shops and refrigerate once opened.

If you don't have olive paste on hand, make your own by pureeing pitted and coarsely chopped Mediterranean black olives in a food processor or blender.

STORAGE TIPS It doesn't stay at its peak long, even refrigerated: give it about 3 weeks, even though it is commonly believed it lasts indefinitely when refrigerated.

Two Provençal Salads

◆◆ INTERMEDIATE PANTRY

Serves 4

They crept into our supermarkets without much fanfare, but one day those delicious and varied greens known as mesclun were everywhere to be found, even the corner grocery.

In Provençal dialect, *mesclun* is the word for "mixture," and it is the variety of these greens that so delights. I add whatever bits of herbs I have on hand, lately throwing in the thinnings from my windowbox garden: teeny lettuces, embryonic nasturtium leaves, wisps of basil and carrot tops. The greens make a perfect bed for nearly anything or can be the basis for the following sun-drenched salads.

Mixed Greens with Hard-cooked Eggs and Olive Paste

On a bed of **olive oil** and **balsamic-dressed greens,** arrange **hard-cooked egg** quarters and nuggets of **olive paste.** Sprinkle with chopped **fresh herbs** if desired and serve immediately.

Goat Cheese Truffles on a Bed of Mesclun

Roll **garlic- or herb-flavored goat cheese** into small balls; smooth out with a few drops of **olive oil or cream** for a smoother texture if need be. Mix **olive paste** with chopped fresh **rosemary, thyme** or **basil** and coat goat cheese balls with this mixture. They should resemble black truffles. Serve several "truffles" atop each plate of **olive oil-and-balsamic- or red-wine-vinegar-dressed mesclun.**

Little Chive-Omelet Canapés with Olive Paste

◆◆ **INTERMEDIATE PANTRY**

Serves 4 to 6

These little omelets, filled with chives and cheese, then served at room temperature topped with olive paste, make a delicious picnic snack on a sun-dappled afternoon along with a salad of sweet tomatoes, or they can be served as an appetizer for a midsummer's night supper.

6 eggs, lightly beaten
1/4 cup to 1/2 cup freshly grated Parmesan cheese
1/4 cup chopped fresh chives
2 tablespoons olive oil or as needed

1/2 loaf baguette or other crusty French or Italian bread, sliced and spread with unsalted butter
Several tablespoons olive paste

1. Mix eggs with Parmesan and chives.
2. Heat olive oil in skillet, then add about 1/4–1/2 cup egg mixture at a time to make 4 to 6 small, pancake-like omelets, setting each golden brown omelet aside to cool as you cook remaining egg mixture. Don't stack them or they will get soggy.
3. When cool, serve omelets or pieces of omelet atop slices of buttered bread, each canapé topped with a dab of olive paste.

◆◆◆◆◆◆

Peanut Butter Peanut butter and jelly sandwiches are quintessentially American. My European friends find them the height of exotica. "I've heard about them," one friend exclaimed over a plate of pâté and crusty bread, "and I've seen them in the movies, but I didn't realize that people actually ate them."

But, sans jelly, peanut butter is adored all over the world, from the spicy peanut sauces of Southeast Asia and China, the tomatoey stews of Africa, and the *moles* of Mexico, as well as the spicy sauces from South America.

Keeping a jar of peanut butter in your pantry means you can add its richness to sauces and stews such as a Mexican *mole* or a savory chili-seasoned soup of bean sprouts, celery, and cabbage. Peanut butter also is good added to spicy soy sauce–seasoned vinaigrettes, especially good served over cucumbers.

Spicy Asian Peanut Dip

◆ BASIC PANTRY

Serves 4 to 6

Whether I am catering parties or hosting my own, without a doubt this is the recipe I get asked for the most. It's sweet and spicy, very versatile, a fine interpretation of the genre.

It's also great last-minute fare, since I usually have all the ingredients in my pantry, and if I don't have any long-marinated chicken wings to serve with it, there are always carrot sticks, and they're equally good for dipping.

Without the cilantro, this sauce will last up to 2 weeks in a jar in the refrigerator. Add cilantro when ready to eat.

3 garlic cloves, chopped
1 cup peanut butter (chunky or smooth)
About 2 tablespoons brown or white sugar
One 1/2-inch piece fresh ginger, chopped
1/2 jalapeño chili, chopped, or hot salsa or chili paste to taste

1/2 cup water
1 to 2 tablespoons soy sauce
1 tablespoon fresh lemon juice
2 tablespoons chopped fresh cilantro
2 tablespoons Asian (toasted) sesame oil

1. In a blender or food processor combine garlic, peanut butter, sugar, ginger, and chili. Blend well.

2. Add water and soy sauce, and when well mixed add lemon juice, cilantro, and sesame oil. Taste and adjust seasoning if necessary.

◆◆ INTERMEDIATE PANTRY

Chinese Peanut Sauce

Add a tablespoon or two of hoisin sauce to above recipe, and serve garnished with a generous sprinkling of chopped **green onions or fresh chives.**

Serve with take-out Chinese roast duck, or your own hoisin-roasted duck, along with a stir-fry of broccoli sprinkled with Asian sesame oil and soy sauce.

◆◆◆◆◆◆

Pickled Jalapeños Hot and tart, jalapeño chilies pickled with spices and vinegar are also called *jalapeños en escabeche.* Sometimes they have other vegetables added such as carrots, cauliflower, onions, celery, etc., much like Italian giardiniera.

Pickled jalapeños are delicious added to burritos and tacos, to sandwiches (especially melted cheese ones), and to quesadillas. I also love these pickled chilies with boiled potatoes and melted cheese or a cheesy sauce, and they're good seasoning a soft taco of scrambled eggs.

Jalapeño, Onion, and Lemon Relish

◆ **BASIC PANTRY**

Makes 1 cup

This tangy salsa is adapted from a Brazilian relish prepared with the local pickled cayenne-type peppers, and served with everything from seafood to grilled steaks or hamburgers.

◆◆◆◆◆◆

To prepare mix 1 cup chopped **white or yellow onions** with 3 to 4 chopped **pickled jalapeños** (or to taste) and the juice of 1 **lemon.** Add **salt** and **pepper** to taste.

◆◆◆◆◆◆

Pickles Every culture and cuisine has some form of pickles. They were originally prepared as a way of preserving summer vegetables (and in more rural societies, this is still true), since salt, spices, sugar, and vinegar are excellent preservatives. But a vegetable's flavor changes in pickling, becoming tangy and supercharged; and we soon develop a hunger for the pickled version. We all have our favorites when it comes to pickles, from the sweet and spicy cucumber slices and clove-scented sweet gherkins favored in the Midwest, to the garlic-redolent kosher dills that not long ago were sold in wooden barrels, the scent of garlic and dill perfuming the air. (I still think the smell of kosher pickles is one of life's best sensations.)

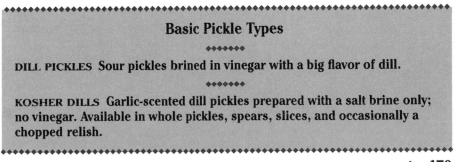

Basic Pickle Types

◆◆◆◆◆◆

DILL PICKLES Sour pickles brined in vinegar with a big flavor of dill.

◆◆◆◆◆◆

KOSHER DILLS Garlic-scented dill pickles prepared with a salt brine only; no vinegar. Available in whole pickles, spears, slices, and occasionally a chopped relish.

SWEET PICKLES Tasting vaguely of cloves, they are sweet and tart at the same time. Pickle relish is a finely chopped mixture of sweet pickles with onions and other seasonings; often it is mixed with mustard or catsup.

◆◆◆◆◆◆

CHOWCHOW, PICCALILLI Sweet and tangy mixtures of pickled vegetables, often seasoned with mustard seed, sweet red bell pepper, and celery seeds.

◆◆◆◆◆◆

GHERKINS Miniature sweet pickles with an intensified sweet-tangy cucumber flavor and a satisfying toothsome crunch.

CORNICHONS Tiny French pickles preserved in vinegar and seasoned with masses of tarragon. Cornichons are the classic accompaniment to pâtés, pot au feu, cold meat, etc.

◆◆◆◆◆◆

BREAD-AND-BUTTER PICKLES Classic Americana, with a sweet and tangy mustard-and-celery-seed-flavored brine.

◆◆◆◆◆◆

OTHER PICKLED CONDIMENTS

PICKLED VEGETABLES Giardiniera (a mixture of carrots, cauliflower, celery, etc.; see page 146); cocktail onions; pickled jalapeños with mixed vegetables.

◆◆◆◆◆◆

BRANSTEN PICKLE A British import much like chutney. Classically eaten with cheese.

◆◆◆◆◆◆

PICKLED CHERRY AND OTHER PEPPERS Sweet or mildly hot, these add great savor to all sorts of American fare. I like them tucked into a Philly cheese steak.

Thirteen Things to Do with Pickles
◆◆◆◆◆◆

While most of us enjoy pickles on the side of the plate, as a sort of lively counterpoint to simple foods, pickles can be used as a condiment and ingredient in other dishes. Here are some suggestions:

◆ **PAN-BROWNED LAMB OR SOLE WITH PIQUANT SAUCE** Dice cornichons and add to the pan you browned the meat or fish in, along with a pinch of tarragon and a few tablespoons of vinegar or white wine to deglaze pan. Swirl it about, then whisk in a little unsalted butter. Pour over meat or fish.

◆ **HAM AND CHEESE SALAD** Delightfully déclassé, and very, very good: mix equal parts diced ham and sharp Cheddar with a few spoonfuls drained diced pineapple (canned is fine). Dress with mayonnaise, season with whole-seed mustard, and add several spoonfuls of diced bread-and-butter pickles. Serve on whole-wheat bread with alfalfa sprouts or shredded lettuce.

◆ **DILL-SEASONED MEAT PIES** Chopped dill pickles, chopped fresh dill, and a bit of sour cream added to browned ground beef makes a good filling for a savory pie or tart.

◆ **SWEET GHERKINS** alongside chopped liver, with red onions on the side: an American version of the classic French combination of cornichons with pâté.

◆ **MIDDLE EASTERN FLAVORS** Serve slices of sour dill pickle atop a spicy Middle Eastern salad such as tabbouli (page 199), or falafel (page 321).

◆ **PICKLE AND MELTED CHEESE SANDWICH** Top whole-wheat bread with thin slices of sweet or kosher dill pickles, then top with sharp Cheddar cheese and broil until bubbly and lightly browned on top. This unlikely-sounding sandwich is absolutely delicious.

◆ **MIDWESTERN CURRIED EGG SALAD** Add several chopped sweet gherkins to egg salad seasoned with whole-seed mustard, celery, onion, parsley, and more than a whiff of curry powder.

◆ **DILL MEATLOAF** Add chopped dill pickles to taste to your favorite meat-loaf recipe, along with a bit of the juice from the pickles and lots of chopped fresh dill.

◆ **ROULADEN** Onto slices of braising steak, cut thinly and pounded flat, sprinkle some chopped onion, a pinch of marjoram, a slice of bacon, and a dill pickle spear. Roll up, dredge in flour, then brown and braise for about an hour in a mixture of red wine and broth, seasoned generously with garlic, paprika, thyme, and a half cup or so tomato sauce.

◆ **RUSSIAN POTATO SALAD** To 1 cup basic potato salad, add 1/2 tart apple, diced; 1/2 cup mixed vegetables such as peas, green beans, and carrots; and 1/2 dill or kosher dill pickle, diced.

◆ **SAVORY BEEF CANAPÉS** In a blender or food processor, mince a cup or so of leftover roast beef chunks. Add 1 diced dill pickle, blend, then bind it all together with a small amount of mayonnaise. Season with black pepper and spread on thin slices of baguette as a canapé or appetizer.

Plum Sauce This thick, purple-brown Chinese condiment sauce, prepared from plums, is sweet, tart, and spicy in a chutney-like way. Classically used for Peking duck, Mandarin pancakes, mushu pork or vegetables, and the like, it's also good combined with other Chinese sauces to make barbecue sauce, dipping sauce for a warming Chinese hot pot, and so forth.

STORAGE TIPS Keep in a jar (transfer from can if it came in one) in refrigerator for up to three months.

Salted Turnips, Chinese (Choan Choy) A very pungent seasoning made by salting Chinese turnip strands. Chop and use in stuffings based on bland meats, such as the fillings for dumplings, wontons, etc. (see page 370). A little goes a long way, but they add a distinctive flavor of their own.

Salsa At least 1 jar each of a good green and red salsa is indispensable for any pantry, ready to transform the simplest ingredients: tortillas, eggs, fish, salad, etc., into spicy Mexican fare.
Green salsa is based on the puckery green tomatillo, or husk tomato, and green chilies, while red is based on ripe red tomatoes and green chilies.

STORAGE TIPS Once opened, salsa should be kept in the refrigerator. Generally, commercial salsa will keep up to about 2 months before growing a forest of strange life forms. Homemade salsa doesn't last more than a week; don't try to keep it longer unless you prepare it specially for canning, as chilies and garlic provide a good medium for the growth of botulism (so do olives if they don't have enough salt in them—salt acts as a preventative to botulism).

Red Snapper Tacos with Green Salsa

◆ BASIC PANTRY

Serves 4

A good salsa in your pantry and a stack of tortillas in your freezer means you never have to be without tacos: any savory bit of meat, chicken, or fish can be doused with spicy sauce, rolled up in a warmed tortilla, and eaten with gusto. Try these fish tacos, a dish favored in seaside areas of Mexico.

3 red snapper fillets, 12 to 14 ounces total
Salt and pepper to taste
1 teaspoon ground cumin
1 teaspoon mild chili powder
1/2 teaspoon dried oregano, crumbled
2 garlic cloves, chopped
1 tablespoon olive oil
Juice of 1/2 lemon or lime
8 corn tortillas
Tiny amount of oil for heating tortillas
Green tomatillo salsa or taco sauce as desired
2 tablespoons chopped fresh cilantro
2 tablespoons chopped onion

1. Preheat oven to 450°. Place fish in a baking dish, then sprinkle with salt and pepper, cumin, chili, oregano, garlic, olive oil, and lemon. Cover tightly and bake for 15 minutes, or until just cooked through.

2. Remove from oven and keep warm.

3. Heat tortillas by first brushing with water and then warming them gently, one at a time, in a lightly oiled heavy skillet over medium-low heat. A non-stick pan is also excellent for this. Stack them onto a heavy plate, covering them as you go to keep them warm and pliable.

4. To assemble tacos: break fish into bite-sized pieces, then roll them up into tortillas, sprinkling with salsa, cilantro, and onion before rolling tightly. Serve immediately, with extra salsa for dipping.

NOTE Since many bottled green taco sauces don't have a tart enough flavor, you can improvise by combining 1/2 cup canned tomatillos, peeled and slightly mashed, with several tablespoons of green salsa.

◆◆◆◆◆◆

Soy Sauce No doubt soy sauce is on the shelf of nearly every pantry in America. Its all-purpose savor has long been splashed into Western dishes as well as Eastern ones: marinades, soups, sauces, pasta, etc. Even when I was growing up, my grandmother used soy sauce to make her pot roast browner, to add zest to her roasting chicken, and to season her kasha (buckwheat groats). My grandfather called it "bug juice," and took me out to a Chinese lunch every week, just the two of us. I remember sitting in my highchair (I must have been less than three years old at the time) and touching the deliciously salty black liquid to my lips, directly from the container. I have better eating manners now.

Soy sauce is made from fermenting soy beans, wheat, and salt, with caramelized sugar added for coloring. It comes in light and dark, or American all purpose, which is pretty dark and is saltier than the fuller-flavored Chinese sauces. Dark is used for braises and heartier flavors, while the light is used for lighter-colored and -flavored foods. There is also a low-salt soy sauce on the American market, but I don't like it much—I always end up adding extra salt to the dish.

Chinese-flavor Dipping Sauce

◆◆◆ ADVANCED PANTRY

Makes 1/2 cup

This deep, dark soy-tasting sauce adds a sharp and welcome accent for bland foods such as steamed dumplings, chunks of steamed fish, or green-onion-and-ginger-steamed chicken.

1/4 cup soy sauce, all purpose or dark
2 green onions, thinly sliced
2 tablespoons rice wine vinegar or sherry vinegar
1 tablespoon Worcestershire sauce
2 tablespoons sugar
2 tablespoons chopped fresh cilantro

2 teaspoons Asian (toasted) sesame oil
2 teaspoons chopped fresh ginger
2 garlic cloves, minced
1/2 to 1 teaspoon Chinese chili oil or a generous dash Tabasco sauce or Chinese chili paste with garlic

Combine all ingredients.

Soy-marinated Grilled Chicken Wings

◆ BASIC PANTRY

Serves 6

This Asian-American marinade permeates the chicken wings and creates a savory crispness as they grill. Perfect for an outdoor barbecue, this recipe can be doubled and tripled indefinitely. Many times I've made these for parties of 150 people or more. They are simple to put together, and have the good grace to get better as they sit in their marinade. In fact, if you can marinate them for 2 to 3 days in the refrigerator—but no longer—they will be fantastic.

2 pounds chicken wings, cut into 2 parts (drumette and wing tip, or just use drumettes)	2 tablespoons honey or sugar
	One 1-inch piece fresh ginger, chopped
3 garlic cloves, chopped	3 green onions, thinly sliced
1/3 cup soy sauce	2 tablespoons Asian (toasted) sesame oil
3 tablespoons dry sherry or rice wine	Spicy Asian Peanut Dip, page 178

1. Combine chicken wings with the next 7 ingredients.

2. Place in a bowl or big plastic bag and let sit in refrigerator for at least an hour or up to 3 days.

3. Turn every so often during marination.

4. Grill over an open fire or broil until crisp. Serve accompanied with the peanut dip sauce.

◆◆◆◆◆◆

Sun-Dried Tomatoes In the land that bakes in Italy's midday sun, the region called the Mezzogiorno, summer's ripe tomatoes are salted and laid out under the open sky to dry to a leathery finish. They are put up in jars of olive oil, topped with a leaf of basil, and left to enjoy in winter, when ripe tomatoes are nowhere to be found. During August you can see wire mesh—and often beds, for bedsprings make a great drying surface—stretched out in the sunny yards, covered with drying tomatoes.

Sun-dried tomatoes have an intense, bright flavor that actually tastes of the summer sun. When dry, they are chewy; marinated, they should be plump and tender. After you use all the tomatoes, use the seasoned oil marinade for salads, or to sauté onions for soups or sauces. Until recently, most of the dried tomatoes sold in our shops came from Italy, but these days Northern California also produces the sun-dried delicacies.

Usually the Italian ones are marinated. Some are wonderful, and others are not. The sun-dried tomatoes that are brighter red in color and plumper in form taste best, and their price tag reflects their quality.

Sun-dried tomatoes are delicious added to crusty French bread sandwiches, pan sauces for roasting chicken, or just plopped onto bread. California dried tomatoes usually come dried rather than in oil, and are very reasonably priced.

Marinated Sun-dried Tomatoes

◆ BASIC PANTRY

Makes 10 to 15 tomatoes

Marinated tomatoes have more flavor than the plain dried ones. Here's how to marinate them yourself.

10 to 15 sun-dried tomatoes
1/4 cup extra-virgin olive oil,
   or enough to cover tomatoes

2 to 3 garlic cloves, sliced
3 to 5 leaves fresh basil or fresh
   thyme sprigs

1. Pour boiling water to cover over the sun-dried tomatoes and cook for 2 minutes. Remove from heat, cover, and let stand for 2 to 3 minutes; drain.

2. Place rehydrated tomatoes in a bowl and layer with remaining ingredients, then pour olive oil over all.

3. Cover and let marinate at room temperature for at least an hour, or refrigerate for up to 5 days.

Sun-dried Tomato and Chèvre Canapés

Generously spread thinly sliced **baguettes** with **goat cheese** (plain, or garlic or herb flavored). Top with a julienne of **marinated sun-dried tomatoes,** above, and a bit of chopped **fresh basil.**

Sun-drenched Swordfish

◆◆ INTERMEDIATE PANTRY

Serves 4 to 6

Swordfish's hearty flavor lends itself to robust flavors: lemon, garlic, sun-dried tomatoes, herbes de Provence, olive oil. Forget the prim and proper here: bring on the lusty flavors!

Accompany with crusty peasant bread, of course, to soak up the cooking juices, and serve with a salad of mesclun and fresh herbs tossed in vinaigrette. And have ice cream or frozen yogurt for dessert, with a few cookies such as Caribbean Coconut Shortbread, page 314.

1-1/2 garlic heads (about 30
   cloves), separated but not
   peeled
1/4 cup extra-virgin olive oil
1 to 1-1/2 pounds swordfish
   steaks
1 to 2 lemons
1 cup dry white wine

1/2 teaspoon herbes de
   Provence
15 marinated sun-dried
   tomatoes, cut into halves and
   quarters
Fresh herb sprigs for garnish
   (rosemary, thyme, oregano,
   etc.)

1. Preheat oven to 375°. Arrange garlic cloves in a baking dish with about half of olive oil. Bake for 15 to 20 minutes, or until fragrant and beginning to become tender.

2. Remove from oven. Add swordfish to pan, arranging garlic cloves around and on top of fish.

3. Slice lemons thinly (about 1/8 inch) and remove seeds. Place a slice or two on each fish steak, then pour remaining olive oil over fish, along with wine. Sprinkle with herbes de Provence.

4. Return to oven and bake for about 10 minutes, then add sun-dried tomatoes and continue baking until fish is cooked through, about 10 more minutes. Serve immediately, each portion of the fish accompanied with a few garlic cloves and sun-dried tomatoes, and garnished with herbs.

Sun-dried Tomato Vinaigrette

◆ **BASIC PANTRY**

Makes 1/2 cup

Sun-dried tomatoes make a particularly tangy vinaigrette. Serve on a salad of butter lettuce and frisée topped with feta and basil, or splashed over Kasha Salad, page 198.

6 to 8 sun-dried tomatoes, cut
   into small pieces
3 garlic cloves, minced
1/4 cup olive oil

2 tablespoons red wine vinegar
Generous pinch thyme and/or
   basil

1. In a blender or food processor, whirl garlic, then add sun-dried tomatoes, olive oil, and vinegar.

2. Whirl until well mixed, then season with thyme and/or basil.

Garlic-roast Eggplant with Sun-dried Tomato Vinaigrette

It's a toss-up as to which is better: eating it or smelling it as it cooks. The eggplant is studded with cloves of garlic, then rolled around in a bit of olive oil and baked to fragrant tenderness.

The sweet, perfumed flesh is balanced by the sharp sun-dried tomato vinaigrette and a fresh bed of lettuce and herbs. Good summer or wish-it-were-summer food.

Serves 4

1 medium to large eggplant
5 to 10 garlic cloves, cut length-
    wise into large slivers or
    quarters
Olive oil for rubbing
1/2 recipe Sun-dried Tomato
    Vinaigrette, page 187

Juice of 1/4 lemon
2 tablespoons chopped fresh
    parsley or basil
Bed of lettuce
Crusty French bread

1. Preheat oven to 350°. With a sharp paring knife, make incisions all over eggplant and stuff each incision with as much garlic as it will hold.

2. Rub all over with olive oil, then place in a baking pan and bake until flesh is soft and tender, about 40 minutes. Eggplant will appear deflated and a bit sad.

3. Let cool, then scrape flesh from tough skin.

4. Place flesh in a bowl and dice or cut up. Mix with vinaigrette and lemon juice, and sprinkle with herbs.

5. Serve at room temperature, on a bed of lettuce, accompanied with bread to spread it on.

Zucchini and Sun-dried Tomato Frittata Pizza

[SCARPACCIA ALLA CALIFORNIA]

Serves 4

The Italian name for this homey dish translates as "old shoe," though no one is sure exactly why. Is it that the dish is as comforting to eat as an old shoe is to wear? Or was it the specialty of the village shoemaker?

This mixture of zucchini and sun-dried tomatoes bakes into a flat pancake-like dish, crisp around the edges, tender and delectable inside. Serve in squares or wedges as an appetizer or a savory snack with a glass of wine, or for a late-night supper.

2 eggs, lightly beaten
1/4 cup grated Parmesan or
    other pungent grating cheese
1 cup water
About 1/2 cup flour
1-1/2 to 2 pounds zucchini,
    thinly sliced

3 tablespoons chopped sun-
    dried tomatoes
1/2 teaspoon chopped fresh
    marjoram or other strong-
    flavored herb
1/2 cup olive oil
Salt and pepper to taste

1. Preheat oven to 375°. Mix eggs with Parmesan cheese, then add water. Beat in flour, mixing well, to make a batter the consistency of heavy cream.

2. Add zucchini, sun-dried tomatoes, and marjoram.

3. Pour half of olive oil into a large flat baking dish, about 18 by 12 inches. Pour vegetable-filled batter into pan, then drizzle with remaining oil. Sprinkle with salt and pepper to taste.

4. Bake for 45 minutes to an hour, or until edges are crisply browned and top golden. Underbaking will result in a doughy, sodden consistency; you will not like it.

5. Remove from oven and let cool to room temperature. No matter how nice it smells, it tastes best at room temperature.

New Wave Onion Soup

◆◆ INTERMEDIATE PANTRY

Serves 4

Sauté 3–4 sliced **onions** in 2 tablespoons of **sun-dried tomato oil** and **unsalted butter.** Add 4–5 cups **broth,** using vegetable and beef or chicken broth, and season with **herbes de Provence** and chopped **fresh basil.** Simmer 30–40 minutes, then serve each bowl topped with a big slice of **dry crusty bread** with a slice of Jack, asiago, fontina, or a similar **cheese** melted atop it.

◆◆◆◆◆◆

Tahini High in protein and calcium, tahini, or ground sesame seeds, has no animal fat, yet it makes a creamy, rich sauce spiced with garlic, olive oil, lemon, yogurt, etc. Tahini has been eaten in the Middle East probably as long as sesame seeds have been growing there.

It was in the sixties that tahini found its way into American cuisine. Tahini has since become de rigueur in the American pantry as an accompaniment to falafels, which are now as American a street food as tacos, egg rolls, and hot dogs.

The dawning of the jet age and the discovery of Middle Eastern food by the baby boom generation helped to call attention to foods like tahini, as did the natural foods movement (weren't they often the same?), and immigration from the war-torn Mideast also contributed. In addition we Americans were developing an adventurous palate, hungering for bright strong flavors. And tahini fits the bill. Try it added to vinaigrettes, or spooned over Mediterranean spiced vegetables. Use it as a sauce for grilled lamb or lamb burgers in pita bread, or mixed with fire-roasted eggplant for baba ghannoush. Try tahini with lots and lots of chopped parsley, cilantro, and fresh mint to make an emerald-colored sauce that tastes of the Middle East at its best. And of course, when tahini is added to ground cooked chick-peas, you have hummus.

But the thing about tahini—also known as tahina—is that it needs to be spiced with a generous hand: cumin, curry, lots of garlic and lemon. Without these strong flavors, tahini has all the excitement of library paste.

Tahini-Yogurt Sauce

Makes about 1-1/2 cups

This tahini sauce varies a bit from the standard in that it has an addition of yogurt, which lightens the sesame paste and enlivens the tanginess of the sauce. Double the amount of yogurt in the tahini for a lively sauce to dip vegetables in.

2 garlic cloves, chopped	Juice of 1 lemon
2/3 cup tahini paste	2 tablespoons water
1 teaspoon cumin seeds, or 1/2 teaspoon ground cumin	Salt and hot pepper sauce to taste
1/4 teaspoon curry powder	2/3 cup low-fat plain yogurt

Mix garlic with tahini paste, then slowly add remaining ingredients, blending until smoothly mixed. A blender or food processor is good for this.

◆◆◆◆◆◆

Truffles and Truffle Paste Keeping truffles in your pantry means that you are either crazy about the fragrant fungus or, considering how expensive truffles are, just plain crazy. Like caviar, its price only adds to its allure.

Truffles are elusive gifts from nature, along with porcini and other delicious wild fungi. They grow just beneath the ground, giving no indication of their presence. The spot that last year was prolific may this year lie barren. Or vice versa.

In the Southwest of France they are often hunted with pigs, in Italy with dogs (though many French farmers are switching over to dogs as well—the pigs get greedy and can be very quick to gobble up the valuable delicacies).

There are many different types of truffles, the most famous being the "black diamonds" of France's Perigord, as well as the pungent black truffles of Italy's Umbria and the white truffles of the Italian Piedmont. In fact, truffles grow in many other parts of the world, but they lack their cousins' aromatic mushroom presence. (Many efforts have been

Three Ways to Serve Tahini-Yogurt Sauce

◆◆◆◆◆◆

◆ Serve Tahini-Yogurt Sauce with an assortment of vegetables: steamed cauliflower, diced tomatoes, English cucumbers, grilled eggplant slices, and whatever vegetables you wish. Good with whole-wheat pita bread, lightly toasted or heated.

◆ As a sauce for meatballs made from chopped lamb, seasoned with pine nuts and ground cumin.

◆ Stir a few spoonfuls into a stir-fry of diced eggplant seasoned with mustard seeds, ground turmeric, and diced tomatoes.

made to "farm" truffles rather than depend on nature's inconsistency, but farmed truffles lack the magic of the wild ones, at least so far.)

The Perigord region of France combines truffles with omelets, rich pâtés, soups and stews, goose and duck livers—and the Piedmontese throw their white truffles into risotti, polenta, and vegetable and game dishes. But Umbria is where my heart lies, at least trufflewise: that is where they toss black truffles nonchalantly into buttered or lightly cream-splashed pasta.

In season, truffles are sold in gourmet shops, especially on the East Coast. They're often packed in rice, which can then be cooked as truffle-flavored rice. Fresh truffles are exorbitantly expensive unless considered as an alternative to buying a small car. Truffle shavings in a can and truffle paste in a tube is what I choose when I'm paying the bill. And I nearly always have one or the other on my pantry shelf, bought when I'm feeling flush, eaten when I'm not.

Last winter I was given a big bag of fresh truffles as part of a publicity stunt (failed) to promote "truffle water" (awful). I considered making pâté and I considered making duck liver. But this pasta dish is what I made—and made—and made, until the last little truffle was gone.

Truffled Garden Pasta

◆◆◆ ADVANCED PANTRY

Toss buttered al dente **pasta** with **sautéed julienned vegetables**—celery, carrots, and zucchini—and as much **truffle paste** as you can afford and delight in. A judicious whiff of **garlic** and **anchovies or a splash of cream** is a delicious addition.

Truffle Vinaigrette

◆◆◆ ADVANCED PANTRY

Makes about 1/2 cup

Add 2 tablespoons **truffle paste** to 1/2 cup **vinaigrette** made from olive oil and red wine vinegar. Serve on a salad of **mesclun** and **herbs** topped with a warm grilled **salmon** fillet.

◆◆◆◆◆◆

Vine Leaf Kopanisti is an intriguing puree of grapevine leaves; try adding a little to a mayonnaise along with a bit of crushed capers, and serving it with grilled fish, peppers, and artichokes. It's quite good, too, with smoked ham such as Westphalian.

Purchase in specialty food shops. Though the jars last up to a year on the pantry shelf, once opened they should be refrigerated and will last only 2 weeks.

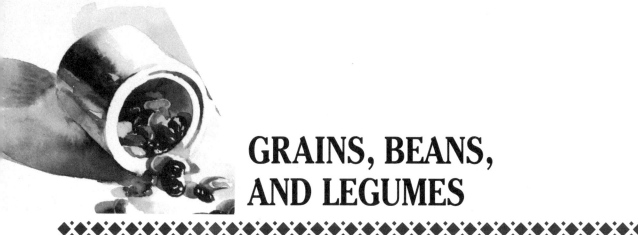

GRAINS, BEANS, AND LEGUMES

Grains, beans, and legumes have sustained much of the human race since time began. They are all seeds that if planted would result in a growing plant, and as such are concentrated nuggets of nutrition and fiber. And nothing fills a hungry stomach as well.

In the pantry, a shelf lined with jars of grains, beans, and legumes is beautiful to gaze at, a kaleidoscope of colors and textures. Remember when as children we made "pictures" from beans, grains, and pastas, gluing them onto paper, enjoying the feel of coarse or smooth textures and marveling at the variety of shapes and hues?

These days we're cooking them, using a global array of flavors.

About Grains

Grains have recently undergone an image overhaul, transforming themselves from humble porridge and starchy side dishes to natural foods and haute cuisine. Seafood with beans, sausage with lentils, savory whole-grain mixtures: what a change of eating from the not-too-distant past when steak and salad was considered by the American public as the epitome of good eating and grains were considered starch, pure and simple.

But a diet of grains has proved to be healthier than that steak and salad, and it certainly is ecologically kinder, as it takes less land to grow grains than to sustain the animals we eat as meat. Vegetarianism is becoming gourmet, and many people eat vegetarian meals not necessarily for health or economics, or out of moral conviction, but simply because they like vegetables and grains best.

A variety of grains kept in the pantry gives our cuisine a shape and form on which to hang everything else: fresh vegetables; spices and condiments; meat, poultry, and fish. And they look so beautiful, these jars of assorted brown and cream-colored nuggets, each a different size and shape and texture.

Grains are the seed-bearing fruits of the plant. Beneath their tough protective husk are the three main parts of the grain: the outer coat, or bran, that high-fiber wonder; the germ, with its rich oil content (and as such, the first part to go rancid); and the endosperm, with its high starch and protein content.

Grains are processed in a variety of ways, each depending on the grain and the result desired. The selection of grains and groats is staggering and often confusing, ranging from whole berry to cracked, flaked, shredded, polished, or ground into flour.

The whole grain, or berry, its husk removed, is known as a groat. Brown rice and wheat berries are examples, as is kasha, or buckwheat groats (a classic of the Russian kitchen, delicious toasted, then cooked with broth, fried onions, and short wide noodles). Natural foods shops sell a variety of other groats. Groats have a whole-grain flavor and take longer to cook (think of brown rice vs. white rice). Polishing grains scrapes away the bran and germ from the endosperm, resulting in a lighter-flavored grain that cooks in a shorter period of time. Without its bran and germ, it keeps in the pantry much longer. Of course, the nutrition also is reduced. White rice, pearl barley, polenta, and couscous are among the grains that have been treated this way.

Cracking is a process that involves coarse grinding and often soaking, which turns grains into grit-like nuggets. Some are cracked from the whole grain, such as bulgur and rye, or from the already processed grain, such as hominy.

STORAGE TIPS Grains should be stored in tightly covered containers to guard against insect infestation and kept in a cool, dry, and dark location, as heat, light, and air all accelerate their decline. Whole grains spoil quickest, doomed by their nutritious oil-rich germ. They last about 5 months, but can be stretched somewhat by refrigeration. Further-processed grains such as white rice, hominy, barley, etc., last up to a year.

Now that we've discovered the goodness of grains they're becoming our staff of life, too. Grains satisfy as no fish fillet or stalk of broccoli can. The trouble is, since they take up to 45 minutes to cook who has time to wait for them to cook at the end of the day? I find that if I cook a large pot of whole grains at the beginning of the week and keep it in the refrigerator, I can dig into it at will for several days. These leftover grains are delicious in casseroles, muffins and breads, soups, meatloaf, stir-fries, and so on. Brown rice goes into pudding, stuffed vine leaves, or cabbage rolls, barley into creamy cabbage soup. You also can freeze individual portions of cooked grains (a good idea for leftovers) and defrost for weekday meals.

A Brief Guide to Cooking Grains

Grain by the Cup	Amount of Liquid	Cooking Time	Yield
Barley	2-1/2 cups	35 minutes	3-1/2 cups
Buckwheat groats	1 to 1-1/2 cups	10 to 15 minutes	1 cup
Bulgur, coarsely milled	3 to 4 cups	20 to 25 minutes	3 cups
Bulgur, finely milled	2 cups	15 minutes	2-1/2 cups
Cornmeal, coarsely milled (polenta)	4 cups	30 minutes or more	4 cups
Cornmeal, finely milled	4 cups	6 to 10 minutes	4 cups
Couscous	1 cup	5 minutes	2 cups
Hominy grits	4 cups	15 to 20 minutes	4 cups
Millet	1-1/2 cups	20 to 25 minutes	4 cups
Oats, rolled	2 cups or according to box	15 minutes	3 cups

RICE			
Arborio rice	3 cups or more	25 to 30 minutes or more	2-1/2 to 3 cups
White rice (short or long grain)	1-1/2 cups	15 minutes	3 cups
Basmati rice	1-1/2 cups	15 minutes	3 cups
Brown rice	2 cups	40 to 45 minutes	3 to 4 cups
Wild rice	6 (!) cups	45 minutes or more	3 cups
Wheat berries	4 cups	1-1/2 hours	3 cups

Barley This hearty cousin of wheat comes in a variety of types and was one of the first grains cultivated by humans. Three thousand years ago the Lake-Dwellers of Switzerland used several kinds of barley. Barley is mentioned in the Old Testament as one of the foods destroyed by the plagues of Egypt. In ancient Greece and Rome it was a staple food, and it was later embraced by England, Scotland, Turkey, Scandinavia, and others.

Until the 16th century barley was the basis of most European bread, but when wheat became more available its higher gluten content made it the grain of choice and gradually it supplanted barley. By the beginning of the 17th century, barley was being grown in America.

Pearled barley, with the bran and germ removed, is readily available and eaten often in hearty soups, especially those of Eastern European origin. Barley groats and grits are eaten in parts of North Africa and the Middle East, often combined with yogurt or soured milk and lots of fresh herbs: green onions, dill, cilantro. Barley is delicious combined with hearty foods such as lamb and root vegetables in Scotch Broth, page 196, or with chili powders in Winter Mesa Beef and Barley Stew, page 196.

In America, much of our barley crop is fed to our meat animals or sprouted and used to make malt and beer; in Scotland barley is an essential ingredient in whiskey.

A word of warning: barley expands thirstily, taking over the lion's share of any liquid. When cooking what seems to be a small amount of barley, don't be tempted to add more. It plumps up dramatically.

Winter Mesa Beef and Barley Stew

◆◆ INTERMEDIATE PANTRY

Serves 4 to 6

Hearty with mild but robust chili powder, stewed meat, and butter beans, this barley casserole encompasses the regional flavors and rustic quality of the traditional foods of America's Southwest. The dish is no more authentic than that, first pulled together from the ingredients I found lining a Southwestern pantry, accompanied with chewy pita-like Navajo fried bread, and eaten outside under a starry Northern New Mexico winter's sky. The brittle cold was tempered by the warmth of hot springs bubbling up from the rocky mountainside and warming us like a central heater.

2 onions, thinly sliced
About 2 teaspoons vegetable oil
2 carrots, diced
1/2 cup diced tomatoes (canned is fine)
2 teaspoons cumin seeds
1-1/2 tablespoons New Mexico chili powder or other good-quality chili powder
3 pieces Canadian bacon or other thick-sliced bacon, diced, or smoky-flavored vegetarian bacon bits
6 cups beef broth or more
About 1 pound chuck steak or other stewing meat, cut into bite-sized pieces
1 cup pearl barley
1/2 cup dry butter beans
1/2 to 1 teaspoon dried oregano, crumbled

1. Brown onions quickly over high heat in a heavy skillet, using only a little oil. You want them to brown darkly and char slightly, but not burn.

2. Add carrots, tomatoes, cumin seeds, chili powder, bacon, broth, and meat. Let simmer an hour, or until meat is nearly tender.

3. Add barley and beans and continue cooking another hour and a half, adding more liquid if necessary to keep mixture somewhat soupy and not a solid mass. Stir every so often to keep barley from sticking to bottom.

4. Serve in individual bowls, each portion sprinkled with a bit of crumbled oregano and accompanied with warm flour tortillas.

Scotch Broth

◆◆ INTERMEDIATE PANTRY

Serves 4

A bowlful of steaming Scotch broth is one of the most welcome dishes imaginable on a chilly, rain-soaked afternoon or evening. The creamy flavor and texture of barley gives the soup its distinctive character, along with grassy leeks, nuggets of turnip, and earthy yellow split peas.

2 quarts lamb or beef broth
1/2 pound lamb, cut into bite-
   sized pieces
3 tablespoons pearl barley
3 tablespoons yellow split peas
1 leek, cleaned and coarsely
   chopped

1 turnip, diced
2 carrots, diced
2 new potatoes, diced
Salt and black pepper to taste

1. Place broth and lamb in a pot and bring to a boil. Reduce heat and simmer, covered, until lamb is very tender, about 2 to 3 hours. (Leftover cooked lamb may be used in place of stewed fresh lamb.)

2. When lamb is almost tender, add barley and split peas, simmer 30 minutes, then add remaining ingredients.

3. Continue cooking another hour or so, until vegetables, meat, and grains are tender, stirring every so often so that barley and split peas do not stick to bottom of pot and burn.

◆◆◆◆◆◆

Buckwheat Buckwheat is one of those foods that can inspire rhapsodies in those who grew up eating it and induce great yawns of boredom from those who didn't.

It is believed that buckwheat was first cultivated in ancient China, then spread to Europe by migrating tribes, finding a gastronomical home in the cuisines of Eastern Europe and Russia, where it is known as *kasha*. With a flavor that is distinctively nutty and grassy at the same time, it is a sturdy grain that requires confident seasoning to rescue it from dullness.

Kasha should be lightly toasted on an ungreased skillet or in a heavy pan before cooking liquid is added. Sometimes a lightly beaten egg is stirred into the toasting kasha grains to keep each kernel separate as they cook.

Cook toasted kasha in broth with lots of sautéed onions and mushrooms, and serve alongside an old-fashioned selection of assorted meats as my grandmother does: a chunk of roast beef chuck or lamb, a whole chicken, and a scattering of meatballs. The chicken flavors the meatballs, which flavor the beef or lamb, and the beef, lamb, and meatballs return the courtesy.

Kasha Salad with Sun-dried Tomato Vinaigrette

Serves 4

The following salad of cold buckwheat groats on a bed of tender raw spinach leaves is brought to life with sun-dried tomato vinaigrette.

If you have no sun-dried tomato vinaigrette, splash with any vinaigrette and scatter the salad with a few diced sun-dried tomatoes.

2 cups medium-grain buck-
    wheat groats
2 cups hot vegetable, chicken,
    or beef broth
1 bunch tender fresh spinach,
    washed and dried

1 recipe Sun-dried Tomato
    Vinaigrette, page 187, or an-
    other vinaigrette plus diced
    sun-dried tomatoes

1. Toast groats in a dry heavy skillet over medium heat. Toss groats to keep them from burning. Let them turn toasty brown.

2. Add hot broth, reduce heat to medium or medium-low, cover, and cook about 10 minutes, or until kasha grains are cooked through but still resist the teeth somewhat. Stop cooking before kasha turns mushy. Add more liquid as it cooks if mixture seems too dry. (The exact cooking time for kasha depends on the degree of fineness the groats are milled to. If you purchase the kasha in a box, cooking instructions should be on the side, especially geared to the groats you've bought.)

3. Remove from heat, cover, and let cool.

4. Arrange spinach leaves on each plate, then place several spoonfuls of kasha on top.

5. Dress with vinaigrette.

◆◆◆◆◆◆

Bulgur Bulgur wheat is made by partially milling and steaming whole-wheat kernels, then cracking them into gritlike bits. It is available in three basic grinds: fine, medium, and coarse. Since bulgur is partially cooked, it requires only soaking to be crunchily edible and brief cooking to be soft and porridgelike. It contains quite a bit of the fiber and nutrition of whole wheat, but is easier to prepare and eat.

Bulgur, one of the oldest forms of processed wheat, has been eaten for centuries in the Middle East and farther north in the Caucasus region of the U.S.S.R. We produce great quantities of it in the United States, sending much of it to developing nations or using it in other foodstuffs such as bread sticks.

The great thing about bulgur is that since it is already precooked it need only be soaked to be edible. It can be cooked to softness for puddings, pilafs, and the like; the choice is up to the cook. Take care, though, not to overcook or to use too much liquid—bulgur quickly and easily turns mushy. Bulgur is great added to breads, simmered with milk and honey for a comforting pudding, and used as stuffing for a Thanksgiving turkey. The Armenians stuff it into vine leaves (dolmas or dolmades) and steamed mussels.

The most famous dish featuring bulgur wheat is without a doubt tabbouli. Originally a Lebanese dish of soaked bulgur mixed with fresh mint, green onions, and parsley, and dressed with lots and lots of olive oil and lemon juice, this zesty salad has in recent years become almost as standard in American delicatessens as potato salad, macaroni salad, and coleslaw.

Curried Bulgur Salad with Green Beans and Yogurt Sauce

♦ BASIC TO
♦♦ INTERMEDIATE PANTRY

Serves 4

Sort of a cross-pollination between the ubiquitous tabbouli and the lesser-known Sephardic barzagan, with the spicy flavors of India thrown in for good measure, this makes great picnic fare. Try it also as a bed for grilled swordfish, or grilled curry-spiced ground or sliced lamb: surround the whole platter with crisp-tender green beans and offer the yogurt sauce for each diner to spoon over as he or she wishes.

2 cups medium-grind bulgur wheat
2 tablespoons olive oil
1 onion, chopped
3 garlic cloves, coarsely chopped
1/4 cup pine nuts or cooked and drained chick-peas
1 teaspoon ground coriander
1/4 teaspoon ground cloves
1 teaspoon curry powder

1 cup diced fresh or drained canned tomatoes
1/4 cup raisins
Salt and cayenne pepper to taste
1/4 cup *each* coarsely chopped fresh mint and cilantro or parsley
2 tablespoons fresh lemon juice
1/4 pound tender thin green beans, cooked al dente and cooled
Yogurt Sauce, following

1. Place bulgur in a bowl and cover with water to soak.

2. Sauté onion, garlic, and pine nuts or chick-peas in olive oil until onions soften. Sprinkle in spices and cook a minute or two longer to cook out rawness.

3. Add tomatoes and raisins, raise heat, and cook until mixture has thickened a bit. Remove from heat.

4. Drain bulgur and squeeze dry, then add to tomato mixture. Season with salt, cayenne, mint, cilantro, and lemon juice.

5. Let cool to room temperature and serve garnished with green beans and spicy-tart Yogurt Sauce.

Yogurt Sauce

Mix 2 teaspoons **tikka paste** (or other curry paste or powder to taste) with 1/3 cup low-fat plain **yogurt.**

♦♦♦♦♦♦

Cornmeal Corn was first cultivated by the Indians of Mexico (though some claim it originated in Peru). Samples of this New World grain's ancestor were found in caves once inhabited by ancient tribes. The antique corn was grasslike, with ears about 1 inch in size, each miniature ear wrapped in its own tiny husk. Over ensuing centuries, the Indians bred and cultivated the grain until they had a wide variety of colors and qualities, from sweet corn for nibbling to chalky, starchy corn for grinding, from black corn and red corn to popcorn and corn used as animal feed, to name but a few. The grain migrated to Peru, where it grew with even more vigor.

When Christopher Columbus returned to Spain, he brought back a pocketful of golden corn kernels. Corn flourished in Europe, and was probably on Magellan's ship when he set sail, because by the early 1500s corn was reported growing in the Philippines. By the mid-century it was growing in China, where today there are regions that eat more corn than rice. The Portuguese brought it to West Africa, where it nourished the people so well that it contributed to a marked growth in the population.

The settlers in what is now New England came to depend on corn to nourish them through the cold early winters of their New World existence. Down South in Virginia, cornmeal soon became a staple. Settlers in both the North and South developed all sorts of dishes, no doubt adapting Indian recipes to their European tastes. Such specialties as johnny cakes, corn pone, and succotash were Indian and colonist collaborations.

Today corn is a vital ingredient in many European cuisines as well as in New World ones. Mamaliga is the staple of Romania, a porridge of boiled cornmeal served buttered and eaten with sour cream for breakfast, sliced and fried to serve with cured meats or grilled sausages for dinner. In Italy, polenta is the equivalent: golden mounds of soft, creamy cornmeal, often embellished with rich cheeses, sage leaves, ragù sauces, and served as a bed for grilled quail and sausages, for chicken livers, and other rich, savory foods. Polenta is used as the base for tarts and simple sweet cakes.

Try, too, making cornmeal crepes by using cornmeal for half of the flour in a basic crepe recipe. Top with apple slices steamed in maple syrup for a sweet treat, or with rosemary-scented sautéed mushrooms for a savory sensation.

Basic Polenta

♦ BASIC PANTRY

Serves 4

1 quart water
1 teaspoon salt

1 cup coarse-ground yellow cornmeal

1. Stir 1 cup water into salt and cornmeal. Mix well, then let sit for 15 minutes.
2. Stir in remaining water, then bring mixture to boil. Reduce heat to medium-low and cook, stirring occasionally with a wooden spoon (it really does make a better pot of polenta) until thick and creamy and no longer gritty. Cooking time will vary from 35 to 40 minutes. The package will advise you on cooking time.
3. Eat immediately, warm and creamy, puddled with melted butter, and cheese or one of the following sauces.

VARIATION FOR CORNMEAL MUSH Follow basic recipe, but use fine ground cornmeal. Cook cornmeal only 15 to 20 minutes.

Toppings for Warm Soft Polenta

◆ BASIC PANTRY

Vanilla-scented Polenta

Mix a few drops of **vanilla extract** into the **cooked polenta;** serve it puddled with **unsalted butter,** and sprinkled generously with sugar.

Polenta and Sausages

Add a bit of chopped **fresh rosemary** to the **cooked polenta;** top with baked or pan-browned **Italian sausages,** along with sautéed **peppers** and **tomatoes.**

◆◆ INTERMEDIATE PANTRY

Polenta with Sage Butter and Cheese

Melt a lavish amount of **unsalted butter** in a heavy pan along with a handful of whole **fresh sage leaves.** When butter is melted and a tiny bit browned and sage is getting crispy, pour the butter onto each portion of **polenta** and sprinkle with freshly grated **Parmesan cheese** and **Gorgonzola cheese or cream.** Add **black pepper** to taste and garnish with a few of the crisp fried sage leaves (save the rest for other dishes).

◆◆◆ ADVANCED PANTRY

Polenta with Sautéed Mushrooms and Cream

Sauté lots of sliced **fresh mushrooms** (enhanced by a handful of rehydrated **dried porcini** if possible) with **onions** and **garlic,** then splash in a bit of **white wine** and raise the heat, boiling off the alcohol. Swirl in a bit of **cream,** then spoon over **polenta,** and pass the **Parmesan.**

Polenta con Ragù e Carciofi

Make your favorite long-simmered tomatoey **ragù,** adding a few **artichoke hearts** and whatever leftover bits of **meat** might be languishing in your refrigerator: chicken, sausage, prosciutto, etc. Serve spooned over the creamy **warm polenta** and pass **grating cheese.**

Cold Cooked Cornmeal for Slicing

◆ BASIC PANTRY

In parts of Europe (Romania and Italy) as well as America (the South and Northeast) cooked cornmeal is routinely poured out onto a board and left to cool, then cut into slices and pan browned, grilled, casseroled, etc. In Romania, it is called "bread of gold" when served this way, and eaten with rustic vegetable soups and garlicky beef sausages.

TO PREPARE Pour **cornmeal mush or polenta,** page 201, onto a big wooden board and let cool into a firm, loaflike mass. Slice it up and fry in **oil** of choice until crispy and nicely browned. Serve for a Yankee breakfast with sausages and maple syrup, or top with Fontina or Gorgonzola cheese and broil until sizzling. From Northern Italy: grill the slices on an open fire, baste with olive oil or sage-infused butter and served with grilled quail or duck.

Baked Tomato-sauced Cheese-topped Polenta Casserole

[POLENTA AL FORNO]

Arrange leftover **cold sliced polenta** in a casserole; sprinkle with chopped **garlic** and fresh **rosemary,** then spoon on **tomato sauce;** top with slices of Fontina, Gruyère, jack, Parmesan, or any flavorful white **cheese** or mixture of cheeses and bake in a preheated 450° oven until casserole is hot, lightly browned on top, and sizzling fragrantly.

Mess o' Greens Soup (Greens and Cornmeal Bisque)

◆ BASIC PANTRY

Serves 4 to 6

Cornmeal, especially leftover cooked cornmeal, is often used to thicken vegetable and bean soups in the corn-eating regions of the world.

I really like this soup's frugality: cabbage leaves (the big green ones from garden cabbage, which would otherwise be discarded; usually they are by the time the cabbages reach the supermarket) and leftover cooked cornmeal. Of course, if you have no cabbage, any hearty greens may be substituted: chard, spinach, dandelion greens, or a combination of greens (sometimes specialty shops or restaurant supply firms will market "winter greens" or "greens for sautéing"). And if you've no leftover cooked cornmeal, cook some from scratch. It's worth the effort because this is an unexpectedly delicious soup.

About 1 quart leafy greens such
  as green outer cabbage
  leaves, chard, dandelion, etc.
3 garlic cloves, coarsely
  chopped
2 leeks, cleaned and coarsely
  chopped
2 tablespoons unsalted butter
2 tablespoons flour
2 cups chicken or vegetable
  broth
2 cups milk
2/3 to 1 cup leftover cooked
  cornmeal, softened into a
  paste with the back of a
  spoon
1/4 teaspoon ground cumin
1 carrot, shredded

1. Blanch greens in boiling water. Rinse with cold water, then drain
well. When cool enough to handle, squeeze dry and coarsely chop into
thin ribbonlike slices. You should have about 2 cups. (Any extra greens
are delicious added to minestrone-type soups or tomatoey pasta sauces
or dressed in extra-virgin olive oil and red wine vinegar and served as a
salad.)

2. Lightly sauté garlic and leeks in butter until leeks are softened.
Sprinkle in flour, let cook a few minutes, then stir in broth. Continue
cooking until thickened.

3. Add greens, milk, and cooked cornmeal, cumin, and carrot, then
heat together until thickened and savory, about 5 minutes.

4. In a blender or food processor, puree half of soup and greens,
and return mixture to pan. Serve immediately.

◆◆◆◆◆◆

Couscous Couscous is a pasta made from milled semolina, a high-
gluten, high-protein wheat. It is probably the descendant of the world's
first pasta, no matter what the Chinese or Italians claim.

To make couscous, semolina flour is mixed with water into a paste
and rolled into pellets. It is then dried and stored until needed.

Couscous is a staple food throughout North Africa and parts of the
Middle East. It is also very popular in Paris, due to the large Algerian
population there.

The term *couscous* refers to not only the pasta, but to the amazing
dish—or rather, the wide variety of dishes—that couscous is the basis
for. The simple description is a spicy stew ladled over steamed couscous,
but that is an understatement indeed. Couscous, to those who have become addicted, is ambrosial, a meal of sensual pleasures, preferably

eaten with the hands. There are few restrictions on a couscous, and each home in each city, town, and village throughout North Africa and parts of the Middle East makes couscous differently. I remember fondly a couscous "joint" I used to frequent in Tel Aviv; their platters of couscous were ringed with plump meatballs that had peas in them. I will never forget those meatballs and walking back and forth from the restaurant along the sea next to the old city of Jaffa, under the starry black sky. In Italy I ate a couscous of ginger-scented fish stew, and in Paris I used to order my couscous with charcoal-grilled merguez (spiced lamb sausages) and lots of harissa on the side, in case the merguez weren't spicy enough. For those lucky enough to live in the San Francisco Bay Area, wonderful couscous dishes are served at Joyce Goldstein's Square One.

For a selection of couscous dishes, refer to any good book on Middle Eastern cooking, such as Claudia Roden's 1968 classic *A Book of Middle Eastern Food*. My copy is worn out from cooking, and half the pages are partially burned away, having been dropped into the oven when I was particularly absorbed in a baking bastilla and simmering tajine.

Ginger-scented Couscous and Tomato Salad

◆◆ INTERMEDIATE PANTRY

Serves 4 to 6

Cook couscous according to package directions, using **chicken broth** as cooking liquid. When tender, dress generously with **extra-virgin olive oil** and **lemon juice,** a teaspoon or two of grated fresh **ginger,** and 3 diced **ripe tomatoes.** Season with salt and black or red pepper, and sprinkle with chopped fresh parsley and mint.

◆◆◆◆◆◆

Hominy Hominy is a particular type of dried corn that has been soaked in a wood ash solution to expand its flesh and loosen its tough outer husk, then cooked in fresh water until plump and tender. It has a rich, bland flavor that regular corn does not possess, much like that of tortilla flour or masa harina.

The English name *hominy* comes from the Indian word *rockahominie*, and the food originated with the Indians, who saved American colonists from starvation by sharing their native foodstuffs and growing techniques.

On the East Coast hominy is cooked with garden vegetables, beans, and bacon, but it comes into its glory in the Southwest and South of the Border, where it is cooked with spices and chilies. The Mexican pozole is a perfect example of this, the round chewy nubbles of hominy floating in a simple broth, and the dish enlivened with fresh chili salsa and a range of condiments and seasonings. Pozole is traditionally based on pork (the head is said to make the best pozole), but lamb and beef broths also can be the basis of hominy soups.

Hominy also may be crushed or ground into a paste, seasoned with chili spices, and wrapped in a banana leaf to be steamed for Central American–style tamales. In parts of West Africa it is cracked into chunks and cooked into a couscouslike mixture.

When hominy is ground into a coarse meal it is called hominy grits, or just plain grits. It can be purchased in three forms: regular, which takes 20 to 25 minutes to prepare; quick cooking, which is ready in 6 to 7 minutes; and instant, which needs only a bath of boiling water to turn it into a bowl of cozy cooked grits. Grits is a Deep South breakfast specialty, usually found next to a slice of country ham.

Venezuelan "Tamales"

[HALLACA]

◆◆ INTERMEDIATE PANTRY

Serves 4 to 6

These hominy-based tamales are equally good unfilled, accompanying a spicy stew.

Two 8-ounce cans hominy, preferably white, drained
1/3 cup shortening
1 teaspoon New Mexico or ancho chili powder, or to taste
1 teaspoon salt
Banana leaves or aluminum foil

Assorted fillings: A cup or so chili-braised or pot-roasted meats, cut into bite-sized pieces; 3 tablespoons raisins; 1/4 cup or so pitted black olives (ripe or a mild Mediterranean-cured olive); mild green chili strips

1. In a blender or food processor, puree hominy into a moist meal. Add shortening, chili powder, and salt and mix well.

2. Warm banana leaves over high heat and, when pliable, cut into lengths of 12–15 inches. Spread 3–4 tablespoonsful of pureed mixture onto each one, then fold over—sides first, then top and bottom. This will form a parcel, flattish at the edges, thicker in the middle. If filling,

place a small amount of filling on top of hominy mixture before closing each parcel.

3. Place parcels in a steamer and steam over a high heat for 35 to 40 minutes.

Chilied Hominy and Peanut Soup, Equadorean Style

Serves 4

A hearty, satisfying soup with autumnal overtones in both color and flavor. The peanut butter is not a strong presence; it just gives a rich roundness to this slightly spicy South American peasant soup.

1 green bell pepper, diced
1 red bell pepper, diced
1 onion, diced
4 to 5 garlic cloves, coarsely chopped
3 tablespoons olive oil
1/2 to 1 jalapeño chili, chopped (include seeds for heat; discard for a less *picante* flavor)
Good pinch ground cumin
5 cups combined lamb and chicken, beef, or pork broth

1 teaspoon mild chili powder such as ancho, New Mexico, or pasilla
4 cups cooked hominy, drained
2 tablespoons crunchy peanut butter
Pinch of cayenne pepper, or to taste
Salt to taste
Wedges of lemon

1. Lightly sauté green and red peppers, along with onion and garlic, in olive oil until softened; add chili and cumin and cook a minute longer.

2. Add broth, chili powder, and hominy. Bring to a boil, then reduce heat and simmer for 10 minutes or long enough to meld flavors. Stir in peanut butter and season with cayenne pepper; add salt if needed.

3. Serve with wedges of lemon.

◆◆◆◆◆◆

Millet Though eaten as a grain, millet—like wild rice—is actually the seed of a grass. Since it thrives in inhospitable soils and climates, it is an important part of the diet of much of Africa, Asia, and India. It also comes in a variety of colors not available here: white, brown, red, and black in addition to the familiar yellow. It has a bland, slightly nutty flavor, somewhat like corn or hominy, and it pairs well with spicy stews and curry, while its powerful nutrition sustains.

Millet is an ancient food that was grown in China even before rice was. In many regions, the Chinese still depend on it as a staple, making pancake-like breads and savory porridges. In India it is simmered into pilafs and baked into flatbreads, while in Ethiopia it is ground and made into injera, the spongy tortilla-like staff of life that their spicy stews, or wats, are ladled onto. Until recently, most of the American supply of millet went to feed birds. These days, however, fiber-consciousness has changed that, with varieties of grains sought after.

NOTE When cooking millet, toasting before simmering brings out its nutty flavor and helps it keep its crunch.

Swiss Cumin-scented Millet-Cheese Pilaf

[HIRSOTTO]

◆◆ INTERMEDIATE PANTRY

Serves 4

This dish will win you over if you've never eaten millet—and will add to your repertoire if you're an old millet hand. The dish is Swiss, a delicious relic of the pre-industrial age when wheat bread was not available to the common person but unground grains were. *Hirsotto* tastes of onions and cheese and nutty, crunchy millet, enlivened by the bite of cumin seeds. Serve as you would any rice or grain side dish.

1 medium onion, coarsely chopped
2 tablespoons unsalted butter
1/2 cup millet
2 teaspoons cumin seeds
3 cups broth of choice

4 ounces Gruyère cheese, coarsely grated (about 3/4–1 cup)
Pepper to taste (broth and cheese are both salty so you probably won't need to add salt)

1. Sauté onion in butter, then, when softened, add millet and cumin seeds.
2. Raise heat and let millet and cumin lightly brown.
3. Add broth, reduce heat to medium, cover, and cook for 15 to 20 minutes.
4. Fork in cheese and toss well, letting it all melt into a delicious, though somewhat messy, potful.

Oats Most of us grew up eating oatmeal, discarded it, then lived through the oat bran dictatorship whereby if one didn't worship at the altar of oat bran the punishment was worse than eternal damnation: clogged arteries and guilt.

Oatmeal is good unless it's cooked to a gluey mess. It has a subtle, pleasantly starchy flavor and consistency. Raw, it is great added to meatloaf or made into a muesli.

Oats are available hulled, steel cut, or rolled (with variations on this rolled theme: instant and precooked); there also is oat bran and oat flour. I don't buy oat flour, but do grind my own occasionally, using a blender to whirl dry oatmeal until it reaches the consistency of flour. Mix it with regular flour and add it to recipes at will. I sometimes add it to wheat flour for tortillas de harina. The oatmeal adds a somewhat sweet quality reminiscent of the flatbreads of Italy's Emilia-Romagna region, making tortillas great breakfast fare, especially spread with sweet butter and strawberry jam.

Indiana Oatmeal Pie

◆ **BASIC PANTRY**

Serves 6

The following crustless tart is pure American country, refined from its Indiana origins with the addition of almond flavoring. It's a chewy, informal sweet, perfect for accompanying mugs of hot coffee or tea on a chilly afternoon. The batter may also be prepared in a square pan like brownies, or poured into a crust and baked like a pie.

4 eggs, lightly beaten
1 cup brown sugar
2 tablespoons flour
2 teaspoons ground cinnamon
1/4 teaspoon salt
1 cup light corn syrup or
English golden syrup

2 tablespoons soft unsalted
butter
1 teaspoon almond or vanilla
extract
1 cup old-fashioned oatmeal

1. Preheat oven to 350°.
2. Mix eggs with sugar, flour, cinnamon, salt, and corn syrup or golden syrup. Whisk in soft butter, then add extract and oatmeal.

3. Pour into a pie tin and bake for 30 to 40 minutes, or until top is crusty.

4. Let cool and enjoy at room temperature.

Chive-flavored Oat and Cheddar Crackers

◆◆ INTERMEDIATE PANTRY

Makes 2 dozen crackers

Homemade crackers are crisp and hearty. These, based on oat bran and cheese, are seasoned with chives and topped with coarse salt, and cumin, caraway, and sesame seeds.

1 cup unbleached all-purpose flour	6 ounces sharp Cheddar, finely shredded (about 1-3/4 cup)
1/2 cup oat bran	1/2 cup chopped fresh chives
1/2 teaspoon salt, plus a little extra for sprinkling	1 egg yolk, beaten with 2 tablespoons cold water
Pinch cayenne pepper	Several tablespoons *each* cumin, caraway, and sesame seeds
4 tablespoons cold unsalted butter, cut into small pieces	Salt for sprinkling

1. Preheat oven to 375°.

2. Mix flour with oat bran, salt, and cayenne. Cut in butter, using two knives or a pastry cutter, until it resembles fine crumbs. Then add cheese, cutting in until it looks like coarse crumbs.

3. Add chives and egg yolk mixture, adding up to 2 tablespoons more of water in order to make a well-moistened dough. Gather dough into a ball.

4. Divide this into several balls, place on a lightly floured board, and roll each ball into a disc roughly 1/8 inch thick. Cut into shapes with a cookie cutter, or use a knife and cut the dough into long, thin triangles (the shape I like best for these crackers, since the points get particularly crunchy).

5. Lightly grease a baking sheet and arrange dough shapes. Press seeds onto each cracker and sprinkle with salt.

6. Bake for 15 to 20 minutes, or until edges are starting to brown and bottoms are golden.

7. Cool on wire racks and store in airtight containers for up to 2 weeks.

NOTE Crackers may be frozen for up to 3 months, though they will probably need crisping in the oven. To recrisp, place in low oven for 10 minutes or so.

◆◆◆◆◆◆

Rice Indigenous to Asia, rice has been cultivated for a very long time. Whether it was first grown in 6000 or 5000 B.C.E. in Southeast Asia or China, or whether it was much later, in India in 3000 B.C.E., no one knows.

The Moors brought it to Europe in the Middle Ages, and the explorers carried it to the New World, where it resisted cultivation until the 17th century. Now America is the world's largest exporter of rice. In fact if you drive through California's Central Valley at certain times of the year, the freeway inevitably will pass over a huge paddy, as the massive fields are flooded for cultivation.

Rice is capable of supplying 80 percent of the body's nutritional requirements and is the staple food for most of Asia. There are over 40,000 varieties known, each varying as to length of grain—short, medium, or long—and degrees of stickiness. Preferences vary all over the world, and a well-rounded pantry stocks a sampling of the basic types. Arborio rice, for example, has a distinctive texture and flavor, making it the only choice for risotti, while short-grained Japanese or California rice is the choice for sushi or any dish where the rice's ability to cling together is prized: stuffed vine leaves, puddings, fritters. Basmati has a fragrance and consistency that lends itself brilliantly to Indian pilafs; try, too, Basmati Rice with Lime Segments, Cilantro, Green Onions, and Jalapeños, page 215. Brown rice makes the most comforting of puddings, a hearty filling for stuffed vine leaves, and a bed for spicy red beans. And plain white rice—both long and short grained—can be served in a great number of ways, not the least of which is lavishly buttered and seasoned with salt and pepper, to be eaten with a spoon when you are very tired.

Long-grained rices cook up fluffy and separate, while short-grained rices are thicker, and cook up into softer grains that tend to stick together. Long-grain rice is the choice for pilaf, while short-grained rice should be served with Japanese dishes. This dictum holds true for both brown and white rice, by the way.

STORAGE TIP Store raw rice as you would other grains; cooked, it lasts about 5 days in the refrigerator.

ARBORIO RICE A short, stubby rice grown in Italy's Po Valley. California Pearl may be used in place of Arborio in some dishes; Spain, too, grows a similar, delicious short-grain rice. Arborio has a distinctive texture and aroma, and its density lends itself particularly well to risotto.

Rice is usually cooked to a dry, fluffy state, with stirring and the removal of the lid during cooking *verboten*. Risotto, on the other hand, is cooked with no lid and stirred all the while it cooks. The result is a creamy sauce binding together nearly al dente plump grains. It can be soupy or thick and porridgy, and almost any food can be added to it.

When done right, preparing risotto is almost a meditation, stirring and stirring the broth and wine into the rice, adding more as the thirsty grains absorb the liquid, demanding more. By the time the grains of rice are tender, your tensions may have vanished. Then again, all that stirring could be nerve-wracking.

Microwave aficionados rave about microwaved risotto, saying it eliminates the constant stirring and attention. I resist, not necessarily because it doesn't taste as good, but because I like to feel what I am cooking, plain and simple. When a dish is encased in a black box, making strange humming noises and emitting harmful rays, the fun is all gone.

There are several risotti located in other chapters of this book. Try Risotto al Mare or Green Risotto with Pesto (page 367). Arborio is also delicious added to soups, such as the following hearty winter potage thick with rice, red beans, winter squash, and chard.

Thick Soup of Winter Squash, Red Beans, Chard, and Rice

[MINESTRA DI ZUCCO, FAGIOLI, E VERDURI]

For those who think of pumpkin and winter squashes as holiday fare, all buttered and sugared and whipped into a pie or casserole, this soup is a revelation. The slight sweetness of the squash gracefully balances the green freshness of the chard, the chewiness of the Arborio rice, and the zestiness of the spicing.

Serve along with crusty bread to dip into the bottom of the bowl, and follow with warm roast duck or shortribs braised in Zinfandel, then pears baked with brandy and cream for dessert. And if you're in

Serves 4

the mood for a risotto instead of a soup, decrease the liquid to 2-1/2 to 3 cups and stir, stir, stir. (Cook the squash in a separate pan, then add it when the risotto is almost done to avoid getting a squash puree instead of chunks in your risotto.)

4 garlic cloves, minced	**1 cup coarsely chopped or**
2 tablespoons olive oil	**thinly sliced chard**
2 cups diced peeled winter	**Salt and pepper to taste**
squash, preferably Hubbard	**1/4 teaspoon dried oregano,**
1/2 cup Arborio rice	**crumbled**
6 cups chicken or other broth	**Grated Parmesan cheese**
1 cup tomato sauce	**2 tablespoons chopped fresh**
1 cup cooked and drained	**parsley**
kidney beans	

1. Lightly sauté garlic in olive oil until fragrant and golden. Do not brown. Add squash and toss to coat with garlic oil.

2. Add rice, broth, and tomato sauce, then cook over medium heat, covered, until squash is tender and rice cooked through. This should take 35 minutes or so.

3. Add beans, chard, salt, pepper, and oregano and heat together to cook chard and combine flavors, about 10 minutes.

4. Serve immediately, sprinkled with Parmesan and parsley.

Cucumber-Mango Rice

For a tropical accent to **plain buttered rice,** add diced ripe but firm **mango** and **cucumber,** then season with lots of **lime juice,** a dash of **salt** and **pepper,** and a sprinkling of chopped **fresh chives.**

Sushi Rice

Makes 5 cups, serves 4 to 6

Cook 2 cups short-grained white **rice** and let cool. While rice is cooling, heat 1/3 cup **rice vinegar** with 3 tablespoons **sugar** and 1 teaspoon **salt** just until sugar dissolves. Pour onto the still warm but not hot rice, mixing gently with a wooden spoon. Transfer rice to a ceramic bowl, taking care not to break up grains too much, and let rice sit and absorb vinegar.

When cooled, add 1 **green onion,** thinly sliced, 2 tablespoons diced **cucumber,** and 1 teaspoon thinly sliced **pickled ginger.**

Serve Sushi Rice garnished with diced fresh **raw tuna**—the silken tuna bits are a delicious contrast to the sweet-tart rice and fresh cucumber. Thin strips of **hijiki seaweed,** first soaked in **soy sauce**–seasoned water to make it pliable, is a traditional garnish, as is a sprinkling of **toasted sesame seeds.**

East-West Sushi Rice

Garnish a mound of **sushi rice,** above, with thin strips of **arugula** and **prosciutto or smoked salmon** and slices of **papaya or melon** sprinkled with some sweetened **rice vinegar.**

◆◆◆◆◆◆

BASMATI RICE Long, slender-grained, and fragrant, basmati rice is favored in India, Pakistan, and parts of Iran for pilafs and biryanis. (Texas grows a delicious basmati rice called Texmati.) Its taste and aroma is hauntingly distinctive, and the grains keep their integrity rather than becoming mushy when cooked. The character of basmati is due in part to its horticultural heritage and genetics, in part to the soil and climate where it is grown, but in addition, it is aged a year, while other rices are not. While white basmati is most commonly available, having been favored in India, increasingly you can find brown basmati rice. Simply increase the cooking time as you would for any whole grain, and consider its nutty flavor when pairing it with other foods.

Coconut Basmati Rice with Raisins

◆◆ INTERMEDIATE PANTRY

Makes 3 to 4 cups

Slightly sweet from the coconut milk and raisins, this rice dish is perfect to pair with a sleek and spicy fresh chutney or salsa and grilled marinated kebabs.

2 cups basmati rice
5 cups water
1/3 cup unsweetened coconut milk
3 tablespoons unsweetened

dried or fresh shredded coconut
Pinch of salt
3 tablespoons golden raisins
Pinch ground turmeric

1. Boil rice in water until rice is slightly more than half cooked. Rice will be nearly tender, but still crunchy inside.

2. Drain, then return to pot. Add coconut milk, coconut, salt, and raisins, then place a clean cloth or paper towel over top of pan and cover with a lid.

3. Cook over very low heat for about 10 minutes, or until rice is just tender. Sprinkle with turmeric and serve.

Basmati with Lime Segments, Cilantro, Green Onions, and Jalapeños

◆◆ INTERMEDIATE PANTRY

Serves 4

Rice with lime, cilantro, green onions, and fresh chilies is a bracing combination eaten in many regions of the world: Mexico, the Middle East, Southeast Asia, India. It is a dish of elegant simplicity, with intense flavor and spunk. Try to take the trouble to peel the lime segments; it gives the dish a suaveness.

◆◆◆◆◆◆

TO PREPARE Cook 2 cups basmati rice as you would ordinary long-grain rice, by boiling, then cooking covered. When just tender, **butter** generously. Top hot buttered rice with segments from 1 to 2 small **limes,** peeled of pith and membranes (if you cannot be bothered peeling pith, simply coarsely chop lime flesh), 3 to 4 thinly sliced **green onions,** 1/4 cup coarsely chopped **fresh cilantro** leaves, and 2 **jalapeños,** seeded and chopped or thinly sliced.

VARIATION Use 2 tablespoons chopped **fresh mint** for 2 tablespoons of the cilantro.

◆◆◆◆◆◆

BROWN RICE The macrobiotic crowd hail it as the cure-all food, alleviating all the ills of both body and soul. But take away the mystical mumblings and you have a good healthy food that can keep a person alive and happy with very few other additions to the diet.

Brown rice has the added nutrition and fiber of whole versus milled grain. It also has a nutty flavor and chewy texture that are wonderful additions to many dishes where white rice would be insipid.

TO PREPARE Place 2 cups short or long grain brown rice in a pot with 4 cups water and 1/2 teaspoon salt. Bring to boil, cover, and reduce heat to a low simmer. Cook for 30–40 minutes. Do not uncover or stir. When tender, fluff with fork and season as desired with butter, soy sauce, and so forth.

Brown Rice–stuffed Grape Leaves

[DOLMADHES]

◆◆ INTERMEDIATE PANTRY

Serves 6 to 8 as a first course or appetizer

Greek stuffed vine leaves are filled with rice or meat and rice. The rice of choice is usually white, but brown rice will accept stronger spicing, resulting in a tastier packet.

Dolmadhes are one of those foods that had its 15 minutes of fame and was then relegated to the ethnic food festival category. But good stuffed grape leaves are a wonder to eat. These are seasoned in the way I used to enjoy them on Crete, with a good shot of cumin and a delicious balance of sweet, tangy, fresh, and spicy.

8 to 10 garlic cloves (coarsely chop 3 cloves)
2 cups cooked brown rice
1-1/4 cups plain yogurt
6 to 10 green onions, thinly sliced
1-1/2 teaspoon ground cumin
1/2 to 1 teaspoon ground cinnamon, or to taste
1/4 cup raisins
1/4 cup coarsely chopped fresh

mint leaves, or 1 tablespoon crushed dried mint
1 egg, lightly beaten
Juice of 1 lemon
One 8-ounce jar grape leaves
1/4 cup extra-virgin olive oil
1/4 cup Kalamata olives, for garnish
1 lemon, cut into wedges
Yogurt-Mint Dipping Sauce, following

1. Combine 3 chopped garlic cloves with brown rice, 1/4 cup yogurt, green onions, cumin, cinnamon, raisins, mint, egg, and lemon juice.

2. Remove grape leaves from bottle and rinse under cold water to remove excess salt.

3. Place 1 grape leaf, vein side up, on plate or in palm of hand and top with about 1 tablespoon filling near bottom of leaf. Fold bottom of leaf over filling, fold in sides, then roll toward top. Repeat with remaining filling and leaves.

4. Arrange stuffed leaves in a steamer with enough water on bottom to get good steam but to not touch grape leaves. Cut remaining garlic cloves into halves and tuck them around stuffed grape leaves. Drizzle with olive oil, cover, and steam over a high heat for 45 minutes, adding more water to steamer if it gets low and threatens to burn.

5. Let cool and serve at room temperature, garnished with Kalamata olives, wedges of lemon, and a bowl of yogurt-mint dipping sauce.

6. Dolmadhes will keep, covered and refrigerated, up to a week.

Yogurt-Mint Dipping Sauce

Combine 1 cup plain **yogurt** with 1 chopped **garlic clove** and 2 teaspoons chopped **fresh mint or** 1 teaspoon crushed **dried mint.**

Brown Rice Pudding

◆ BASIC PANTRY

Serves 4

Hearty and comforting even when nothing is wrong, brown rice pudding is a cozy bowl of nutty rice simmered creamily with a little sugar or honey, lemon zest, and vanilla. It makes good cold-weather breakfast food, eaten warm while trying to summon the courage to face the cold and gloom.

My trick is to make this dish the day after a Chinese take-out supper. I order an extra portion of plain brown rice. The next morning it's waiting for me in its little cardboard container, all ready to be warmed through with milk and turned into pudding.

4 cups cooked unseasoned brown rice
Tiny pinch of salt
2 cups milk
Zest of 1/4 lemon (wash well to rid it of pesticides and dirt) left in one large piece or finely minced

1/4 cup honey or sugar, or to taste
2 eggs, lightly beaten
1/2 teaspoon vanilla extract
1/2 teaspoon ground cinnamon

1. Combine rice, salt, milk, lemon zest, and honey or sugar, and heat over medium heat until milk is boiling. Reduce heat and cook over medium heat until about two-thirds of milk is absorbed.

2. Add a spoonful or two of rice mixture to beaten eggs and mix well, then, off heat, stir eggs into hot rice and milk mixture. Return pan to stove, and over very low heat or in a double boiler, simmer and stir until thickened. Do not let heat get high or egg will curdle.

3. Add vanilla (and remove lemon zest if desired), then pour pudding in a large bowl or individual bowls. Sprinkle with cinnamon.

4. Eat immediately or let cool.

Gelato di Riso

Prepare above pudding, decreasing the amount of rice to 2 cups, and using **Arborio rice** in place of brown. For the liquid use 1 cup **heavy (whipping) cream** in place of 1 cup of milk. Prepare pudding, then freeze as you would ice cream, stirring and scraping the sides every so often to break up ice crystals and grains of rice.

Black Rice Pudding

This is a Western adaptation of the simple sweetened glutinous rice dishes of Southeast Asia.

◆◆◆◆◆◆

TO PREPARE Use **black rice** in place of brown in the Brown Rice Pudding recipe, page 217. For Black Rice Pudding Ice Cream, prepare as for Gelato di Riso, above.

Other Rices for Your Pantry

◆◆◆◆◆◆

BLACK AND RED Newly cultivated in California, these exotics are usually added to rice blends; the black, which occasionally will be found on its own, cooks up to a rather sticky, inky-colored, but delicious potful.

GLUTINOUS Also known as sweet, or sticky, rice, glutinous rice sticks together and is sweeter and more strongly flavored than plain rice. Eaten as the daily rice in parts of Thailand and Laos, it is usually relegated to sweets in other parts of Asia, where it is often cooked with coconut milk and tossed with ripe mangos.

LONG-GRAIN EXOTICA Thai jasmine-scented rice and Louisiana wild pecan rice are both worth picking up if you find them. They cook like other long-grained rices, with the flavor overtones their names suggest.

WHEANI (also known as wehani) is a California hybrid brown rice with a genetic link to basmati rice. It has a reddish color, is very aromatic, and is usually found only in rice combination mixes.

RICE PRODUCTS Rice is found in our pantry shelves in a growing variety of forms other than the grain. Puffed rice crackers give delicious satisfaction and crunch yet deliver little in the way of calories or fat. There are also rice noodles from Asia, with their soft noodle quality and subtle rice flavor, and cereals and pilaf mixtures. Rice paper from Vietnam is a delicious curiosity and a boon for any pantry: simply moisten with water and wrap up morsels of spicy foods and fresh herbs. And don't forget rice flour, which contributes a brittle crispness when added to fritter batter, especially the Indian ones based on chick-pea flour, or besan.

Other Grains for Your Pantry

AMARANTH The Aztecs called amaranth "grain of the gods" because of the mystical qualities attributed to it. On ceremonial occasions it was mixed with honey and human blood to form wafers. By the time of the 16th Century Spanish occupation, possession of amaranth had become a crime, the punishment for which was having one's hands cut off. This hearty grain is good in pilaf, soups, spicy stews, and so on. Its leaves make a delicious addition to green salads.

QUINOA High in calcium and protein, this ancient Peruvian grain thrives at very high altitudes: it was first grown on terraces on the mountains that surround Machu Picchu. Quinoa looks somewhat like a cross between mustard and millet. The tiny grains cook up in about 15 minutes. It should be light and delicate but presents two pitfalls: it must be rinsed well (at least twice under running water) to rid it of any bitterness. And it should be cooked in abundant water, then drained before serving, as the grain exudes a sticky, viscous substance called saponin, reminiscent of okra or nopales. Quinoa is often cooked into pilaf-type dishes and eaten as a savory grain dish, and is good as a grain salad with nuts, dried fruit, and fresh herbs, dressed with vinaigrette.

RYE dates back to the Roman empire, though now it is most popular in Eastern Europe, Germany, and Russia for use in sourdough and heavy black pumpernickel breads. Rye is sold ground into flour, rolled into flakes and used in cereal mixtures, and as whole berries, much like wheat. In fact, a pilaf of wheat and rye berries is fantastic.

TEFF A highly nutritional wheat-like grain, teff is the size of a pinhead. It's the staple food of Ethiopia, where it is ground into flour and made into large tortilla-like pancakes.

TRITICALE Recently developed, this grain combines the good qualities of wheat and rye in regard to protein content, gluten, and high yield. Often used in bread. May be used in any way that wheat or rye berries are.

Wild Rice Wild rice is the seed of an aquatic grass (*Zizania aquatica*) indigenous to North America. It was so valuable to the Indians of the Great Lakes region that at one time they used it as currency. Most of the wild rice sold these days is grown largely in Minnesota and Idaho, though California has enthusiastically entered the arena.

The traditional Great Lakes type of wild rice can grow grains of up to an inch in length. Length is the guideline for judging quality and market value. These days much of the "wild" rice available is cultivated in paddies like regular rice, and though its length is not as luxurious as the purely wild, its price is much more appealing. And regardless of length, look for grains that are whole, not broken.

Wild rice is at its best paired with other grains, since by itself it is a bit intense. There are numerous combinations of wild and other exotic rices available these days, most of them grown in California's Central Valley. A bag or two on your pantry shelf means you always have a simple, hearty accompaniment to a roast chicken or braised pot roast, or a means of adding interest to a virtuous pot of steamed vegetables. Wild rice and rice combinations are good cooked at the beginning of the week and added to other foods such as waffles, pancakes, muffins, and soups as the week progresses. It lasts up to about 5 days refrigerated; let your nose be your guide. You can also freeze several portions to use as desired.

Basic Wild Rice

◆◆ INTERMEDIATE PANTRY

Makes 3-1/2 to 4 cups

While these are the basic cooking guidelines, they are just that. As with other grains and legumes, the age of the grains helps determine the cooking time. I once had some very old wild rice that took what seemed like hours to cook. But it tasted fine.

◆◆◆◆◆

TO PREPARE Rinse and drain 1 cup **wild rice**. Bring 3 or 4 inches **lightly salted water** to a boil in a medium (2 quart or so) saucepan. Add wild rice and boil uncovered over high heat until grains are barely tender, 40 minutes to an hour.

Drain (saving liquid for soup) and cover; let sit in its own steam for 10 minutes or so.

Wild Rice Waffles with Porcini Butter and Sausages

◆◆◆ ADVANCED PANTRY

Serves 4

Leftover wild or wild and brown rice makes a very good waffle—the juxtaposition of luxurious wild rice and homey waffle is enticing. Wild rice waffles are delicious with wild mushroom butter, and with sausage and sage leaves; enjoy for an autumn brunch or supper.

1 ounce dried porcini mushrooms	2 eggs
4 tablespoons unsalted butter, softened	1-1/2 cups milk
	2/3 cup oil or melted butter
2 cups unbleached all-purpose flour	1 cup cooked wild or mixed wild and brown rices
1 teaspoon salt	1 pound fennel-scented or hot Italian sausages
1 tablespoon baking powder	Fresh sage leaves

1. Rehydrate porcini by pouring hot water over them, soaking, and squeezing dry (see page 138). Chop coarsely and mix with softened butter. Set aside.

2. Sift flour, salt, and baking powder together.

3. Mix eggs with milk and oil or butter, then stir cooked wild rice into liquid.

4. Mix liquid ingredients with dry ingredients, stirring only until just combined. Overbeating results in tough waffles.

5. Set batter aside while you brown sausages. Add sage leaves to pan when sausages are about half cooked and let them cook. Alternatively, skewer sausages with sage leaves and broil or grill over an open fire.

6. Heat waffle iron, oil lightly, and bake waffles. Serve waffles topped with a nugget of melting mushroom butter and a skewer or portion of browned sausage and sage leaves.

VARIATION Omit mushroom butter, sage, and Italian sausages and instead serve **waffles** topped with **maple syrup** and American sage-seasoned breakfast **sausages.**

Wild Rice and Turkey Soup with Porcini Mushrooms

Serves 4 to 6

The autumnal scent of turkey simmers with wild rice and porcini or other wild mushrooms for this rustic, robust soup.

6 ounces uncooked boned turkey thigh meat, cut into bite-sized (1 inch) pieces (about 1 cup)
1 onion, chopped
1/2 carrot, diced
1 bay leaf
3 tablespoons extra-virgin olive oil
1 tablespoon flour
1 cup wild rice

2 baking potatoes, peeled and diced
6 cups chicken or vegetable broth
1 ounce imported dried mushrooms such as porcini
1/2 pound fresh mushrooms, thinly sliced
1/4 cup dry sherry, Madeira, or Marsala
Salt and pepper to taste

1. Sauté turkey with onion, carrot, and bay leaf in 1 tablespoon olive oil until onion is softened and turkey is lightly browned. Sprinkle in flour and stir well.

2. Add wild rice, potatoes, and broth. Bring to a boil, then reduce heat and simmer until wild rice is nearly tender, 45 minutes or so.

3. Meanwhile, rehydrate mushrooms (see page 139), saving their soaking liquid for soup.

4. Sauté fresh mushrooms in remaining olive oil, then add rehydrated mushrooms to mixture. Cook until lightly browned and fragrant, then add to simmering soup along with strained soaking liquid.

5. Pour in sherry, Madeira, or Marsala and season to taste. Serve immediately.

About Beans and Legumes

Beans and legumes were grown in Asia, Africa, and the Americas long before the start of the Common Era. Beans have been found in Bronze Age deposits in Europe dating from circa 3000 B.C.E. Beans played an important part in the burial rituals of ancient Egypt, Rome, and Greece, where they were placed in tombs to nourish the departed on their journey to the next world. In Greece, they were used as a voting tool with a white bean indicating "for," and a black bean "against."

Beans were an important part of the American Indian diet and culture when the colonists arrived. No doubt the first pot of Boston baked beans was put together during that first shatteringly cold winter.

Along with grains, dried beans and legumes (including lentils, split peas, and black-eyed peas) sustain more of the world than any other food. Full of protein and complex carbohydrates, they are available in winter when little emerges from the cold earth.

With 15,000 species of beans and legumes, deciding what to keep on your pantry shelf might seem overwhelming. Not to worry: only 20 or so types of beans and a handful of legumes are readily available.

The flavors and textures of beans and legumes range from the chestnut-like chick-pea to the grassy flageolet, the starchy pinto, and the creamy butter bean. Black beans have a distinctive flavor not easily confused with anything else, plus they have the good manners to make their own inky sauce.

With their bland flavor and starchy consistency, beans take readily to strong seasonings, and they grow more delicious the longer they are cooked. This makes them a star in the ethnic kitchens of the world, where beans are often tossed into liquid and set in a slow wood-burning oven or over an open fire. *Cholent* is the classic dish of this genre, prepared for centuries by observant Jews, the beans mixed with grains, meats, and seasonings, then placed in a slow oven as a meal for the sabbath or the following day, when religious law prohibits the lighting of stoves. This idea spread to the Puritans and migrated to the New World, where it evolved into Boston baked beans.

Dried beans are usually available in wide variety in natural foods shops and specialty grocers, but they are also available in an increasingly interesting array in ordinary supermarkets.

STORAGE TIPS Beans and legumes keep their flavor and tenderness for up to a year; after that they can be tough and their flavor diminishes steadily. Store in tightly sealed jars to protect against insects, and keep in a cool, dry place. Once damp they will absorb moisture and spoil.

Cooked beans should be stored in the refrigerator, where they will last 1 to 4 days before going sour. Beans and legumes will thicken as they cool and solids will sink to the bottom; stir well before reheating so that the solids at the bottom don't burn, and add more liquid if necessary to get the consistency you want.

Beans The biggest drawback to beans is their cooking time; they take hours. At the end of the day, when faced with a choice of waiting three hours for a pot of beans and having a plate of pasta within ten minutes, only the diehard beanophile would choose to wait. A little advance preparation can make beans as easily available to your table as that fish fillet or plate of spaghetti.

Simply cook up batches of beans in advance and freeze them in 1- or 2-cup portions. They will last up to 5 months and, like a good Girl or Boy Scout, you'll always be prepared. The other thing to do is keep your pantry supplied with canned beans in addition to dried and frozen cooked beans. Canned beans are surprisingly acceptable. Though many are rather salty or mushy, that can usually be remedied by rinsing them and decreasing their cooking time with other ingredients. I have always railed against them, but recently changed my ways when I found out that some delicious beans I had been happily forking up were in fact canned. I'm no snob—canned beans have since become a part of my pantry. Note, though, that they should be rinsed if they are to be used in a salad, and they're best when used as part of a dish rather than the focus.

Pantry List: Beans and Legumes

◆◆◆◆◆◆

BEANS

Anasazi	Flageolets	Pinquito
Appaloosa	Great Northern	Pinto
Azuki	Jacobs cattle	Red
Black	Kidney (red, white,	Runner
Borlotti	brown, and black)	Soldier
Butter	Lima	Soy
Cannellini	Mung	Swedish brown
Chick-peas	Navy	White
Cranberry	Pink	Yellow-eye
Fava		

LEGUMES

Black-eyed peas (pigeon peas)	Indian lentils (red, white, black, oily, etc.)	Puy lentils Yellow split peas
Brown lentils		
Green split peas		

MISCELLANEOUS

Mixtures of grains, beans and legumes sold for soup

Bean Basics

One pound dried beans equals 2 cups dried and 5 to 6 cups cooked, except for limas, which make slightly less, and mung beans, which make slightly more.

ANASAZI (Cooking time after soaking: 1 to 1-1/2 hours)—Named after the Anasazi Indians, who originally cultivated the purple-and-white mottled bean. They may be used in the same ways as pinto beans for a rustic Southwestern flavor.

APPALOOSA (Cooking time after soaking: 1-1/2 to 2 hours)—Like anasazi and Jacobs cattle beans, Appaloosas are from the Southwest, and are notable for their earthy flavor and satisfying, starchy consistency, as well as their mottled colors. Appaloosas are speckled black on a white background and, like Jacobs cattle beans, although their markings fade with cooking, they do not entirely disappear.

AZUKI (Cooking time after soaking: 1 to 1-1/2 hours)—Tiny beans from Japan with a deep red color. Azuki have a pea-like flavor and are eaten with brown rice by those on macrobiotic diets.

BLACK (Cooking time after soaking: 1-1/2 hours)—Their rich distinctive flavor is an important part of the cuisines of many regions of Central and South America. Black beans combine brilliantly with spicy foods and other hearty flavors for sustaining stews; as purees they are spread on tortillas and sandwiches; as sauces they are ladled over steamed rice. In parts of Mexico the inky cooking liquid is used to cook rice and to mix with ground corn for tortillas. The Brazilian *feijoada* is a feast meal based on rice and black beans, accompanied with a wide variety of grilled sausages and meats, sliced oranges, and cooked greens. Black bean soup is eaten in parts of the South and the Caribbean.

BORLOTTI (Cooking time after soaking: 1-1/2 hours)—Similar to the cranberry bean, this Italian bean is plump and striated with red, and cooks into a pink-brown solid color. Borlotti are cooked in risotti, soups, stews, and the like. Usually more available in the United States in cans rather than dried, it is occasionally found fresh. Cranberry beans may be substituted for borlotti.

BUTTER (Cooking time after soaking: 45 minutes to 1 hour)—A creamy, buttery texture and mild flavor makes this flat, wide kidney-shaped bean a favorite on the American table. It also takes less time to cook, so can be added to soups, stews and other dishes without pre-cooking, by adding a bit of time to the cooking.

CANNELLINI (Cooking time after soaking: 1-1/2 hours)—Italian white kidney beans, cannellini are delicious as a base for soups (especially minestrone), tomatoey stews, and pureed with garlic as a zesty appetizer spread. In America they are more often found in cans than dried.

CHICK-PEAS (Cooking time after soaking: 1-1/2 to 2 hours)—Nutty and firm, with a distinct round shape and golden color, chick-peas (aka garbanzo beans) are favored throughout the Mediterranean and India. They may be mashed into hummus or cooked with pasta, tossed with couscous or stewed with lamb; in some parts of the Middle East they are soaked and coated with a sugar shell, then eaten as a candylike nibble.

CRANBERRY (Cooking time after soaking: 1-1/2 hours)—Nutty and slightly sweet, with a somewhat mealy texture, cranberry beans are delicious added to soups and Italian and Latin American/Caribbean dishes. Also known as shell beans, these New World natives are one half of the corn-bean pairing that is succotash.

FAVA (Cooking time after soaking: 1 to 2 hours)—Small or large, fava beans are possibly the oldest bean known. They are a mainstay in Egypt, where they are ground into felafel or drizzled with olive oil, garlic, and lemon, or stuffed into pita with raw vegetable salad. Favas are one of the more distinctively flavored beans: slightly bitter, with a pungent, almost primitive taste.

FLAGEOLET (Cooking time after soaking: 1 to 1-1/2 hours)—Green-white oval beans favored in France as the traditional accompaniment to garlic-roast lamb; they make a good addition to soups, pasta dishes, and stews and have a flavor at once grassy and meaty.

GREAT NORTHERN (Cooking time after soaking: 1 to 1-1/2 hours)—The most commonly available white bean in America, Great Northerns are an all-purpose bean for long-cooked casseroles and stews. Somewhat kidney shaped, they cook up soft with a flavor that is balanced between starch and vegetable.

JACOBS CATTLE (Cooking time after soaking: 1-1/2 to 2 hours)—Hefty kidney-shaped beans with red-brown speckles on a white background that resemble the marks on brown and white cattle. Use as you would pinto beans, white beans, red kidney beans.

KIDNEY (Cooking time after soaking: 1-1/2 hours)—Indigenous to the Americas, kidney beans have a starchy, bland, and slightly sweet flavor, with somewhat tough skins holding the soft flesh in. Red kidney beans are the most popular beans in the United States, eaten in soups and chili con carne, three-bean salads and casseroles, but recently other colors of kidney beans have become more available: white, brown (hearty and delicious for Mediterranean dishes), and black (with a flavor somewhere in between black and kidney beans). I like kidney beans marinated in olive oil, garlic, wine vinegar, ancho or New Mexico chili powder, chopped thyme and cilantro. Superb.

LIMA (Cooking time after soaking: 45 minutes to an hour)—Starchy and mild, lima beans are delicious in hearty winter soups, especially when combined with root vegetables and barley. Lima beans hail originally from Peru, hence the name. They come in small and large, the larger ones being known as butter beans; in their native land, there are varieties of lima beans that grow to the size of duck eggs.

MUNG (Cooking time after soaking: 30 to 40 minutes)—Small and dark-green skinned, mung beans have a strong pea flavor, and are eaten by health food advocates, usually as a salad or in soup. I prefer mung beans sprouted.

NAVY (Cooking time after soaking: 1-1/2 hours)—Also known as pea beans, these roundish small beans are used in long-simmered dishes such as Boston Baked Beans or soups. They have a firm texture, and will keep their shape when cooked.

PINK (Cooking time after soaking: 1 to 1-1/2 hours)—Somewhat of a cross between kidney beans and pinto, these have a similar rich and starchy flavor that go well with Southwestern and Puerto Rican spicing. There is a variety of smallish pink beans that fit into this category, especially in the Southwest.

PINQUITO (Cooking time after soaking: 1-1/2 hours)—Small and round-oval in shape, pinquito beans have a flavor and consistency much like pinto beans.

PINTO (Cooking time after soaking: 1 to 1-1/2 hours)—Variegated when raw and dried, cooking to a pale brown-pink color, pinto beans are the bean of choice for chili con carne and refried beans. Try seasoning pinto beans gently with chili spices and using them as a bed for grilled chicken, garnished with Ancho Chili Mayonnaise (page 155).

RED (Cooking time after soaking: 1 to 1-1/2 hours)—Like kidney beans but slightly smaller, red beans are most famous in New Orleans where they are simmered into the delectable red beans and rice, or simmered into dark, mysterious soups.

RUNNER (Cooking time after soaking: 1-1/2 to 2 hours)—Large and plumply oval, with a mottled skin, runner beans come in a selection of varieties, including scarlet, black, and white runner beans. Use in soups, European peasant braises, and ragouts of Mediterranean vegetables.

SOLDIER (Cooking time after soaking: 1-1/2 to 2 hours)—Long oval whitish beans with dark brown marks that are shaped like tiny soldiers. Mealy textured and good in hearty dishes.

SOYBEAN (Cooking time after soaking: 3 hours)—Their strong vegetable-oil flavor makes them not terribly popular on the table as is, but these Chinese natives are amazingly versatile: ground into a flour, their high protein content boosts any bread or baked good it's added to, and steeped in water they become a milk substitute. Tofu is likely the most well-known soy product: mild and creamy, tofu may be eaten stir-fried, deep-fried, pureed into sauce. Soy beans are often encountered in "texturized vegetable protein" or meat substitutes.

SWEDISH BROWN (Cooking time after soaking: 1-1/2 to 2 hours)—Small round beans with an ochre-brown color. Use for long-baked casseroles, stews, etc.

WHITE (Cooking time after soaking: 1 to 1-1/2 hours)—In between Great Northern and navy beans in both size and flavor, white beans may be used in any soup or stew that calls for a basic white bean. I prefer Italian cannellini or French white beans for their fuller flavor, but they are not as easily available here.

YELLOW-EYE (Cooking time after soaking: 1-1/2 to 2 hours)—About the size and shape of a pinto bean, yellow-eye beans derive their name from their distinctly personalized yellow markings on a creamy white background. Use in cassoulets, especially one made with seafood.

Legume Basics

Legumes need no soaking.

STORAGE TIPS Keep cooked legumes, especially lentils, in the freezer. Ice cubes made from cooked lentils make an excellent spur-of-the-moment thickener for soups and sauces, while several cubes of black-eyed peas add interest to salads, spicy braises, etc.

BLACK-EYED PEAS (Cooking time: 1 to 1-1/2 hours)—Cream-colored kidney-shaped small beans with distinctive black "eyes." The flavor of black-eyed peas is less starchy and more vegetable-like than other beans and lends itself well to spicy flavoring. A favorite in the South, they are served marinated as "Texas caviar" or tossed with rice as "hoppin' John." In the Middle East they are known as *lubiyas* and are eaten in spicy vegetable soups and stews.

BROWN LENTILS (Cooking time: 40 to 50 minutes)—Brown lentils are the most easily available lentils, usually sold in the market as simply "lentils." Their rich, meaty flavor is delicious in soups, stews, salads, and so on. Cooked until just tender, they are marvelous marinated for a salad; cooked beyond that into a soft, thick porridge-like mixture, they make a robust basis for minestrone and vegetarian casseroles. Sausage and lentil combinations have become quite chic in recent years, and well they should: they bring out the best in each other.

FRENCH GREEN (PUY) LENTILS (Cooking time: 40 to 60 minutes)—These brown-green lentils are French in origin, are slightly smaller than our usual brown lentil, and full of robust earthy flavors. The Puy tends to hold its shape better than other lentils and as such is best for lentil salads dressed with a mustardy or walnut oil-based vinaigrette, served on a bed of frisée lettuce.

GREEN SPLIT PEAS (Cooking time: About 60 minutes)—Split peas are the basis of the classic soup, but are also good served as a puree alongside roasts, etc.

INDIAN LENTILS (Cooking time: 40 minutes)—Indian lentils come in a wide array of colors, each with its own distinctive flavor, texture, and aroma. My favorite, and the one I find most useful in my pantry, is the red lentil, or masoor dal, a tiny red-orange legume that cooks up into a soft yellow mush in about 40 minutes' time. Seasoned with curry, ginger, onions and garlic, it is a superb accompaniment to any Indian-style meal, as well as an excellent basis for soups and sauces.

YELLOW SPLIT PEAS (Cooking time: About 60 minutes)—Yellow split peas are similar to green split peas in texture, consistency, and cooking time, but their flavors are not the same. While the green peas have a strong pea flavor, the yellow peas are more like Indian red lentils, and I find that the two can be used interchangeably.

Recipes for Beans and Legumes

Cabbage, Potato, and White Bean Soup with Cilantro-spread Croutons
[SOPA DE PEDRA]

Throughout world folklore weave tales on the theme of stone soup, a soup based on but one stone. The stone is usually brought to the village by some crafty itinerant who proceeds to place the stone in a big pot of water over an open fire in the central square. The locals, never very bright in these stories, gather to watch the wonder of the stone that makes soup. Inevitably they offer odd bits of bacon, chunks of potato, savory onions, wedges of cabbage, and handfuls of beans, all to season the "stone soup." When the mixture is a delectable brew of everything tossed in, the cook fishes out the amazing stone, and sits down to enjoy his soup. In some of the versions of this story the traveler offers to sell the gullible villagers stones just like his.

My particular stone soup originated in Portugal with stopovers in England, Mexico, and California, each adding to the myriad of tastes and textures in the soup.

One particularly endearing aspect of this soup is that it freezes well and, when defrosted, lends itself to enriching other soups and stews.

1/2 onion, diced
1/2 medium cabbage, thinly
   sliced or coarsely shredded
1 pound baking potatoes,
   peeled and cut into 3 or 4
   chunks each
4 ounces meaty ham or thick-
   cut bacon, diced
6 cups chicken or vegetable
   broth

1-1/2 cups cooked cannellini
   beans
2 tablespoons or so olive oil for
   sautéing
4 to 8 slices stale or oven-dried
   baguette
3 to 4 chopped garlic cloves
Cilantro-Garlic-Tomato Spread,
   following
1 jalapeño chili, seeded and
   chopped

1. Combine onion, cabbage, potatoes, ham, and broth. Bring to a boil, then reduce heat and simmer over medium-low heat for 40 minutes, or long enough for potatoes to cook and fall apart a bit and cabbage to soften into rest of soup.

2. Add beans and let simmer with rest of soup for 15 to 20 minutes.

3. Make garlicky croutons (and they couldn't come at a better time: your house will smell like cabbage by now. Best to get that garlic going as soon as you can). Heat a tablespoon or two of olive oil in a heavy pan over medium-high heat and brown baguette slices. Remove from heat and toss garlic with hot browned bread slices.

4. Ladle hot soup into bowls and top each one with a crouton thickly spread with the Cilantro-Garlic-Tomato Spread. Pass chopped jalapeños for each diner to sprinkle on as desired.

Cilantro-Garlic-Tomato Spread

In a blender or food processor, puree 4 to 5 **garlic cloves,** then add 1 chopped seeded **jalapeño chili,** 1 to 1-1/2 diced medium **tomatoes,** juice of 1/2 **lemon,** 2 tablespoons **olive oil,** and 3 tablespoons coarsely chopped fresh **cilantro.**

Whirl to form a chunky paste, then season to taste with **salt.**

Alpine Soup

Bring 1/2 cup dry **red wine** to a boil and cook down to half its volume. Add 2 cups leftover **Sopa de Pedra,** page 230 (good when stored in your freezer) and 1/2 cup **heavy (whipping) cream.** Simmer together a few minutes to meld flavors, then season with **salt** and **pepper** and serve.

Cumin-flecked Black Bean Nachos

◆◆ INTERMEDIATE PANTRY

Serves 6 to 8 as an appetizer

A hearty and irresistible appetizer, perfect for nibbling on a cold afternoon or evening, accompanied with tortilla chips and lively conversation.

If you begin with already cooked or canned black beans, these take only a few minutes to put together. Follow with Mexican chilled orange duck and a spicy peanut salad (Ensalata de Cacahuates, page 251).

1 onion, chopped
2 garlic cloves, chopped (as always, amount could be increased)
2 tablespoons olive oil
2 teaspoons chili powder
2 to 2-1/2 cups cooked black beans, including about 1/2 cup cooking liquid
Salt and cayenne or salsa to taste
10 ounces jack cheese, thinly sliced

1 teaspoon cumin seeds
3 tablespoons chopped fresh cilantro
10 to 15 cherry tomatoes, halved, or 2 ripe tomatoes, cut into wedges
1 or 2 tablespoons pickled jalapeño slices
Sour cream as desired
Yellow- or blue-corn tortilla chips, preferably low-salt

1. Preheat oven to 450°. Sauté onion and garlic in olive oil until softened, then sprinkle with chili powder and cook a minute or two longer.

2. Add black beans and liquid, and cook down to a thickened mixture, mashing the beans slightly as they cook so you end up with a mix that is partly smooth, partly chunky. Season with salt and cayenne or salsa to taste.

3. Spoon bean mixture into a glass pie pan or a rustic ceramic casserole. Top with sliced cheese and sprinkle with cumin seeds.

4. Bake for about 10 minutes, or until cheese melts and lightly browns. Serve immediately, garnished with cilantro, tomatoes, pickled jalapeños, sour cream, and tortilla chips.

Huevos Motul

◆◆ INTERMEDIATE PANTRY

Serves 1 (multiply as desired)

A spicy carnival-colored dish from Mexico's Yucatán Peninsula.

◆◆◆◆◆◆

Spread **chilied black beans** from preceding recipe over a softened **corn tortilla.** Top with a **poached or fried egg,** then garnish with a **mild salsa or chili-seasoned tomato sauce** and sprinkle with colorful bits: **green peas, diced ham,** strips of **roasted red peppers (or chilies),** cubed **mild cheese,** leaves of **cilantro.**

Black Beans and Melted Cheese in Pita

◆◆ INTERMEDIATE PANTRY

Serves 4

Though it sounds like a mish-mash of cultures and cuisines, it is very much like a bean-stuffed bread the Navajo Indians once ate—plus the addition of Old World cheese. The pita turns out hot and chewy, stuffed with melting cheese. Serve with salsa, sour cream, green onions, and cilantro. It's good, too, made with chipotle-seasoned black beans.

4 pita breads, flat-rolled bread dough, or flour tortillas
1 recipe Cumin-flecked Black Bean Nachos, page 232
1/2 pound or so cheese such as queso fresco, jack, asiago,

young pecorino, or not-too-salty feta, crumbled, coarsely grated, or thinly sliced
Salsa, sour cream, chopped fresh cilantro and mint, and green onions as garnish

1. Open pita breads and spread insides with beans, then add a layer of cheese and close up tightly. Very lightly sprinkle with a few drops of water.

2. Brown stuffed pita breads in a lightly greased frying pan until cheese melts and pita breads have lightly browned in spots.

3. Serve immediately, garnished with salsa, sour cream, cilantro and mint, and green onions.

NOTE If using bread dough, roll a lime-size sphere of once-risen dough into a thin pancake. Lightly brown on one side, then spread the cooked side with beans and cheese. Fold over, and cook the stuffed dough until cooked through and flecked with brown. If using flour tortillas, spread beans over 1 tortilla, top with cheese, then add a second tortilla. Cook bean-stuffed disks according to basic recipe directions.

Black Bean Chili with Spicy Sausage and Pumpkin

◆◆ INTERMEDIATE PANTRY

Serves 4 to 6

The deep, dark flavor of black beans combines beautifully with spicy and/or smoked sausages and the sweet earthiness of pumpkin. The flavors come from whichever sausage you add.

1 onion, chopped
6 to 8 ounces spicy sausage, diced (chorizo, smoked, etc.)
2 garlic cloves, chopped
1-1/2 teaspoons cumin seeds
1 jalapeño chili, chopped

2 medium tomatoes, diced, or 1-1/2 cups canned
2 cups broth of choice
2 to 2-1/2 cups pumpkin chunks
3 to 4 cups cooked black beans, with 1-1/2 cups cooking liquid

1. Sauté onion with sausage and garlic, adding cumin seeds and jalapeño once meat has browned a bit.

2. Add tomatoes, broth, and pumpkin. Bring to a boil, reduce heat, and cook until pumpkin is just tender.

3. Mash black beans a little, leaving most whole but enough mashed to thicken sauce. Add to pumpkin mixture, along with enough liquid to give it a soupy consistency.

Hoppin' John Salad

◆ BASIC PANTRY

Serves 4

Usually served hot, hoppin' John is a classic dish of the Southern states, a combination of black-eyed peas and white rice. This dish takes a turn toward "Texas caviar," as well, marinating both beans and rice and serving them cold as a salad. And the whole thing is given a contemporary twist with its bed of nouvelle greens: frisée, baby dandelions, mesclun, radicchio.

Delicious with barbecued foods such as chili-spiked ribs or carnitas duck.

1 cup cooked black-eyed peas	2 tablespoons white wine vinegar
1 garlic clove, chopped	Salt and black pepper to taste
2 teaspoons green salsa	1 cup long-grain white or brown rice
1/2 jalapeño chili, chopped	
1/2 teaspoon cumin seeds, or 1/4 teaspoon ground cumin	1-1/2 cups water for cooking white rice, 2 cups for cooking brown rice
1 green onion, thinly sliced	
3 tablespoons diced or coarsely chopped red bell pepper	2 cups slightly bitter greens such as frisée, baby dandelions, mesclun, etc.
2 tablespoons extra-virgin olive oil	

1. Combine black-eyed peas with garlic, green salsa, chili, cumin, green onion, red bell pepper, olive oil, vinegar, salt, and pepper. Let marinate while you cook rice.

2. Combine rice and water with a pinch of salt. Bring to boil, reduce heat, and cover, then cook over medium-low heat until rice is just tender, but not overdone or mushy, about 10 minutes. Allow 30 to 40 minutes for brown rice.

3. Pour black-eyed peas and marinade over rice, mix gently, then let cool.

4. Serve at room temperature, garnished with greens.

Pureed Pinto Bean Bisque

◆ BASIC PANTRY

Serves 4

This hearty soup is filled with the earthy flavors of beans, onions, and spices. It is smooth and creamy, melting with cheese, and delicious preceding something equally Southwestern in flavor: say, lamb shanks that you've braised with pureed mild red chilies and served with a spoonful of Cilantro-Lime-Paste (page 360), and a varied green salad with lots of frisée.

Pass crusty rolls to accompany, and for dessert: caramelized pecans (page 249) spooned over vanilla ice cream with chunks of fresh pineapple that you've sautéed in butter and brown sugar.

1 onion, minced
2 garlic cloves, chopped
1 tablespoon olive oil
2 teaspoons chili powder
1-1/2 teaspoons ground cumin
1/4 teaspoon dried oregano
1/2 jalapeño, chopped
2 cups refried beans

3 cups vegetable, beef, or
    chicken broth
3 tablespoons tomato sauce
3 tablespoons shredded sharp
    Cheddar, Parmesan, or jack
    cheese
2 tablespoons chopped fresh
    cilantro
3 tablespoons sour cream

1. Sauté onion and garlic in olive oil until softened, then stir in spices. Cook a minute or two longer, then add jalapeño, beans, and broth along with tomato sauce.

2. Bring to a boil, then reduce heat and simmer for about 5 minutes. Stir and taste for seasoning.

3. Serve immediately, garnished with cheese, cilantro, and sour cream.

Tangy Tomato-Yogurt Soup with Lentils and Zucchini

◆ BASIC PANTRY

Serves 4

What a bracing bowlful this is: tart with yogurt and lime, bites of lentil giving texture, zucchini for garden freshness (if zucchini is unavailable or winter bitter, omit). It tastes vaguely Middle Eastern and very tropical, as if it came from a fictitious island in the Caribbean once ruled by the Byzantines but now inhabited by gentle dairy and citrus farmers.

The ingredients are those I nearly always have on hand, and while the lentils take 40 minutes to cook, popping in a few ice cubes of already cooked legumes brings this soup to the table in about 15 minutes.

Serve as a first course for any spicy meal; as this is a relatively light soup, you could follow it with something sustaining and deliciously heavy.

1/4 cup dried brown lentils,
    or 1/2 cup cooked lentils
2 tablespoons olive oil

1 large onion or 2 small ones,
    coarsely chopped
2 garlic cloves, chopped

1/2 fresh jalapeño chili,
chopped
1/2 cup coarsely chopped fresh
or canned tomatoes
4 cups chicken or vegetable
broth
2 teaspoons chopped ginger

Pinch each of sugar and salt
1 small or medium zucchini,
diced
1-1/2 cups plain yogurt
Juice from 1 lime or lemon
(2 tablespoons)

1. If using dried lentils, place in a pan with water to cover. Bring to a boil, then reduce heat and simmer until lentils are just tender, 35 to 45 minutes. Drain, reserving lentils to add to soup, if needed.

2. In olive oil, lightly sauté onion, garlic, and jalapeño until vegetables are soft, then add tomatoes, broth, ginger, sugar, and salt.

3. Bring to a boil, reduce heat, and cook for 5 to 10 minutes, or long enough to combine flavors, then add zucchini and cook until tender.

4. Stir yogurt to rid it of any lumps, then stir a spoonful or two of hot broth into yogurt and mix until smooth.

5. Add this broth-lightened yogurt to simmering soup, and heat together until hot but not boiling, then stir in lemon or lime juice.

6. Serve immediately.

Sauce Indienne

◆ BASIC PANTRY

Serves 4

This piquant and suave sauce is based on pureed lentils and yogurt with a hint of spicy-sweet chutney. It is delicious pooled on the bottom of a plate, French style, and topped with grilled lamb and a fine scattering of chopped cilantro. Or serve as an accompaniment to an Indian feast, or a tandoori chicken breast resting on a bed of curry-spiced spinach. This is so rich, it is difficult to believe that it's really quite a lean sauce.

1/4 cup dried brown lentils,
or 1/2 cup lentils cooked
in broth
2 cups broth, if using raw
lentils
1 whole garlic clove
2 green onions, cut into several
pieces or coarsely chopped

2 tablespoons mango chutney
One 1-inch piece fresh ginger,
chopped
2 cups plain yogurt
Juice of 1/2 lemon or lime
Tabasco or similar hot sauce

1. Place lentils in a pot with broth, garlic, and onions. Bring to a boil, reduce heat, and simmer for 40 minutes, or until lentils are tender. (May be made ahead and frozen.)

2. In a blender or food processor, puree chutney to break up any large pieces of fruit, then add cooked lentils, broth, and ginger. Puree until smooth.

3. Stir in yogurt, then chill until ready to serve. Before serving, add lemon or lime juice and hot sauce to taste.

Balkan-Flavors Red Lentil Chowder

◆ BASIC TO
◆◆◆ ADVANCED PANTRY

Serves 4

Creamy nuggets of butter beans or lima beans, bites of carrots and potatoes, and a sprinkle of cumin and thyme give lovely hearty flavors to this soup.

1/4 cup dried butter beans or lima beans, or 1/2 cup cooked beans
2-1/2 cups water (if using dried beans)
1 onion, chopped
1 tablespoon butter or vegetable oil
2 carrots, thickly sliced
1 turnip, diced
2 waxy boiling potatoes, diced, or 1 large baking potato, peeled and diced

1 quart chicken or vegetable broth (plus 1 cup if using already cooked beans)
1/2 cup red lentils (masoor dal) or yellow split peas
1/4 to 1/2 teaspoon dried thyme, crumbled
1/4 to 1/2 teaspoon ground cumin
Dash of hot pepper seasoning

1. If using dried butter beans, place beans in a saucepan and add water. Bring to a boil, then reduce heat and simmer until beans are cooked, 45 minutes to an hour. You should have 1-1/2 to 2 cups liquid; if not, add a little extra water.

2. Lightly sauté onion in butter or oil and, when softened, add remaining ingredients.

3. Bring to a boil, then reduce heat and simmer over low heat until vegetables are cooked through and lentils have dissolved into a thick soup.

West Indies Split-Pea Stew with Whole-Wheat Croutons and Toasted Sunflower Seeds

◆ BASIC PANTRY

Serves 4

A consummately sustaining potful.

◆◆◆◆◆◆

Prepare the **Balkan-Flavors Red Lentil Chowder** on the preceding page, omitting butter beans and using a combination of 1/2 cup *each* **green and yellow split peas** in place of the 1/2 cup red lentils. If you don't have a turnip, potato, or carrot, don't worry about it; they're optional. Do, however, add 2 cups **tomato sauce** in place of water or some of broth. Season with 1 **bay leaf**, 1/4 teaspoon **curry** powder, and a good pinch of ground **cinnamon** and **cloves** in addition to the cumin, thyme, and hot pepper seasoning called for in the basic recipe.

When split peas are cooked through and mixture is thick and chunky, taste for seasoning; it should be zesty and highly flavored.

To make whole wheat croutons: Brown in a little **olive oil** 6 pieces of **whole-wheat bread** that you've cut into bite-sized cubes; add 3 tablespoons or so shelled **sunflower seeds** to toasting bread and let them brown as well. Serve with a generous amount of croutons and sunflower seeds resting atop mixture.

NUTS, SEEDS, AND DRIED FRUITS

✦✧✦

Nuts, seeds, and dried fruits are among the most sustaining foods in your pantry. Nuts and seeds, being the germs of developing plants, are filled with all the proteins plants need to grow. Dried fruits are nutritionally sustaining in a different way: with much of their water evaporated, the sugar is concentrated in their flesh, giving them a nearly candylike quality. Nuts, seeds, and dried fruits are available in supermarkets, natural foods shops, and specialty food shops. Nearly every pantry has several of these foods, even if only a bag of peanuts, a jar of sesame seeds, and a box of raisins.

These seemingly ordinary ingredients can transform other dishes in surprising and wonderful ways. A handful of toasted pine nuts is delicious sprinkled over pasta, as are almonds or cashews over a savory pilaf. Nuts may also be ground into sauces such as a rich pistachio sauce for chicken, and a cashew nut–enriched Pacific Rim pesto. Add toasted nuts, coarsely or finely ground, to your favorite shortbread. Seeds may be toasted and eaten as a snack, or ground into sauces such as tahini or pipián. Then there is peanut butter and the other nut butters: cashew, almond, etc. Seeds such as poppy, sesame, sunflower, and pumpkin add a delicious crunch to cuisines the world over. Try kneading bread dough with poppy seeds and grated sharp Cheddar, or sprinkling toasted sesame seeds over soy-braised meat. Ground poppy seeds, sweetened, make a delectable Eastern European filling for pastries. Dried fruits, too, are a boon to have in the pantry: soak a dried fruit of choice in brandy or liqueur for a bracing midwinter treat over ice cream, or add a handful of prunes to a pan of poaching pears. Raisins added to curry-spiced meatballs are excellent, as are apricots added to a nutty pilaf.

Nuts and seeds are at their best when roasted to bring out their warm foresty flavor. There are few more enticing nibbles than fresh roasted nuts. To roast, place nuts or seeds in a baking dish and toss with a drizzle of oil. Bake in a 500° oven, turning once or twice to ensure even browning. The cooking time will depend upon the nut or seed you are roasting. Another way is to slowly cook oil-tossed nuts or seeds in a heavy frying pan on top of the stove over a medium heat, stirring for even browning.

The tiny bit of oil helps brown the nuts and give a fuller, rounder flavor, as well as a crispier crunch. However, you can omit the oil and toast the nuts or seeds in a dry pan instead.

Storage Tips

NUTS AND SEEDS Shells protect nuts against rancidity. Unshelled and stored in a cool dry place, they can last for up to 2 years. Shelled, however, they can go rancid in as little as 6 weeks. Stored in airtight containers, they will keep in the refrigerator for 6 weeks to several months. Frozen, they last from 6 to 12 months.

DRIED FRUITS Store in a dry, cool place. Dried fruits last varying lengths of time, depending upon the fruit, how it is dried, etc. A good gauge is about 6 months, with some fruits lasting longer, some less.

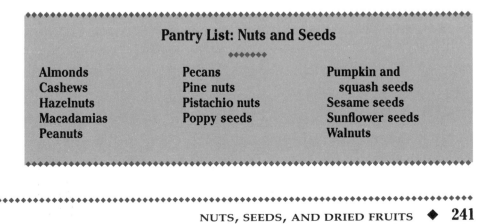

Pantry List: Nuts and Seeds

Almonds	Pecans	Pumpkin and
Cashews	Pine nuts	squash seeds
Hazelnuts	Pistachio nuts	Sesame seeds
Macadamias	Poppy seeds	Sunflower seeds
Peanuts		Walnuts

Almonds Cultivated since antiquity in the Mediterranean and Asia, the almond was once considered a fertility symbol by the ancient Greeks. In the Bible, Sampson is said to have courted Delilah with almonds.

The almond is a member of the rose family, as well as a cousin to peaches, apricots, cherries, raspberries, and plums. Note that each of those fruits benefits from a dash of almond essence to bring out its own characteristics.

There are two basic types of almonds: bitter and sweet. Almond essence is made from bitter almonds, while sweet almonds are the ones for eating. America's largest almond-growing region is California's Central Valley, cultivated originally by the early Spanish missionaries.

Almonds may be purchased whole, with or without their skins; they also may be bought halved, slivered, chopped coarsely, crushed to a meal, roasted and salted, and sometimes smoked or seasoned. Almond paste, also known as marzipan, is a blend of ground almonds, sugar, and sometimes butter, sold in logs or cans to be used for baking.

Almond Biscotti

[BISCOTTI DI PRATO]

◆ **BASIC PANTRY**

Makes about 2 dozen cookies

Subtly tasting of almonds and delightfully crunchy, biscotti are eaten throughout Italy. You will see them piled into baskets and in gleaming jars perched atop espresso cafe counters, especially in Tuscany, where biscotti are said to have originated around the 13th century.

Italy, however, is not the only place where biscotti are eaten with a passion. These crunchy crisp rusks are all the rage in West and East Coast cafes and groceries, sometimes embellished with hazelnuts and chocolate.

Biscotti usually contain little or no fat and bake up to a bone-dry crunch rather than being crumbly. The traditional way to enjoy them is by dipping the hard cookies into a glass of sweet vin santo, a dessert wine from Tuscany. It's a happy marriage indeed: the nutty flavor of the sherrylike wine complementing the nuts in the cookies and vice versa.

1-1/2 cups whole unblanched almonds	1 teaspoon baking soda
	Pinch of salt
2 cups unsifted all-purpose flour	3 large eggs
	1 teaspoon vanilla extract
1 cup sugar	

1. Preheat oven to 400°. Toast almonds by spreading them on an ungreased baking sheet and baking for about 20 minutes, or until lightly

browned. Turn once or twice. Let cool, then coarsely chop, using a nut chopper or food processor.

2. Combine flour, sugar, soda, and salt in a bowl.

3. In a separate bowl, combine eggs and vanilla. Make a well in dry ingredients, as if you were making pasta, and pour egg mixture into center. Mix well, gradually incorporating dry ingredients into dough.

4. Mix nuts into dough, using your hands to mix if a spoon is not strong enough.

5. Let dough sit at room temperature for 30 to 60 minutes.

6. Preheat oven to 300°. Butter and flour a baking sheet or spray with nonstick coating.

7. Form 1 long loaf or 2 smaller ones, and place on baking sheet. Bake for 45 to 50 minutes, or until golden. Remove from oven and let cool slightly.

8. When cool enough to handle, slice into 1/2-inch-wide diagonal slices. Do not let loaves cool completely—when cold they are as easy to slice as concrete.

9. Place slices onto an ungreased baking sheet and return to oven. Bake for 35 to 50 minutes, depending on how brown you like them. Turn once to bake each side.

10. Cool on a rack, then store in a paper bag. I find that they improve after 3 or 4 days. Their texture becomes crispier and drier, the flavor more subtle.

Thin Tart of Marzipan and Pears

◆◆ INTERMEDIATE PANTRY

Serves 6

A thin layer of pears bakes on top of a sweet layer of marzipan, all resting in a flaky pie shell. Simple to prepare and perfect on a chilly autumn evening, accompanied with a small glass of brandy and the first wood fire of the season.

1 recipe Basic Pie Dough, page 363
1 cup Almond Paste, following, or one 8-ounce package marzipan
1 egg
3 to 4 firm but ripe and flavorful pears, peeled and thinly sliced

2 tablespoons brown sugar or less if using Amaretto
1/2 teaspoon almond extract, or 1 tablespoon Amaretto liqueur
1 to 2 tablespoons unsalted butter, in small bits

1. Preheat oven to 400°. Roll dough out about 1/8-inch thick onto a baking sheet.

2. In a blender or food processor, puree almond paste with egg.

3. Spread almond mixture over dough, folding edges over to form shallow sides.

4. Mix pears with almond extract or liqueur and layer over almond paste. Sprinkle with brown sugar and butter bits.

5. Bake for about 15 minutes or until edges of tart are golden brown. Take care not to let delicate fruit burn.

6. Serve immediately.

Almond Paste

◆ BASIC PANTRY

Makes about 2 cups

2 cups unskinned almonds
1/2 cup sugar or to taste
2 to 3 tablespoons unsalted
 butter

1/4 teaspoon pure almond extract, or a larger amount imitation almond extract, 1 teaspoon or to taste

1. In a blender or food processor, mince, then pulverize almonds.

2. Add sugar, butter, and almond extract. Keep mixing until smooth and well combined. Keep stored in freezer for up to 2 months.

◆◆◆◆◆◆

Cashew Nuts This rich and meaty nut is a New World native, prized in the Yucatán as much for its sweet fruit as for its nut.

Cashews are deliciously addictive simply toasted and salted, but they are delicious, too, in a wide variety of other dishes. They're brilliant added to stir-fries or pilafs, or sprinkled over hot fudge sundaes.

Chicken, Pepper, Water Chestnut, and Cashew Stir-Fry

◆◆ INTERMEDIATE PANTRY

Serves 4

This is so simple and endlessly adaptable. I make it with almonds or peanuts if I've no cashews, and with duck or tofu if I've no chicken.

2 chicken breast halves,
 skinned and boned
 (6 to 8 ounces total)
1 tablespoon cornstarch

2 tablespoons dry sherry
2 tablespoons chicken broth
1 teaspoon soy sauce
2 garlic cloves, chopped

1 piece fresh ginger, chopped
2 tablespoons mild vegetable
  oil
1/2 cup quartered or sliced
  water chestnuts
1/2 green bell pepper, cut into
  large dice
1/2 red bell pepper, cut into
  large dice

1/4 cup hoisin sauce
1/4 cup toasted cashew nuts,
  either purchased or home-
  prepared according to directions on page 241
2 teaspoons chopped green
  onions or fresh cilantro

1. Cut chicken into large dice or small bite-sized pieces. Combine with cornstarch, sherry, broth, and soy sauce. Set aside.

2. In a wok or heavy skillet, stir-fry garlic and ginger for a moment in 2 teaspoons vegetable oil, then add water chestnuts and peppers. Cook a minute on high heat, then remove from pan and set aside.

3. Take chicken from marinade (reserve for sauce) and stir-fry in remaining oil over high heat. Cook a minute or two until barely translucent, only half done, then add stir-fried vegetables, reserved marinade for sauce, and hoisin sauce.

4. Let mixture thicken, adding a few spoonfuls extra liquid such as water or broth if it seems too thick, then add cashews. Serve immediately, sprinkled with green onions or cilantro.

Wide Noodles with Salmon and Pacific Rim Pesto

◆◆ INTERMEDIATE PANTRY

Serves 4 to 6

Inspired by Genoese pesto, aromatic seasoning pastes may be made with differing herbs and nuts, instead of the traditional basil and pine nuts. Here the crunch of rich cashews combines with pungent fresh ginger and cilantro for an East-West pesto. If salmon is unavailable, use any seafood; alternatively, the dish is just as delicious without it.

PESTO
2 garlic cloves, chopped
1/2 jalapeño, chopped, with
  or without seeds as desired
2 teaspoons chopped fresh
  ginger
4 tablespoons mild vegetable
  oil
2 cups fresh cilantro leaves

1/4 cup toasted cashew nuts,
  coarsely chopped (cashews
  can be either commercially
  roasted or home-toasted
  according to directions on
  page 241)
Juice of 1 lemon or lime
1-1/2 tablespoons soy sauce

(*continued*)

1 pound fresh wide noodles, or
  12 ounces dried wide noodles
1 teaspoon *each* soy sauce and
  Asian (toasted) sesame oil

8 ounces salmon steaks,
  skinned, boned, and cut into
  bite-sized pieces
Salt and pepper to taste
2 tablespoons minced fresh
  cilantro or mint for garnish

1. Prepare the pesto: In a blender or food processor, puree garlic with jalapeño, ginger, and 3 tablespoons oil, then add cilantro and blend until mixture is coarsely chopped. Add cashews, lemon or lime juice, and 1/2 tablespoon soy sauce, and blend together coarsely.

2. Cook noodles in boiling water until just tender, then drain well and toss with soy sauce and sesame oil. Set aside.

3. Saute salmon nuggets briefly in remaining 1 tablespoon vegetable oil for 2 minutes, or until just cooked. Add salt and pepper.

4. Serve soy-and-sesame-dressed noodles studded with salmon nuggets, then top with several spoonfuls of sauce. Garnish with chopped cilantro or mint.

◆◆◆◆◆◆

Hazelnuts Also known as filberts, *noisettes* (in French), and *nocciole* (in Italian), these small round nuts have long been popular in Europe. In fact, the ancient Celts revered the hazelnut, and fed them ceremoniously to salmon as part of their mystical rituals. From hazelnut wood they whittled "magic" wands.

In recent centuries the hazelnut has been added to tender chocolates and cream sauces, toasted and used to top noodles and casseroles, used as a coating for fish, and pureed into a paste for pastries and ice creams. But it wasn't until recently that hazelnuts entered the American food scene in a big way (though I read that the Native Americans liked hazelnuts added to Brussels sprouts; so do I. See recipe that follows). In recent years American chefs have been exploring this nut's potential in sauces, meringues, herb butters, and the like, and now home cooks are following suit. Oregon is currently the largest domestic producer of hazelnuts, keeping up with America's appetite for their woodsy crunch in such items as oat-nut breads and granola cereals.

Hazelnuts have a hard outer shell, so I prefer buying them already shelled unless I'm serving them in a bowl accompanied with a nutcracker. Shelled hazelnuts can have their skins or be skinless. I don't recommend buying chopped hazelnuts, since all the flavor seems to have fled while they sat in their package. The skin of the hazelnut is astringent and papery and should be removed. To do this, lightly toast the nuts in an ungreased pan over medium heat. When skins turn brown, remove and place in a clean towel, rubbing vigorously against each other until skins fall away (or toast them in a 400° oven for 10 minutes instead of on top of the stove).

Brussels Sprouts with Hazelnuts and Browned Butter

◆◆ INTERMEDIATE PANTRY

Serves 4

Buttery toasted hazelnuts echo the autumnal flavor of Brussels sprouts. This dish, adapted from the Native Americans of New England, is one of those surprisingly perfect pairings that makes you fall in love with both partners. It's a great make-ahead dish for any winter holiday gathering, as it tastes better at room temperature than it does hot.

2 pounds fresh Brussels sprouts
1/2–2/3 cup hazelnuts, toasted and peeled (see above)

1/2 cup (1 stick) unsalted butter
Salt and pepper to taste

1. Steam or parboil Brussels sprouts until just tender and bright green, about 5–6 minutes. Drain and set aside.
2. Coarsely chop hazelnuts in a blender or food processor, leaving some whole, others in halves, quarters, and tiny bits.
3. Over medium or medium-high heat brown nuts in an ungreased pan until toasty and browned in spots.
4. Remove from heat, add butter, and return to heat, reducing the temperature to medium or medium low, so that butter gently browns and takes on a nutlike flavor. Take care to remove before butter burns.
5. Toss sprouts with nuts in their browned butter, shaking to coat well. Add salt and pepper to taste. Serve at room temperature.

BLT, Corn, and Spinach Salad

◆◆ INTERMEDIATE PANTRY

Serves 4

This recipe, the essence of summer with its tomatoes and corn, bacon and spinach, is courtesy of chef Phillipe La Mancusa.

1 cup hazelnuts, toasted and peeled (see above)
1/2 pound thick-cut bacon, diced

1/3 cup olive oil
1/3 cup hazelnut oil

(continued)

1/4–1/3 cup balsamic vinegar
Juice of 1/2 lime
Salt and pepper to taste
Kernels from 4 ears fresh corn

6 Roma tomatoes, diced
4 to 6 cups young tender spinach leaves, torn into bite-sized pieces

1. Chop hazelnuts coarsely. Take one-eighth of this mixture and grind finely. Set aside.

2. Cook bacon until cooked through but not crisp. Drain and set aside.

3. Make dressing: Combine olive oil with hazelnut oil, balsamic vinegar, and lime juice, finely ground hazelnuts, salt, and pepper.

4. Return bacon to pan with corn and sauté quickly, then add 1 cup dressing and tomatoes. Heat through and remove from stove.

5. Arrange spinach leaves on plates and dress with some of reserved dressing. Then pour hot tomato, bacon, and corn and warm dressing over. Sprinkle with reserved toasted hazelnuts and serve immediately.

Macadamia Madness

◆◆◆ ADVANCED PANTRY

Serves 4

My best friend got married and went to Hawaii on her honeymoon. She brought me back a jar of macadamia nuts.

It was the middle of winter so I turned up the heat in my apartment, wrapped myself in a flowered sarong, and headed into the kitchen to fix the macadamia-encrusted fresh tuna she described. I am probably the only person I know who gets culinary descriptions from other people's honeymoons.

It's always hard for me to believe that the exotic landscape rife with tropical forest, swaying palm trees, fiery volcanos, and East-West culture is really part of America. These days, too, the macadamia nuts that were once available only on "The Islands" are sold in every supermarket in the country, and are increasingly available even in Europe.

Macadamia nuts, round and rich and addictive, are natives of the Hawaiian Islands. These oil-rich nuts have a full flavor and a particularly satisfying crunch, and are usually sold toasted and salted, either whole or in small pieces. They are good as a solitary nibble, equally good paired with sweet chocolate or coconut, and good, too, with savory things such as the following macadamia-encrusted tuna steak, served with tender spinach and tomato-lime-ginger butter.

5 tablespoons unsalted butter,
  at room temperature
4 fresh tuna steaks, about 6
  ounces each
1/2 cup coarsely chopped macadamia nuts, or as needed
1 bunch spinach leaves, cleaned
  and stemmed

1 garlic clove, chopped
3 tablespoons fresh lemon or
  lime juice
1 teaspoon tomato paste
1 tablespoon finely grated fresh
  ginger
Salt and pepper to taste

1. Preheat oven to 500°.

2. Melt 1 tablespoon butter and brush onto tuna steaks. Place in a shallow baking dish, then top with chopped nuts pressed on tightly to form a somewhat even layer.

3. Meanwhile, steam or blanch spinach. Rinse with cold water and squeeze dry.

4. Combine garlic and lemon or lime juice in a skillet or saucepan and bring to a boil. Let cook over high heat until liquid has evaporated nearly completely, leaving only about 2 to 3 teaspoons at bottom of pan.

5. Remove from heat, then stir tomato paste and half of ginger into pan. Using a whisk, swirl in remaining butter in bits, adding more as each lot is added. The mixture should be thickened and somewhat fluffy. Add the remaining ginger, and salt and pepper to taste. Set aside and keep at room temperature.

6. Bake fish until nuts form a golden crust and fish is just firm to touch, about 6 minutes.

7. Arrange a bit of spinach on each plate, then place a hot crusty tuna fillet next to it. Place a knob of tomato-lime-ginger butter alongside and serve immediately.

Caramelized Pecans

◆◆ INTERMEDIATE PANTRY

Makes 3/4 cup pecans

Pecans are an essential flavor of the American South: pecan pie, Creole pralines, pecan-studded ice cream. I have overly fond memories of a chicken breast from the same neighborhood, breaded and fried, served in a cream gravy, and scattered with lots of toasted pecans.

This recipe caramelizes the pecan, giving sweetness to the deeply flavored, slightly bitter nut. The caramelized nuts can be used in a wide variety of ways: as a nibble with a glass of chilled dry sherry or a mint julep, strewn across a bowl of rich ice cream, or scattered atop a slice of pound cake. For an unusual play of sweet and savory, use the caramel-ized nuts to garnish a salad or braised meat dish.

| 3/4 cup pecans | 2 tablespoons sugar |

1. In an ungreased pan over medium-high heat, or on a baking sheet in a preheated 400° oven, bake pecans until they are half toasted, about 10 minutes.

2. Remove from stove or oven, sprinkle with sugar, and return to finish toasting. They are ready when sugar is lightly caramelized, about an additional 7 minutes in oven. Remove and let cool.

Sonoma Salad

Serve **caramelized pecans,** above, strewn across a salad of drained steamed **spinach** and pan-broiled fresh **goat cheese,** all dressed with a vinaigrette of **olive or nut oil** and **balsamic vinegar.**

Chicken Breasts with Pistachio Cream

[POULET À LA PISTACHE]

◆◆◆ ADVANCED PANTRY

Serves 4

Pistachio nuts are a traditional snack throughout the Middle East, especially in Iran, where they are roasted, salted, and dyed that distinc-tive garish red color. In California, roasted pistachios are usually pre-pared au naturel. Pistachio nuts are used in sweet pastries such as baklava, and in the famous pistachio paste and chocolate concoctions of Paris's patisseries.

Ground nuts are traditionally used to thicken sauces in many of the world's cuisines, from Turkish Circassian chicken to Indonesia's peanut sauces. Ground pistachios are particularly elegant, especially when added to a French cream sauce. The result is creamy and delicate, with a distinctive, classic taste.

4 chicken breasts, skinned, boned, and lightly pounded if very thick	1/2 cup shelled untoasted and unsalted pistachio nuts, finely ground
3 tablespoons unsalted butter	Dash of white pepper (add salt only if not using canned broth)
1 cup dry white wine	
1 cup chicken broth	
1/2 cup heavy (whipping) cream	

NOTE Untoasted, unsalted pistachio nuts can often be purchased at natural food shops or ordered by mail.

1. Gently sauté chicken breasts in butter until just gilded and half cooked, a minute or two per breast. Remove to plate.
2. Pour white wine and chicken broth into pan, raise heat to high, and cook to reduce to about 1/2 cup. Pour in cream and continue cooking a minute or two longer.
3. Lower heat and stir in pistachio nuts, breaking up any lumps that might form. Add half-cooked chicken breasts and any pan juices to pistachio sauce, and warm through gently. Season with salt (if needed) and pepper.
4. Serve immediately.

Romaine Lettuce with Peanuts, Crisp Fried Chili, and Grated Cheese

[ENSALADA DE CACAHUATES]

◆◆ INTERMEDIATE PANTRY

Serves 4

Peanuts may have New World origins, but they have become one of the world's most universal nuts. Used in savory as well as sweet dishes, peanuts add crunch and richness to foods from Asia to Africa, South America to the Mediterranean to our own South. Peanut butter has become an American classic spread between slices of bread, fueling generations of schoolchildren. It also adds a nutty creaminess to sauces, stews, and soups, especially spicy ones; see page 175.

In the following salad a generous amount of crushed peanuts adds a robust crunch to crisp sweet romaine lettuce. Tossed with a mildly spicy chili oil dressing, shredded sharp cheese, and thin strips of toasted New Mexico or California chilies, this is an excellent salad to accompany a pasta dish, especially one that has no cheese in it, such as one based on fish or seafood.

1/2 mild dried red chili such as New Mexico or California, cut into thin strips with scissors
1/4 cup olive oil
1-1/2 tablespoons white wine vinegar

2 garlic cloves, chopped
1/2 teaspoon dry mustard
Pinch of sugar
Salt and black pepper to taste
1 head romaine, washed, dried, and cut or broken into bite-sized pieces

(continued)

2 to 3 ounces sharp hard cheese such as pecorino, Romano, asiago, dry jack, finely shredded or grated (about 1/4–1/3 cup)	1/2 cup dry-roasted peanuts, coarsely crushed (leaving some crushed, some in halves, and others nearly whole)

1. Fry dried chili strips in olive oil for 2 to 3 minutes, or until they change color and darken but do not burn. Remove from pan and drain on absorbent paper. Pour oil into a heat-resistant container to cool (this will be red in color, perfumed with the flavors of the peppers, and become the base for your dressing).

2. Mix cooled chili oil with white wine vinegar, garlic, mustard, sugar, salt, and pepper. Use a whisk to combine it into a creamy consistency.

3. Just before serving, dress lettuce with vinaigrette, toss together with cheese and peanuts, and top with fried chili strips.

Spanish Pine Nut Macaroons

◆◆ INTERMEDIATE PANTRY

Makes about 2 dozen cookies

Pine nuts are the kernels from the pine tree, small soft oval nuts enclosed in a tough brown-black shell. They're most commonly sold with the shell removed, but have more of a piney aroma and flavor the sooner they are eaten after shelling. My grandmother remembers buying paper cones of pine nuts from the candy kiosk in the streets of old New York as a treat. They called them "Indian nuts," and sitting on the front stoop trying to crunch the shells between young teeth was a whole afternoon's entertainment.

Pine nuts are used extensively in Italian and Middle Eastern cooking: In Genoa they are ground with basil for pesto; in the Southern regions they are tossed into pasta, or combined with raisins for a sweet and savory effect. Focaccia breads might have pine nuts kneaded in, as might meatballs, while in the Middle East the tiny nuts are added to the filling for stuffed vine leaves.

The following cookies are a culinary souvenir from a visit to Spain. They beckoned to me from the window of pastry shops so chic and elegant it looked as if they were selling jewelry rather than cookies and cakes.

Crunchy around the edges, chewy toward the middle, these simple-to-make cookies have flavor in each pine-nutty bite. To keep their shape, they should be baked on aluminum foil or parchment, then cooled directly on the foil or paper; peel off the paper when the cookies are cool. If you bake directly on a baking sheet and try to remove the cookies with a spatula, they will deform themselves into gnomelike lumps, and their crisp exterior will shatter. They will still be good, but not as attractive.

1 roll (8 ounces) almond paste cut into small pieces	**1 teaspoon grated lemon zest**
2/3 cup sugar	**Whites from 2 eggs**
	1 cup pine nuts

1. Heat oven to 325°; line baking sheet with aluminum foil or parchment paper.

2. In a blender or food processor, whirl almond paste until it is smooth, then add sugar, lemon zest, and egg whites, whirling until all is combined.

3. If dough is malleable, wet hands and make balls, then roll balls in pine nuts, then plop onto baking sheets. If dough is more like a batter, you can mix nuts into batter and spoon it onto baking sheets.

4. Bake 15 to 25 minutes or until cookies seem firm and are lightly colored and somewhat glazed on top.

5. Remove and let cool on foil- or paper-lined cookie sheets. If not using liners, carefully remove cookies with a spatula and place on plates or wire racks to cool. They will last 3 to 4 weeks in a cool, dry place, and taste better several weeks into the process. Freeze for up to 2 months, then reheat in a slow oven to crisp up.

Spinach and Ricotta Ravioli in Pureed Walnut Cream

[PANZOTI]

◆◆ INTERMEDIATE PANTRY

Serves 4

My first taste of Europe came in Genoa, Italy. Genoa is not a tourist town, so rather than getting caught in a crowd of my fellow Americans, I was able to poke around through the centuries-old cobbled streets absorbing the flavor of the ancient seaport Christopher Columbus came from (I often passed his little house). I ate pesto on everything until I thought that I too would turn green if faced with another basil leaf.

Outside my window was a panoramic view of the harbor, and wonderful cooking scents wafted up from the trattoria downstairs. They served the following dish of spinach pasta in walnut sauce; like pesto, this sauce is a feature of Genoese cooking.

1 cup walnuts
2 to 3 garlic cloves, chopped
2 tablespoons olive oil
1/2 cup grated Parmesan cheese
1 cup heavy (whipping) cream
Up to 1/2 cup boiling water, as
needed

1/4 to 1/2 teaspoon dried
oregano
Salt and pepper to taste
1 pound fresh or frozen
spinach-and-ricotta-stuffed
ravioli

1. Finely grind walnuts in either a blender or food processor. Set aside.

2. Gently heat garlic in olive oil until fragrant, then add to walnuts and whirl until well mixed, then add cheese and cream. Continue to whirl, adding enough boiling water to reach a creamy consistency. Season with oregano, salt, and pepper.

3. Cook ravioli until just al dente, then drain and nap each portion with a bit of walnut sauce. Serve immediately.

Cross-Country Mixed Nut Pie

◆ BASIC TO
◆◆◆ ADVANCED PANTRY

Makes two 8-inch pies

Crunchy toasted nuts baked in a sweet near-glaze, this is a variation of the classic pecan pie, except in this version anything goes, nut-wise.

Whichever nut you use gives the pie a taste of the region it comes from: pecans give a distinctly Southern flavor; hazelnuts, a taste of the Northwest; walnuts, an All-American savor; and an assortment of mixed nuts gives each bite a variety of nut flavors and textures.

Double recipe Basic Pie Dough,
page 363
1 cup sugar
Pinch of salt
1-1/4 cups dark corn syrup
1/4 cup brandy or whiskey, optional (if not using, increase
corn syrup to 1-1/2 cups)
1/2 teaspoon ground cinnamon

4 tablespoons unsalted butter
1-1/2 teaspoons vanilla extract
4 eggs, lightly beaten
2-1/2 cups coarsely broken up
and partially chopped un-
salted toasted nuts of choice
(pecans, walnuts, hazelnuts,
cashews, almonds, etc.)

1. Prepare pie dough and roll out into 2 circles; use to line two 8-inch pie pans and crimp edges of dough. Preheat oven to 325°.

2. Combine sugar, salt, corn syrup, brandy or whiskey, and cinna-

mon and bring to a boil, stirring to dissolve sugar. Boil for about 5 minutes, then remove from heat.

3. Beat in butter, vanilla, and eggs; mix well, then stir in nuts.

4. Pour into pie shells and bake 50 to 60 minutes, or until knife comes out clear.

5. Let cool and serve either warm or cool.

Mixed Nut Tartlets

Prepare as for Mixed Nut Pie, but use tiny tart pans and prepare individual nut tarts. Decrease baking time to about 25 minutes, or until edges of crusts are golden and centers are set.

Josephine's Sunflower Bread

◆ BASIC PANTRY

Makes two 9-by-5-inch loaves

Sunflowers growing with their faces turned toward the sun are a heady sight, conjuring up visions of van Gogh's Provence. They grow exceedingly well in the sunnier areas of the United States as well. When I was growing up in California's Central Valley, my Russian-born grandfather always had a row of them in the backyard garden.

Sunflowers are particularly prized for their oil and for nibbling in Russia; in Israel sunflower seed munching is so widespread that there are signs in buses, movie houses, and other public places forbidding the spitting of sunflower seed shells onto the floor.

Sunflower seeds are good toasted and salted in their shell, or with the shell removed and a little soy sauce added before toasting. Sprinkle toasted seeds onto ratatouille, pasta, cheese sandwiches on wholewheat bread, or salads. Cubes of cheese are nice dipped into a combination of toasted sunflower and cumin seeds.

The following bread takes advantage of the nutty flavor and texture of sunflower seeds. Since excellent bread is available in most major urban areas, I usually just purchase a fresh crusty loaf. But sometimes on a gray winter's day the idea of baking bread appeals. When I bake bread I want a loaf that tastes of wheat, made from an adaptable recipe that lets me add whatever grains and seeds are lying around my pantry. This is such a recipe, developed by my baking assistant, Josephine Aspin.

This bread is particularly good with cheese or toasted and served with a rustic soup or hearty salad.

1 package (2 teaspoons) active dry yeast	About 2-1/2 cups unbleached all-purpose white flour
1/4 cup warm (105° to 115°) water	1-1/2 teaspoons salt
3 tablespoons honey	1-1/2 cups sunflower seeds, shelled
2 tablespoons vegetable oil	1 egg white, beaten with 1 tablespoon water
2-1/4 cups lukewarm (85°) water	
3 cups whole-wheat flour	

1. Add yeast to 1/4 cup warm water, stir to dissolve, and let sit until foamy, about 10 minutes.

2. In a large bowl, combine honey, oil, and lukewarm water with dissolved yeast mixture.

3. Add whole-wheat flour and mix well with a wooden spoon, or use a heavy-duty mixer equipped with a dough hook. When flour is mixed in, add white flour and salt.

4. Place dough on a lightly floured board and knead well with floured hands for about 10 minutes, adding more flour 1 tablespoon at a time if needed. About halfway through kneading process add 1 cup sunflower seeds. Dough is ready when it springs back after being poked.

5. Rub a large bowl lightly with vegetable oil, then place dough inside, turning so that whole lump of dough is lightly oiled.

6. Cover with a clean cloth and let rise in a warm spot (80° to 85°) until doubled in bulk, 1-1/2 to 2 hours.

7. Punch down and turn onto floured board to knead again for five minutes.

8. Divide dough in half and form into 2 loaves. Roll loaves in remaining 1/2 cup sunflower seeds, pressing seeds into sides of loaves. Place each loaf in a lightly oiled 9-by-5-inch loaf pan. Let rise again until doubled in bulk (about 45 minutes). Meanwhile, preheat oven to 375°.

9. Brush top of loaves with egg white mixture and sprinkle with any leftover sunflower seeds. Bake for 35 to 45 minutes, or until loaves feel hollow when tapped.

India Aspin's Seeded Three-Grain Bread

Decrease amount of white flour by 1 cup in preceding recipe, adding 1/2 cup **oatmeal,** 1/3 cup **bulgur,** and 1/3 cup **millet** to dough, along with 3 tablespoons **poppy seeds.**

Cubes of Cheese Rolled in Toasted Sunflower and Cumin Seeds

◆◆ INTERMEDIATE PANTRY

Serves 2 to 4 as a snack

Sunflower and **cumin seeds,** toasted together and used to coat cubes of **cheese,** are very simple but very good. The seed mixture is good, too, sprinkled over Cheddar and Olive Pâté, page 173.

1/4 cup sunflower seeds	8 ounces jack, white Cheddar,
1 tablespoon cumin seeds	or other cheese of choice, cut
	into 1/2- to 3/4-inch cubes

1. In an ungreased heavy skillet, toast sunflower seeds over medium-low heat for about 5 minutes, or until they just start to turn golden.

2. Add cumin seeds and continue toasting until sunflower seeds are brown and cumin seeds are fragrant and lightly browned in color.

3. Let cool, then roll cheese cubes in seed mixture, or serve cubes of cheese on toothpicks surrounding a small saucer of seed mixture for individual dipping.

Yucatecan Pumpkin Seed Sauce

[PIPIÁN]

◆ BASIC TO
◆◆ INTERMEDIATE PANTRY

Makes about 2 cups
(Serves 4 to 6)

Pumpkin and other squash seeds have long been a favored food in the Americas, with sauces prepared from them dating back to ancient times. No doubt, along with chilies and dried corn, pumpkin seeds were one of the first foods of the New World pantry.

While pumpkin seed sauces are still adored throughout most of Mexico, they are especially doted on in the Yucatán Peninsula. That cuisine differs strikingly from the foods of the other regions of that vast nation. While much of the food of Northern and Central Mexico reflects an Aztec heritage, the food of the Yucatán is distinctly Mayan. Among the culinary characteristics setting it apart from other regions are its seasoning pastes. In the central market of Mérida you'll find huge piles of these pastes, or *recados*, each color reflecting its seasoning base: red for achiote and red chilies, yellow for roasted chilies and spices, black for charred-until-black chilies, and green paste for pumpkin seeds.

In addition to their use in pipián sauces, pumpkin seeds are squeezed to extract their essential oil, which is then drizzled over dishes such as *papadzul* (egg- or black-bean stuffed tortillas) as a condiment. They might also be simply toasted to a crisp, brittle state and seasoned with mild chili powder; one of my editors, a Yucatecaphile, dotes on lima beans tossed with these slightly *picante* pumpkin seeds.

This particular pipián sauce is much thinner than most; it's also tangier, more like tahini or hummus. No surprise, really, when you think about the large Middle Eastern community in Mérida, the capital of Yucatán.

Serve this sauce surrounded by wedges of pita or French-style bread, and garnish with lots and lots of watercress—its freshness is a welcome balance to the sharpness of the sauce. This pipián is also good spooned onto grilled lamb kabobs, but, then again, what isn't?

2/3 cup unsalted raw hulled pumpkin seeds	1/2 to 1 jalapeño chili, chopped, with or without seeds, as desired
2 teaspoons cumin seeds	Hot pepper sauce to taste
6 garlic cloves, coarsely chopped	Salt and black pepper to taste (no extra salt if canned broth is used)
1/4 cup olive oil	
1 to 1-1/3 cups chicken or vegetable broth	3 green onions, thinly sliced
1/3 cup fresh lime juice (juice of 4 to 5 limes)	Pita wedges
	About 1 cup watercress sprigs

1. In an ungreased skillet over medium heat, toast pumpkin seeds with cumin until seeds begin to pop.

2. Puree in a blender or food processor to a fine powderlike meal.

3. Heat garlic in olive oil for a minute or two until garlic is golden in color and smells fragrant.

4. Pour garlic and oil into ground pumpkin seeds in a blender or food processor and whirl to mix well. Then, with machine on, add broth, lime juice, and chopped jalapeño. Taste for seasoning, then add hot pepper sauce, salt, pepper, and green onions. Whirl a minute or two longer to combine, but not long enough to puree bits of green onion.

5. Serve garnished with pita and watercress.

Sesame Seeds Sesame seeds come in both black and beige, hulled and unhulled, and usually are sold raw. Toasting releases their nutty fragrance. Tahini is made from toasted hulled sesame seeds (see page 189). Toasted sesame seeds ground with a little sea salt makes gamacio, a Korean sesame salt much favored by natural foods advocates.

Korean Sesame Salt

[GAMACIO]

◆ BASIC PANTRY

Makes 1 cup

Sesame salt is delicious on any savory grilled meat or fish, and with steamed rice or baked sweet potatoes. I like it sprinkled over fat rice noodles that have been cooked in broth then seasoned with a bit of soy sauce and Asian sesame oil. Chopped green onions sprinkled over the top adds a finishing touch.

**1 cup hulled or unhulled
  sesame seeds**

2 teaspoons salt

1. Toast sesame seeds in an ungreased skillet until golden.
2. Grind in blender with salt.
3. Store, covered, for up to 4 months.

Dried Fruit

Dried fruits are an expected ingredient in sweet and healthful snacks, but they are not commonly used in savory dishes. They should be!

The choice of dried fruits available is wide and varied: chewy apples and pears, plump apricots from Turkey, chewy figs from Greece, cherries and prunes from California.

BUYING TIPS When buying fruit, look for a moist and chewy product with good color. Much of the fruit that fits this description has had sulfur added, as sulfur helps preserve the color and texture. Many believe that sulfur, as well as all other additives, should not be used. However, studies have shown that unless you have a sensitivity or allergy to sulfur, its presence in dried fruit is not harmful. I continue to buy fruits that are moist and flavorful. The dried unsulfured ones are often (though not always) browner and more leathery. Natural foods and imported food stores are the best places to find the widest range of fruits.

STORAGE TIPS Keep in a well-sealed container in a cool place. This slows darkening of color and unpleasant changes in flavor.

Pantry List: Dried Fruits

◆◆◆◆◆◆

Apples	Golden raisins	Prunes
Apricots	Peaches	Raisins
Cherries	Pears	Tropical fruits such as
Figs	Pineapple	papaya

Recipes Featuring Dried Fruits

Apricot Hamantaschen

Makes about 1 dozen

Five Simple Things to Do with Dried Fruit

◆◆◆◆◆◆

◆ Add a generous amount of raisins to curry-seasoned ground meat.

Hamantaschen are triangle-shaped pastries eaten at the Jewish festival of Purim, the name taken from the evil Haman who threatened the Jews of ancient Persia. His plot was foiled, and since then this delicious cookie has been his namesake.

The hamantaschen from my childhood were baked by large, flour-covered Russian women. The hearty cookies were shortbread or yeast dough on the outside, disappointment on the inside. That is because invariably they were filled with prunes, and I waited until maturity to appreciate prunes.

Hamantaschen can, however, be filled with any seed or dried fruit filling. Ground poppy seeds simmered in milk and sugar along with a cinnamon stick are good, but my favorite is apricot, especially in the following recipe, which is as good during the rest of the year as it is at Purim.

Form into meatballs and simmer in tomato sauce, or make into patties and grill.

◆◆◆◆◆◆◆

◆ Add a handful of dried figs to red wine when poaching pears or peaches.

◆◆◆◆◆◆◆

◆ **PRUNE ICE CREAM** Simmer a handful of pitted prunes in brandy until they soften and plump. Drain any excess liquid, reserving it for another use, then roughly chop prunes and mix them into softened vanilla or coffee ice cream; refreeze to firm. Serve sprinkled with ground cinnamon or cardamom.

◆◆◆◆◆◆◆

◆ **PRUNE POUND CAKE** Fold diced prunes into your favorite rich pound cake, such as one made with sour cream.

◆◆◆◆◆◆◆

◆ **ALMOND PASTE— STUFFED APRICOTS** Stuff a spoonful of almond paste into each pitted apricot and enjoy as a sweetmeat with mint tea or brandy.

DOUGH

3/4 cup (1-1/2 sticks) unsalted butter, at room temperature

2/3 cup sugar

1 egg

2 cups sifted flour

1/4 cup milk combined with 1 teaspoon vanilla or almond extract

APRICOT FILLING

8 ounces (1 cup) dried apricots

1 cinnamon stick

1/4 cup water

3 tablespoons sugar or to taste

1. To prepare dough: Cream butter with sugar.
2. Mix milk with eggs and extract.
3. Beat in 1/4 cup flour, then alternately add remaining flour and milk mixture in 3 batches.
4. Cover or wrap in plastic and place in refrigerator for at least 1 hour.
5. To make filling: Combine dried apricots with cinnamon stick, water, and sugar.
6. Bring to a boil, then reduce heat and simmer for about 10 minutes, or until apricots have turned tender. The amount of time this takes will depend on the apricots you use.
7. Remove cinnamon stick and puree apricots with cooking liquid until smooth.
8. Preheat oven to 350°. Roll dough about 1/4 to 1/8 inch thick. Cut into circles about 3 inches in diameter. Place 1 tablespoon or so of apricot filling in center, then fold up three sides, sealing them halfway up sides, to form a triangle with an opening in center with filling peeking through.
9. Arrange pastries on a baking sheet and bake for 15 minutes, or until pastries are pale golden in color. Enjoy warm or cool.

Dried Cherry and Exotic Fruits Compote

Dried cherries are tart-sweet pie cherries that are pitted (usually) and dried to raisin-like nuggets; they are also known as sun-dried cherries. Nibble as a pick-me-up snack, or rehydrate and add them to vinaigrettes (especially for duck salad) or sweet savory sauces. Pureed and

Serves 4

strained, sweetened, and seasoned with a dash of almond extract, they make a fragrant frozen ice or sorbet.

While cherries may be rehydrated by soaking in water, a combination of half water and half brandy gives them even more flavor.

1 cup hot water, or 1/2 cup hot
  water and 1/2 cup hot brandy
1/2 cup dried pitted cherries
Selection of juicy fresh ripe
  tropical fruits: pear, kiwi,
banana, sliced pineapple,
  blood orange, guava, caram-
  bola, etc., depending on
  availability
Honey to taste

1. Pour hot liquid over cherries; let sit, covered, at room temperature overnight.

2. Peel and dice fresh fruit, then combine with cherries and their soaking liquid. Sweeten with honey and chill before serving.

Moroccan Honey Lamb with Prunes

Serves 4 to 6

Savory roasted lamb, tender bits falling off the bone, awash with spices and honey and punctuated with prunes. The spices, especially the saffron, give a refreshingly bitter edge to an otherwise sweet dish. This delicious dish shakes the palate up in a delightful way.

Serve for a feast also starring a vegetable couscous, and perhaps a savory salad and some spicy-hot relish, along with a big bowl of cool yogurt.

8 ounces (1 cup) pitted prunes
1-1/2 cups hot water or tea
2-1/2 pounds lamb stewing
  meat, cut into chunky
  portions
1 onion, chopped
1/2 cup chopped fresh parsley
1/2 teaspoon ground ginger
1/2 teaspoon curry powder
Pinch of ground nutmeg
Large pinch of black pepper
About 2 teaspoons ground
  cinnamon
1/4 teaspoon saffron
1/4 to 1/2 cup honey, to taste
About 1 cup beef broth
  (optional)
1/4 cup almonds, toasted (see
  page 239)

1. Rehydrate prunes by pouring hot water or tea over them to cover, and let sit for at least an hour.

2. Preheat oven to 350°. Combine meat with onion, parsley, and spices and place in a roasting pan. Bake for 2 hours, or long enough to brown meat and render it tender.

3. Add prune soaking liquid and honey (along with 1 cup or so of beef broth if it seems dry) and return to oven. Continue to bake another 20 minutes or so, turning every so often so that meat caramelizes, then add prunes and heat through together.

4. Serve lamb, which by now should be falling off its bones, with prunes, all topped with a scattering of toasted almonds.

Green Island Beef and Guinness Stew

◆ BASIC PANTRY

Serves 4 to 6

Stew—a hearty, simmering potful of meat and vegetables—is no doubt the national dish of Ireland. Whatever is available goes into the stewpot, and the result is a nourishing one-pot meal capable of sustaining a large family.

Now, about the addition of the prunes to this stew: they add an indefinable richness of flavor, a certain elusive richness, and a mysterious deep flavor. And though the original recipe called for Guinness stout, I use a combination of beer (or ale) and port, since that is what was in my pantry the first time I made the dish and I liked it so much I've made it that way ever since.

2 pounds boneless chuck or other stew beef, cut into bite-sized pieces	1/2 cup port
	1-1/2 cups beef broth
7 to 8 onions, sliced thinly lengthwise	1 bay leaf
	1/4 teaspoon dried thyme
1 tablespoon vegetable oil, or 1 piece bacon, diced	1 tablespoon chopped fresh parsley
1/2 cup all-purpose flour	Tiny pinch of ground cloves
2 carrots, sliced 1/4 inch thick or diced	Salt and black pepper to taste
	10 prunes, pitted
1 bottle (12 ounces) beer, ale, or stout	Champ, following

1. Brown meat along with half of onions in oil, or cook bacon to render fat, then remove bacon bits to brown meat and onions. When meat is lightly browned, sprinkle in flour and stir, cooking for several minutes.

2. Add carrots, then pour in beer, port, and broth, and add bay leaf, thyme, parsley, cloves, salt, and a generous shake of black pepper.

3. Simmer, covered, until meat is almost tender, about 1-1/2 hours.

4. Add prunes, then return to stove and simmer until completely tender, another hour or so.

5. By now prunes should have disappeared into a dark, deeply flavored sauce. Serve immediately, accompanied with Champ.

Champ

Also known as skelk, this rich Irish dish consists of creamy mashed potatoes enriched with lots of green onions that have been wilted in simmering milk. Traditionally, skelk is served with a lump of sweet butter melting down over it in luscious rivulets.

6 large all-purpose potatoes, peeled and quartered, or cut into chunks
1/2–3/4 cups milk

6–10 green onions, thinly sliced
4 tablespoons butter
Salt and pepper to taste

1. Put potatoes in pan with water and cover. Bring to boil and cook over medium heat for 15 minutes or until potatoes are tender when pierced with a fork. Drain well and keep warm over a low heat while you wilt the onions.

2. Combine milk and onions and bring to boil. Reduce heat and simmer about 5 minutes, until onions are soft.

3. Mash potatoes, gradually adding milk (as needed), onions, and butter. Season generously with salt and pepper.

THE PASTA PANTRY

❖◆

Despite our current rapture over fresh pasta, we shouldn't forget how very good dried pasta can be. And it's the perfect pantry food, waiting patiently on a shelf or in the freezer to be cooked and eaten.

Dried pasta can be a humble dish of everyday nurturing or an elegant dish of sophistication, and it's ready within but a few minutes, not counting the sauce.

Though the Chinese claim that they taught Marco Polo the fine art of pasta making, records show that noodle eating was going on in the West well before 1298, the year Polo returned from his travels to the Far East. It is generally believed that pasta originated in the neolithic Middle East as a pounded paste of toasted grains; eventually it would be boiled into a pasta-like mixture.

The first record we have of pasta being eaten in Italy is a bas relief carved on a fourth-century tomb, about 30 miles outside of Rome. It shows tools of pasta making, and they look amazingly like the tools used today.

The Western passion for pasta has continued unabated. In Cicero's day, the Romans ate a flat ribbonlike pasta called lagunum, much like our contemporary lasagne. By the thirteenth century, pasta was an important part of the Italian diet. And while flat noodles were still in vogue, someone wrapped a sheet of pasta around a knitting needle, and the round macaroni was invented. By the fifteenth century a wide variety of pasta shapes existed.

Thomas Jefferson brought pasta back from Italy to the New World, along with a pasta machine and huge supply of Parmesan cheese (his favorite dish was spaghetti with butter and cheese). However, it wasn't until large groups of immigrants started arriving in America and operating restaurants that pasta—known then to the American public simply as spaghetti or macaroni—became part of the American diet.

Even today, when we have a large pasta industry, the best dried pasta comes from Italy. Made from durum wheat semolina, it absorbs water but doesn't get gummy or soft unless overcooked.

Other ethnic groups have contributed to our pasta consciousness as well. The German immigrants brought over wide flat noodles and casseroles that became staple foods in the Midwest; more recently, Asian immigrants have brought a wide variety of spicy and sprightly pasta dishes based on noodles made from either rice or bean flour, in addition to their own unique wheat noodles.

As with beans, cooks inevitably end up with small amounts of pasta left in the bag. Instead of wasting space with accumulating partially full bags, pour the last little bits of pasta into a big jar. Break spaghetti into small pieces. At some point when the jar begins to fill, you will want to make minestrone or pasta fagioli, and you will have an interesting collection of pastas for it.

Pasta: Fresh vs. Dried

The passion for fresh pasta nearly pushed dried pasta off the pantry shelves for a while. Happily, the infatuation cooled and settled into a mature love, and now both live together happily in our kitchens.

They are both made from flour and water (though fresh pasta often has eggs added while dried seldom does), but fresh pasta and dried pasta are almost two different foods, with completely different qualities.

Fresh Pasta, at its best, is light and tender. It should have very little, if any, chewiness and no doughiness (except for thick udon noodles).

It comes in a wide variety of shapes and sizes, ranging from tagliarini, fettuccine, lasagne, gnocchi, Chinese noodles, and wonton/ egg-roll wrappers; it is sold stuffed, as ravioli, tortellini, agnolotti, pelmeni, wontons, and so on. Often fresh pasta is sold with flavoring kneaded into the dough: in Italian delicatessens you'll most often find pasta green from chopped spinach or pale green from herbs. In trendier pasta shops, the noodles are likely to be flavored with wild mushrooms, hot chili peppers, squid ink, lemon zest, and black pepper, and on and on.

The hallmark of fresh pasta is its delicate nature. It should be cooked in simple ways that enhance it: a glistening of butter, a sprinkling of herbs; or a dab of caviar or olive paste; try a drizzle of Asian sesame oil and soy sauce, with a sprinkling of chives. Save the heartier sauces for dried pasta. (With one exception: a rustic ragù, simmered from all sorts of savory meats, makes a delectable contrast served on tender fresh noodles.)

Fresh pasta cooks extremely quickly—usually in only a few minutes' time. Add an extra minute to that and you might have a pot of mush.

Dried Pasta is everything a pantry food should be. It takes up little space on the shelf, needs no refrigeration, is nutritious, gives itself to endless variations, and is strongly appealing.

Though some dried pastas are delicate, by and large they are sturdy, chewy, and robust. They do take longer to cook than fresh, some taking up to 8 minutes, depending upon the thickness, but they should never be cooked beyond al dente, or just yielding to the teeth.

Dried pasta comes in such a wide variety of shapes and sizes, it would probably be impossible to catalogue them completely. Just when you thought you had covered every type available, you'd notice a new package tucked away in the corner of some ethnic delicatessen or specialty food shop.

The best dried pasta comes from Italy, and is made from hard durum wheat. But Greek pastas have their own cozy taste, and Asian pastas have enriched our pantry and cuisine immeasurably.

Dried pastas are also available flavored with vegetable purees, herbs, seafood essences, spices, and so on. One of my current favorites is an Italian import of sturdy, chewy spaghetti flavored and colored with a variety of vegetables: its multihued appearance is as delightful as its subtle vegetable flavor. Italian whole-wheat pasta has a nutty flavor, delicious combined with potatoes and green beans; and Japanese buckwheat pasta is wonderful not only in a classic broth, but in East-West dishes such as Buckwheat Soba with Crab, Peas, and Cream (page 281).

In general, dried pasta benefits from a sharper or stronger sauce than does fresh pasta. Dried pasta can support hearty flavors and so adds immensely to the possibilities of pantry cuisine.

STORAGE TIPS Dried pasta lasts about 2 years on the pantry shelf. Whole-wheat and flavored pastas will deteriorate within about 6 months. Fresh pasta may be kept in the freezer up to 3 months.

I adhere to the Italian way of eating pasta: in a shallow soup bowl. The official explanation is that the pasta stays warmer longer, since it remains in a smaller area and doesn't have the whole plate to straggle out to, cooling off in the process. But that doesn't explain the way pasta just tastes better in a bowl. I accept it as Italian magic.

And as for sprinkling Parmesan: keep a large chunk of Parmesan or other dry grating cheese to pass, along with the grater, from diner to diner, so that each person can enjoy a flurry of freshly grated cheese over his or her pasta.

Pasta Basics

LONG THIN STRANDS OF PASTA Spaghetti, vermicelli, long fusilli, spaghetti integrale (whole wheat); flat pastas: fettuccine and linguine; round thickish pastas with a hole in their center: bucatini, perciatelli, Greek thick round pastas; very thin pastas: capellini (also known as angel hair, or fideos), fedelini, spaghettini, tagliatelle; tonnarelli (square cut)

TINY PASTAS FOR SOUP Anellini (little loops), alphabets, stelline (stars), orzo or semini di melone (seed shapes), acini di pepe (the size and shape of peppercorns); tubetti (tiny tubes)

SHORT THICK MACARONI Small and large elbows; small and large conchigliette (seashells); cavatelli, orecchiette (flat round ovals); round hollow quills such as rigatoni and penne; fusilli, rotelle, farfalle (bow ties), lumache (shaped like snails); dumplinglike gemelli (chewy twists) and gnocchi

FLAT NOODLES Lasagne, flat wide noodles, pappardelle, trenette

VEGETABLE AND SPECIALTY PASTAS Spinach, multicolored vegetable, corn, artichoke, squid ink, porcini, saffron, tarragon, basil, lemon, chili, etc.

STUFFED PASTA Dried cheese-stuffed tortellini, tricolor tortellini

ASIAN PASTA Buckwheat soba, mung bean vermicelli (bean threads), wide and thin rice vermicelli (rice sticks), ramen-type noodles, Japanese thick udon (dried or vacuum packed, usually in refrigerator section of Asian shops)

FREEZER Potato gnocchi, agnolotti, tortellini, and ravioli stuffed with traditional meat, cheese, chicken, or spinach fillings, as well as contemporary ones: mushroom, seafood, red pepper and sausage, porcini and veal, Cajun crab, sun-dried tomato, and so forth, in pastas of various colors and flavors: tomato, beet, herb, porcini, chili, etc.; wonton noodles; fresh Chinese rice noodles; fresh Chinese thin egg noodles

The Basic Pasta Pantry

◆◆◆◆◆◆

spaghetti, capellini, fettuccine	alphabets	vegetable-flavored pastas of choice
elbows, farfalle, seashells	ramen wonton noodles	lasagne noodles

The Intermediate Pasta Pantry

◆◆◆◆◆◆

To the above list, you'll add:

orzo, tubetti	Italian whole-wheat pasta	gnocchi
orecchiette	rice noodles	pappardelle
fusilli corti (short)	mung bean thread	lasagne flavored with spinach or herbs
dried stuffed tortellini or ravioli	fresh Chinese rice noodles	udon
buckwheat soba		

Recipes Featuring Pasta

Perigord-style Tomato Broth with Acini di Pepe

◆◆◆ ADVANCED PANTRY

Serves 4 as main course,
6 as first course

This comforting tomato-scented broth is seasoned with thyme and enriched with the tiny pasta known as acini di pepe. The size and shape of peppercorns, these small, perfectly round, and slightly chewy bits of pasta add a delightful texture to the soup. While I love acini di pepe, any of the other tiny pastas may be used. In the Perigord region of France, often the soup is served with thin capellini, broken into short lengths.

1 onion, chopped
3 garlic cloves, chopped
1/2 teaspoon dried thyme
1 carrot, diced
2 to 3 tablespoons olive oil
2 cups diced fresh or canned
  tomatoes

1 cup tomato juice
3 cups chicken, beef, or vegetable broth
4 to 6 ounces acini di pepe or
  other small soup pasta
Freshly grated Parmesan cheese

1. Sauté onion, garlic, thyme, and carrot in olive oil until softened and lightly golden. Add tomatoes and continue cooking another 3 to 5 minutes.

2. Add tomato juice, broth, and pasta. Bring to a boil, then reduce heat and let simmer until pasta is tender, about 10 minutes, depending on pasta. Be very careful not to overcook the pasta.

3. Serve immediately, offering each person freshly grated Parmesan to sprinkle on his/her soup.

Udon with Green Onion Custard

◆◆ INTERMEDIATE PANTRY

Serves 1 as a main lunch or supper course, 2 as a first course

Udon are thick, slightly doughy, Japanese noodles. They are sold dried and in vacuum packs in the refrigerated section of Asian groceries with a small packet of seaweed- and/or bonito-based broth. Dried udon are inferior to the vacuum-packed fresh ones in that they're flatter and lack chewiness and juiciness. If using dried udon, boil until tender, then use in soups, casseroles, and so on, as you would the fresh.

As do ramen, they make a cozy bowlful, delicious topped with nearly any small bits of savory foods. My favorite is the following extremely simple one, made for me long ago when my daughter was a baby and I hired a delightful Japanese foreign student to babysit.

A variation of egg drop soup, a layer of egg and onions is steamed on top of the soup rather than drizzled into it in strands. The recipe makes 1 serving, to correspond with the single serving packets, but of course it can be doubled, tripled, or multiplied at will to serve as many as you'd like.

1 vacuum-pack udon, with packet of broth flavoring
1 egg

1 green onion, thinly sliced
Dash soy sauce

1. Prepare udon and broth according to package directions.

2. Beat egg, then add green onions, soy sauce, and a teaspoon or two of prepared broth.

3. When broth is hot, reduce heat to medium, then pour egg and onion mixture on top of simmering broth. Cover and let cook over low medium heat for about 5 minutes, or until egg is set. Serve immediately, with either chopsticks or large ceramic spoons.

Turkey Soup with Autumn Vegetables and Stelline Pasta

Serves 6 as a first course, 4 as a main course

This is a comforting soup full of gentle yet lively flavors, the stelline and sprinkling of Parmesan adding an Italian accent.

Vary this recipe according to whatever is in your pantry: if you have no stelline pasta, use any sort of small soup pastas: anellini, tiny squares, orzo; in place of turkey, use diced boneless chicken. As with most soups, this is best when made with a homemade broth; think about it after Thanksgiving when you're faced with that turkey carcass and wondering what to do with it.

1/2 pound, 8 ounces (1 cup) turkey thigh, boneless, skin removed and cut into bite-sized pieces	1 tablespoon olive oil
	1 tablespoon flour
	6 cups chicken or turkey broth
	1/4 cup tomato sauce
1/2 onion, chopped	1 bay leaf
1/2 carrot, chopped	1 tablespoon chopped fresh parsley
1 garlic clove, chopped	
1/4 turnip, diced	1/2 cup fresh or frozen peas
1/2 red bell pepper, diced	1/4 to 1/3 cup stelline pasta
1 large slice pumpkin or other winter squash, peeled and diced (about 3/4–1 cup)	Grated parmesan for sprinkling

1. Sauté turkey with onion, carrot, garlic, turnip, red bell pepper, and pumpkin in olive oil until lightly browned. Sprinkle in flour and cook a minute or two longer.

2. Pour in broth, tomato sauce, bay leaf, and parsley, and simmer 20 minutes or so, then add peas and pasta, and simmer for another 10 minutes, or until vegetables and pasta are tender and soup is rich in flavor. Serve hot with a sprinkling of Parmesan cheese.

Orzo and Peas with Prosciutto in Garlic-Saffron Cream

Serves 4 as a first course

Orzo (and other similar pastas such as semini di melone) are tiny rice-shaped pastas favored not only in Italy, but throughout the Mediterranean. Often they are served simply, in soup, but they also give themselves easily to sassy saucing, especially in Greece, where they might be blanketed with a tangy egg-lemon sauce or, my favorite way, mixed with a bit of tomato sauce and the drippings from a savory herb-scented lamb roast.

In the following recipe they are combined with peas, punctuated with bits of prosciutto, then sauced with a rich garlic-saffron cream. A sublime dish to spoon up any time you are tending towards indulgence.

1/2 pound orzo or similar pasta
4 to 5 garlic cloves, coarsely chopped
2 tablespoons unsalted butter
2 cups chicken broth
1 cup sour cream or crème fraîche
2 to 3 ounces prosciutto or Serrano ham, cut into thin strips or dice

1 cup fresh or frozen peas
Large pinch saffron dissolved in 1 tablespoon cool water
Black pepper to taste
About 1/4 cup grated Parmesan cheese for sprinkling (or pass a large chunk for each person to add as desired)

1. Cook orzo in boiling salted water until just al dente. Drain and set aside.

2. Lightly heat garlic in butter, then add broth and cooked orzo. Heat until bubbly around edges.

3. Stir sour cream or crème fraîche so that it becomes creamy, then off heat stir it into hot orzo mixture. Add prosciutto, peas, and saffron, and warm together. The mixture should remain a bit soupy but thicken somewhat. Season with black pepper to taste. Serve immediately, each portion sprinkled with Parmesan cheese.

Italian Countryside Pasta with Prosciutto, Sage, Olives, and Garlic Butter

[PAPPARDELLE ALLA COMPAGNIA]

◆◆ INTERMEDIATE PANTRY

Serves 4 as a main course for polite people or as a first course for hearty eaters

A pasta of pantry luck, thrown together one summer evening in a Tuscan villa I had rented. What little we had to eat was on the shelves, as the shops hadn't reopened for the afternoon as I had thought they would.

I foraged: pasta, of course, and a sage bush fortuitously growing next to the front door, a handful of olives and a slice of prosciutto I had salvaged from lunch.

Dinner that night in the open air with the sounds of neighboring villages echoing across the valley was one of the most memorable meals of my life. I saw my first fireflies that night, and perhaps a hundred million shooting stars. And the pasta was very, very good.

12 ounces dried delicate wide
flat noodles
2 tablespoons unsalted soft
butter
1 tablespoon olive oil
3 to 4 garlic cloves, minced
1 to 2 tablespoons fresh sage
leaves, coarsely chopped

2 ounces prosciutto (about 4
slices), cut into thin shreds
1/4 cup black oil-cured olives,
pitted and halved
3 tablespoons grated Parmesan
cheese
Black pepper (and salt, if
needed) to taste

1. Cook noodles in boiling salted water until al dente. Do not over-cook; delicate noodles cook very quickly.

2. Meanwhile, heat butter gently and, when melted, add olive oil, garlic, and sage leaves. Warm together but do not sauté.

3. Toss hot drained pasta with aromatic butter-oil mixture and add prosciutto and olives.

4. Serve immediately, topped with a generous sprinkle of Parmesan cheese.

Auntie's Napa Cabbage Salad with Crunchy Chinese Noodles, Nuts and Seeds

◆◆ INTERMEDIATE PANTRY

Serves 4 as a main lunch
dish, 6 as a side dish

Ramen noodles have, in a short period of time, gone from the Asian pantry to the all-American one. Lasting nearly forever on the shelf, they cook up in about 5 minutes. Some of them are very good; most of them are very salty. They come in a huge variety of flavors, from the chicken to some frightening flavor combinations. There also is natural foods ramen, with whole-wheat noodles and seaweed-based vegetarian broths.

Here they are with a handful of nuts fried to a crispy brown and topping a Napa cabbage salad. It is strikingly good, the sort of dish to make for a summer barbecue, accompanied with grilled soy-marinated chicken or fried chicken with pecans, Georgia style. The recipe can be multiplied for a large group.

1 big head Napa cabbage, including stalks and core, base
trimmed
6 green onions, thinly sliced
1 package chicken-flavored
ramen noodles, with packet
of seasoning

1/4 cup butter or vegetable oil
1/3 cup sesame seeds
2 ounces slivered almonds or
unsalted dry-roasted peanuts
(1/2 cup)
One 1/2- to 3/4-inch piece fresh
ginger, coarsely chopped

3 tablespoons soy sauce	1/4 cup rice vinegar
1/3 cup vegetable oil	1/3 cup sugar
2 tablespoons Asian (toasted) sesame oil	Salt and black pepper to taste

1. Coarsely chop cabbage. Combine with green onions and set aside in refrigerator.

2. Lightly crush noodles while still in package.

3. Melt butter or heat vegetable oil, then brown sesame seeds, almonds, and ramen noodles, adding seasoning powder from packet. When toasty, crunchy, and deliciously browned, after 5 to 8 minutes, remove from heat.

4. Mix dressing by combining ginger, soy sauce, vegetable oil, sesame oil, rice vinegar, and sugar in a blender, then whirling to mix well. Season with salt and pepper. (The dressing will seem sweet and not exciting, but it works well with the rest of the salad.)

5. When ready to serve, toss cabbage and green onions with dressing, then top with a generous sprinkling of seeds, nuts, and crispy noodles.

6. Serve immediately. (If making ahead, prepare all the components, then toss together at the last minute.)

Perciatelli or Bucatini with Sardines and Fennel, Sicilian Style

[PASTA CON LE SARDE]

◆◆ INTERMEDIATE PANTRY

Serves 4 to 6 as a main course

Pasta con le sarde is a classic of the Sicilian kitchen, with as many variations as there are cooks on that sun-washed Mediterranean island. The dish may be made with either fresh or canned sardines, and served warm or cold, like a salad or picnic dish.

This version makes good use of the pantry including sardines and anchovies, pine nuts and golden raisins, and toasted bread crumbs; in fact, aside from the fresh fennel, it is a pantry-only pasta.

1/4 cup dry bread crumbs	Generous pinch of saffron dissolved in 1/2 cup cool water
1/3 cup plus 1 tablespoon olive oil	2 tins boneless sardines, drained and cut up
1 onion, chopped	Pinch of fennel seeds
3 anchovies, cut up into pieces	
1/4 cup pine nuts	
2 tablespoons golden raisins	

(continued)

1 pound thick round pasta such
as perciatelli or bucatini,
broken into bite-sized
lengths

1 bulb fresh fennel, cut into
julienne
1/2 cup or more coarsely
chopped fennel greens
Salt and pepper to taste

1. Lightly brown bread crumbs in 1 tablespoon olive oil. Set aside.
2. Sauté onion and anchovies in 1/3 cup olive oil until onion is soft and anchovies fall apart. Add pine nuts, raisins, and saffron water and boil for a minute or so, then add sardines and fennel seed. Set aside.
3. Cook pasta in boiling water; when half done, after 3–4 minutes, add fennel. At this point the pasta should be pliable, but too crunchy to eat.
4. When both pasta and fennel are al dente, after about 4 minutes, drain and toss with sauce. Sprinkle with chopped fennel greens and toasted bread crumbs; add salt and pepper to taste.

Treasure Hunt Pasta in Herbed Tomato Cream

◆◆ INTERMEDIATE PANTRY

Serves 4

At its best when prepared with a wide selection of stuffed pastas: each forkful becomes a new discovery, as you eat your way through a bowlful, searching for edible treasures.

I find that the best way of having a selection of varied stuffed pastas is to go to the neighborhood pasta shop and buy a selection, then repackage them into parcels, each containing 4 or 5 different types, and freeze the extras. If fresh filled pastas are not available, dried ones, which have become so easily available, will take their place gracefully.

4 garlic cloves, chopped
4 to 5 mushrooms, chopped
2 tablespoons butter
2 cups coarsely chopped peeled
and seeded fresh or canned
tomatoes, drained of excess
juice
1/4 cup tomato paste
2 cups heavy (whipping) cream
2 ounces (about 4 slices) prosciutto, Serrano ham, bacon
(2 slices) or pancetta, diced

Salt and pepper to taste
Large pinch dried, or several
sprigs fresh, marjoram
1 to 1-1/2 pounds mixed fresh
stuffed pastas: spinach and
ricotta, porcini, sausage, etc.
Grated parmesan cheese, for
sprinkling
Chopped fresh parsley, basil,
or marjoram

1. Lightly sauté garlic and mushrooms in butter, or, if using bacon or pancetta, brown along with garlic and mushrooms; you will probably not need butter. When softened, add tomatoes and tomato paste and cook over medium heat to a thick sauce, about 5 to 10 minutes.

2. Stir in cream, cook another 5 minutes or so to meld flavors, then add prosciutto (if using) and marjoram. Season with salt and pepper and set aside.

3. Cook pasta in rapidly boiling salted water until just tender; drain.

4. Toss cooked pasta with sauce and serve immediately, each portion sprinkled with Parmesan cheese and fresh herbs.

Esther's Apple-Noodle Kugel

◆ **BASIC PANTRY**

Serves 4 to 6 as a side dish

This kugel is blissfully buttery, rich with cinnamon and apples and reminiscent of the Old Country. Kugel, for those uninitiated, is a rich baked pudding of noodles, fruit, cheese, sugar, and spices. It is a specialty of the Jews from Eastern Europe and Russia and, despite its rich sweetness, is served as part of the meal, not as dessert—though I remember an elderly relative serving it as a snack.

This particular kugel came to my table from Russia, via a 50-year stopover in Nebraska. It is courtesy of my friend Esther Novak, who grew up on a cattle ranch in Nebraska. Her father had dreamed of owning his own land when he was a boy in Eastern Europe; in Nebraska his dream became a reality. In the Midwest, far away from his countrymen, who were migrating to New York and the other urban areas, Esther's father surrounded himself and his family with cows and fields of corn. At the Jewish holidays, however, Midwest farm cooking gave way to the Old World specialties, such as this kugel.

Delicious as this kugel is, it always tastes better when I remember this elderly Jewish farmer's stories of cow-raising and country life.

1 package (12 to 16 ounces) broad noodles	2 medium unpeeled apples, coarsely grated
1/2 cup (1 stick) unsalted butter	2 teaspoons ground cinnamon
1/2 cup small-curd cottage cheese	1 cup sugar
3 large or 4 small-to-medium eggs, lightly beaten	1/2 cup raisins
	1/2 teaspoon baking soda
	Tiny pinch of salt

1. Preheat oven to 350°. Cook noodles in boiling salted water until just tender. Drain and set aside.

2. Melt butter.

3. Combine noodles with butter and rest of ingredients in a rectangular baking pan.

4. Bake until brown and crusty, 1 to 1-1/2 hours. Serve immediately.

Summer Day Yellow and Green Cool Pasta

◆◆ INTERMEDIATE PANTRY

Serves 4 to 6 as a summer lunch, 6 as a first course or side dish

Combining yellow and green pasta has been popular in Italy for several years; it's called *paglia e fieno*, or "straw and hay," since the colors are reminiscent of the stacks and mounds of straw and hay dotting the Italian countryside.

Cooked al dente and served cool, the classic "straw and hay" becomes a spunky salad. Each of the savory and varied ingredients gives a differing flavor and texture, from the strong briny accents of olives to the nearly sweet strips of pepper, from salty-sweet prosciutto to tender asparagus and sweet basil, all of it bound up in that rich garlic balm, aïoli.

This makes a sensational lunch, along with a plate of mesclun, and maybe a cold roast chicken. For dessert I wouldn't mind sweet garden-fresh cherries tossed with ice cubes (instead of chilling them in a refrigerator, which can dull garden freshness), or a tiny piece of something richly chocolate.

By the way, using homemade aïoli in this dish is important. If eating raw eggs seems a bit risky because of possible salmonella infection, be sure to use organic free-range eggs from a safe source, or substitute Cheater's Aïoli on page 155.

1/2 pound *each* dried yellow and green pasta such as fusilli, seashells, or 3/4

pound each fresh yellow and green pasta (fettuccine, linguine, etc.)

FOR THE AÏOLI
2 garlic cloves
1 egg
Dash of lemon juice
1 tablespoon Dijon mustard
1 cup extra-virgin olive oil

1/2 pound asparagus tips, steamed al dente and cooled
1/2 cup roasted red peppers, cut into strips

1/4 cup Greek olives,
   pitted and halved
4 ounces prosciutto (8 slices),
   cut into strips

Salt and pepper to taste
1/4 cup sweet basil leaves,
   cut into strips

1. Cook pasta in lots of rapidly boiling salted water until al dente; drain. Rinse in cold water to stop cooking.

2. To make aïoli: in a blender or food processor, puree garlic, then add egg, lemon juice, and mustard. With machine on, add olive oil in a thin stream until sauce has thickened.

3. Toss cooled pasta with sauce, and add asparagus, red pepper strips, olives, and prosciutto. Season to taste.

4. Chill until ready to serve, then sprinkle generously with basil.

Whole-Wheat Spaghetti with Black and Green Olives, Tomatoes, and Goat Cheese

[SPAGHETTI INTEGRALE ALLA ZINGARA]

◆◆ INTERMEDIATE PANTRY

Serves 4 to 6 as a main course, 6 to 8 as a first course

Whole-wheat spaghetti from Italy is nutty tasting, with a good, supple quality that lends itself to robust saucing. This dish is a great example: "gypsy-like" colors and flavors, with two types of olives, chopped tomatoes, garlic, and the tangy creaminess of goat cheese.

1 pound whole-wheat pasta imported from Italy
15 black Italian-style olives,
   pitted and halved
15 green Mediterranean-type olives, pitted and halved
3 garlic cloves, chopped
4 medium ripe tomatoes,
   seeded and diced

1/3 cup olive oil
3 to 4 ounces fresh goat cheese such as Italian caprina, French Montrachet, or California chèvre, crumbled
1/2 cup fresh basil leaves, torn or coarsely cut
Black pepper to taste

1. Cook pasta in boiling salted water until al dente; drain.

2. Meanwhile, combine black and green olives with garlic, tomatoes, and olive oil.

3. Toss hot drained pasta with this mixture, then add goat cheese, basil leaves, and black pepper. Serve immediately.

Capellini with Tomatoes, Mushrooms, and Roasted Garlic

◆ BASIC PANTRY

Serves 4 as a main course, 4 to 6 as a first course or side dish

Confartarse congli aglietti is a Calabrese saying that means "console yourself with garlic." I take this advice seriously.

In this dish the garlic is lavish indeed, but, cooked whole until soft, it is not sharp at all. The roasted whole cloves of garlic have a mild fragrance and sweet earthy flavor that pull together the freshness of the tomatoes and heartiness of the mushrooms.

The choice of pasta is important here: capellini, a thin pasta, deliciously traps the sauce between its delicate strands.

4 whole garlic heads
6 tablespoons olive oil
4 ounces fresh mushrooms, thinly sliced (cultivated, shiitakes, chanterelles, oyster, etc.)
5 large tomatoes, peeled, seeded, and chopped
2 to 3 tablespoons tomato sauce, optional (use if tomatoes are a bit listless or acidic, or if dish simply needs more sauce)
12 ounces dried capellini
Salt and pepper to taste
3 to 4 tablespoons freshly grated Parmesan cheese
1 tablespoon chopped fresh thyme or oregano

1. Heat oven to 350°. Cut off just enough of tops of garlic heads to expose cloves inside. Rub all over with olive oil, and place cut side down in a shallow baking pan. Roast for 35 to 45 minutes, or until bulbs have softened. Turn occasionally if they begin to brown.

2. Remove from oven and let cool.

3. When cool, hold uncut end and with your fingers squeeze out soft flesh. Set aside.

4. Heat 2 tablespoons of olive oil in a skillet and lightly sauté mushrooms until golden but still firm. Remove from pan and reserve, then add tomatoes to pan and lightly sauté them in remaining olive oil, stirring occasionally until they thicken. Add tomato sauce.

5. Cook pasta in a large pot of boiling salted water for just 3 or 4 minutes, or until al dente. Drain.

6. Meanwhile, add reserved mushrooms and roasted garlic flesh to tomatoes and heat until piping hot. Add hot drained pasta and toss together. Season to taste.

7. Serve immediately, sprinkled with Parmesan cheese and thyme or oregano.

Capellini with Multicolored Tomatoes in Balsamic Vinaigrette

Serves 4

An exquisite collection of ripe tomatoes, preferably a full palette of reds, yellows, oranges, and greens, in a variety of sizes and shapes— for this you need a very special greengrocer or garden. The farmer's market is good for ripe red tomatoes in season, and the pantry provides the rest.

The dish is no more than pasta tossed with garlic and olive oil, then topped with balsamic-and-herb-marinated tomatoes. Keep the pasta, olive oil, and balsamic vinegar in your pantry, waiting for high tomato season.

1 pound dried capellini or other very thin pasta	10 to 15 beautiful ripe small or medium tomatoes, preferably in a rainbow of colors
5 garlic cloves, finely chopped	1 tablespoon balsamic vinegar
1/4 cup extra-virgin olive oil	1 tablespoon or so chopped fresh herb such as thyme or marjoram
Salt and pepper to taste	

1. Boil pasta quickly; it will cook in only 3–4 minutes. Drain.
2. Toss drained pasta immediately with 3 garlic cloves, olive oil, salt, and pepper. Set aside to cool to room temperature.
3. Quarter tomatoes and marinate with remaining garlic, balsamic vinegar, salt, and pepper, plus a dash of sugar if tomatoes are acidic. Let marinate for at least 15 minutes, or up to 2 days, in refrigerator.
4. Serve room-temperature garlic-olive oil pasta topped with marinated tomatoes and sprinkle with herbs.

Buckwheat Soba with Crab, Peas, and Cream

Serves 4 as a first course or side dish

Buckwheat noodles are adored throughout regions of Japan and Korea, and often are served icy cold, topped with assorted spicy condiments, as a refreshing summer dish. Hot chili oil, chopped green onions, diced tofu, and a drizzle of soy sauce are favored toppings; so, too, is a poached egg served atop buckwheat soba in broth.

Soba is delicious served in Western dishes as well, and I love the way creamy sauces and shellfish are enhanced by the nutty flavor of this pasta.

Soba is sold dried in Asian stores and in supermarkets with a large Asian food section. When choosing soba, be sure to choose one that is not too thin; I find that these dissolve too readily when cooking and don't accept Western-type sauces well. Choose a width that approximates fetuccine if possible.

8 ounces buckwheat soba	1-1/2 cups heavy (whipping) cream
4 tablespoons unsalted butter	
2 garlic cloves, chopped	1 cup freshly grated Parmesan cheese
1/2 to 3/4 pound cooked fresh crab meat	
2 cups fresh or frozen baby peas	Salt (if needed) and pepper to taste

1. Cook pasta in boiling water until just tender. Drain.

2. While pasta is cooking, melt butter with garlic, then add crab and warm together. Add peas and cream, and heat until bubbles form around edge of pan.

3. Toss hot drained pasta with crab-cream mixture, then toss with Parmesan and season with salt and pepper to taste. Serve immediately.

Homey Greek-style Macaroni and Cheese, with Vegetable Juice, Cinnamon, and Oregano

◆ BASIC PANTRY

Serves 4 as a cozy supper dish

This is one of my family's comfort foods, evolved from a winter spent in Greece. I'm not certain it belongs in a cookbook: it is a private sort of dish, one that my daughter and I share when no one else is looking.

12 ounces short pasta such as seashells, elbows, penne, etc.	1 cup vegetable juice such as V-8
2 garlic cloves, chopped	About 1/8 teaspoon *each* ground cinnamon, ground allspice or cloves, and dried oregano
2 tablespoons olive oil or butter	
2 tablespoons flour	12 ounces jack cheese, diced (1-1/2 cups)
2 cups milk	Salt and pepper to taste

1. Cook pasta in rapidly boiling salted water until just al dente. Drain.

2. Lightly sauté garlic in olive oil or butter; sprinkle on flour, stir to cook through, then remove from heat. Slowly stir in milk, pressing any

lumps against side of pan to dissolve them. Return to heat and cook, stirring, until mixture thickens, about 5 to 7 minutes.

3. Add vegetable juice and continue simmering until sauce thickens once again and flavors concentrate. Season with cinnamon, allspice, and oregano; you will probably need more than specified in the recipe—I find that the dish tastes best when it has more cinnamon and allspice than seems reasonable.

4. Stir in cheese and let melt, then toss it all with pasta. Add salt and pepper, then serve immediately.

THE ROOT CELLAR

Before the advent of the refrigerator, each home had a root cellar, a cool dark place for storing root vegetables, onions, cabbages, etc., to protect them from spoilage and preserve them through the long winter.

We may all have refrigerators these days, but most of us still keep a few dark drawers or a similar space for storing vegetables as well as some long-keeping fruit: oranges, apples, lemons, limes, etc. (I remember my grandfather storing his backyard's winter orange crop in a chest of drawers; as a small child it gave me great delight to find dozens and dozens of round orange fruit rolling around in the place where I expected to find underwear and socks.)

The root cellar is a traditional extension of the pantry, updated here to be more contemporary. Here is a short list of suggestions for root cellar foods to keep on hand.

STORAGE TIP Apples can be stored in a cool room or a cold damp cellar, as can all root crops such as carrots, beets, kohlrabi, potatoes, parsnips, turnips, and rutabagas.

Root crops can also be stored in damp sand, but take care not to let the submerged vegetables touch each other or they will rot.

Always keep potatoes in complete darkness to prevent the formation of a green layer under the skin. This green layer is toxic, and potatoes that display it should either be well peeled or discarded.

Brussels sprouts are best kept on their own stalk. Onions, garlic, and winter squashes can be kept in a cool dry place out of the sun's way; onions and garlic are most effectively and attractively kept when they are braided and hung up.

Potatoes in the Pantry: A Guide

The following list of potatoes is divided into basic, intermediate, and advanced sections, based on availability. Despite the wide array of colors, flavors, sizes, and shapes of the potatoes listed, there really are only two types: mealy and dry fleshed, which are perfect for baking, mashed potatoes, and fries, etc., but that fall apart when boiled; or the waxy, firm-fleshed types, which hold their shape when boiled but are too moist to be mashed, baked or fried. Waxy potatoes are perfect for salads, or to lightly brown in butter.

Basic

IDAHO OR RUSSET POTATOES Large and brown, these potatoes are mealy textured, with a dryish floury flesh and a tough brown skin. Use for baking, "fries," mashed potatoes, most soups, and to thicken other dishes.

RED "NEW POTATOES" Waxy textured, these have a moist flesh, with a slightly sweet overtone. Boil for use in salads and in any dish in which you want the potatoes to keep their shape.

WHITE WAXY POTATOES Thin skinned, with waxy flesh. Much like red potatoes, without the distinctive, slightly sweet edge. Particularly good diced and cooked in olive oil, onions, garlic, and seasonings, or browned with chorizo and green beans.

Intermediate

TINY WHITE OBLONG BITE-SIZED POTATOES Sometimes called finger potatoes, royals, Jerseys, or cornichons. They have a waxy flesh with a light, pleasing potato flavor. Boil quickly and serve as is or brown in a little butter or olive oil with herbs (fresh rosemary, thyme, sage, etc.) and sprinkle with coarse salt.

SMALL RED NEW POTATOES Also known as creamers, these waxy-fleshed potatoes are much like their larger red siblings, but with a more delicate yet more pronounced flavor. Boil, steam, or pan brown until just tender. Serve al dente, at room temperature, along with steamed yellow (wax) and green beans, and a selection of multicolored tomatoes. Garnish with hard-cooked eggs and pungent niçoise olives, and dress with Anchovy Vinaigrette, page 41.

FINNISH YELLOW POTATOES With their golden color, moist waxy flesh, and nearly buttery flavor, they beg to be served on their own, and are able to eschew being buttered at the table. Boil until just tender; to gild the lily, top with sour cream and lots of chopped fresh dill and green onions.

Advanced

PINK FIR Long and narrow, somewhat smaller and knobbier than red new potatoes, they are very firm fleshed, waxy, and succulent. Boil or steam whole and serve garnished with lots of sprigs of fresh herbs and, if it is in season, tender shoots of asparagus. Serve with a sauce of yogurt combined with mayonnaise to taste, seasoned with grated lemon zest, a squeeze of lemon juice, chopped fresh tarragon, and a pinch of cayenne.

BLUE POTATOES With a startling gray-blue waxy flesh, these potatoes have a pleasingly hearty earthy flavor. Boil until just tender. Serve as an accompaniment to New Mexico–style pork with green chilies or alongside a grilled steak, with a nugget of New Mexico Chili Butter, page 349, to melt atop both.

Recipes Featuring Ingredients from the Root Cellar

Leah's Apple Flan

◆ BASIC PANTRY

Makes one 8-inch pie

Anyone who has been involved professionally with food has, at one time or another, catered parties. Occasionally I still do it, and sometimes when I don't I miss it: the sense of camaraderie among the staff, the theatrical aspect of getting it all together and making it brilliant from beginning to end.

This apple flan is adapted from a recipe of one of the nicest clients I ever catered for, Peggy Meyers. She made these apple-custard tarts to end a Mediterranean-inspired dinner party I prepared for her and her guests.

I call it Leah's Apple Flan, however, because my daughter adores apples in all guises and immediately adopted the dish as her favorite, streamlining it in the process. I can usually tell when important school exams are coming up by the presence of my daughter in the kitchen, accompanied with the sweet smell of baking apple flan.

1 recipe Pie Dough, page 363	1 tablespoon brandy or fruit brandy (eau-de-vie), optional
2 large or 3 medium tart green apples, peeled and sliced	1/2 teaspoon vanilla or almond extract (1 teaspoon if not using brandy)
2 tablespoons soft unsalted butter	1 teaspoon ground cinnamon
2 beaten eggs	
3 tablespoons sugar	

1. Preheat oven to 375°. Prepare dough; roll out and use to line an 8-inch pie pan, crimping edges of crust.

2. Layer apples into pie crust and bake for 30 minutes, or until apples are becoming tender and pastry is getting golden.

3. Mix remaining ingredients and pour over apples into pie shell.

4. Return pie to oven and continue baking for another 15 minutes. Serve warm or cool.

Beets in Curried Tomato Vinaigrette

◆◆ INTERMEDIATE PANTRY

Serves 4 to 6 as an appetizer or side dish

Beets might be an acquired taste, along with caviar, pungent olives, and strong-smelling cheeses.

I remember as a child hating, really hating, beets: the way they bled, turning everything around them a sickly scarlet hue. But as I traveled I grew impassioned by the beet as I discovered how sharp and strong flavors could balance its sweetness and the way olive oil seems a natural with it.

France was where I made the change: there the beets are sold already cooked in the marketplace. I would buy a basketful of the hot, still steaming red roots, then take them home and douse them with olive oil and a dash of raspberry vinegar to bring out their fruitiness.

In Greece it was a coarse, rustic olive oil that dressed the beets, along with an equally coarse vinegar and a topping of chopped onions and black olives.

The irony is that just when I grew affectionate towards the rather messy red beets, golden beets made their appearance in my local markets. And while they have a pleasing flavor, somehow without the streak of vermillion left behind on both my hands and plate, they don't seem quite like real beets.

My current favorite beet recipe is an eclectic mix of Mediterranean and Indian flavors, with a nod toward California. Use either red or golden beets, or a combination of both (in which case they should be served immediately rather than left to marinate, turning the golden beets as red as their bowlmates).

6 medium beets, tops removed but unpeeled	Pinch *each* curry, ground cumin, ground turmeric
2 garlic cloves, chopped	2 tablespoons olive oil
2 teaspoons sugar	Salt and pepper to taste
2 tablespoons wine vinegar	1 teaspoon chopped fresh
2 tablespoons chopped fresh or canned tomatoes	cilantro, or Cilantro-Lime Paste, page 360.

1. Preheat oven to 350°. Place beets in a shallow baking pan and bake for 30 to 40 minutes, or until tender when pierced with a knife. (Young, tender specimens will take less time, and older ones will take longer.)

2. Let cool. When cool enough to handle, peel. The skin will slip off easily.

3. Dice beets, then toss with garlic, sugar, and vinegar, and let sit a few minutes to absorb flavors.

4. Add remaining ingredients. Serve immediately, or chill and enjoy later. They will last up to about 4 days in the refrigerator.

Brighton Beach Root Cellar Borscht

This is a robust hot vegetable borscht, with cabbage, tomatoes, and potatoes in addition to beets. I grew up eating this, and I was reminded of it recently in New York's Brighton Beach. Once known as the home of Coney Island, or perhaps the birthplace of Neil Simon, nowadays it is

Serves 4 to 6 generously

called "Little Odessa" because of the Soviet emigrés settling there. The shop signs are bilingual, and walking through the streets is like being in an Isaac Bashevis Singer novel—the feeling is of another world and time.

In the restaurants you won't find snooty waiters or waitresses urging you to try the latest trendy offering; you'll get Olga or Natasha, a big no-nonsense woman eager to feed you borscht.

I'm going to make the ambitious claim that this borscht will win over even the most vehement beet-hater. That's because, with its flavors of other vegetables and its tangy sweet-sour seasonings, this soup doesn't taste only of beets.

1 onion, chopped
1 carrot, diced
4 medium beets (3 diced and 1 coarsely shredded)
2 cups diced fresh or canned tomatoes
4 to 6 medium waxy boiling type potatoes, peeled and cut into bite-sized chunks
1 small to medium head green cabbage, thinly sliced

1 quart vegetable, beef, or chicken broth
3 tablespoons sugar
2 to 3 tablespoons cider or white wine vinegar
1 to 2 teaspoons chopped fresh dillweed, or a large pinch of dried dill
Salt and pepper to taste
About 1 cup sour cream

1. Place onion, carrot, and diced beets in a pot along with tomatoes, potatoes, cabbage, and broth.

2. Bring to a boil, then reduce heat and simmer until potatoes and cabbage are tender, about 40 minutes. Be sure you cook vegetables long enough; borscht is not meant to be al dente.

3. Add reserved shredded beets to soup and season with sugar and vinegar. Continue cooking for another 10 minutes, or long enough for sugar and vinegar to give up their harshness and become sweet-sour. Adjust sugar and vinegar if necessary.

4. Season with dill, salt, and pepper, then ladle into bowls. Garnish with dollops of sour cream and eat up, with a big piece of buttered rye bread alongside.

Russian Beet, Carrot, and Almond Cake

◆ BASIC PANTRY

Makes 2 9-by-9-inch cakes

This recipe came to me via a Soviet emigré. My daughter was horrified when I began to grate the beets for this cake, but an hour later we were sitting at the table, tea mugs in one hand, squares of this moist, wholesome cake in the other. It's delicious frosted, but if you're feeling lazy, sprinkle brown sugar over the top for its final 15 minutes of baking. The sugar will caramelize and get crunchy.

Beets serve the same function in this cake as carrots do in carrot cake: to give it a rich, moist texture. The cake also may be made by using all beets, or both red and golden beets.

4 eggs, lightly beaten
2 cups sugar
1 cup vegetable oil
2 cups unbleached all-purpose flour
2 teaspoons baking powder
1-1/2 teaspoons baking soda
1 teaspoon ground cinnamon
Pinch of salt
1 teaspoon vanilla extract

2 cups coarsely shredded peeled beets
1 cup coarsely shredded peeled carrots
1-1/2 cups coarsely sliced almonds
2/3 cup raisins
Sifted powdered sugar for dusting, or Cream Cheese Frosting, following

1. Preheat oven to 350°. Beat together eggs, sugar, and oil until emulsified, light, and fluffy. Set aside.

2. Sift together flour, baking powder, baking soda, and cinnamon. Add egg mixture and stir well.

3. Add vanilla, beets, carrots, walnuts, and raisins.

4. Pour into 2 9-by-9-inch baking pans (either buttered and floured or nonstick ones) and bake for 35 to 45 minutes, or until firmish to the touch on top and golden brown in color.

5. Let cool a few minutes, then remove from pans to cool thoroughly.

6. Serve dusted with a bit of powdered sugar or frosted with cream cheese frosting.

VARIATION Use whole wheat pastry flour instead of white for a sturdy, wholesome cake.

Cream Cheese Frosting

Whip 8 ounces (1 cup) room-temperature **cream cheese** with 1/2 cup (1 stick) soft, unsalted **butter.** When well mixed, add 2–3 cups **powdered sugar** and a dash of **vanilla or almond extract** to taste.

Celery Root and Carrots in Caper Rémoulade

◆◆ INTERMEDIATE PANTRY

Serves 4 to 6

Raw shredded celery root makes a rustic salad that tastes and looks a bit like crab meat. Combined with shredded carrots and bound up in a caper-tarragon mayonnaise, it makes a hearty first course with the flavors of a Mediterranean winter.

It is particularly good served as part of a selection of composed salads, French country style.

1 medium celery root	2 teaspoons capers, plus a little
2 carrots	of their brine
3 tablespoons mayonnaise,	Generous pinch diced, or
or enough to bind mixture	1/2–1 teaspoon fresh,
2 teaspoons Dijon, milder	chopped tarragon
French mustard, or American	Salt and pepper to taste
brown mustard	

1. Peel gnarly brown-skinned celery root. Be careful, as it is tough and difficult to peel. Coarsely shred and set aside. Coarsely shred carrot and mix with celery root.

2. Add mayonnaise, mustard, capers, and tarragon; season with salt and pepper.

Icy Citrus Rounds

◆ BASIC PANTRY

Serves 6 to 8

The simplicity of this dish beguiles me. I devised these treats to amuse a child once. It was so much fun to pop the whole slice of frozen fruit into our mouths, rind and all. The fruit is tart-sweet, and the crystalized sugar topping is crunchy, almost like a cookie.

Enchanting after a spicy curry or Mexican meal.

Try to get organic, unsprayed fruit; otherwise, wash the skins extremely well before using.

2 lemons
2 limes
2 oranges (1 regular and 1 blood
   orange, if possible)

Sugar for sprinkling, about
   1/3 cup total

1. Wash fruit well and dry.
2. Slice thinly and arrange on waxed-paper lined cookie sheets.
3. Sprinkle each round with about 1/4 teaspoon sugar.
4. Freeze until hard. Best eaten within a day or two of freezing.

Jerusalem Artichokes with Roast Duck

◆◆ INTERMEDIATE PANTRY

Serves 4

I sampled this delightful combination in Ireland and found that the earthy, slightly sweet root flavor of the Jerusalem artichoke paired well with rich roast duck.

◆◆◆◆◆◆

TO PREPARE Roast 2 **ducks** in a 350° oven with an **onion, apple** slice, and piece of **celery** in each cavity. When skin is golden brown and flesh is tender, they are ready (about 1 hour). Pour off fat as you go along; when ducks are tender, deglaze pan with 1 cup **dry white or red wine** and 1 cup of **beef, chicken, or duck broth.** Set aside.

Peel 1 pound **Jerusalem artichokes;** slice, then boil or steam for 10 minutes, or until they are just tender. Toss them with Garlic-Parsley Butter, page 350, or Shallot-Thyme Butter, page 351, and serve with roast ducks and their pan sauce, the ducks' juices mingling with the savory vegetables. Turnips may be served in the same way.

Tiny Onions Baked in Olive Oil and Balsamic Vinegar

◆◆ INTERMEDIATE PANTRY

Serves 4

The slight sweetness of balsamic vinegar brings out the natural sweet flavors of tiny onions. Serve as a vegetable side dish or as a relishlike accompaniment.

2 cups tiny onions
3 tablespoons olive oil
2 tablespoons balsamic vinegar

Salt and pepper to taste
1 tablespoon chopped fresh
   parsley

1. Preheat oven to 350°. Blanch onions in boiling water for 2–3 minutes; drain and rinse with cold water, then slip their skins off.

2. Toss onions with olive oil, vinegar, salt, and pepper and bake for 20 minutes, or until browned in places and tender when pierced.

3. Serve hot or at room temperature, sprinkled with chopped parsley.

VARIATIONS Anchovies, **sun-dried tomatoes, pine nuts,** and **raisins** are traditional additions to these tiny onions.

Red Wine–braised Lamb with Peas and Gnocchi

Tiny **braised onions** are a delicious addition to savory wine-braised meats such as **Red Wine Lamb Ragout with Garlic, Herbs, Peas, and Gnocchi,** page 406. This also is an excellent way to use leftover onions.

Warm Leeks in Mustard Vinaigrette

◆◆ **INTERMEDIATE PANTRY**

Serves 4

Leeks are a delicious, subtle member of the onion family, adding their distinctive character to soups, stews, braises, and other dishes. They're also lovely simply poached in water or broth, then drained and dressed in a vinaigrette of choice.

4 to 6 leeks, well cleaned
Mixture of half water, half chicken broth (enough to cover leeks) for poaching

1 recipe Garlic-Mustard Vinaigrette, page 41
1 tablespoon minced fresh parsley

1. Slice cleaned whites of leeks, plus an inch or two of their tender greens, crosswise into 3/4-inch pieces (though they look nicer cut lengthwise, cutting them crosswise makes for easier eating: no long strings to get caught in the throat).

2. Place leeks and liquid in a saucepan. Cover and bring to a boil. Reduce heat and simmer until leeks are just tender, about 6 minutes.

3. Drain, reserving liquid for another use (it makes wonderful soup).

4. Toss warm leeks in vinaigrette and serve slightly warm, sprinkled with parsley.

VARIATION Honey mustard or Creole mustard makes a lively dressing for the warm leeks.

Mashed Potatoes with Olive Oil, Provence Style

◆ BASIC PANTRY

Serves 6

Traditional Provençal potatoes get their distinctive taste from a good rich olive oil. Serve with slices of rare rosemary-and-garlic-scented lamb, sauced with its own pan juices and sprinkled with diced Kalamata olives. Spinach, quickly cooked in a little olive oil and garlic, is lovely on the side.

5 pounds russet potatoes, peeled and quartered
1/2 cup milk or cream

1/2 cup olive oil
Salt and pepper to taste

1. Cook potatoes in boiling water to cover until just tender. Drain.
2. Mash, adding milk or cream and olive oil a little at a time, letting potatoes absorb each addition of liquid as you go along.
3. Season generously with salt and pepper.

Potatoes Browned with Mustard Seeds and Cumin

◆◆◆ ADVANCED PANTRY

Serves 4

Simple and savory, with the good strong flavors of India. The mustard seeds are at once nutty and slightly spicy, and tossing the crusty, browned potatoes with fresh ginger and chili gives a new dimension to a dish of very simple ingredients.

Serve as a side dish with any sort of curry-flavored meal, or for breakfast, to accompany eggs scrambled with diced tomatoes and seasoned with garlic and green onions.

5 large russet potatoes, peeled and cut into large dice
2 tablespoons vegetable oil or unsalted butter
2 teaspoons black mustard seeds
1 teaspoon ground cumin

Salt to taste
2 teaspoons grated fresh ginger
1 jalapeño or Anaheim chili, seeded and chopped (or to taste)
Juice of 1/2 lime

1. Brown diced potatoes in oil or butter, along with mustard seeds. When potatoes are nearly tender, about 6 to 8 minutes, sprinkle in cumin, then continue cooking for another few minutes to bring out flavors and aromas. Season with salt and remove from heat.
2. Toss hot cooked potatoes with ginger and chili, and serve immediately, lime juice squeezed over.

Spiced Browned Potatoes in Yogurt

Prepare **preceding recipe,** let cook slightly, and combine with 2 cups low-fat plain **yogurt,** 1 chopped **garlic clove,** 2 tablespoons chopped **fresh cilantro,** and 1 **green onion,** thinly sliced. Chill and serve cool as an Indian-flavor potato salad, sprinkled with a little **paprika** and **cayenne** if desired.

Charcoal-grilled Potatoes with Assorted Mayonnaises

◆ BASIC TO
◆◆ ADVANCED PANTRY

Serves 4

The potatoes are first parboiled, then cut into big thick slices, almost like steaks. These are then marinated in olive oil, a dash of vinegar, and a sprinkling of herbs, before being grilled over an open fire. They are sensational.

Serve as a separate course, accompanied with a few peppers thrown onto the fire along with them if desired, and any of the suggested savory mayonnaise sauces.

3 pounds large russet potatoes, unpeeled
1/2 cup olive oil
4 garlic cloves, coarsely chopped
2 teaspoons dried herbes de Provence, 1/2–1 teaspoon crumbled, dried oregano, or 1 teaspoon fresh, chopped rosemary

1 tablespoon vinegar
1/4 teaspoon salt
Mayonnaise of choice: Ancho Chili Mayonnaise (page 157) or Olive-Pesto Aïoli (page 159)
10 niçoise olives and a handful of arugula, frisée, or mesclun for garnish

1. Cook whole potatoes in a large pot of boiling water until not quite tender (a knife inserted into center should meet with some resistance), about 20 minutes. Drain and cool until cool enough to handle but still warm enough to absorb dressing.

2. Cut each potato lengthwise into 1/2-inch-thick slices and arrange in a large shallow dish or pan. Drizzle oil over all and sprinkle with garlic, herbs, vinegar, and salt. Cover and let sit for 1 hour at room temperature.

3. Meanwhile, light a fire in an open grill. After fire burns out the coals will eventually change from red to white; at this point they should be ready. Arrange potatoes on grill and cook over high heat until brown in spots, about 3 minutes on each side.

4. Serve potato slices immediately, each napped with a bit of sauce and a garnish of olives and greens.

Mediterranean Potato Hash with Eggs and Cheese

◆ BASIC PANTRY

Serves 3 to 4

This hearty, comforting dish is one of the foods I make when everything else in life seems complicated or off-balance and I need something cozy and familiar.

Such omelets are eaten throughout the Mediterranean, the character of the dish varying as to the choice of cheese and herbs. I'm fondest of feta, but garlic jack is a close runner-up, and when I recently brought home a chunk of sheep's milk cheese from Spain, this omelet is what most of it went into.

This recipe makes a somewhat messy omelet; for something a bit more tamed and frittatalike, see the following recipe.

6 russet potatoes, peeled and
  thinly sliced
About 3 tablespoons olive oil
8 ounces cheese (about 3/4 cup
  diced or coarsely crumbled)
  feta, pecorino, asiago, garlic
  jack, Fontina, Cheddar, etc.

4 eggs, lightly beaten
1 teaspoon crumbled dried
  oregano leaves, or to taste
Salt and pepper to taste

1. In a skillet fry potato slices in olive oil until golden and crisp in places, soft in others.
2. Toss cheese into pan with potatoes, then add eggs. Let cook a bit on bottom, then lift sides and let eggs run underneath; toss once or twice into a sort of scramble until cheese is melted and crisp in parts, and eggs are holding the whole delicious mess together.
3. Serve immediately, sprinkled with oregano, salt, and pepper.

Flat Potato and Cheese Omelet

Prepare **above recipe,** using a skillet with a heatproof handle. When you add cheese and eggs to pan, cook on top of stove undisturbed for a few minutes to brown and set bottom.

When bottom is set, place whole pan under a preheated broiler and broil until top is set and lightly golden. Serve immediately, sprinkled with oregano, salt, and pepper.

Peruvian Potato Salad with Lemon, Chilies, and Pickled Vegetables

[CAUSA A LA LIMONO]

◆ BASIC PANTRY

Serves 4 to 6

This spicy salad of mashed potatoes dressed with olive oil and lemon juice is a classic from Peru that in my kitchen evolved into a piquant mixture studded with pickled vegetables or diced olives, depending upon my pantry.

I think *causa* is at its best with lots of wild and unrefined flavors: the mashed potatoes nearly beg for a good lashing of olive oil and lemon juice, and even throw in a little of the brine from either the pickled jalapeños, vegetable giardiniera, or olives. The only way to ruin this dish is to be timid with the seasonings.

3 pounds russet potatoes, peeled and quartered or cut into chunks
1-1/2 pounds onions, chopped
1/2 cup fresh or frozen lemon juice
1/2 cup extra-virgin olive oil
1/2 teaspoon dried red pepper flakes, or to taste
1/4 to 1/2 fresh chili, chopped

1/2 to 1 pickled jalapeño chili, chopped, plus 1/2 to 1 teaspoon chili marinade
1/2 cup coarsely chopped giardiniera or pimiento-stuffed olives, plus a tablespoon or two of brine
Lemon wedges and lettuce greens for garnish

1. Boil potatoes until just tender. Drain and mash.
2. Add onions, lemon juice, olive oil, red pepper flakes, fresh chili, pickled jalapeño, marinade, chopped vegetables, and a bit of their brine. Taste for seasoning—it should taste flamboyant.
3. Serve cool, garnished with lemon wedges and greens.

Sunday Supper Potatoes

◆ BASIC PANTRY

Serves 4 to 6

Chunks of potatoes bake leisurely in a bath of broth, seasoned with lots of garlic and glistening with olive oil. As the potatoes cook they get crusty, and the broth is absorbed and evaporates into flavorful crispy bits at the bottom of the pan.

If you don't have frozen homemade broth, improvise by simmering a mixture of half canned chicken broth and half water along with a chunk of onion, several garlic cloves, a chopped tomato, and a pinch of your favorite herbs.

8 large russet potatoes, peeled and cut into big and medium chunks

6 to 10 garlic cloves, cut up haphazardly, but not quite chopped

3 tablespoons olive oil

Enough broth to reach two-thirds up side of potatoes

Salt and pepper to taste

1. Preheat oven to 350°. Place potatoes in a baking pan and add remaining ingredients.

2. Bake for about 30 minutes. With a spatula, turn potatoes to brown on other side.

3. Raise heat to 375° and continue to bake for another 30 minutes, tossing with a spatula several more times during that time. Potatoes should be crisp and crusty when done, having soaked up all flavors from broth. Salt and pepper if necessary.

Garlic Potato Gratin

◆ **BASIC PANTRY**

Serves 4

Use any type of waxy potato for this gratin, except perhaps blue potatoes. This makes a seriously delicious gratin, fragrant with the scent of garlic, crusty on top, and meltingly tender within, yet simply prepared from ingredients in the pantry.

Serve as an accompaniment to crisp pan-browned turkey fillets on a bed of watercress.

10 medium waxy potatoes, peeled and sliced thin (about 3 cups total)

1/4 cup extra-virgin olive oil

Salt and coarsely ground black pepper, to taste

5 to 7 garlic cloves, coarsely chopped

1/4 cup milk

4 ounces grated sharp Cheddar or similar cheese combined with 2 tablespoons chopped fresh chives

1. Preheat oven to 325°. Drizzle a little olive oil in the bottom of a baking dish or casserole. Then layer potatoes and garlic, drizzling with milk and remaining olive oil, as well as salt and pepper, as you go.

2. Bake for 1 hour, or until potatoes are tender. Then top with cheese mixture and return to oven.

3. Continue baking another 15 minutes, or until cheese has melted and browned lightly.

Winter Squash Baked with Garlic, Thyme, Paprika, and Wine Vinegar

◆ BASIC PANTRY

Serves 4

This Native American food is at its best when combined with strong, untamed flavors such as garlic, herbs, olive oil, and vinegar. It tastes of its own savory self, but is delightfully enhanced.

2 pounds Hubbard, acorn, or other winter squash, seeded and peeled	1 teaspoon red wine vinegar
	1/2 teaspoon paprika
3 garlic cloves, chopped	Pinch of dried or teaspoon fresh thyme leaves
1 to 2 tablespoons olive oil	Salt and pepper to taste

1. Preheat oven to 400°. Cut squash into chunks, then score to allow flavorings to seep in.

2. Sprinkle squash with remaining ingredients.

3. Bake until tender, about 30 minutes. Serve hot or warm.

Hearth-roasted Sweet Potatoes or Yams with Red Chili Butter

◆◆ INTERMEDIATE PANTRY

Serves 4

Place 4 washed **sweet potatoes or yams** into hot coals or wrap in aluminum foil and place on top of a grill. Alternatively, they may be simply baked in the 375–400° oven. Each way will take 45–60 minutes.

When the sweet flesh is meltingly tender, remove and cut open, filling each gash with a generous nugget of **New Mexico Chili Butter,** page 349.

Spicy Winter Squash Soup with Cabbage, White Beans, and Pasta

Serves 6

This soup evolved from the Pureed Pumpkin Soup in *Hot & Spicy*. I had some left over, but not enough for a group just come back from flea-market shopping on a chilly day. I searched my pantry for hearty ingredients that would turn my small amount of soup into a full meal, and ended up with this rustic, satisfying dish.

4 garlic cloves, chopped
1 small onion or 1/2 medium onion, chopped
1 tablespoon olive oil
1 tablespoon flour
1 pound winter squash, seeded, peeled, and diced
1 tablespoon mild chili powder such as New Mexico, ancho, or pasilla
Large pinch dried oregano
1 cup tomato sauce
3 cups chicken broth
1/2 medium cabbage, thinly sliced
About 1/2 cup broken-up spaghetti or soup pasta

1 cup cooked white or butter beans
1 cup milk
1 jalapeño chili, seeded and chopped
2 tablespoons chopped fresh cilantro (or omit jalapeño and cilantro and use 1 tablespoon Cilantro-Lime Paste, page 360)
Salt and pepper to taste
6 slices or so dry French bread, each rubbed with a cut garlic half
1 cup Gruyère or Emmenthal cheese, coarsely grated

1. Sauté garlic and onion in olive oil until softened, then sprinkle in flour and cook and stir 2 to 3 minutes. Add diced squash and cook a few minutes, then sprinkle with chili powder and oregano and cook a few minutes longer.

2. Stir in tomato sauce and broth, then bring mixture to a boil. Reduce heat and simmer until squash is tender, about 15 to 20 minutes.

3. Remove squash from soup. Puree, then return to soup. Add cabbage and pasta, then continue cooking until cabbage is tender and pasta al dente.

4. Add beans, milk, chili, and cilantro and simmer another 5 minutes, or long enough to meld flavors. Add salt and black pepper.

5. Serve each bowl of steaming hot soup topped with a garlic-rubbed croûte, and sprinkled generously with a flurry of grated cheese.

THE DRY GOODS PANTRY

◆◆◆

The words "dry goods" always remind me of the scenes in Western movies when the prairie family went into town and shopped at the dry goods store. As a child, the guns and the rough living conditions shown in these films horrified me, and I confess that I often wondered as to the state of their bathrooms. In most ways I was relieved to be living in the twentieth century, only envying one thing about frontier life: the dry goods store. I would have gladly sat through an entire movie filmed in that setting, with its wonderful array of barrels and burlap bags filled with all sorts of long-keeping ingredients.

We all keep an array of dry goods in our pantry. My list may not include your favorite staples and many basic "dry goods" are found in such chapters as "Grains and Legumes," and "Pasta." Space prohibits me from describing in detail things such as cornstarch and yeast. But I do want to describe less-usual dry goods, such as chick-pea flour, that don't seem to fit into any other chapter, and I want to put some common ingredients in a new light. Foods such as leftover dry bread, which may seem too common to mention, add a wealth of flavor and gastronomy to the table. And they satisfy my craving for kitchen frugality, because if they are not saved and used, they will be thrown into the rubbish.

STORAGE TIPS Store dry goods in tightly sealed containers to guard against moisture or insects. Salt, flour, and sugar last for about 2 years; other ingredients, such as yeast, will have expiration dates stamped on their packaging. Packaged foods such as crackers and tortilla chips go stale quickly after the bag is opened, and should be sealed tightly.

Pantry List: Dry Goods

Baking supplies and thickening agents (yeast, baking soda, baking powder, cornstarch, arrowroot, etc.)

Bread, bread crumbs, dried bread, and bread sticks

Candies

Coconut

Cookies and cookie crumbs

Falafel mix

Flours

Indian crispy snack (Sev)

Jams, jellies, and preserves

Matzo

Popadums (Indian flatbreads)

Popcorn

Rice paper

Salt cod

Seaweed

Soy-based meat substitutes

Sugars

Syrups and honeys

Tortilla chips

Bread At its best, bread is fresh and crusty, a substantial food ready to scoop up every little bit of sauce and vinaigrette. But bread's freshness is transitory indeed; by the next day that delightful soft and yielding loaf has started in the direction of hard and dry. Do not throw it away. Now is the time for frugality, since dried bread in the kitchen is one of the most versatile and delicious foods you can have around.

Whoever has a loaf of bread in his or her kitchen has access to all sorts of delicious things that bread can turn into: soft fresh crumbs, toasted browned crumbs, croutons to toss into a savory salad, a big croûte topped with melted cheese afloat in a bowl of steaming soup, or a dish of rich bread pudding.

Bread crumbs are as good as the bread they are made from, and are always better homemade than purchased. Bread crumbs may be made from fresh bread with a soft, fluffy consistency, or they may be made with stale bread and browned in a heavy skillet in a little butter or olive oil to make them crunchy.

STORAGE TIPS Stale and leftover bread and crumbs should be thoroughly dried in an oven for long storage, then kept in a tightly sealed jar. Discard if any moldy smell or appearance occurs. To dry fresh bread crumbs, place on baking sheet and bake in a preheated 300° oven for about 20 minutes. (You may drizzle olive oil over, and season them with garlic, paprika, salt, and pepper if you like, before baking.)

FRESH BREADCRUMBS An especially good coating for chicken breasts or duck breasts, as they help keep lean meat juicy. Mixed with chopped garlic and parsley, they distinguish cassoulet from plain old bean casserole, and are a good topping for fish fillets Catalan style. Bread crumbs may be stirred into a sauce to thicken it with a Germanic or Alsatian accent; large croutonlike crumbs are delicious browned in butter and scattered on soup.

Crumb-coated Mustard-spread Leg of Lamb

◆ BASIC PANTRY

Serves 4 to 6

This is more a description than a recipe, and as such does not demand exact amounts. Make incisions all over a **leg of lamb,** then stuff each incision with a half clove or sliver of **garlic** and several leaves of **rosemary. Salt** and **pepper** the roast. Mix 2 cups or so (depending on size of lamb) fresh white country (baguette, sourdough, etc.) **bread crumbs** with 5 or so chopped **garlic cloves,** several tablespoons of **olive oil,** and 3 tablespoons chopped fresh **parsley.** Place lamb in a roasting pan surrounded by a head of **garlic** per person, spread the roast with a generous amount of **sweet-hot mustard** such as a Mendocino type, and pat crumbs all over roast, pressing them into coating. Roast in a preheated 350° oven until lamb is one-third cooked (use a thermometer and cook it no further than rare; that is, rare after it has been removed from oven and has set a few minutes—during which time temperature will continue to rise), then remove it from oven, spoon off any fat from bottom of pan, and pour in a bottle of **Merlot** and a cup or so of **broth.** Continue cooking until rare inside and crusty brown on outside.

Remove lamb from pan, and if pan juices are not sufficiently saucy, deglaze pan with a bit more broth or red wine, cooking liquid down until deeply flavorful.

Transatlantic Christmas Pudding with Boozy Citrus Sauce and Lime Sorbet

◆◆ **INTERMEDIATE PANTRY**

Serves 6

Fresh bread crumbs are an indispensable ingredient for a proper Christmas pudding.

The Midwest and East Coast still preserve a little bit of Olde English Christmas tradition in the form of the long-steamed pudding (the "figgy pudding" of which we all sang of when we were kids, but about which I, for one, hadn't the foggiest notion).

Prepared with dried fruit, beef suet, and spices, Christmas puddings are the fragrant center of attention when they are carried aflame to the table after the excesses of the holiday meal, with blue tendrils of fire licking up their sides. In recent years these hefty desserts have given way to more contemporary ones, it is true, but the pudding still remains a tradition, evoking simpler times and old-fashioned holidays.

As tantalizing as such puddings might be, they do present several problems. The first is that they must be made weeks, even months ahead of time—as a good fruitcake (which a pudding strongly resembles) must. The second is that preparing a proper pudding requires large quantities of suet, or beef fat. And not only do I not want to be bothered with dicing and dealing with suet, I don't want to eat it, either.

That is why this recipe is so good. It requires about 10 minutes of preparation time, then a leisurely 2-hour steam bath. And forget about that nasty suet—this pudding is bound with butter. The traditional cloying "hard" sauce has been replaced by a thin sauce of citrus and spice, accompanied with the contemporary touch of a tart lime sorbet.

This nearly nouvelle pudding is the work of cookbook author and illustrator Leslie Forbes, and it reflects her transcontinental lifestyle: a North American living in London, she spends much of her time travelling all over the world.

Forbes says that this recipe is very accepting of additions: chopped lightly toasted almonds, candied citrus peel, and so on, while cookbook author Myrtle Allen of Ireland's Ballymaloe Restaurant (and cooking school) adds the flesh of a cooked apple or two to her steamed puddings.

3/4 cup (1-1/2 sticks) soft butter (Include a pinch of salt if using unsalted butter.)
1/3 cup dark brown sugar
2 to 2-1/2 cups loosely packed fresh whole-wheat bread crumbs (about 4–6 trimmed bread slices, whirled in a blender)
3 eggs, well beaten
3 heaping tablespoons jam or preserves dissolved in 1 tablespoon of hot water

(continued)

1/2 teaspoon baking soda
Generous handful *each* raisins
and mixed candied fruits
2 tablespoons brandy, rum, or
Irish whiskey

Boozy Citrus Sauce, following
Lime sorbet or not-overly sweet
sherbet

1. Cream together butter and sugar.

2. Stir in bread crumbs, eggs, jam, baking soda, raisins, candied fruits, and brandy, rum, or whiskey.

3. Pour into a 2-quart soufflé dish, pudding dish, or heatproof bowl, then cover with a piece of buttered aluminum foil. Secure tightly with a string.

4. Place bowl in a steamer pot, or in a heavy pot, then fill pot with hot water that reaches halfway up the side.

5. Steam pudding for 2 hours, adding water to bottom of pot or steamer if needed.

6. Serve hot, accompanied with citrus sauce and lime sorbet or sherbet.

NOTE If you want to flame the pudding, heat several tablespoons of alcohol of choice in a ladle until hot but not boiling (if you boil the alcohol off it will not catch fire), then pour over pudding. Set fire to pudding with a match. The alcohol may catch fire by itself as it heats, so in the interest of your eyebrows (I once singed mine), keep your face safely away.

Boozy Citrus Sauce

Juice of 3 lemons
6 tablespoons orange
marmalade
1/2 teaspoon ground allspice
3/4 cup (or 1-1/2 sticks) butter,
melted

7 ounces alcohol of choice:
sherry, rum, brandy, whiskey, Cointreau, etc.

Heat together all ingredients until marmalade melts and sauce bubbles around edge. Serve immediately, or make ahead and reheat.

DRIED BREAD CRUMBS Dried bread crumbs are a pantry basic, but one that is often taken for granted. I've recently grown to appreciate their delicious versatility. Like other ingredients, there are mediocre bread crumbs and there are good ones. Good bread crumbs are made from good bread; avoid the prepackaged stuff. I used to make crumbs when my bread was still relatively fresh, but lately I've been letting the bread go stale in large chunks and grating the crumbs when I need them. Grating bread over the large holes of a cheese grater makes lovely crumbs, lighter and more flavorful than those made in a blender. And I brown the crumbs in butter or olive oil. Delicious.

Butter-browned dried bread crumbs add a crispy veneer to the top of any casseroled dish, helping to seal in the juicy interior in the bargain. Lightly cooked cauliflower tossed with toasted bread crumbs makes an old-fashioned supper dish that I welcome anytime, especially if it has a little melted sharp Cheddar on it.

One of the best things anyone can do with browned bread crumbs is to toss them with noodles. In the Midwest, especially in the Mennonite and Amish areas, buttered crumbs are the traditional topping for home-made noodles. A Venetian specialty is pasta cooked in a seafood broth sprinkled with olive oil-toasted crumbs, and a California pasta dish is capellini tossed with bread crumbs, shreds of coppa or other lean, spicy cured meat, and strips of thinly sliced grilled vegetables, all seasoned with olive oil and balsamic vinegar.

Piquant Pasta with Autumn Vegetables and Butter-browned Crumbs

◆◆ INTERMEDIATE PANTRY

Serves 4 to 6

Pasta tossed with fresh and marinated vegetables, seasoned with balsamic vinegar and rosemary, the whole dish pulled together with the crunch of toasted bread crumbs. I came up with this dish at the end of a cold winter; the colorful slashes of red, orange, and green hinted of the warm season waiting in the wings, while the heartiness of the dish satisfied.

1/2 to 2/3 cup dried bread
  crumbs
1/4 to 1/3 cup olive oil
1/2 cup thin strips marinated
  roasted red peppers
8 ounces winter squash,
  seeded, peeled, and diced

1/2 cup cooked greens such as
  chard or spinach, cut into
  bite-sized pieces and
  squeezed dry (about 2–3
  cups raw, loose greens)

(continued)

2 teaspoons chopped fresh rosemary	1 pound dried pasta such as spaghetti
1 teaspoon balsamic or wine vinegar	3 garlic cloves, chopped
	Salt and pepper to taste

1. Brown bread crumbs in 2 tablespoons oil. Remove from pan and set aside.

2. Heat 1 tablespoon oil in pan and add peppers and winter squash, cooking for about 5 minutes, tossing to cook squash evenly.

3. Add greens and rosemary to peppers and squash, pour in vinegar, and cook a minute longer. Remove from heat.

4. Meanwhile, bring a large pot of salted water to a boil and cook pasta until al dente. Drain and toss with remaining olive oil plus chopped garlic.

5. Add pasta to vegetable mixture and toss together. Add salt and pepper.

6. Serve immediately, tossed with browned bread crumbs.

◆◆◆◆◆◆◆

DRIED BREAD That fragrant loaf of bread, so irresistible when minutes old, is another story as the clock ticks by. Within 24 to 48 hours the ravages of time turn the tender loaf into a heavy, dry object more suitable for use as a doorstop than a meal. No wonder, then, that the Mediterranean kitchen, always as frugal as it is full of flavor, has a wealth of dishes prepared with stale bread.

STORAGE TIP Cut day-old bread into thin slices, bake in a low oven until very dry, then store in an airtight container and use as desired. If a bit tired tasting, refresh slices by heating in a preheated 300° to 350° oven for 10 minutes or so. Bread will last for several months this way, but if you see any indication of decline—an off smell or spots of mold—discard the entire amount.

Eight Things to Do with Dried Bread

◆◆◆◆◆◆◆

◆ Drizzle with lots of olive oil, toss with garlic and Parmesan cheese, and bake at 400° until crispy golden brown. Serve with roasted red peppers, liver pâté, or goat cheese as an appetizer.

◆ Cut into bite-sized cubes for use in fondues.

- Toss torn pieces of stale pita bread with ingredients for a Greek salad (cucumber, tomatoes, peppers, red onion, chopped mint and parsley, feta cheese, and olives). Dress with lots of olive oil and lemon juice and serve a bowl of yogurt on the side.

- Brown cubes of stale bread in olive oil, adding several cloves of chopped garlic once bread has browned. Serve in soups or sprinkled onto pasta. For an Andalusian soup, puree your favorite gaspacho with enough of these garlicky croutons to thicken the mixture into a creamy, savory cold soup.

- Toss olive oil–browned croutons into scrambled eggs, especially ones that contain sautéed wild mushrooms.

- Scatter olive-oil-and-garlic-seasoned croutons, just before serving, over a tomato-braised whole fish, along with such Mediterranean seasonings or herbs such as chopped fresh oregano, fennel, orange zest, Italian parsley, and rosemary.

- Rub a thick slice of toasted rye bread with garlic, then top with shredded Gruyère. Broil until bubbly. Or omit cheese and top garlic-rubbed rye bread *croûte* with Mediterranean White Bean Pâté, page 31.

- Make Panzanella Bread Salad: Layer very dry bread, sliced or in chunks, with sliced ripe tomatoes, chopped garlic, chopped fresh herbs (or chopped fresh parsley plus a few spoonfuls of defrosted frozen pesto), lots of olive oil, a bit of broth, and a splash of wine vinegar. Chill and serve garnished with Greek-style olives or nuggets of olive paste.

Bread Soup

[PAPPA COL POMADORO ALLA SIENESE]

◆ BASIC PANTRY

Serves 4

When made with excellent bread, ripe tomatoes, and aromatic olive oil, this dish is sublime. *Pappa* is comfortingly soft and easy to chew, therefore perfect for those who do not yet have strong teeth as well as those for whom strong teeth are a thing of the past.

4 to 5 garlic cloves, minced
2 tablespoons extra-virgin olive oil
2 large flavorful tomatoes, or 4 canned tomatoes, diced
1 cup tomato sauce

1 cup chicken or vegetable broth
About 3 cups dried bread slices or large croutons
1/4 cup coarsely chopped fresh Italian parsley or basil

1. Lightly brown garlic in 1 tablespoon olive oil, then add tomatoes and cook a few minutes to make a saucy, aromatic mixture.

2. Add tomato sauce and broth, then simmer a few minutes longer.

3. Add bread and continue simmering until liquid is absorbed. Break up some bread with a spoon, and let rest remain in more or less large pieces.

4. Serve immediately, each portion sprinkled with parsley or basil and drizzled with a little remaining olive oil.

NOTE This dish will vary wildly depending on the bread you choose. Fresh rosemary bread and sourdough are my favorites, especially when combined. If you use a dark bread, as is traditional in Florence, add a little chopped onion, celery, and sage to the sautéing garlic.

Crunchy Garlic Bread with Chive-Oil Puree and Balsamic-dressed Tricolored Tomatoes

◆◆ INTERMEDIATE PANTRY

Serves 4 to 6 as a first course, or 4 as an alfresco lunch dish

With flavors redolent of a sultry summer afternoon, this is an elaboration of bruschetta, that Italian dish of garlic-rubbed toast topped with tomatoes, peppers, seafood, beans, greens, or nearly anything. It radiates American enthusiasm in its abundance of flavors and the freshness of its ingredients.

While I adore this with tricolored tomatoes of yellow or orange, green, and scarlet, if I can't find them in my market I use Roma tomatoes.

When tomatoes are ripe and rich, I tend to find even olive oil a distraction, and a discreet sprinkle of balsamic vinegar is what I crave. It brings out the fruity quality of the tomatoes, much as it does with strawberries.

1 loaf Italian country bread or baguette, preferably stale, sliced 3/4 to 1 inch thick
1/2 cup extra-virgin olive oil
1/4 cup coarsely chopped fresh chives
About 2 cups ripe tomato wedges (if possible, choose a combination of yellow or orange, ripe green, and red)

4 garlic cloves
1 teaspoon balsamic vinegar, or to taste
Generous pinch *each* of sugar and salt
Pinch of crumbled dried thyme or marjoram, or 1 tablespoon chopped fresh basil or parsley

1. Arrange bread in a flat pan or on a baking sheet. Drizzle with 3 tablespoons olive oil, then place in a 275° to 300° oven and let dry. Remove and cool. (Toasted bread may be stored in a paper bag for up to a month. As long as it's dry and there is no sign of mold, it should be fine to eat.)

2. In a blender or food processor, combine chives with remaining 5 tablespoons oil and whirl until chives are well chopped and mixed with oil. Set aside.

3. Dress tomato wedges with 1 garlic clove, minced, balsamic vinegar, sugar (or honey) and salt, and herbs.

4. Assemble dish just before serving: cut remaining garlic into halves (save any remaining garlic for another use) and use to rub onto bread.

5. Spread each garlic-rubbed toast with a little pureed chives, and top each with several wedges of marinated tomatoes and a drizzle of marinade. Eat at once.

New Orleans Creole Bread Pudding

◆ **BASIC PANTRY**

Serves 4 to 6

Making sweet pudding from layered stale bread and custard is one of the kindest things you can do to old bread. The transformation is Cinderella-like: what was once a bag of dry, not very nice bread suddenly becomes one of the most delicious desserts you could eat. Bread puddings are eaten throughout the country. In the Midwest a particularly rich bread pudding is steamed, as a Christmas pudding might be; in New Mexico bread pudding is traditionally made with sweet wine and a mild cheese such as jack. And in recent years bread pudding has been the star of the comeback trail, with upscale innovative restaurants adding it to their menus, sparked with such ingredients as chocolate chips or sun-dried cherries.

Though it's become an American classic, bread pudding no doubt has its antecedent in the bread and butter pudding of Britain. While it may have originated as a way of using up dry bread, few desserts evoke so much passion—or greed—as a good bread pudding. With none of the airy attributes that mark most first-rate desserts, it has a homey sturdiness, a faintly caramelized crusty exterior and creamy insides, and a buttery-boozy topping to pull it all together.

You can make puddings in individual baking dishes instead of one large one for a more elegant presentation, and you can use whiskey in place of brandy—it's often the choice in New Orleans.

Twelve 1/4- to 1/2-inch-thick
French or Italian bread slices
(about 3 cups)
1/2 cup (1 stick) butter (a mixture of unsalted and salted
butter seems to taste best
here)
1/2 cup sugar

2 cups milk
1/2 cup brandy
2 egg yolks
1/4 cup golden raisins
1 tablespoon butter for dotting
on top
Brandy Sauce, following

1. Preheat oven to 375°. Cover bottom of a 9-by-13-inch baking pan with bread slices, broken if need be to fit in pan more or less evenly and flat.

2. Heat butter, sugar, milk, and brandy until sugar is dissolved. Cool.

3. Beat in egg yolks, then add raisins and pour custard over bread layers, jostling them a bit to let raisins fall between cracks. Press bread down with your hands if you need to, to get bread pieces to soak up liquid on top.

4. Dot top with butter, then bake until golden brown, about 45 minutes to 1 hour.

5. Serve each portion topped with a spoonful of brandy sauce.

Brandy Sauce

4 tablespoons butter
1/2 cup brown sugar, packed

1/4 cup brandy

Combine all ingredients and heat over a medium heat until sugar is dissolved and alcohol is burned off. Let boil just a minute or two for a caramelized flavor, but do not cook too long or you will have a hard toffee that refuses to budge from the pan once cooled a bit.

Fondue

◆ BASIC TO
◆◆ ADVANCED PANTRY

Serves 6 to 8 as an appetizer

Fondue is a consummate pantry food, having originated in Switzerland as a way of making hard bread and last summer's cheese soft enough to eat during the long cold winter. By heating the cheese in a pot of warm wine, then dipping the bread into it, all of the ingredients became edible again. Here is my version of the Swiss classic.

One 1-pound loaf sourdough
(or other crusty, hearty
bread), preferably stale
2 cups fruity but dry white
wine such as Riesling, Char-
donnay, or Fumé Blanc
1 to 2 chopped garlic cloves
12 ounces (1-1/2 cups) jack
cheese (or other creamy, mild
cheese), cut into small dice or
cubes
3 tablespoons flour
1/2 to 1/3 cup coarsely grated
dry jack cheese, aged asiago,
or Parmesan
Pinch *each* of cayenne and
ground nutmeg
2 tablespoons kiwi brandy or
other eau-de-vie

Accompaniments:
Several crisp sweet-tart apples
or pears, cut into wedges for
dipping
Plate of roasted red peppers,
cut into strips
Crisp-tender steamed broccoli
florets, cooled
2 to 3 tablespoons lightly
toasted cumin seeds (to toast,
see page 241)
Several mustards: whole seed,
tarragon, herbes de
Provence, California sweet
and spicy, etc.
Tiny cornichon pickles

1. Cut bread into bite-sized cubes, leaving a bit of crust on each cube. Arrange in a shallow baking pan and bake in a 250° oven for about an hour, or until dry.

2. Combine wine and garlic, and bring to boil.

3. Mix cheese cubes with flour. Reduce heat under wine to low, then mix in cheese cubes, stirring well in one direction until they melt. When nearly melted, stir in grated cheese. When melted, in just a minute or two, add cayenne, nutmeg, and brandy, and stir well.

4. Light a fondue pot and place in center of table, adjusting heat as needed so that mixture stays just warm enough for dipping and does not burn on bottom.

5. Serve simmering melted cheese mixture surrounded by a selection of accompaniments: bread, apples, and vegetables for dipping; seeds, mustards, and pickles as condiments for varying each mouthful.

WISCONSIN FONDUE **Sharp Cheddar** and **beer,** accompanied with **marinated tomatoes, whole-seed mustard,** and **bread and butter pickles.**

Four Ways to Wrap a Breadstick

◆◆◆◆◆◆◆

◆ Spread it with garlicky Boursin or goat cheese and roll a slice of Westphalian ham around it.

◆ Spread it with soft unsalted butter seasoned with olive paste, then wrap a silky slice of prosciutto around it.

◆ Spread it with garlic-parsley butter, then wrap it with a thin slice of bresaola, or air-dried beef.

◆ Spread the stick with cream cheese seasoned with lots of chopped fresh chives or shallots, then wrap a slice of smoked salmon around it.

NEW MEXICO FONDUE Add a shot of **tequila** in place of brandy; have **soft tortillas** for dipping and a selection of spicy condiments: **dried-chili pastes** and **fresh relishes, chopped herbs,** and so on.

PACIFIC NORTHWEST FONDUE **Watercress sprigs** to spoon warm cheese over.

NEW YORK LITTLE ITALY FONDUE Lots of **garlic** and **tomatoes** sizzling in the basic cheese mixture sprinkled with chopped fresh **oregano.**

◆◆◆◆◆◆◆

BREADSTICKS Always in my pantry, for nibbling on when a big crunch is in order, or for serving with cheeses, salads, or soups, or just dipping naughtily into soft butter.

Bread sticks, or *grissini,* are found in Italian bakeries; when my teen-aged daughter was little, our neighborhood Italian bakery always made sure she had a bread stick in her chubby fist. They are delicious, and I would love them even if I didn't have such pleasant memories. Search out a good bakery-made bread stick—it will be irregularly shaped and hopefully very long. If it has seeds, even better.

Coconut The dried coconut I keep in my pantry is sweetened, chewy, and lends itself to making sweet and tropical-accented desserts. For savory dishes I use either canned or frozen coconut milk (unsweetened) or I get ambitious and make my own (see page 135).

Caribbean Coconut Shortbread

◆ BASIC PANTRY

Makes one 9-inch rectangle

Sweet coconut is delectable sprinkled onto a whipped cream–frosted sponge cake (fill the center layer with tropical fruit). It doesn't demand much from the cook, but it tastes very special indeed. So does the following shortbread, which hails from the Cayman Islands and tastes somewhat like a terrific macaroon, but with the texture of shortbread.

1/2 cup (1 stick) unsalted butter, at room temperature
Pinch of salt
1/2 cup powdered sugar

1 cup unbleached all-purpose flour
2 cups flaked coconut
1 teaspoon vanilla extract

1. Preheat oven to 350°. Mix together butter, salt, and half of powdered sugar until well combined. Quickly add flour, then coconut and vanilla. This is easily done in a food processor.

2. Spread out about 1/2 inch thick on an ungreased baking sheet, patting out with your fingers. With a knife, make criss-cross lines marking pieces into diamond shapes.

3. Bake until very lightly browned, about 20 minutes.

4. Remove from oven and sprinkle with remaining sugar, using a sifter so there are no lumps. While shortbread is still warm, cut it into serving pieces using scored lines as guidelines.

Coconut Shortbread Tarts Filled with Peach Frozen Yogurt and Raspberries

Press **shortbread dough,** above, into bottom of individual tiny tart pans. Bake as above, then cool in pans. When firm and cool, carefully remove from pans. Serve filled with **frozen peach yogurt** and spoon **fresh raspberries** over the top.

◆◆◆◆◆◆

Cookies and Their Crumbs Cookies—good-quality ones such as gingersnaps, amaretti, ladyfingers, and biscotti—are good for more than an afternoon snack, a clandestine nibble, or as companions to the late show.

Cookies in the pantry are an excellent basis for desserts, such as the deliciously simple one of cookies crumbled onto ice cream, or cookies soaking in liqueurs and layered with fruit or mousse. But they also make a surprisingly good thickening ingredient for savory foods: Northern Italian pumpkin ravioli, for example, thickened with amaretti crumbs, or German sauerbraten, with its tart and sweet-spicy sauce thickened with gingersnaps.

STORAGE TIPS Store cookies in a loosely covered container in a dry place. Recrisp in a 300° oven if necessary. To keep soft cookies soft, store with a piece of bread. When the bread gets dry, replace it. And don't put both soft and crisp cookies together—the soft ones will sog up the crisp cookies and the crisp cookies will sap the moisture of the soft ones.

New England Pork Chops and Mushrooms

Serves 4

The following dish uses gingersnaps as a thickener for a mysteriously lilting result: not so much sweet or spicy, just subtly different.

2 medium onions, thinly sliced top to bottom
2 tablespoons vegetable oil
4 thick pork chops, at least 8 ounces each
2 cups (1 bottle) full-flavored beer
1 cup beef broth
1 tablespoon cider vinegar
1 bay leaf
6 gingersnaps, crushed
1/3 cup heavy (whipping) cream
1 pound mushrooms, thinly sliced
1 garlic clove, chopped
1 tablespoon brandy
Salt and pepper to taste

1. Sauté onions in 2 teaspoons oil until softened and lightly browned, then add pork chops, pushing onions aside to lightly brown chops.

2. Add beer, broth, vinegar, and bay leaf, then simmer over a low heat for 15 to 20 minutes, or until meat is tender. Stir in gingersnaps and cream, and continue cooking until sauce thickens, another 5 minutes or so.

3. Quickly sauté mushrooms with garlic in remaining 4 teaspoons oil. Pour in brandy and cook over high heat to evaporate alcohol.

4. Add mushroom mixture (plus accumulated juices) to pork chops, and simmer together for another 5 to 10 minutes. Season with salt and pepper if needed, and serve with casserole-roasted potatoes and crusty bread.

NOTE Since pork is often so lean these days, the braising doesn't always make it as tender as it should. If the meat you use in this recipe cooks up on the dry side, cut it into bite-sized pieces and eat the dish as a sort of mushroom and pork stew. Preparing it a day ahead and reheating it gets the flavors into the meat and mellows the dish.

Lime Cheesecake in a Ginger Crust

Serves 6 to 8

The richness of the cheesecake filling is tamed by the spicy lift of a ginger crust. Serve this rich, citrusy cheesecake with a spoonful of mixed berries or a garnish of tropical fruit.

CRUST

3/4 cup gingersnap crumbs
1 tablespoon sugar

3 tablespoons melted unsalted butter

FILLING

12 ounces (1-1/2 cups) cream cheese, at room temperature
1/3 cup sugar
3 large eggs, at room temperature

1-1/2 tablespoons grated lime zest
1/3 cup fresh lime juice

TOPPING

1 cup sour cream
1 teaspoon sugar
1 teaspoon fresh lime juice

An assortment of mixed berries and/or slices of tropical fruits such as mango, papaya, kiwi, etc.

1. To make crust: Combine gingersnap crumbs with sugar and butter, then press into bottom and sides of a glass pie pan or cheesecake pan. Chill for at least 30 minutes or, preferably, 1 hour.

2. Preheat oven to 325°. To make filling: Mix cream cheese with sugar, eggs, zest, and juice. (This is easiest to do in a food processor or blender.)

3. Pour filling into chilled crust and bake for 35 to 40 minutes, or until it looks nearly set, but is still somewhat liquidy or jiggly. The top should not appear firm. If it does it might crack when it cools (though the crack can be camouflaged by sour cream or yogurt topping and fruit).

4. Combine ingredients for topping and pour it evenly over hot cheesecake; return cake to oven for 7 to 8 minutes, or until it appears set.

5. Cool and chill, well covered, in the refrigerator for at least 2 hours or overnight.

6. Serve accompanied with an assortment of berries and/or fruit.

VARIATION Instead of sour cream topping, top above cheesecake with 2 cups **lime-flavored yogurt** and return it to oven for only 5 minutes.

Gingersnaps or Biscotti Layered with Whipped Cream

◆ **BASIC TO**
◆◆ **INTERMEDIATE PANTRY**

Serves 4

I consider desserts my weak spot when it comes to cooking, so I'm always looking for a sweet that is simple, undemanding to prepare, and out of the ordinary. This one, given to me by my agent, Teresa Chris, is all those things. It's the sort of messy thing I always wanted to eat as a child but wasn't allowed to. And it's nice enough to serve to polite company.

3/4 cup heavy (whipping) cream   About 16 gingersnaps or 8 to 10
Sugar to taste   large biscotti

1. Whip cream and lightly sweeten it with sugar.
2. In a glass bowl or dish, layer cookies and cream.
3. Chill for at least 2 hours. Serve with fresh fruit or chopped preserved ginger.

Little Italy Amaretti-baked Apricots

◆◆ **INTERMEDIATE PANTRY**

Serves 4

Amaretti means "just a tiny bit bitter," because of this cookie's distinctive bitter-almond flavor. The famous cookie develops its crunch through a long and slow baking.

Amaretti were originated in the early 1700s in Saronno, Italy, by a young baker who created them for a visiting cardinal, and wound up winning the hand of the woman he loved. It was her idea to wrap the cookies in the pastel-colored papers, and the descendants of that baker and his wife still make these cookies today.

12 ripe sweet apricots, halved   1 to 2 tablespoons sugar
    and pitted   Vanilla ice cream or frozen
8 amaretti, roughly broken up   yogurt

1. Preheat oven to 400°. In a shallow baking dish, layer apricots with amaretti, sprinkling with sugar as you go. Cover tightly with aluminum foil, then bake for about 20 minutes, or until apricots and amaretti are a sweet, fragrant, messy mixture.
2. Serve each portion topped with scoops of vanilla ice cream or frozen yogurt.

Fresh Peach and Amaretti Mousse

Serves 4

Fruit, yogurt, and crème frâiche make a light mousse, contrasting with its crunchy sweet topping of amaretti crumbs. Simple to prepare, but lovely and vibrant.

1 cup heavy (whipping) cream
2 tablespoons powdered sugar
1/2–1 teaspoon vanilla extract
6 ripe sweet peaches
Juice of 1/4 lemon

1 container (6 to 8 ounces)
 apricot- or peach-flavored
 fromage frais or yogurt
10 to 12 amaretti cookies,
 crumbled

1. Beat cream until thick; add sugar and vanilla.
2. Mash or puree peaches with lemon juice.
3. Mix peaches with fromage frais or yogurt, then fold in whipped cream.
4. Sprinkle mousse with a heavy layer of amaretti crumbs.

Nectarine Mousse with Oatmeal Cookie Crumbs

Use **nectarines** in place of peaches and **oatmeal cookie crumbs** in place of Amaretti.

Four More Things to Do with Amaretti

◆◆◆◆◆◆

◆ Nibble, by yourself or with a friend, along with a glass of red wine.

◆ Add crumbled amaretti to egg white batter for meringues.

◆◆◆◆◆◆

◆ BRANDIED FRUIT WITH AMARETTI CRUMBS Slice peaches or nectarines, toss in brandy and sugar to taste, then serve over vanilla ice cream along with a generous sprinkle of crumbled amaretti and a handful of tart fresh raspberries.

◆◆◆◆◆◆

◆ CARROT-AMARETTI ICE CREAM Cook 2 carrots until very tender, mash, add 1 tablespoon of Amaretto liqueur, and place over heat for a minute or two to absorb excess liquid. Combine with 1 pint softened vanilla ice cream and a dash of almond extract if you like an almond scent as much as I do, then fold in 6 or so somewhat broken-up amaretti cookies and return to freezer to firm up. Serve when just firm, sprinkled with cinnamon if desired.

Candies I always keep a jar of some sort of really good hard candy on hand, though not necessarily for nibbling on—hard candy can be a trial for even the toughest of teeth (though I have fond memories of spending afternoons sticking peppermint sticks into lemons and sucking the combination of sweet and sour).

Candies in the pantry make great flavorings, coarsely crushed and added to other desserts. The simplest is crushed peppermint or lemon drop candy added to ice cream, or peppermints added to whipped cream and rolled up in a fudgey roulade, or simply plopped onto a chocolate tart.

Chocolate espresso beans are a personal favorite; use them to garnish a whipped cream–topped cappuccino milkshake, or just nibble a handful when no one is looking.

Toffee Crunch Fresh Fruit Cream Gâteau

◆ **BASIC PANTRY**

Serves 8 to 10

English toffee, crushed, is the basis for a delectable celebration cake that was, at one stage of my catering career, my signature dish. I made them small enough for a child's birthday, and large enough for a wedding for hundreds. For my daughter's birthday one year I made this cake in the shape of a yellow submarine and rented the movie to coordinate the theme. Ten years later it is the cake that she remembers.

2 homemade or bakery sponge layers, about 12 inches in diameter
A generous sprinkling of brandy or liqueur (optional)
1/2 pound hard English toffee covered with chocolate and almonds
3 cups heavy (whipping) cream
1 teaspoon vanilla extract
1/4 cup or more powdered sugar
Strawberries, kiwis, nectarines, bananas, or any other fresh soft fruit, alone or in combination

1. In a blender or food processor chop toffee into an uneven mixture of part chunks, part crumbs. Set aside.

2. Whip cream until firm, adding powdered sugar and vanilla halfway through.

3. Place 1 layer of sponge cake on a plate or platter, sprinkle with brandy if using, then spread with a thin layer of cream. Over that, layer

two thirds of candy mixture. Top with a thick layer of whipped cream and second cake layer.

4. Sprinkle cake with brandy or liqueur, then ice with remaining whipped cream.

5. Sprinkle remaining crushed toffee around sides of cake, and garnish with fresh fruit, peeled and cut into slices.

◆◆◆◆◆◆

Falafel Mix While I usually don't recommend using packaged mixes, falafel mix is an exception, since it is basically seasoned ground dried chick-peas and bulgur wheat. Every brand I've ever used has made reasonable falafel croquettes, and most of them are very good.

In addition, falafel mix is a great seasoning for other foods: add it to chopped lamb as a way of extending the meat and turning it into exotically seasoned meat logs, or use it to stuff red, yellow, and green bell peppers. As a variation on the theme, roll the falafel mix–seasoned-meat into tiny balls. Brown and serve with a yogurt or tahini-spice dip, or simmer the meatballs in cinnamon-and-curry-scented tomato sauce along with peas, spinach, eggplant, or whichever vegetables are in season. Use falafel mix to thicken stews or hefty soups.

Tel Aviv Central Bus Station Falafel

◆◆ INTERMEDIATE PANTRY

When you make falafel, be sure it is a really trashy street-food version: pile the fried **chick-pea balls** into warm **pita** halves, along with a salad of chopped **cucumbers,** diced **tomatoes,** chopped fresh **cilantro,** lots of spicy **Tahini-Yogurt Sauce** (page 190), **sauerkraut,** pickled **chilies** such as jalapeños, and, for good measure, several **potato chips.** And there you have the gaudy concoction I used to munch on at the Tel Aviv Central Bus Station.

◆◆◆◆◆◆

Flour Always on hand, flour is indispensable in the kitchen. There is a wide variety of flours on the market, and here again your pantry can be as basic or as extravagant and ambitious as you like. Each flour has a specific use and character, from all-purpose white to nutty whole wheat, rustic rye to soft fine rice flour.

A Guide to Flours in the Pantry

◆◆◆◆◆◆

BASIC

ALL PURPOSE, BLEACHED OR UNBLEACHED Soft, powdery, and white, used in thickening sauces; baking sweets such as cakes, pie crusts, and cookies; in pastas and roux; and for combining with whole-wheat and other flours for breads, pastries, etc.

WHOLE WHEAT Light brown in color, soft and powdery with a bit of texture, this is used anywhere you want added nutrition and fiber along with a nutty grain flavor.

MASA HARINA Pale cream to light yellow in color, this is soft and powdery but with a small amount of gritty texture. Use for tortillas, tamales, to thicken Mexican sauces and Tex-Mex chili con carne, to mix with white flour for baking Southwestern breads, etc. This definitely belongs in the Basic Pantry of anyone who loves Mexican food.

"WONDRA" INSTANT FLOUR Very floury, this usually is sold in a round canister for shaking, and it dissolves instantly. Use to thicken sauces smoothly without having to be mixed with melted fat, and to dust on foods to be browned.

◆◆◆◆◆◆

INTERMEDIATE

To the above selection of flours add:

BREAD FLOUR High gluten, sometimes called "strong flour," this is used for bread, pasta with a bit of chewiness, etc.

WHOLE-WHEAT PASTRY FLOUR Smooth and powdery, pale brown in color, this finely ground pastry flour made from whole wheat is used in pastries, pie crusts, cakes, cookies, etc.

CAKE FLOUR Very silky soft and fine textured, cake flour is used for cakes, pastries, and delicate steamed Chinese noodles (see page 324).

CHICK-PEA FLOUR Ochre-golden in color, powdery in consistency, with a definite scent of the chick-peas it is milled from. Use in batters for frying Indian foods, in Indian candies, and for thickening sauces; used in Provence for the niçoise specialty, socca, a chick-pea pancake.

BUCKWHEAT FLOUR This pale gray-brown, soft flour with a small amount of texture is used in breads, dumplings, noodles, and crepes.

SOY FLOUR Pale yellow-ochre in color, soy flour is milled from soybeans and has their distinctive scent and flavor. Combine with other flours to up the protein content of breads and baked goods. Soy flour adds a hearty, satisfying quality to breads.

◆◆◆◆◆◆

ADVANCED

To the basic and intermediate flours, add:

BARLEY FLOUR Pearly beige-cream in color, with a slightly gritty texture and a distinctive barley flavor. Use with other flours for breads.

RYE Steely pearl-grey in color, soft with a hint of texture, and tasting of rye. Combine with white flour for breads, dumplings, pasta.

RICE FLOUR These fine white grains are combined with chick-pea flour for Indian batters; used in Chinese cooking as a coating mixture for meats, kneaded into dough for noodles and pastries; and dusted onto some breads.

OAT FLOUR Grayish beige in color, with a slightly glutinous quality once cooked. Combine with white and whole-grain flours to increase the fiber in baked goods.

Saffron Spaetzle

◆◆◆ ADVANCED PANTRY

Serves 4

The following dumplings are easily made. Saffron from the pantry makes them distinctive, but they are delicious as well without the saffron.

1-1/2 cups unbleached all-purpose flour
1 teaspoon salt
2 eggs
1/2 cup milk

1/2 teaspoon or more saffron threads, dissolved in 3 tablespoons warm water (if not using saffron, use only water)
3 tablespoons unsalted butter
Salt and pepper to taste

1. Combine flour and salt.
2. In another bowl, beat eggs with milk and saffron water, then stir liquid into flour and combine well.

3. Bring a large pot of salted water to a boil. Using a colander (the kind with large holes) set over boiling water, pour in batterlike dough and, using a large spoon, force it through holes, forming squiggly dumplinglike shapes. (It will fall like straggling lumps into the water and you may wish that you had more than 2 hands at this point. Regardless of how unpromising it looks, in about 5 minutes you will have delicious dumplings.) Cover pot and boil for 5 minutes, releasing cover if it threatens to boil over.

4. Drain dumplings and place in a bowl of cold water to firm, 15–30 minutes. Don't be tempted to skip this step or they will be gummy. They may be kept in their cold bath for up to 2 hours.

5. Melt butter and let it warm to a golden color, then drain dumplings and toss them in butter over low to medium heat, gently tossing and warming through. Take care not to break them into mush. Add salt and pepper and serve.

VARIATIONS Add lots of chopped **garlic** to butter, **and/or toasted bread crumbs.** Or, omit saffron from batter, and serve dumplings with sautéed chopped rehydrated **wild mushrooms** such as shiitakes, cèpes, or morels.

Very Delicate Chinese Steamed Noodles

◆◆ INTERMEDIATE PANTRY

Serves 4

I owe this method to cookbook author Rhoda Yee. While she taught me many secrets of the wok, it was these delicate, quivering noodles that most captivated me. Serve on their own, or with any sort of stir-fry, such as broccoli and Chinese roast duck, with a sprinkling of toasted sesame seeds, chopped fresh cilantro, and green onions.

2 cups cake flour
1/4 cup cornstarch
1 teaspoon salt
1/3 cup vegetable oil
2-2/3 cups cold water
Asian (toasted) sesame oil

Soy sauce to taste
Chopped green onions, fresh
    cilantro, diced ham or
    shrimp, toasted sesame
    seeds, or julienned roast
    pork for garnish

1. Combine cake flour, cornstarch, salt, oil, and water in order given, mixing until batter is smooth and lump free.

2. Drizzle a bit of sesame oil into bottom of a pie tin, then ladle in 1/3 cup of batter, turning pan to coat bottom evenly.

3. Place in a steamer and steam for 5 minutes, or until noodle firms, then roll it out of pan and repeat, drizzling sesame oil onto pie pan, ladling batter, and steaming. If you use several pie pans, you can keep process going smoothly.

4. Serve immediately, sprinkled with soy sauce and rolled around any of garnishes, then sliced.

VARIATIONS Roll noodles out of pan and let cool. Omit garnishes. Slice to thickness desired and use as fresh noodles, topping them with a variety of savory stir-fried meats, fish, vegetables, etc. Or, when you ladle batter into pie tin, sprinkle any of garnishes on top of soft batter before steaming. Serve unrolled noodles at room temperature, garnished with a drizzle of soy sauce, a sprinkling of crushed peanuts, and chopped cilantro and green onions.

Crisp Fish Strips with an Indian Flavor

◆◆ INTERMEDIATE PANTRY

Serves 4

Finely milled chick-peas make a rich, nutty flour, prized in the Indian kitchen for a variety of dishes ranging from savory fritter batter to a rich cake-like fudge. Nearly as high in protein as soy flour, chick-pea flour has a flavor unlike that of any other. Peruse Indian cookbooks for other recipes using chick-pea flour, also known as *besan*.

Often paired with chick-pea flour is rice flour, which adds a delicate, light crispness to the hearty bean flour.

In the following traditional North Indian dish, tender strips of white-meat fish are seasoned assertively, then tossed in chick-pea and rice flour and fried to crispness. This method also is used for small whole fish such as smelts and fresh sardines, and for freshwater fish such as trout.

Serve simply in a napkin-lined basket, with a squeeze of lime or lemon, a sprinkle of chopped cilantro, a shake of hot pepper seasoning.

1 pound firm white-fleshed fish fillets	1 teaspoon ground cumin
2 lemons or limes	1/2 teaspoon curry powder
2 garlic cloves	Salt and black pepper to taste
2 tablespoons minced fresh cilantro	1/2 cup chick-pea flour
Shake of hot pepper seasoning	1/4 cup rice flour or cake flour
	Vegetable oil for frying

1. Cut fish fillets into strips. Sprinkle with lemon or lime and coat well.

2. Toss with garlic, cilantro, hot pepper seasoning, cumin, curry powder, salt, pepper, chick-pea flour and rice or cake flour.

3. In a large, heavy skillet, heat oil to a depth of 1/2 to 3/4 inches and, when very hot, shake off excess flour and spices from fish, then plunge them into hot oil in several batches and fry quickly until lightly browned. It won't take more than a few minutes for each batch. Do not overcook.

4. Drain on absorbent paper and serve immediately, accompanied with wedges of lemon or lime and a sprinkling of cilantro.

Crisp Fried Cilantro-Mint-stuffed Fish Steaks

Here, fish steaks are stuffed with a cilantro-mint-chili paste, then dusted with the flour mixture and fried. It makes a slightly more ambitious, refined dish.

CILANTRO-MINT PASTE

3 chopped garlic cloves	Juice of 1/2 lemon
1/2 to 2 chopped jalapeño chilies	Salt to taste
	Pinch of curry powder
1/2 cup chopped fresh cilantro	4 firm white-fleshed fish steaks
1/2 cup chopped fresh mint	

1. Combine all ingredients for Cilantro-Mint Paste.

2. Cut a pocket in each fish steak by placing it on a flat surface and cutting into it with a sharp knife.

3. Stuff each pocket with a tablespoon or two of the Cilantro-Mint Paste, then proceed as in above recipe, tossing with spices and flours, then frying until crisp and lightly browned. Allow a few more minutes of cooking time, as fish steaks are thicker than strips.

◆◆◆◆◆◆

Indian Crispy Snacks (Sev) These crisp fried squiggles are based on spiced chick-pea flour. Keep some on your shelf to serve as a cocktail snack or in the following dish.

Indian Yogurt Bowl with Sev, Potatoes, Chick-peas, Cilantro, and Mango Chutney

◆◆◆ ADVANCED PANTRY

Serves 4

Stir 2 cups plain **yogurt** to smooth out any lumps, then place 1/2 cup in each of 4 bowls. Top each bowlful with 1/2 cold boiled **waxy potato,** diced, a handful of cooked **chick-peas,** a spoonful of **Cilantro-Lime Paste** (page 360), a spoonful of **mango chutney,** and a sprinkling of **sev.** Eat immediately.

◆◆◆◆◆◆

Jams, Jellies, and Preserves Bitter-tangy lime marmalade for spreading onto hot scones, thick strawberry preserves for spooning onto a butter croissant, red currant or raspberry jelly to melt and glaze a tart with. There are so many exceptional jams, jellies, and preserves on the market it's a shame to stock your pantry with only commercial ones from the supermarket.

Many fine jams and preserves have a somewhat reduced sugar content so that the flavors shine through, and others, especially the imported French ones, taste so strongly of the fruit that eating them is a constant exercise in stopping yourself from eating them with a spoon. Several years ago there was an imported jelly made from orange blossoms. It was heaven, but unfortunately is nowhere to be found these days.

A selection of jams and jellies on your pantry shelf can do much more than serve as a spread for toast. Try adding a tiny spoonful to a salad dressing, or mixing raspberry jam with whole-seed mustard and using it as a glaze for ham. Apricot jam makes a good tart-spicy accent sauce (see Turkey Fillets with the Flavors of Southeast Asia, page 136), or a good filling for a rich sponge cake when combined with soaked and pureed dried apricots and a dash of brandy.

STORAGE TIPS Because of their high sugar content, syrups may be stored on the pantry shelf; they will keep for about a year, though refrigerated they will keep for up to 2 years. Jams, however, should be stored in the refrigerator once opened. Most jellies and jams will last, in the refrigerator, for several months. Low-sugar ones, however, will not keep longer than about a month.

Blood Oranges with Rose Petal Sauce

◆◆◆ ADVANCED PANTRY

Serves 4

Rose petal jam may sound like an oddity, but it is a flower-perfumed sweet that makes itself as welcome on a slice of soft, crisp-crusted, crumbed white bread as it is sandwiched between thin slices of sponge cake (frosted with whipped cream, of course, and garnished with lots of fragrant fresh unsprayed rose petals).

Rose petal jam can be easily turned into rose petal sauce and enjoyed on ice cream or with fresh fruit. This dessert of ruby red oranges lying in a pink pool of fragrant sweet rose petal sauce is no less than stunning. It looks like a sunset and smells like an exotic garden in bloom.

4 blood oranges	Rose petal sauce, page 45

1. Peel blood oranges and cut into thick slices.
2. Spoon a bit of rose petal sauce onto individual plates, then arrange orange slices on top.
3. Serve immediately.

VARIATION This sauce will keep, refrigerated, for up to 2 weeks, though it might need another hit of rose water as its delicate scent fades. Try spooning it over **vanilla ice cream, brandy-soaked figs, and pistachio nuts.**

◆◆◆◆◆◆◆

Matzo Made from no more than flour and water with a bit of salt, matzo appears much like a cracker or any flatbread. But matzo is much more than that. It is a ritual food eaten at the Jewish holiday of Passover, the symbol of unleavened bread the fleeing Hebrews baked quickly on the desert's hot rocks in flight from an angry Pharaoh long ago.

I always have a box of matzo in my pantry; it's comfortingly good broken up into a bowl of hot soup, then poked at until it softens somewhat. It is a good no-fat alternative to crackers for dipping, and I love it best used in place of leavened bread for a chicken salad sandwich; the matzo's crunchiness is perfect next to the richness of the chicken salad. Matzo can be crushed into matzo meal (or bought that way), which can be used in place of bread crumbs or to make *kneidelach,* or matzo balls.

Matzo Brei

◆◆ INTERMEDIATE PANTRY

Serves 2

As with other ethnic dishes, there are variations of matzo brei for each and every family, and for each member within each family. Matzo brei, or fried matzo, is simply softened matzo combined with eggs and fried. But here the disagreements begin. Soak in milk or water? Warm or at room temperature? Lots of egg, or just enough to disappear into the maze of matzo? Fry it up flat and custardy inside, or broken up into crisp bits? Cook it in chicken fat, butter, vegetable oil? And what to serve it with—sweet things like jam or syrup, or with salt?

Regardless of how you cook it, matzo brei is one of the ultimate pantry foods. Made from ingredients I almost always have on hand no matter how tight the budget has been, nothing makes things seem quite so right as does a pan of matzo brei. If the following dish doesn't thrill you, it might be that you have to grow up eating it to fully appreciate its charm.

The following recipe is the way I like it, crispy and salty. It's followed by a variation for a sweet pancake-like matzo brei.

2 pieces matzo	2 to 3 tablespoons vegetable oil
2 eggs, lightly beaten	or olive oil
	Salt to taste

1. Break matzo up with your hands into relatively bite-sized pieces. (A variety of sizes helps make a good matzo brei to my taste.)

2. Place in a bowl and pour cold water to cover over matzo (some use hot water, but I think it softens matzo too much). Let sit a minute or two, then pour off water, draining as much as possible.

3. Add eggs to soaked matzo and mix well.

4. Heat a heavy skillet, then add oil. Add matzo mixture and fry over medium heat until it starts to set. Turn with a spatula, breaking up the whole pancake-like mixture, and fry a bit more. Occasionally turn the chunks and clusters, letting them brown and crisp in some places and remain tender and eggy in others. Add more oil if necessary.

5. When crispy on the outside, remove from pan with a slotted spatula (drain on absorbent paper if necessary). Sprinkle with salt and serve immediately.

Sweet Matzo Brei, Pancake Style

Soak **matzo** in **milk** rather than water, and add a dash of **ground cinnamon** and **sugar** when you add egg (I knew someone who added pistachios and vanilla extract). Fry mixture in **butter,** as if it were a pancake, letting it brown first on one side, then carefully turning it to other side. Serve sizzling hot and golden, accompanied with **jam and/or cinnamon sugar.**

◆◆◆◆◆◆

Popadums are ethereally thin Indian flatbreads made from specially prepared ground lentils. They are purchased, even in India where the entire cuisine is crafted by hand, and look much like thin though sturdy wafers. They must, however, be fried to reach their brittle crispness.

Popadums are usually imported from India, and come in a variety of sizes, from only an inch or two in diameter to a whopping 12 inches or more. They may be plain, or studded with dried garlic, red chili, black peppercorns, and other savory bits. Popadums may be fried several hours ahead of time and kept in a dry place.

STORAGE TIPS Popadums will last nearly indefinitely stored in a dry place.

Indian Appetizer Plate

◆◆ INTERMEDIATE PANTRY

Serves 4 to 6

In many Indian restaurants a plate of popadums is brought out, accompanied with a selection of condiments, while you make your dinner choice. They make a great home appetizer, like tortilla chips with salsa. For parties I often serve a tipped huge basket with masses of popadums tumbling out.

Oil for frying
8 to 12 popadums
Condiments: Mango chutney, ripe mangos mixed with chopped jalapeño chilies, Tomato-Cilantro-Chili relish (following), Pickled Onions (following), Spiced Yogurt Dip (following), leftover sambaar or any Indian spiced red lentil dish

1. Heat oil for frying. (I use a wok since it reaches the highest heat using the smallest amount of oil, and is similar to the Indian pot used for this purpose.)

2. Fry popadums in small batches. (They will sizzle and nearly explode in hot oil, expanding as do rice noodles when they are deep-fried. They will go from being tough to being crisp and delicate.) Fry quickly on each side, until lightly golden brown, then remove from wok to paper towels.

3. Serve with a choice of condiments and sauces.

Tomato-Cilantro-Chili Relish

Dice 6 ripe **tomatoes** and combine with 1/2 to 1 chopped **jalapeño** and 2 tablespoons chopped fresh **cilantro.** Add salt to taste.

Pickled Onions

Thinly slice a mild **onion** and toss with 1 to 2 tablespoons fresh **lime or lemon juice.** Add **salt** and dried **mint** to taste.

Spiced Yogurt Dip

Season plain **yogurt** with a pinch of **curry powder,** a little chopped **garlic,** and a dash of either **chutney or powdered tamarind** and a sprinkle of **mint,** either fresh or dried.

◆◆◆◆◆◆

Popcorn Introduced to the New Americans by the Native Americans at the first Thanksgiving, popcorn is probably our number-one national snack. High in fiber, it can be a healthy thing to munch on, especially when made with a skimpy hand on the oil and salt. Its satisfaction factor is high: it delivers massive crunch with each mouthful. Good for nervous nibbling. My brother claims that without it, getting through law school would have been impossible; my own salt-and-butter-stained computer keyboard "snitches" on me, even if I do hide the bowl when I clean up for guests.

But popcorn, like so many other healthful foods, is even more delicious when festooned with deliciously harmful substances. I'm thinking about caramel corn and its relations.

Chocolate-Macadamia Popcorn

◆◆◆ ADVANCED PANTRY

Serves 6 to 8

When I was a child, before the advent of huge shopping malls, downtown was the gathering place in my town, as it was in most others across the country. We went downtown to shop, to eat out, and to go to the movies. Next to the movie house was a shop that sold caramel corn. Movie goers could buy a bag and bring it in, and hungry shoppers could stop for a snack. Buttery-sweet smells spilled out onto the street, making walking by a nearly intolerable experience if I couldn't go in. I remember that caramel corn with almost indecent affection. But with social changes and the migration to the suburbs, the shop eventually closed, and the main street turned into a mall frequented mostly by vagrants. And I gave up caramel corn, preferring to spend my calories on sauces and wines.

Then one day I visited my aunt, who had a bag of dark-colored caramel corn. I resisted offers of the nibble until after we had talked a long time and I was hungry. "It really is good," she said, with the tone of voice that implied I might be a food writer but shouldn't be a snob.

It was really good, too, the dark color a result of the caramel melting with chocolate, studded with small crunchy bites of macadamia nuts. I must warn you, however, that you make this at your own risk. It tastes much better than the stuff bought at the mall, and it is alarming how often I find my hand full of the chewy sweet mixture heading towards my mouth.

8 cups unbuttered, unsalted popped popcorn (approximately 1/3–1/2 cup popcorn kernels)

One 3-1/2-ounce jar macadamia nuts, quartered and halved

1 cup light brown sugar

1/4 cup syrup such as golden syrup, or half dark and half light corn syrup

1/2 cup (1 stick) unsalted butter

1/2 teaspoon salt

3 heaping tablespoons unsweetened cocoa

1/2 tablespoon baking soda

1. Toss together popcorn and macadamia nuts, and pour into a shallow baking dish or onto a cookie sheet.

2. In a heavy saucepan, combine brown sugar, syrup, butter, salt, and cocoa.

3. Bring to a boil over a medium heat and continue boiling for 5 to 7 minutes, or until syrup reaches 260° on a candy thermometer, or forms a ball if a drop or two is dropped into a glass of cold water.

4. Remove from heat and add baking soda; it will foam up.

5. Quickly pour over popcorn and nuts, mixing well so that caramel

coats popcorn and holds much of it together; let cool. Caramel will be very hot and hard to handle, then cool very quickly.

6. When cool enough to handle, break up into smaller pieces. Keep in a relatively dry place. I keep it lightly covered with paper on a pantry shelf for however long it lasts.

◆◆◆◆◆◆

Rice Paper Southeast Asian and Vietnamese rice paper is an edible sheet made from rice dough, rolled thinly onto bamboo trays, then steamed and finally dried into waferlike rounds or triangles that will keep indefinitely on the pantry shelf. When dipped into lukewarm water, it rehydrates and becomes a translucent noodle-like pancake amenable to being eaten as is, accompanying a platter of fresh fruit or platters of savory stir-fries and salads. It may be filled and eaten as a spring roll, or fried to a golden crispness.

Tropical Fruit Rolls

Try wrapping rehydrated **rice paper rounds** around a selection of **tropical fruit** such as papayas, kiwis, and bananas, then brushing parcels with melted **butter**. Bake in a preheated 425° oven until parcels have turned golden. Serve with a **puree of mango,** slightly **sweetened** and hit with a little **rum or tequila,** and a cloud of lightly **whipped cream.**

◆◆◆◆◆◆

Salt Cod Hearty and savory once soaked and cooked, salt cod is not salty at all. Choose a creamy colored slab; cod that's too white indicates an overabundance of salt. The fish should be soaked in several changes of cold water. The problem is that a piece of salt cod can take 2–36 hours to refreshen. It's best to get exact refreshening directions from your fish source.

One pound dried, boneless cod rehydrates up to 1-1/2 pounds. Refreshed cod can be gently simmered Mediterranean style in a wide variety of sauces, from creamy to tomatoey. Soaked (but uncooked) it can be torn into bite size bits and dressed with olive oil, garlic, diced ripe tomatoes, and a garnish of pungent black olives to make Esqueixada, the classic Catalan salad.

Seaweed (Hijiiki and Nori) Thin strips of seaweed, to be used as a garnish for soups, sushi, sashimi, and so on. Cut the seaweed very thinly using a pair of scissors. Hijiiki makes a good topping for Sushi Rice, page 213.

Soy-based Meat Substitutes For vegetarians and those who want to cut down on their meat consumption, soy-based meat substitutes are good in curries, pilafs, spaghetti sauces, and in any dish where you would ordinarily use ground meat or simmered meat chunks. I find that dry ones tend to be much more flavorful and practical than canned ones.

Sugars An innocent by-product of photosynthesis, sugar has been named in recent decades as the cause of nearly every ill known to humankind, both physical and mental; recently, however, fats have taken over the role of evil incarnate and those of us with a sweet tooth can breathe a sigh of relief.

These days we're likely eating less sugar, or at least trying to; but the sugar we are eating comes in a wide array of flavors, textures, consistencies, and forms. I keep a selection of sugars on my pantry shelf, in addition to the basic white and brown for baking, cooking, etc. I adore offering several different types of sugar to accompany tea or coffee.

Search for Parrot Brand sugar cubes, the brownish ones that come in a gaily colored rectangular box. They are exorbitantly expensive, but there is nothing like a nubby rounded cube, with its slight whiff of molasses, held between the fingers and dipped into a bowl of café au lait, and sucked on until the cube melts in the mouth, all sweet gritty grains. Bliss.

Try also crystalized rock sugar, usually available in a light golden brown color though sometimes sold in garish carnival hues of pink, blue, and green. Cubes of Demerara sugar, brown and granulated, with a markedly molasseslike flavor, are good with coffee or tea, and their shape is neat and tidy.

Raw, pale beige-brown sugar is a good spoon-on in place of its bland white brother, and maple sugar is concentrated maple flavor.

Syrups and Honeys Natural foods stores have some interesting syrups such as rice bran syrup, and blackstrap molasses. They're high in minerals and vitamins, and if the strong flavor needs getting used to, it can nonetheless be a bit addictive. Good on breakfast cereals or in hot milk.

CORN SYRUP In both light and dark versions, it is used for confections, and to give a smooth sweetness to baked goods and sweets where no sugar granules are desired. English golden syrup (treacle), a lightly caramelized thick sugar syrup, gives the same practical results but has a rich, round sweet flavor; seek it out. Molasses is briefly discussed in "A Brief Guide to Sugar," below.

HONEY is available in a wide array of consistencies, thicknesses, flavors, and colors. Some honeys are scented by the flowers the bees had fed on, such as lavender or sage; some are thick and darkly sweet, while others are as light and delicate as nectar. Choose raw, unheated honey when possible, as its flavor and nutrition remain undiminished.

Whipped honey is a personal favorite; I love spreading it onto hot toast or spooning it up alongside a cup of bitter, strong coffee. Vanilla and other flavored whipped honeys are available in specialty shops, and they are delectable, the apricot nearly as delicious as the vanilla.

Sometimes honey is sold in combs, to chew on like a candy, spitting out the wax after all of the honey has been chewed away.

MAPLE SYRUP has a pleasingly bitter edge and depth to its sweetness; see page 154 for information and a recipe.

FRUIT SYRUPS Italian and French fruit syrups come in a wide variety of flavors such as lemon, bitter cherry, mint, and almond. Keep several on hand as nonalcoholic mixers with chilled mineral water; they're good too as a summer treat drizzled over shaved ice.

LIME SYRUP Used in many mixed drinks, thinned with ice water or cold mineral water, lime syrup is the basis for my favorite summertime wine cooler: sangría Guadalajara. Simply pour a glass of rough red wine over an ice cube, then, using the back of your spoon to keep syrup from mixing with wine, pour 1 ounce of lime syrup slowly into glass.

A Brief Guide to Sugar

GRANULATED Ordinary white sugar, ground into somewhat coarse crystals. Sugar is usually milled from either beets or cane, and while many extole the virtues of one over the other, I notice no difference.

SUPERFINE Granulated sugar ground to a finer consistency that is readily dissolvable in iced drinks, etc.

(POWDERED) CONFECTIONER'S Soft, powdery sugar that has been very finely ground along with cornstarch to create its distinctive texture. Powdered sugar is usually used for icings, for dusting onto cakes and cookies, for making fudge and other confections, etc.

RAW SUGAR Less refined than ordinary granulated sugar, raw sugar still has some molasses flavor and nutrients left in. Its texture is slightly more coarse than that of granulated sugar.

BROWN SUGAR comes in two varieties, dark and light. Dark brown sugar has a rich molasses color and flavor, while the light is subtler, with a softer, almost sandlike texture. If brown sugar becomes hard, soften it by placing it in a covered bowl with a few drops of water, then placing the whole thing in a just-warm oven for 15 to 20 minutes. Do not process very hard brown sugar in a processor or blender, as the chunks can get so hard as to damage the blades of the machine.

LARGE CONFECTIONER'S GRANULES White sugar in the form of tiny cubes that hold their shape in baking, used primarily to sprinkle onto pastries. Usually available only from bakers' supply shops and some specialty shops.

VANILLA SUGAR Sugar impregnated with the sweet scent of vanilla. To make your own, open a vanilla bean and scrape out some seeds, then mix them with sugar. Place in a canister with sugar to cover and let it sit for several days before you start to use it. Add more sugar as you go along, for a nearly endless supply of a fragrant sweet to sprinkle onto cookies, buttered toast, bowls of hot cornmeal mush, and whatever else takes your fancy.

SUGAR CUBES come in nearly as wide a variety as do other forms of sugars. White cubes are the most easily available, sold in several different sizes. Brown sugar cubes are imported from Britain and are occasionally available here; they have a lovely molasses flavor and are particularly good in coffee. French "Parrot Brand" sugar cubes are my favorites. Chunky and rough textured, they are available in both white or brown.

CRYSTALIZED SUGAR LUMPS Amber-colored candylike sugar chunks, delicious served with tea or coffee, and nearly as pretty to look at as they are delicious to nibble. Sometimes pink, blue, and other colors are sold, but I find the colors off-putting.

MAPLE SUGAR Made from evaporating maple syrup, this is very sweet with slight bitter or woodsy overtones and a distinctive flavor of its own. Usually sold as a sweet, sometimes in the shape of maple leaves or little people, etc.

Sliced Apples and Pineapple with Caramel Dipping Sauce

◆ BASIC PANTRY

Serves 4 to 6

Soft, sweet caramel pairs as readily with the apples and pineapple in this dish as it does with caramel apples on a stick. Consider this the grown-up version.

1 cup sugar
1/2 cup (1 stick) unsalted butter, cut into bits
1/2 cup heavy (whipping) cream
Tiny pinch of salt

1/2 teaspoon vanilla extract
3 tart crisp apples
1/4 fresh sweet ripe pineapple, peeled

1. In a heavy saucepan, gently heat sugar until it melts and caramelizes, then turns brownish. Do not let burn.

2. Remove from heat and add butter gradually, stirring, then add cream and stir well to combine. Add salt and vanilla, then return to heat and bring to a boil. Cook another minute or two longer, then let cool.

3. When cool it should be almost creamy in consistency, much like caramel apple coating.

4. Slice apples and pineapple into bite-sized pieces and arrange on a platter. Serve with caramel sauce.

◆◆◆◆◆◆◆

Tortilla Chips So common as to be overlooked, well-made tortilla chips can add lots of flavor to other dishes as well as being great on their own for crunchy snacks.

Low-salt or unsalted are best, as are some of the specialty corn chips: blue corn with their earthy, dusky flavor, and corn chips with pureed black beans in the dough (but not the ones with imitation cheese and similar phony flavorings). Crushed tortilla chips can be used to thicken savory Mexican-style sauces or as coating for oven-fried foods. I especially like adding a generous handful of crushed tortilla chips to a sauté of thin strips of beef, red and green peppers, tiny edible cob corn, tomatoes, and lots of ancho or a similar chili seasoning paste.

Tortilla chips added to a spicy scramble of Mexican seasoned eggs give you *migas,* a Texan specialty: add chips to pan just after adding eggs, and as they cook into soft curds, tortilla chips will soften. Top with cilantro and serve with lots of salsa and beans of some sort on the side. And tortilla chips are superb added to any good rich broth, along with a sprinkle of chopped fresh cilantro and a splash of fresh chili, with a wedge of lemon to squeeze over it all.

I'm amused by "Frito-pie," the 1950s state fair snack of a bag of corn chips opened and stuffed with chili con carne, topped with grated cheese, onion, shredded lettuce, etc. Mark Miller of New Mexico's Coyote Cafe is orchestrating this brilliant comeback, a nose-thumbing at our food snobbism, and why not? Frito-pie is good. So are nachos: a layer of tortilla chips topped with melted cheese and chilies. They are delicious when made well, with good chips, chopped chili, and, for my taste, refried beans.

Tortilla Soup

◆ BASIC PANTRY

Prepare a simple vegetable soup by simmering julienned **carrot, zucchini,** and **red and green bell peppers** in **broth** along with chopped **tomatoes and sliced green chilies** to taste. Serve ladeled into large bowls over diced **cheese** and low-salt **tortilla chips,** a scattering of chopped fresh **cilantro, fresh chilies,** and a wedge of **lime.** Serve right away.

Macaroni à la Mexicana

◆ BASIC PANTRY

Top a **macaroni and cheese casserole** that you've seasoned forcefully with sautéed **chorizo** with crumbled **tortilla chips** and more shredded **cheese.** Bake to melt and brown. Top with chopped **onion, cilantro,** diced **tomatoes,** a dollop of **sour cream.** Accompany with **Basic Salsa** (page 368).

THE FROZEN PANTRY

I have somewhat mixed feelings about highlighting the freezer as an extension of the pantry. Too many people already live out of the freezer, putting whole meals in the deep freeze, then heating them up in the microwave. I recently heard a caterer on a local talk show saying that she freezes everything and takes it out of the freezer directly to her car, letting it all defrost as she goes about her errands. When she arrives at the party the food is all ready. Having tasted her food, I wasn't surprised.

Although some things freeze well, freezing changes the basic structure of food. It breaks down the cell walls, letting the fluids seep out, so that the texture of the food is altered as well. And the flavors fade, without a doubt.

But for long-term storing of fresh, and some cooked, ingredients, a freezer is fine. With a freezer we can have vegetables in the middle of winter that still have flavor and bright color, even if their crunch has softened. Summer's bounty of fruit goes into suspended animation, ready to offer its taste of sunshine in winter when the only thing warm is the radiator. We can toss into the freezer bits and pieces of things that would otherwise spoil, then when we have enough to work with, pull it all out. I always do this with chicken giblets and parts: the livers become chopped liver, the gizzards become Cajun "dirty rice" (along with a liver or two), the necks become chicken soup.

Stock or broth is another thing that freezes beautifully. Not only can you turn the waste of bones into flavorful broth, you can have at your fingertips a broth that isn't heavily salted like most canned ones. That means you can boil stocks to reduce them, then use them as the basis for sauces. You can make the most of that duck carcass, the handful of fish frames given to you by your fishmonger, the bone from a leg of lamb. While frozen chicken is not as nice as fresh, it's invaluable to have on hand—just spice it up a bit more forcefully. Already-cooked poultry and meats don't freeze well; they tend to get dry and lose their flavor. But you can rescue the odds and ends from cheeses to use for grating and for mixing with other foods.

Baked goods such as breads and doughs take well to freezing. With several loaves of half-baked or raw bread in your freezer you are always less than an hour away from home-baked bread. And already-made bread can be rebaked to a near bakery-fresh quality. Frozen pie dough and filo in your pantry means that you can prepare flaky delicate pastries quickly and easily. Even cakes like pound or sponge, while they lose moisture in freezing, are good layered with liqueurs and whipped creams or custards, sweetened ricotta, and so on, as trifles and cassatta-like cakes. (My editor confesses to freezing half-eaten birthday cakes and occasionally slicing off pieces to eat frozen with tea or coffee. I thought I was the only person who did this! The icing is great, like a frozen confection.)

STORAGE TIPS A freezer temperature of 0°F is best. If your freezer cannot keep ice cream solid, do not store other foods for longer than a week or two. For each 5 degrees above 0°, storage time is cut in half.

Label packages, if they're not self-evident. Save plastic containers and use for freezing; glass jars can get brittle and break in the deep freeze (though tell that to my grandmother, who's been freezing chicken soup in them for years); leaving space for expansion in glass containers will help prevent breaking. Wrap other foods tightly in aluminum foil, preferably using two layers. Don't freeze too much at one time—it puts a strain on the freezer.

To Refreeze or Not to Refreeze; That is the Question

You may safely refreeze partially frozen food if it has been thawing in the refrigerator and is still somewhat icy. If the food is completely defrosted, do not refreeze it; you may, however, cook it and refreeze it cooked. Do not refreeze food that has been cooked and frozen, then defrosted and reheated. Any bacteria that has accumulated will flourish.

Shellfish spoil quickly after thawing. Don't refreeze—you cannot detect any spoilage by smelling or looking at it. Poultry or meat that has been frozen raw may be refrozen after cooking.

In general, broth (and any meat or poultry in broth) may be kept in the freezer for up to 6 months; most home-prepared foods can be kept for up to 2 months, though the seasonings fade a bit with deep-freeze storage. Unsalted butter lasts for months in the freezer.

Broths and stocks (chicken, beef, fish, duck, and so on; duck and fish stocks are especially useful for making sauces and braises that accompany duck or seafood, and for giving a distinctive flavor to soups and pasta sauce)

Butter (unsalted; flavored, or compound, butters)

Cakes (pound and sponge cakes for making cassata, celebration cakes, etc.)

Cheeses (for grating and cooking rather than for out-of-hand eating, as freezing destroys much of their delicate texture)

Chicken: breasts (boneless and lightly flattened, for quickly prepared meals), livers for chopped liver, gizzards and necks for soups and rice dishes, a whole chicken for roasting)

Red Chili-Citrus Paste, page 128

Cured meats: the odds and ends of prosciutto, pancetta, ham, sausages, etc., for making ragù-type long-simmered sauces and minestrones, or for a sausage supper

Duck: breasts, whole, gizzards, livers, etc. (see chicken, above)

Filo dough

Fruit: unsugared

Fruit juices and drinks

Herb and spice seasoning pastes

Ice creams, sorbets, and frozen yogurts

Juice bars

Lemon grass (chopped and frozen in plastic bags)

Pasta (fresh noodles; stuffed pastas such as ravioli; wonton wrappers for preparing your own ravioli, cannelloni, and the like)

Pesto

Pie dough

Puff pastry

Salsas

Smoked fish such as salmon or trout

Tortillas (both corn and wheat)

Turkey (individual pieces for braising, roasting; chopped turkey for meatballs, soups, etc.)

Vegetables: a selection of peas, corn, spinach, lima beans, artichokes

Wonton and egg roll wrappers

Broths and Stocks Stocks are one of the most useful ingredients you can store in your freezer. They give body and depth without the heavy dose of salt that commercial stocks have. In addition to chicken, beef, lamb, pork, and vegetable broth, duck and fish stocks give you distinctive flavors that you cannot simply run to the store and purchase. Making your own stocks means that every little bit and scrap in your kitchen can be used. I love the serendipitous way stocks can vary: one batch might have a sweet garlic scent, another batch might taste of fennel, another of grassy herbs. Be sure to label them well.

I'm only including two basic stock recipes: one for fish stock, the other for a mild chili-scented duck stock. I include them because they are less common; most other cookbooks have recipes for chicken, beef, turkey, lamb, and veal broth.

The basic procedure for a light-colored stock is to place the meat (chicken, turkey, veal, or beef, etc.) in a pot and cover it with cold water. Add aromatics—onion, bay leaf, leeks, seasonings, and herbs of choice—and I tend also to add a few bouillon cubes instead of salt, to help the soup on its way. Bring to a boil, reduce heat, and simmer for several hours, or until the broth is richly flavored. Skim off any scum that rises to the surface and, when done, strain the soup and discard the used-up vegetables.

For a brown stock (used with beef, lamb, etc.), first roast the meat and bones in a hot oven, along with onions, carrots, and celery, etc., until very dark brown and crusty. Use these bones and vegetables as the basis for your stock, and pour water into the pan to scrape up the bits of concentrated flavor that gather there. Continue as for light-colored stock.

Remember to always cool the stock thoroughly before freezing, or the warmth will lower the temperature of the entire freezer, unleashing the perils of food poisoning.

Fish Stock

Makes about 2 quarts

Especially good as a basis for fish stews, this recipe makes a cauldron of steaming, well-seasoned broth into which you can toss whatever the ocean has to offer that day. Fish stock can also be used to make sauces and to cook pasta, rice, paella, etc.

1 to 1-1/2 pounds fish bones, heads, trimmings, with gills removed (any fish except salmon)	1 cup clam juice or chicken broth
1/2 onion	Several sprigs of parsley
Several garlic cloves, whole	1 bottle dry white wine
	3 cups water

1. Combine all ingredients. Heat to boiling, skim scum off surface, reduce heat, and simmer over low heat for 20 minutes.

2. Strain and discard solids. (If you're feeling ambitious, take cheese-cloth, pour solids into it, and squeeze tightly to extract flavor. Let extracted juices drip into broth; discard solids.)

3. Reduce broth by boiling for 10 minutes. Fish stock, unlike meat and poultry stock, should not cook longer than 30 minutes, as it can turn bitter.

4. Cool completely before freezing.

Red Chili-scented Duck Stock

◆◆ INTERMEDIATE PANTRY

Makes 2 quarts

This is flavored with mild red chili, but it doesn't taste hot; the chilies merely give it a warm depth. If you like, substitute red bell pepper or omit chilies altogether.

Use this mildly chilied duck stock for sauces, gumbo, and red beans and rice, or to cook rice in, along with lots of chopped celery, onion, green pepper, thyme, and bits of duck meat, liver, and gizzard, for a Cajun "dirty duck rice."

Since duck bones are usually not plentiful, I make this using a short-cut, beginning with chicken broth (and I confess it's usually canned) and adding a few scraps, such as the odd duck wing stashed away in my freezer. Sometimes I freeze duck carcasses leftover from dinner parties, expressly for this purpose.

Bones from 1 duck
1 onion, cut in half
Several garlic cloves, whole and unpeeled
1 stalk celery, cut into several pieces
1 bay leaf

1/4 cup chopped fresh or canned tomatoes
3 cups chicken broth
2 cups water
2 large dried mild chilies such as New Mexico or California, cut open and seeds removed

1. Combine all ingredients in a saucepan and bring to a boil.

2. Reduce heat and simmer, covered, for 2 hours, or until flavor is good.

3. Let cool, then remove bones and vegetable debris. Discard, removing any bits of meat from bones to nibble on or to give to the cat.

4. Strain through cheesecloth for clarity, or just pour off liquid, leaving behind sediment that remains at bottom.

5. Chill broth and spoon off congealed fat from top.

6. Use as is or freeze. May be boiled down and reduced to a more concentrated form before freezing.

◆◆◆◆◆◆

Bread Dough Whether homemade or commercial, frozen bread dough is invaluable in a good freezer pantry.

Twelve Things To Make With Defrosted Frozen Bread Dough

◆ BASIC PANTRY

Bread Sticks

Makes 8 to 10 bread sticks

Roll **dough** into balls about the size of large walnuts, then roll in between olive-oiled hands into strands about 1/4 to 1/2 inch round. Brush with **beaten egg white**, then coat well with **dried onion flakes, caraway seeds, poppy seeds,** and a sprinkling of **coarse salt.** Lay out on an ungreased baking sheet and bake in a pre-heated oven at 425° until golden, about 12 to 15 minutes.

Grilled Flatbread

Makes 8 to 10 flatbreads

Roll **dough** out onto a piece of aluminum foil as thinly as you can, brushing with **olive oil or melted butter.** Sprinkle with chopped fresh **rosemary** and **coarse salt,** then bake by placing on a hot grill. Bake first on side with foil, then remove and bake other side directly on grill. It won't take more than a few minutes on each side. Enjoy with a selection of **grilled sausages** to wrap around.

Caper and Red Onion Pizza

Serves 4

Top thinly rolled bread dough with a layer of tangy **tomato sauce,** then a generous sprinkling of **capers,** thinly sliced **red onion,** and a layer of **asiago, Fontina, or jack cheese,** a sprinkling of **Parmesan,** and a drizzle of **olive oil.** Bake in a preheated 425° oven for 20 to 30 minutes, or until bubbly, crisp edged, and inviting.

(Each bite of this conjures up memories of the saucy slices I munched one midday in Florence's Piazza Santa Maria Novella. The sun was fierce, and so were the voracious pigeons, who fought us for every mouthful. Yet that day of eating zesty pizza in the still, white light remains a memory of how good life can be.)

Chocolate-stuffed Fried Bread Puffs   Makes 4 to 6

Take individual **dough** rounds and wrap around squares of **bittersweet chocolate;** fry quickly until golden brown. Each delicate doughnutlike pastry will ooze hot melted chocolate.

Gnoccho Frito   Makes 3 to 6

Crisply fried on the outside, soft and doughy on the inside, enclosing pungent blue cheese and the sweet freshness of basil. Roll **dough** into 6 (for appetizer portion) or 3 balls, then roll these into flat discs. In center of each disc, place a slice or two of **blue cheese,** a sprinkling of chopped **garlic,** and several **basil leaves.** Fold over and seal, then brown in a hot heavy skillet with just enough **oil** to cover bottom. Cook, several pastries at a time, until golden and lightly brown-flecked. This will take only about 5 minutes. Serve hot, rubbed with **garlic** if desired.

Pizza d'Asparagi   Serves 4

Spoon quickly cooked **asparagus** and a fresh **garlicky tomato sauce** onto rolled-out **dough.** Bake in a preheated 425° oven for 20 minutes, or until cooked through.

◆◆ **INTERMEDIATE PANTRY**

Navajo Fry Bread   Serves 4 to 6

Flatten into 3- to 4-inch individual **rounds;** fry to a golden brown and serve smeared with any **mild chili paste,** or serve plain, to accompany any spicy-sauced Mexican or Southwestern dish. Or serve with jam and butter for breakfast, with a mug of coffee or tea.

New Mexico Tostadas

Serves 4 to 6

Roll **dough** out and fry as for Navajo Fry Bread, then serve spread with **black beans** and sautéed **chorizo.** Top with a **fried egg,** sprinkle with chopped fresh **cilantro,** and pass the **salsa.**

Perestroika Pizza

Serves 4

Roll **dough** out to a thickness of about 1/2 inch. Brush with **olive oil** and sprinkle with **green onions.** Bake in a preheated 375° oven until golden, about 20 minutes, then serve while still hot, spread with **cream cheese, smoked salmon,** thinly sliced **red onions,** and, if you're feeling flush, a spoonful or two of **caviar.**

Hazelnut Focaccia

Serves 4 to 6

Roll **dough** out thinly, lightly coat with **olive oil,** then spread with a layer of finely ground **hazelnuts** mixed with chopped **garlic, Parmesan cheese,** and **olive oil;** sprinkle with a little **thyme** and **coarse sea salt** and stud the whole thing with about 1/2 cup of small flavorful **black olives** such as Nyons or niçoises. Let rise until doubled in bulk, then bake in a preheated 375° oven until top is crusty and dough appears to be baked through, about 30 minutes.

◆◆◆ ADVANCED PANTRY

Double-Onion Nan

Serves 4 to 6

Roll bread **dough** out as thin as possible, then brush with melted **butter** and sprinkle with thinly sliced **green onions.** Fold over, then roll out again, repeating so that onions marble through layers of dough. During last folding add a teaspoon or two of **black onion seeds** (available in Indian grocers). Brush top with butter and sprinkle with onion seeds, then bake in a preheated 425° oven until golden brown and baked through. Serve with any spicy Indian-style dish, or with a wonderful main-course salad with lots of interesting alliums such as garlic shoots and onion sprouts.

Macadamia-Coconut Coffee Cake　　　　　　　　Serves 4

Roll bread **dough** into a flat rectangle, then spread with soft **un-salted butter.** Mix 2/3 cup **brown sugar** with 2/3 cup **shredded coconut,** 3 tablespoons **milk,** and 3/4 cup halved and broken-up **macadamia nuts** (rub off salt with a clean towel if nuts are salted). Spread about half of mixture onto bread dough, then roll up tightly. Spread half of remaining nut mixture onto bottom of a baking pan, then cut roll into 12 slices and arrange slices in prepared pan. Let rise until doubled in size, then top with re-maining nut mixture. Bake in a preheated 375° oven for 35–45 minutes, or until golden brown.

Breads I always keep some of my favorite breads in the freezer: French, pumpernickel, seeded rye, multi-grained sandwich bread, and so on. I even brought a loaf of olive bread back from Italy once and planted it directly in my freezer, where it stayed until I had a festive brunch. And I always have at least one bag of bagels there. (I've spent my life eating bagels, from the freshly baked ones at my grandparents' house to the chewy *bagalehs* sold hanging from a string, eaten on the streets of Jeru-salem on my way home from classes; from slightly sad *beigels* bought still warm after a day of flea marketing in London's Brick Lane, to quin-tessential New York bagels, cut open and slathered with melting sweet butter, and California-style bagels with Brie cheese melting seductively on top.)

Always buy bagels fresh and freeze them yourself. The already frozen ones in the supermarket freezer are last-resort bagels only, usu-ally having about as much flavor as cardboard.

Butters Flavored butter, also known as compound butter, can add ex-citement to the simplest foods. Since it freezes well for up to 2 months, you can freeze small packets and always have a selection on hand to melt onto a grilled chicken or duck paillard, or a broiled fish fillet. You can baste a chicken with it, or spread some onto a grilled ear of corn.

Be sure, though, that it is well wrapped to protect its delicate flavors from other odors that lurk in the freezer.

New Mexico Chili Butter

◆ BASIC TO
◆◆ INTERMEDIATE PANTRY

Makes 1/2 to 2/3 cup

Earthy flavors, with only a gentle warmth rather than the heat you'd expect from a chili butter. Cilantro adds a grassy note.

Use New Mexico Chili Butter to melt into a baked sweet potato, the spicy butter a pleasant contrast with the sweet, caramely flesh. Or spread it onto bread, garlic-bread style, sprinkle with grated dry jack, and bake in a hot oven. Chili butter is good melted onto fish, and on quickly grilled chicken paillards, too.

3 garlic cloves, minced
1/2 to 1 cup chopped fresh
  cilantro
1 green onion, thinly sliced
2 to 3 tablespoons good-quality
  chili powder, preferably New
  Mexico

1/2 cup (1 stick) unsalted butter,
  at room temperature
2 to 3 tablespoons olive oil
Salt to taste

1. In a blender, puree garlic and add cilantro, green onion, and chili powder. Mix until smooth.

2. Add butter, olive oil, and salt to taste and whirl until well mixed.

Rosemary-Mustard Butter

◆ BASIC PANTRY

Makes about 1/2 cup

Serve this piquant tangy butter melting onto any grilled meat, poultry, or fish. It is especially good with Italian sausage and chicken liver kabobs, page 385, or with grilled swordfish.

1 garlic clove, minced
2 tablespoons Dijon mustard
1 tablespoon chopped fresh
  rosemary

1 teaspoon chopped fresh
  parsley
1/2 cup (1 stick) unsalted butter,
  softened
Salt and pepper to taste

Combine all ingredients.

Rosemary-Mustard Butter and Pastrami Shirred Eggs

Place a nugget of **Rosemary-Mustard Butter,** page 349, in bottom of desired number of ramekins, top with a bit of julienned **pastrami,** then break an **egg** into each ramekin. Dot with more butter, then cover and bake in a preheated 350° oven until whites have set.

Chive Flower Butter

◆◆◆ ADVANCED PANTRY

Most fresh herbs are delicious chopped and mixed into fresh unsalted butter: thyme, watercress, tarragon, garlic chives, rosemary, parsley, basil, mint, and so forth. Chive flowers are celestial added to sweet butter. Cut **chive flowers** up enough to combine petals with butter, but to leave some texture to mixture (besides, the lavender color of the chive flowers is beautiful). There is no hard and fast rule as to proportion of herb to butter; you must do this by taste.

Garlic-Parsley Butter

◆ BASIC PANTRY

Makes about 1/2 cup

This classic combination is also known as "escargot butter." It's perfect for garlic bread.

◆◆◆◆◆◆

TO PREPARE Mix 1/2 cup (1 stick) softened **unsalted butter** with as much chopped **garlic** as you dare and enough chopped fresh **parsley** to turn it green. Season with **salt** and use immediately or store in freezer.

Green Chili–Cilantro Butter

◆◆ INTERMEDIATE PANTRY

Makes about 1/2 cup

Particularly good on charcoal-grilled chicken breasts, fish fillets, and baked potatoes.

◆◆◆◆◆◆

TO PREPARE Combine 1/2 cup (1 stick) soft unsalted **butter** with 1/2 to 1 chopped **green chili** (seeded), 3 to 5 chopped **garlic cloves,** and 1/2 cup chopped fresh **cilantro.** Season with a dash of **lemon juice** and **salt.** Use immediately or freeze.

Blue Cheese Butter

◆ BASIC PANTRY

Makes about 2/3 cup

Blue cheese butter is a delicious inclusion to the frozen pantry. It's good melting onto a rare grilled steak, or spread on a baguette topped with rare roast beef and watercress or sweet basil. Or try it on a Cobb sandwich: spread blue cheese butter on black bread and fill with slices of poached chicken breast, crumbled bacon, avocado, tomato, and watercress.

1 garlic clove, chopped
2 to 3 ounces blue cheese
(1/3–1/2 cup loosely
crumbled)
1/2 cup (1 stick) unsalted butter,
at room temperature

Dash of brandy (optional)
Black or cayenne pepper to
taste

Combine all ingredients and mix well.

Shallot-Thyme Butter

◆◆ INTERMEDIATE PANTRY

Makes about 1/2 cup

Mix several chopped **shallots** into 1/2 cup of softened **unsalted butter,** then add 2-1/2 teaspoons chopped fresh **thyme** or 1/2 teaspoon dried, **salt** and **pepper** to taste, and 1 tablespoon **lemon juice.** Serve with grilled salmon or trout.

◆◆◆◆◆◆

Cakes Pound and sponge cakes store well in the freezer. Serve them drizzled generously with liqueurs and/or brandy, then layered with whipped cream or ricotta cheese fillings. These cakes can then be frozen for up to 3 months and retrieved at will; they are sturdy and keep well.

Almond Cream Gâteau

◆◆ INTERMEDIATE PANTRY

Sprinkle a thin layer of **sponge cake** with a generous amount of **almond liqueur** such as Amaretto plus a little **brandy.** Spread with lightly sweetened **whipped cream,** then repeat, using three layers in all. Freeze until ready to eat, and serve partially frozen.

Traditional Custard Trifle

A British confection of sponge cake layers soaked in sherry or other spirits, then layered with custard, whipped cream, chopped fruits, and nuts. The best trifle I ever tasted was editor Paul Richardson's: it was absolutely bathed in grappa, and layered in between the custard and sponge cake were nuggets of fruitcake. It was unforgettable.

◆◆◆◆◆◆

TO PREPARE Place a layer of sliced **sponge cake** on bottom of a deep glass bowl and sprinkle generously with **sweet sherry**—really soak it.

Mix vanilla-scented soft **English custard** with **whipped cream** and spoon onto soaked cake; sprinkle with **glacéed cherries,** sliced **almonds,** and chopped **candied angelica,** then top with another layer of sherry-soaked cake, custard, and so on.

Sicilian Cassata

Makes one 9 inch loaf cake

Mix 1 pound **ricotta cheese** with 2 tablespoons **coffee liqueur or chocolate liqueur,** 2 tablespoons **almond liqueur,** 2 tablespoons **brandy,** and **sugar** to taste. Add 1/4 cup chopped **glacéed fruit or chopped candied orange peel,** and 1/4 cup **chocolate chips.**

Cut one 9-inch **pound cake** into 3 or 4 layers. Sprinkle each layer with a little **brandy and/or liqueur,** then a thick layer of ricotta mixture. Top with another pound cake layer, than sprinkle again and spread with another layer of ricotta. Repeat, ending with pound cake, then sprinkle with brandy and liqueur. Wrap up and let chill in refrigerator overnight or freeze until ready to eat.

This cake may be iced with a simple **chocolate frosting,** but I don't usually bother.

◆◆◆◆◆◆

Chicken Gather up gizzards, necks, and livers chicken by chicken, and soon you will have enough for chopped liver, soup, or ragù. Ditto for duck.

TO FREEZE CHICKEN OR DUCK BREASTS Place on a waxed paper–lined baking sheet and freeze for 1 hour. When solid, wrap well and freeze for up to 2 months.

Grilled Chicken or Duck Paillards with Seasoned Butter

Grill or pan brown flattened **chicken or duck breasts** quickly and serve with a nugget of **flavored butter** melting in.

◆◆◆◆◆◆

Filo Dough can be used to wrap almost anything, turning the simplest foods into great pastry treats. The thing about filo is not that it tastes delicious—it does; and it's not that it is crispy and flaky beyond reason—it is. The great thing is that something so wonderful should be so easy. All it involves is folding, not the delicate manipulations required in other pastry-making. If you can wrap a birthday present, you can make filo pastries.

Filo dough is as versatile as it is delicious. Sweet or savory fillings, small individual pastries or large pies, baked or fried, served sprinkled with spices or sugar, or drenched in a honey-scented syrup—with filo the variety of pastries you can make is nearly endless.

Filo is sold in long rectangles, usually rolled up and sold in 1-pound packages. Generally, there are about 25 sheets of filo per pound. But all filo is not alike. Filo stretched by hand into tissue paper–like sheets has more integrity than machine made filo, and is easier to handle. Hand-made filo dough is generally available commercially in areas with large Greek communities.

Filo dough keeps perfectly well in the freezer, but not forever. After 3 months it dries out, tending to shatter into broken-edged sheets that resist being turned into golden pastries. Therefore you should buy your filo fresh when possible and freeze it yourself. The filo you buy already frozen is like a coy, aging starlet: it doesn't even hint at its age.

Defrost filo and use as you would fresh dough. Filled filo pastries may be frozen unbaked, then placed on baking sheets and baked directly from the freezer, allowing 5 or 10 extra minutes of temperature change.

Three Spectacular and Simple Filo Pastries

North African Almond "Cigars"

◆◆ INTERMEDIATE PANTRY   Makes 8 to 12 pastries

Combine 1 cup **almond paste** with 1 beaten **egg**, 1 tablespoon **rose water**, and 1 teaspoon ground **cinnamon.**

Arrange a sheet of **filo** on a clean waxed paper–lined surface, and brush with melted **unsalted butter.** Place several spoonfuls of almond filling in a rectangular shape in center, then fold over top and bottom and roll up pastry into a cigar shape. Repeat until all filling is used.

Bake in a preheated 375° oven for about 15 minutes, or until golden brown. Serve sprinkled with **powdered sugar** and lots of **ground cinnamon.**

Brik à l'Oeuf

◆ BASIC PANTRY   Makes 1 individual pastry
                                      Multiply as desired

Lay a sheet of **filo** onto a waxed paper–lined working surface. In one corner place 1 teaspoon chopped **onion** and either chopped **fresh parsley or cilantro,** a pinch of chopped **green chili,** and a teaspoon or two of **tuna fish.**

Heat a wok or heavy frying pan with **olive oil.** Working quickly, open an **egg** onto mixture of chopped onion, etc., then fold over and roll, flag-fashion, enclosing egg completely in filo. Toss into hot oil, frying until golden. Remove from oil. The egg will be still quite soft, so pastries may be finished in the oven. This gives you the benefit of being able to serve them hot, all at once.

Serve with **lemon wedges** and **hot chili sauce** of choice.

Greek Island Cheese and Herb Pie

◆ BASIC PANTRY

Coarsely crumble 1/2 pound or so of **feta cheese** and mix with several chopped **green onions,** 3 tablespoons or so coarsely chopped fresh **mint and cilantro,** and a pinch of **tarragon.** Bind together with 1/2 cup **cottage cheese,** 1/4 cup plain **yogurt,** and 1 beaten **egg.**

Brush a sheet of **filo** with **melted butter,** then layer into a baking dish and repeat until you have a layer of 8 sheets or so of pastry. Pour filling into pastry sheets, then fold over edges of pastry and top with 6 or so sheets of buttered filo dough.

Bake in a preheated 375° oven for about 30 minutes, or until pie is golden brown. Serve hot.

Potato and Vegetable Samosas

◆◆ INTERMEDIATE PANTRY

Serves 4

Filo makes a good—though not traditional—pastry for samosas, the Indian savory pastry filled with meat or vegetables, then fried or baked until golden and eaten dipped in a spicy chutney or a yogurt-based sauce.

4 large baking potatoes, peeled and cut into small chunks (about 2 to 2-1/2 pounds)
2 tablespoons unsalted butter
1/2 onion, coarsely chopped
3 garlic cloves, chopped
1/4 to 1/2 jalapeño chili, chopped
1/2 carrot, diced
1/2 teaspoon cumin (ground or seeds)
1 teaspoon fresh ginger, shredded or chopped
1/2 teaspoon ground turmeric

3/4 teaspoon curry powder
1/2 cup fresh or frozen peas
Juice of 1/2 lemon
2 tablespoons yogurt
1 tablespoon chopped fresh cilantro
1 egg, lightly beaten
Salt and cayenne to taste
1/4 to 1/2 pound filo dough, cut into strips about 4 inches wide
3 tablespoons melted butter plus 3 tablespoons vegetable oil, for brushing

1. Preheat oven to 425°. Cook potatoes in rapidly boiling water until tender (about 15 minutes). Drain.

2. Meanwhile, in melted butter sauté onion, garlic, chili, and carrot until vegetables soften, then sprinkle with cumin, ginger, turmeric, and curry, and stir to cook spices through.

3. Mix with drained cooked potatoes, then add peas, lemon juice, yogurt, cilantro, and egg, seasoning with salt and cayenne.

4. Brush strips of filo with melted butter and oil, then place several tablespoons of potato mixture at corner of each strip, working with 1 or 2 strips at a time, but no more than that. Be sure to cover waiting filo with a damp cloth or paper towel. Fold a corner over filling, then continue folding, like a flag, to enclose filling.

5. Place potato-stuffed parcels onto a baking sheet and bake for 15 to 20 minutes, or until pastries are golden brown.

6. Serve immediately, accompanied with yogurt mixed with a little chopped cilantro and mint, seasoned with fresh ginger, salt, cayenne, and a pinch of sugar.

Crisp Filo-wrapped Meatloaf

◆◆ INTERMEDIATE PANTRY

Serves 4

Filo makes a flaky pastry wrapping for meatloaf, a sort of retro food combining the meatloaf of the fifties with the pastry wrapping of the sixties. The important thing is that it is delicious, regardless of which decade or food style it hails from.

◆◆◆◆◆◆

Prepare your favorite **meatloaf recipe** to serve 4 people. (Mine has lots of onions.) Bake and let cool (preferably overnight).

Using **olive oil–brushed filo pastry,** wrap entire meatloaf in from 6 to 8 layers.

Bake in a preheated 400° oven for about 10 to 15 minutes, or long enough to turn pastry golden brown and heat meatloaf through. Serve with any **spicy salsa, and/or sautéed peppers and tomatoes.**

Greek Zucchini and Cheese Pastries

[KOLOKYPHIAPITA]

◆◆ INTERMEDIATE PANTRY

Makes about 25 small pastries

These individual pastries are filled with shredded zucchini and cheese, a delightful change from the more traditional feta-cheese pastries.

4 zucchini, coarsely shredded
3/4–1 cup (4 ounces) jack or Gruyère-type cheese, coarsely shredded
1/2 cup freshly grated Parmesan cheese
2 to 3 garlic cloves, minced
1 egg

1/4 teaspoon dried thyme, oregano, or marjoram
About 1/3 pound filo dough, cut into 4-inch-wide strips
3 tablespoons unsalted butter, melted with 3 tablespoons oil, for brushing

1. Preheat oven to 375°. Place zucchini in a strainer and squeeze to remove excess moisture. Combine squeezed zucchini with cheeses, garlic, egg, and herbs.

2. One strip at a time, brush filo with butter/oil mixture. Place a spoonful of filling at one corner and fold over as if you were folding a flag.

3. Place on a baking sheet and bake for about 10 minutes or until golden brown and crisp. Serve immediately.

◆◆◆◆◆◆

Frozen Fruit They seem almost like dirty words, to be whispered under the breath: *frozen fruit.* But even for those of us who live in areas where so much scrumptious fresh fruit is available, frozen fruit has its place. Cranberries, for example, can be frozen for months, and used to give a tangy tart accent to dishes such as zucchini bread and Cranberry Fool that have no relationship to Thanksgiving season. And frozen fruits of all kinds can be whirled in the blender with a bit of yogurt, buttermilk, or milk and/or juice for refreshing, satisfying drinks.

To freeze fruits yourself, lay them out on a waxed paper–lined baking sheet. Place this in the freezer until the fruits are hard and icy. You must have a good freezer to do this. When frozen solid, remove and place them into plastic bags. Seal and take out by the handful as desired.

Frozen melon lends itself to an exquisite sorbet: puree the fresh fruit and freeze in ice cube trays, then placing the solidly frozen cubes into plastic bags and seal well. When the urge for sorbet hits, place as many cubes as you like, along with a shot of lemon juice, sugar, liqueur, or fruit juice, into the processor, and whirl until it is the consistency you like. Cantaloupe has an affinity for anise-flavored liqueurs, while honeydew is accented by Midori, the melon liqueur, and watermelon is lovely with a bit of rose water.

And don't neglect frozen juices, orange juice especially—use it to sweeten red cabbage or to baste a turkey or duck, along with lots of chili powder. Or whip it into a frenzy with vanilla ice cream and season it with orange flower water.

Cranberry Fool

◆ **BASIC PANTRY**

Serves 4

Tangy and sweet, with the distinctive yet pleasing bitter edge of cranberries. While just the sight of fresh cranberries in autumn grocers triggers my sense of excitement over the approaching holiday season, cranberries can be hard to deal with. They need so much sugar for one thing, and their strong flavor keeps them from readily integrating with other fruit. The truth is, I've always liked delicate summer berries better.

But recently I've come to appreciate the unique qualities of this American berry, and this frothy whip of fruit and creams is one of the reasons why.

1 bag frozen cranberries, partially defrosted but still icy
1-1/2 cups sugar, or to taste

1 tangerine, peeled and seeded
1/2 cup sour cream
2 cups heavy (whipping) cream

1. In a blender, puree cranberries with sugar and tangerine, then add sour cream.

2. Whip heavy cream until it forms firm peaks, then fold into cranberry mixture. Serve immediately.

Mixed Berry Passion

◆ BASIC PANTRY

Serves 2 to 3

1 cup mixed unsweetened frozen berries (blackberries, strawberries, cranberries, etc.)

Juice of 1 lime
1/2 cup apple juice
2 cups lemonade

1. Whirl berries in a blender to chop, then add rest of ingredients and whirl until frothy.

2. Enjoy immediately with a scoop of vanilla ice cream or a splash of tequila.

High-Fiber Fruit Smoothie

◆ BASIC PANTRY

Serves 2, very generously

Well-made smoothies are light, refreshing, and bursting with fruit. This one is based on cranberries, apples, tangerines, and kefir, or liquid yogurt.

1/2 cup (2 ounces) frozen cranberries
2 small apples, cored and diced
2 tangerines, peeled and diced

3 cups strawberry kefir or other sweet liquid yogurt
Dash of vanilla extract

1. Whirl cranberries and apples in a blender until finely chopped. Add tangerines and process until chunkily smooth.
2. Add kefir and vanilla and whirl until frothy. Serve immediately.

Strawberry and Orange Blossom Smoothie

◆◆ INTERMEDIATE PANTRY

Serves 2

A lovely nonalcoholic drink, sophisticated enough for adults, bright and fruity enough for kids.

1-1/2 cups orange juice　　　**Dash of orange flower water**
1 cup frozen strawberries

Whirl everything together until strawberries are well mixed and drink is slushy. Enjoy immediately.

◆◆◆◆◆

Herb and Spice Seasoning Pastes Freeze mixtures of chopped fresh herbs in plastic bags. One of my favorites is cilantro and mint—delicious added to curried dishes. Basil, pureed in oil for pesto (see page 364), is a classic. Following are two of my favorite combinations.

Crisp Chicken Breasts Coated with Primavera Herbs and Parmesan

◆ BASIC PANTRY

Coat boned **chicken breasts** with Primavera Herbs (see below) mixed with finely grated **hard cheese** such as Parmesan. Dredge chicken breasts in **flour** and saute in **olive oil** until just cooked through but juicy, only a few minutes.

PRIMAVERA HERBS Chopped **parsley, chives or green onions, garlic, basil,** and a little grated **orange zest.** Use for soups, sauces, salads, etc.

Cilantro-Lime Paste

Simmer with sauces in which you want a Mexican or Indian flavor. Add to chopped tomatoes, and you have instant salsa.

◆◆◆◆◆◆

TO PREPARE Whirl 5 **garlic cloves** and 2 jalapeño **chilies** in a blender along with 1 cup fresh **cilantro** leaves. Add enough **lime juice** to make a paste or sauce, add **salt** to taste, then freeze if desired in ice cube trays.

◆◆◆◆◆◆

Ice Creams, Sorbets, and Frozen Yogurt Talk about frozen assets—the freezer can be a culinary Fort Knox if you like ice cream as much as I do.

Many store-bought ice creams are so good, doing any more to them than applying a spoon is too much. Still, with a container or two of ice cream, sorbet, and frozen yogurt in the freezer you have great possibilities for creative desserts.

Lavender Honey Milk Ice

Makes 1 quart

"This tastes sooooo romantic" intoned my daughter, with the expression only someone standing on the verge of being sixteen years old could muster.

The lavender in the milk ice is not overpowering, but a sweet elusive perfume. Using milk to lighten the cream produces a clearer, cleaner taste than similar ice creams based on cream and egg yolks.

Lavender ice cream is a specialty of Provence, where lavender fields stretch on endlessly, making a perfumed purple landscape. Many use lavender honey in this recipe, but I think it doesn't have the same perfume as actually steeping the lavender in the honey.

6 tablespoons honey	**2 cups milk**
1 tablespoon lavender buds	**2 cups heavy (whipping) cream**

1. Gently heat honey and lavender together; when honey has melted, let sit several minutes, then strain.

2. Heat milk and cream until bubbles form around edge of pan, then add strained lavender honey.

3. Let mixture cool, and freeze.

Blackberry-Buttermilk Ice Cream

◆ BASIC PANTRY

Makes 1-1/2 quarts

Buttermilk makes a lovely ice cream, especially when paired with blackberries. For the best blackberries: Get up early one August morning, before it gets too hot. Grab a bucket and wander down to the nearest creek, climbing into the thicket where you are most likely to find the best berries. Pick as many as you can carry, and eat as many as you like.

2 cups heavy (whipping) cream
1/4 cup sugar or to taste
2 cups buttermilk

1 teaspoon vanilla extract
2 cups blackberries

1. Combine cream and sugar in a saucepan and bring to a boil. Let cool.

2. Mix sweetened cream with buttermilk and vanilla, then freeze.

3. When soft-firm, fold in blackberries. Return to freezer for half an hour or so, then serve.

VARIATION Puree berries and mix with cream, then freeze.

Mango-Lime Cooler

◆ **BASIC PANTRY**

Serves 2

Frozen fruit juice bars add sparkle to frosty drinks. My daughter discovered this fact around the time that frozen fruit bars were making their appearance in supermarkets. She was inventive and singleminded in her pursuit, showing no interest in anything that wasn't a cold, frothy puree for a very long while. She's moved on to boys and rock music, but *I'm* still interested in those frozen fruit bars and the delicious drinks they make. This is one of my recipes.

1 mango, peeled, pitted, and cut into pieces
2 frozen lime juice bars (or lemon bars if lime bars are very green—the coloring won't look nice pureed with the mango)
1 cup limeade or white grape juice
1 tablespoon fresh lime juice, plus a little grated zest

1. Puree mango and add frozen juice bars, broken up a bit and sticks removed. Whirl, then add limeade, lime juice, and zest.

2. Serve immediately.

◆◆◆◆◆◆

Pie Dough freezes beautifully, and provides the basis for innumerable pastries, from Thin Tart of Marzipan and Pears (page 243) to Cross-Country Mixed Nut Pie (page 254), Leah's Apple Flan (page 287), and Zucchini Tart al Pesto (page 365). It's a great boon to have pie dough in the freezer; there are numerous good-quality frozen pie crusts, but if you make your own, so much the better.

Basic Pie Dough

Makes one 8-inch pie crust

Adding a dash of lemon juice helps tenderize the pastry, and using frozen butter keeps it flaky.

**1 cup plus 2 tablespoons un-
  bleached all-purpose flour**
1/4 teaspoon salt
**6 tablespoons frozen unsalted
  butter, in little pieces**

2 tablespoons cold water
**1 to 2 teaspoons fresh lemon
  juice**

1. Mix flour and salt, then cut in butter using a pastry cutter, two knives, or a food processor. Combine lightly, stopping as soon as mixture resembles coarse meal or tiny peas.

2. Sprinkle with water and lemon juice, and mix lightly, using only enough liquid so that dough holds together when pressed lightly into a ball. (Take care not to handle dough with your hands any more than necessary, as warmth of your flesh will cause butter to melt and dough to become less flaky and a bit tough.)

3. Let rest, wrapped in plastic wrap, in the refrigerator for at least an hour, then roll out on a floured board and use as desired.

4. To freeze: dough may be frozen in a ball that is well-wrapped in plastic wrap, thawed in refrigerator, and, when soft enough to handle, rolled out. Or, dough may be rolled out and laid in a pie pan, then wrapped in plastic and frozen. You may stack several pie crusts, separated by a sheet of plastic wrap, then wrap them together and freeze.

Simple Blue Cheese Savories

Cut strips of **pie dough,** above, and lay out on an ungreased baking sheet. Top with crumbled **blue cheese** and bake in a preheated 400° oven until golden and crispy, about 8 to 10 minutes. Enjoy immediately.

Turnover Filled with Fontina, Red Pepper, Ricotta, and Pesto

My version of an Italian street pastry, filled with cheese and pesto, and at its best when very, very hot, the melted cheese streaming out and each bite a challenge to keep from burning your tongue.

[PANZAROTTI
CARNEVALE]

◆◆ **INTERMEDIATE PANTRY**

Serves 4 to 6

1 recipe Basic Pie Dough,
  page 363, or one 8-1/2- to
  9-1/2-inch pie crust
12 ounces coarsely chopped or
  diced Fontina or jack cheese
  (about 1-1/2 cups)

2 tablespoons roasted red
  pepper strips
2 tablespoons chopped peeled
  and seeded tomatoes
1/4 cup ricotta cheese
1 garlic clove, chopped
1/4 cup Pesto, below

1. Preheat oven to 400°. Prepare pie dough and divide dough into
6 equal parts. Roll out each dough round into a thin disc.

2. Mix Fontina or jack cheese with red pepper strips, tomatoes,
ricotta cheese, and garlic. Set aside.

3. Place a dab of pesto on each disc, then top with a heaping tablespoon or two of cheese mixture.

4. Close up each disc by moistening edges of dough, then folding
over and pressing edges together. (If you have any leftover cheese mixture, save it for other uses: stuffing a flattened boned chicken breast, or
spreading onto slices of baguette and broiling for a sort of crostini.) Cut
gashes in top of pastries and place them on a baking sheet.

5. Bake for 15 minutes, or until golden brown. Serve immediately.

◆◆◆◆◆◆

Pesto Whether homemade or store-bought, pesto keeps extremely well
in the freezer. Like other pastes of chopped or pureed herbs, it is a great
boon to have on hand.

Pesto makes a delicious adornment for a bowl of minestrone, a
spoonful melting into the steaming soup. Pesto may be added as a condiment, spooned onto sautéed eggplant slices simmering in tomato
sauce. In Provence I was fed a rare sautéed lamb steak with a pan sauce
made with fresh tomatoes, a swirl of *pistou* (the Provençal equivalent of
pesto) giving style to the simple sauce.

Pesto also gives great flavor to risotto (see page 367).

Basic Pesto

My pesto is a simple puree of basil, with just enough olive oil to bind
it and lots of garlic. Parmesan cheese gives it body, and while classic
pesto often has walnuts or pine nuts in it, I prefer my pesto without, as
I think nuts tend to develop a rancid flavor as pesto sits.

When I want a nut flavor with my pesto, I scatter a handful of walnuts, pine nuts, or hazelnuts atop a plate of pesto-sauced pasta.

3 to 5 garlic cloves, chopped
2 cups tightly packed, relatively unblemished basil leaves

1 teaspoon salt
1 cup olive oil
3/4 cup grated Parmesan cheese

1. In a blender or food processor mince garlic, then add basil and salt. Whirl to chop finely.

2. Slowly add olive oil to whirling machine, forming a thin, smooth puree, then add cheese and mix in well.

Five Simple Things to Do with Pesto

◆◆◆◆◆◆

◆ Mix equal parts pesto, heavy cream, and blue cheese, seasoning with a little garlic, then tossing it onto pasta.

◆ Arrange ripe tomatoes on a platter and dress with olive oil and balsamic vinegar. Garnish with nuggets of pesto, goat cheese, and black olives.

◆ Add several tablespoons pesto to your favorite recipe for fresh pasta and knead the basil paste into egg noodle dough. Serve the delicate, fragrant pasta tossed with only a bit of unsalted butter.

◆ Toss cooked orzo with a generous amount of pesto and a dash of red wine vinegar. Stuff into hollowed-out tomatoes, and sprinkle with toasted pine nuts.

◆ PESTO-OLIVE AïOLI Mix 1/3 cup pesto with 2/3 cup Olive Aïoli (page 158) for a vibrant dip to accompany vegetables or skewered chunks of poached or grilled chicken breasts alternated with chunks of yellow and red bell pepper.

Zucchini Tart al Pesto

◆ BASIC PANTRY

Serves 6

Pale green with shredded zucchini, richly flavored with pesto and cheese, this is a delightfully savory tart. Enjoy it as an appetizer or for a picnic lunch, or serve larger wedges along with a varied salad for a warm-weather supper.

Though it's delicious warm, I think this is even better cooled to room temperature, when it is perfectly suited for serving as a party appetizer along with asparagus with Olive Aïoli (page 158), a platter of roasted peppers, and baguette slices topped with chèvre and sun-dried tomatoes.

1 recipe Basic Pie Dough, page 363	2 garlic cloves, chopped
1/2 cup shredded dry grating cheese such as asiago, Parmesan, or dry jack	2 eggs, lightly beaten
	1/2 cup half and half
	2 tablespoons Pesto, page 364
4 zucchini, coarsely shredded	Salt and pepper to taste

1. Preheat oven to 350°. Prepare pie dough. Line a 9-inch pie pan with pie dough and crimp edges of dough.

2. Sprinkle cheese over bottom of pie crust. Top with zucchini and garlic.

3. Mix eggs with half and half.

4. Dot pesto over zucchini, then pour egg mixture over zucchini. Add salt and pepper.

5. Bake about 45 minutes until crust is golden brown and filling seems set—that is, not jiggly when shaken.

6. Serve hot, or let cool and enjoy at room temperature.

Pesto-stuffed Turkey Schnitzel

◆ BASIC TO
◆◆ INTERMEDIATE PANTRY

Serves 4

Thinly sliced turkey breasts are fairly new additions to our markets. They are excellent for all sorts of quick sautés and dishes in which veal or chicken breasts are usually used. Their bland and delicate flesh takes exquisitely to all sorts of spicy or piquant seasonings.

In this dish, slices of turkey breast are spread with pesto and quickly browned à la schnitzel. The accompanying sauce of sliced garlic and pimientos is optional—the schnitzel is as good without as it is with it.

8 thin slices raw turkey breast (1 to 2 ounces per slice)	Bread crumbs for coating
1/4 to 1/2 cup Pesto (page 364) or as needed	Several tablespoons grated Parmesan cheese
Flour for dredging	Milk for coating
	Olive oil for sautéing

SLICED-GARLIC-AND-PIMIENTO SAUCE

4 to 5 garlic cloves, thinly
sliced

1/3 cup thinly sliced marinated
roasted red peppers

1 cup dry but fruity white
wine, such as Riesling

Fresh basil leaves for garnish

1. Spread 4 turkey slices thickly with pesto. Top with other 4 slices, sandwich style.
2. Dredge in flour and coat well.
3. Mix crumbs with Parmesan cheese.
4. One at a time, quickly place pesto-stuffed cutlets into milk, then into crumb-cheese mixture, pressing to make it stick well. Place on a plate and let sit for 15 minutes or so to help crumbs adhere.
5. In a heavy skillet, heat olive oil to a depth of 1/8 to 1/4 inch, enough to pan-fry cutlets to crispness but not so much that you are deep-frying.
6. Pan-brown turkey over a medium-high heat, first on one side, then on other, cooking 1 or 2 minutes on each side. Remove to a plate and keep warm while you make sauce.
7. Pour off any fat from pan in which schnitzel was cooked, then add garlic. Cook a minute or two, then add peppers.
8. After a minute longer pour in wine, raise heat, and boil down mixture until wine is reduced to a concentrated sauce.
9. Serve pesto-stuffed schnitzel with a puddle of sauce next to it.

Green Risotto with Pesto

◆◆ INTERMEDIATE PANTRY

Serves 4

Smooth and creamily sauced, this risotto is distinctively green from a generous splash of pesto and is particularly pungent due to the addition of blue cheese. It was adapted from a dish made for me one summer in Italy.

But I developed the recipe out of sheer exuberance at the thought of having pesto in my freezer. This is not hard to understand when I explain that the first time I went to Europe, I planned my trip around Genoa for no reason other than pesto. This isn't mere love; it's passion.

3 garlic cloves, chopped
1 tablespoon unsalted butter
1-1/2 cups Arborio rice
1 quart hot chicken or vegetable broth (preferably low-salt or unsalted)
3/4 cup heavy (whipping) cream
3 to 4 ounces blue cheese, crumbled (about 1 cup)

1/4 cup Pesto, page 364
1/3 cup coarsely grated Parmesan or other grating cheese
1/4 cup coarsely chopped fresh basil

1. Heat garlic in butter and, when lightly golden and aromatic, stir in rice and toss together over heat to coat.

2. Continue to stir, adding 1/2 cup broth and letting rice absorb it. Repeat with another 1/2 cup broth, and when that is nearly absorbed, add another 1/2 cup and repeat until all broth is absorbed and rice is nearly tender.

3. Add cream and continue cooking until rice is just tender but with a slight resistance to the bite. Cream will bubble and boil up, but that is fine.

4. When rice is al dente, stir in blue cheese, pesto, and Parmesan.

5. Serve immediately, each portion topped with a sprinkling of chopped basil.

◆◆◆◆◆◆◆

Salsa Many bottled sauces are delicious, but making your own gives a fresh, distinctive touch to whatever you add it to.

Basic Salsa

◆ BASIC PANTRY

Makes 2–2-1/4 cups

Whirl several **garlic cloves** along with several **chilies,** choosing from quite hot and spicy or mild; chopped **onion** is good, too. Add 2 cups chopped **tomatoes,** a little chopped fresh **cilantro and/or parsley** if desired, and **salt** and ground **cumin** to taste. For a cilantro-flavored salsa, add more cilantro, or use the Cilantro-Lime Paste on page 360.

◆◆◆◆◆◆◆

Tortillas Both flour and corn tortillas freeze admirably, ready to provide for a snack or an entire fiesta. Simply defrost and use as you would fresh. They will not be as soft and pliable, however, and will dry out over time.

Mediterranean Tostadas

My current favorite tortilla topping is more Mediterranean than Mexican. Top large **flour tortillas** with **jack or mozzarella cheese,** along with sliced **pimiento-stuffed olives** and strips of **roasted red peppers.** Broil until bubbly and lightly browned in spots. Serve with your favorite **salsa.**

Crab and Avocado Soft Tacos

Toss fresh cooked **crab meat** with a little **chili powder,** chopped **onion,** and chopped fresh **cilantro;** roll into warm soft **corn tortillas** and garnish with sliced **avocado,** a squeeze of **lemon or lime,** and **sour cream.** Serve with a **salsa** of choice.

Bunuelos

These crisp fried cookie-like pastries are beloved in Mexico and America's Southwest. Fried flour tortillas make a delicious bunuelo-type sweet.

◆◆◆◆◆◆

TO PREPARE Simply fry **flour tortillas,** whole or in wedges, in 1/2 inch or so of **vegetable oil** until golden. Remove and drain on absorbent paper. Serve New Mexico style, sprinkled with ground **cinnamon** and **sugar, or** drizzled with **brown sugar syrup** and **toasted pecans,** New Orleans style.

Bunuelo Ice Cream Sundae

Top **cinnamon-sprinkled bunuelos,** above, with **coffee, chocolate, banana, or pralines-and-cream ice cream,** and plonk the whole thing down into a puddle of **chocolate or caramel sauce.**

Tropical Fruit Chimichangas

Wrap several slices of **fresh fruit**—apple, pear, banana, etc.—in a softened **flour tortilla** (heat in a lightly oiled medium hot frying pan to make it pliable), fold over top and bottom, then roll up tightly and fry until golden. Serve sprinkled with **cinnamon sugar,** resting in a pool of **mango puree** and covered with as much **whipped cream** as you can bear.

Wonton and Egg Roll Wrappers Wonton and egg roll wrappers make excellent ravioli and other dumpling wrappers. They may be filled with any sort of savory fish, meat, cheese, or vegetable mixture, then sealed and steamed or boiled until just tender. Egg roll wrappers make great noodles for lasagne, or for cannelloni. Purchase both in Asian groceries or supermarkets and freeze. They will keep for up to 6 months.

Crisp-fried Noodle Strips to Scatter over Asian Salads

Cut **wonton wrappers** into thin strips and fry quickly in **vegetable oil** until golden.

Rustic Fish Ravioli

◆ BASIC PANTRY

Serves 4 to 6

Combine 1 pound leftover simply **cooked fish** (such as baked, grilled, or braised in tomato sauce), bones removed and broken up with a fork, with 1/2 cup or so cooked chopped **chard or spinach,** squeezed dry; season with chopped fresh **parsley** and **basil, salt,** and **pepper.** Bind with **egg** and use to fill **wonton wrappers.**

Cook quickly in boiling salted water, then serve in **broth,** garnished with chopped **fresh herbs,** a drizzle of **olive oil,** and a squeeze of **lemon.**

Chinese Dumplings

◆◆◆ ADVANCED PANTRY

Serves 6

These are a variation of steamed dumplings, *sui mei,* but here the filling is encased completely in noodle dough. I like to serve them dressed with Asian sesame oil and soy sauce, with dabs of sauces and condiments.

Chinese salted turnips are brownish, thick shreds, somewhat dried, with bits of crystallized salt clinging to them. They smell strong—old socks come to mind—but a small amount adds a distinctive, pungent flavor accent to many foods, especially meatballs or meat fillings.

You can purchase salted turnips in plastic bags from Asian food stores. They last nearly forever—at least a year—but should be kept well-sealed in a cool, dry place.

1 pound ground pork	1 to 2 tablespoons grated or
15 water chestnuts, chopped	chopped fresh ginger
coarsely	1/4 cup cornstarch

1/4 cup chicken broth
1 tablespoon chopped salted
  turnips
2 teaspoons soy sauce
2 teaspoons dry sherry
2 teaspoons Asian (toasted) sesame oil
1/2 cup chopped fresh cilantro
3 to 5 green onions, thinly
  sliced

1 package (about 8 ounces)
  wonton wrappers
Garnishes: Asian sesame oil,
  soy sauce, Chinese garlic-
  chili paste, Green Onion Oil
  (page 78), diced cucumber,
  balsamic or Chinese black
  vinegar, chopped fresh
  cilantro and mint

1. Mix together all ingredients except wonton wrappers and garnishes.

2. Stuff wontons: Place a tablespoon or two of filling in middle of
wonton wrapper. Wet edges of noodle square, then top with a second
wonton noodle and press edges to seal well. Set aside, in a single layer,
on a plate to let the edges dry and "glue" together.

3. Cook in boiling water until just tender, about 3 minutes. Open
one to see if pork filling is cooked through.

4. Serve dumplings on a platter, drizzled with sesame oil and soy
sauce, and accompanied with garnishes of choice.

Lower East Side Pirogi

◆ BASIC PANTRY

Serves 4 to 6

Tender gossamer-thin noodles filled with mashed potatoes, enriched
with lots of golden brown fried onions and served topped with drifts of
sour cream, with maybe a nugget of butter melting in as well.

All over New York's Lower East Side were once family-run luncheon-
ettes that served these tiny gastronomical souvenirs of the Old Country
homeland alongside all-American burgers.

3 onions, chopped or thinly
  sliced
3 tablespoons unsalted butter,
  or as needed
3 cups mashed potatoes
2 eggs, lightly beaten

Salt and pepper to taste
1 package wonton wrappers
  (about 8 ounces)
Melted butter for drizzling
Sour cream for garnish

1. Fry onions in butter until well browned and enticing.

2. Mix potatoes with butter-browned onions and eggs, then season with salt and pepper; they will need more of both than you expect.

3. Make dumplings by taking a wonton wrapper, brushing edges with water, topping with a tablespoon or two of mashed potato filling, then topping with another noodle square. Press edges to seal well.

4. Cook potato dumplings in boiling water for about 2 minutes, or until dough is cooked through.

5. Drain carefully and serve drizzled with melted butter and dolloped with sour cream.

◆◆ INTERMEDIATE PANTRY

Salmon-filled Pirogi

Follow **preceding recipe,** but use this filling: Combine 1/3 cup chopped **shallots** with 2 tablespoons **unsalted butter,** 4 ounces (3/4 cup) mashed cooked **salmon,** 4 ounces (3/4 cup) chopped **smoked salmon,** 3 tablespoons chopped **fresh chives,** 3 ounces (about 1/2 cup) cream cheese, and chopped **fresh dill** to taste.

THE CANNED AND BOTTLED GOODS PANTRY

$\diamond\!\bullet\!\diamond$

It is ironic that in a cookbook based on the contemporary American pantry, the chapter on canned and bottled food should be so small. Canned and bottled foods are not as important to us as they once were. There are, however, a number of excellent foods available in cans and bottles.

Some foods are not too harmed by canning and are convenient to have on hand (such as tomato sauce, tomato paste, and diced tomatoes, beans, hominy, and so forth); foods that are difficult to find fresh (tomatillos, nopales, hearts of palm, vine leaves, etc.); and some fruits (pineapple, mandarin oranges, mangos). And it's nice to have a few cans of comfort foods: cassoulet, corned beef hash, tamales. (We all have some secret favorites, in the pantry, hidden away from the rest of the world.)

Tuna is one of the best all-purpose pantry foods available, one of the few things that's really good in a can (though you can't compare it to fresh tuna). Salmon is good, too, for a quick salad, or a pâté, or as a filling for ravioli-like dumplings. Marinated artichoke hearts are always in my pantry, if not to eat straight out of the jar, then to puree with mayonnaise into a smooth and tangy sauce for fish or chicken. Roasted red peppers are one of the most valuable items in the modern pantry—I could think of endless dishes to prepare and enjoy with them. Enchilada or mild chili sauce is useful, though a bit thin and acidic to be used as is—it needs to be simmered with a rich sweet chili such as ancho, or at least some good sweet paprika.

Juices, especially cranberry and combined juices, are handy not just for drinking: you can simmer fresh cherries with a cinnamon stick in cranberry juice, then enjoy them chilled, with a spoonful of sour cream stirred in. Or use a little cranberry-apricot juice mixed with white wine to simmer chicken, then reduce the cooking liquid and thicken it with whole-seed mustard and sour cream. Fruit juices can be whirled, along with a contrasting fruit, into a frenzy in the blender. Dark cherry juice makes a delectable granita, especially with its flavor oomphed up with a hit of almond extract or Amaretto. Apple-raspberry juice, strawberry lemonade, kiwi nectar, etc., make exotic ice cubes either for adding to other drinks, or for pureeing into a slush.

There are proportionately few recipes in this section, because the ingredients found here are used in other dishes throughout the book.

STORAGE TIPS Use canned or bottled meats, vegetables, or legumes within 18 months; canned fish within 1 year.

Once opened, store foods tightly covered and refrigerated. Remove from tin or can to avoid the metal flavor. Some storage times: fish and seafood, 1 day; fruit, 1 week; broth, 2 days; meat, 2 days; pickles and olives, 1 month; poultry, 1 day; tomato sauce, 1 week; vegetables and legumes, 3 days.

Pantry List: Canned and Bottled Goods

Artichoke hearts, marinated
Beans (kidney, black, chick-pea, white, black-eyed, etc.)
Beans, refried
Broth (chicken and beef)
Chestnut puree (unsweetened and sweetened)

Enchilada sauce, mild chili sauce
Fruit and vegetable juices (cherry, pineapple, apple, mixed fruit combinations, V-8, tomato, etc.)
Hearts of palm
Hominy
Nopales
Roasted red peppers
Salmon

Sardines
Sauerkraut
Tomatillos
Tomatoes
Tomato paste
Tomato sauce
Tuna fish
Vine leaves
Plus several cans of your favorite comfort food (only you know what that is)

Italian Turkey-Chestnut Soup with Porcini Mushrooms

◆◆◆ ADVANCED PANTRY

Serves 4 to 6

Chestnut paste gives any dish an instant flavor of chilled autumn evenings, when the days grow short and the chestnut vendors come out onto the streets to sell their wares.

Chestnuts are sold either whole, in pieces, or in a paste, sweetened or unsweetened. They are also sold as confections, marrons glacée.

Sweetened chestnut puree can make a delicious, hearty dessert: open the can, spread the puree out on a plate, and top with a dab of sour cream and a grating of dark chocolate.

Unsweetened chestnut puree is delicious added to savory rustic soups, such as this one from Umbria. The chestnuts, combined with porcini mushrooms, give the soup a wonderful flavor of the forest.

1 ounce dried porcini mushrooms	6 cups turkey or chicken broth
Warm broth or water for rehydrating	One 6-ounce can pureed chestnuts
1/2 onion, chopped	1 bay leaf
1/2 carrot, chopped	1/4 cup tomato sauce
1/2 red bell pepper, chopped	1 tablespoon chopped fresh parsley
1/2 celery stalk, chopped	Salt and pepper to taste
1/2 rutabaga, chopped	2 tablespoons Madeira, Marsala, or dry sherry
2 tablespoons olive oil	Parmesan cheese to taste
1 tablespoon flour	

1. Rehydrate porcini in warm broth or water (see page 140). Set aside and reserve soaking liquid. Chop porcini coarsely. Sauté in 1 tablespoon olive oil, then set aside.

2. Sauté onion, carrot, red pepper, celery, and rutabaga in remaining 1 tablespoon of olive oil until softened, then sprinkle with flour and cook until slightly browned.

3. Add reserved soaking liquid, broth, chestnuts, bay leaf, tomato sauce, and parsley, and simmer for about 15 minutes, or until soup is flavorful. Add salt and pepper to taste.

4. Add sautéed porcini, simmer another few minutes, then stir in Madeira, Marsala, or sherry, and serve immediately, each portion sprinkled with Parmesan cheese.

Chicken Breasts Dijonaise

Serves 4

Cranberry-apricot juice adds a sweet note to garlicky mustard-cream chicken, rounding the mustard flavor out and giving it depth and complexity.

1 garlic head, cloves separated and peeled but left whole, plus 3 cloves peeled and coarsely chopped
2 tablespoons vegetable oil or butter
1 cup chicken broth
1/2 to 2/3 cup cranberry-apricot juice

2 tablespoons whole-seed mustard
3 bay leaves
3 tablespoons sour cream or heavy (whipping) cream
4 boned chicken breast halves
Salt and pepper to taste (optional)

1. Sauté whole garlic cloves in oil or butter; add broth and simmer garlic cloves until tender, then mash coarsely with a fork; add cranberry-apricot juice and boil down to reduce by about half.

2. Swirl in mustard and bay leaves, then add chicken breasts and gently cook, covered, in sauce. Cook only for a few minutes, as tender breasts can easily be turned into tough, unpleasant pieces of meat.

3. Remove chicken from sauce and keep warm. Reduce sauce if necessary, then swirl in sour cream. Taste for seasoning, adding salt and pepper if necessary. Serve chicken breasts napped with mustard cream sauce.

Fruit Frenzies

Whichever fruit juice and fruit you choose, simply whirl in a blender or processor until frothy and well mixed. A dab of honey could be added, if desired.

Apple juice and raspberries or blackberries
Strawberries and orange juice
Pineapple juice and pomegranate seeds

Tropical fruit juice mixture with mango slices
Banana and apricot chunks with strawberries and kiwi juice

Hearts of Palm Vinaigrette, Brazilian Style

◆◆◆ ADVANCED PANTRY

Serves 4

Cactus (Nopales) Salads

◆◆ INTERMEDIATE PANTRY

Serves 4

Serve canned **hearts of palm** arranged on plates and dressed with a tangy **vinaigrette** (page 81). Garnish with chopped fresh **parsley** and strips of **roasted red peppers.**

Nopales may be bought fresh in a few Latin American groceries, but they are easily available in jars in most Latin groceries and many supermarkets. They are delicious in salsa and gaspacho, as well as tucked into tacos. They have a flavor somewhere in between green beans and okra.

Nopales generally come in a jar, sometimes seasoned with a hot chili, a piece of onion, and a sprig of cilantro. They exude a slightly viscous liquid, which you might find disconcerting at first.

They make an intriguing and refreshing salad directly from the jar, as in the following traditional dishes.

Cactus Salad with Cheese

[NOPALES CON QUESO]

Crumble several ounces slightly salty **fresh cheese** such as feta or queso fresco over the top of 2 cups **nopales.** Top with chopped **red onion,** a bit of **tomatillo salsa,** and a splash of **vinaigrette.**

Cactus Salad with Egg

Top 2 cups **vinaigrette-and-salsa-dressed nopales** with chopped **hard-cooked egg** for an exotic yet friendly salad. Garnish with **chopped onion** and **fresh cilantro.**

◆◆◆◆◆◆

Roasted Red Peppers Among the stars of the modern pantry, these go from salad to sandwich to canapé with grace and aplomb. They're even delicious eaten directly out of the jar.

Fire roasted and peeled of their charred skin, roasted red peppers are as useful as they are good to eat, and there are many quality brands of them on the market.

Nine Things to Do with Roasted Red Peppers

◆◆◆◆◆◆

MEDITERRANEAN PEPPER SALAD Dress with olive oil, balsamic or wine vinegar, and top with crumbled feta, chopped fresh thyme, and/or black Mediterranean olives.

◆◆◆◆◆◆

NEAR EAST PEPPER SALAD Top with sliced boiled potatoes, curried yogurt, chopped fresh cilantro and mint.

◆◆◆◆◆◆

ROASTED PEPPER AND CHEESE SPREAD Puree 1 garlic clove, then add 3 roasted red peppers and puree. When smooth, add 3 ounces cream cheese (1/2 cup) and chopped fresh oregano to taste. Serve accompanied with crusty light wheat bread.

◆◆◆◆◆◆

HARISSA Puree roasted red peppers, then season to taste with ground cumin, hot pepper sauce, chopped fresh cilantro, and lemon juice.

◆◆◆◆◆◆

ROASTED RED PEPPER AND BEANS PASTA Add thin slices of roasted red peppers to tomato sauce, along with a handful of broccoli florets and diced peeled broccoli stems, and 1/2 cup cooked kidney beans. Pour over any al dente pasta.

◆◆◆◆◆◆

RED PEPPER AND CHICKEN SALAD Add strips of tangy red peppers to a simple mayonnaise- or aïoli-based chicken salad.

◆◆◆◆◆◆

RED PEPPER AND GREEN OLIVE RELISH Chop roasted peppers and combine with coarsely chopped green olives, chopped garlic, olive oil, chopped fresh oregano, and a dash of red wine vinegar. Serve with cold meats or as a sandwich relish, in crusty rolls.

◆◆◆◆◆◆

POTATO SALAD Cut strips or chop roasted red peppers and use as a garnish for a vinaigrette- or mayonnaise-based potato salad.

◆◆◆◆◆◆

ROASTED RED PEPPERS RELISH AND FRIED SOLE Thinly slice roasted red peppers and toss with red wine vinegar. Use as a relish for golden-brown sautéed sole fillets, along with a scattering of capers.

Tomatillos Also known as a husk tomato, the tomatillo is a tart, firm vegetable that looks much like a green tomato. Raw, it is tart to the point of puckery and firm-crunchy in texture, and is used as a sour accent in salsas and spicy relishes. Cooked, it softens to an almost mushy consistency, readying itself for endless salsa and sauce possibilities, including salsa verde. Mashed and added to guacamole, cooked tomatillos give the predictable sauce a vibrant lift. One of the simplest Mexican chicken dishes I know is also the most delicious: simmer chicken with tomatillos, cumin, and ancho chili, and season with onions, garlic, chopped cilantro, and green chili to taste.

Vine Leaves Bottled grape leaves add a strong flavor accent to the pantry. As a wrapper they are classic: try the Brown Rice–stuffed Grape Leaves, page 216, or wrap vine leaves around goat cheese and grill. Chicken and meats are also good wrapped in the tangy leaves, as are ham-and-vegetable terrines. Try, too, using vine leaves as a bed for a platter of tabbouli.

STORAGE TIPS Store on the pantry shelf until using; once opened, store in the refrigerator for up to 2 weeks.

Vine Leaf–wrapped Chicken Thighs

◆◆ INTERMEDIATE PANTRY

Serves 4

The following dish is a Provençal/Italian/Greek hybrid in which chicken thighs are wrapped in grape leaves to give them a lovely flavor.

Wrap the chicken in several layers of leaves; the chicken will stay succulent, while the leaves will become crispy and delightfully brittle.

6 skinned and boned chicken thighs
2 garlic cloves, chopped
3 tablespoons olive oil, plus a little extra for sautéing
1-1/2 tablespoons fresh lemon juice
1/2 teaspoon chopped fresh, or dried, thyme, or to taste
6 slices bacon, smoked ham, or pancetta
18 to 24 vine leaves

1. Toss chicken thighs in garlic, olive oil, lemon juice, and thyme.
2. Wrap each thigh in a slice of bacon, ham, or pancetta, then continue wrapping in grape leaves.

3. Arrange in a baking dish and marinate in refrigerator for at least 2 hours.

4. Pan brown leaf-wrapped parcels in just enough olive oil to keep leaves browning crisply.

5. Cook over low to medium heat, letting packages lightly brown. Allow a total of 15 to 20 minutes to cook. The outer leaves should be quite browned and rather crispy, while inside leaves will be moist and succulent. Serve immediately.

◆◆◆◆◆◆

Sardines I always assume that people eat foods like sardines in their own ritualized ways. To me, sardines are meant to be layered onto buttered whole-wheat bread and topped with whole green onions. I'd never serve this to anyone else, but it is blissful to me.

Sardine and Refried Bean Tostadas

◆ **BASIC PANTRY**

Serves 4

Sardines are surprisingly good mashed and added to refried beans. Begin by sautéing an **onion** until softened, then add 2 to 3 chopped seeded **tomatoes** and cook down to a savory mixture. Season with **salsa**, then add 1-1/2 to 2 cups **refried beans.** Cook together a minute to meld flavors, then add 1 can **boneless sardines,** mashed.

Serve spread onto crisp-fried **corn tortillas,** topped with shredded **lettuce** and chopped **fresh cilantro.**

BACON, SAUSAGE, HAM, SMOKED AND CURED MEATS, AND FISH

◆❖

Cured meats have been an important part of the pantry since humans began storing food for winter. In the modern Western world, where most people have refrigerators and freezers, cured meats are eaten more for their distinctive flavor than for their keeping qualities (though in parts of the world where refrigeration is not as available, storage is still an important aspect of cured meats).

Often the bits of cured meats I have in my pantry are leftovers: two slices of mortadella leftover from preparing a lunch (delicious added to lima beans); a merguez not eaten at last week's couscous party (wonderful scrambled with eggs, tomatoes, and peppers); and several strips of bacon (not enough for a breakfast or a BLT, but enough to flavor a pot of beans and rice).

If I'm not able to use these small bits immediately, I wrap them and put them in the freezer. I soon have enough mixed and varied meats for a richly flavored sauce bolognese, or a saucy jambalaya.

America has a heritage of sausage eating, brought over by the English and developed by German, Eastern European, and Italian immigrants. Asian and Latin American pantries, too, offer a selection of sausages, such as the long dry spicy Chinese and Southeast Asian sausages, and the wide array of Mexican and Central American chorizos. In recent years, though, health concerns have focused on the fats, salts, and preservatives that turn sausage into a dietary taboo. Sausage-makers have responded by producing either sausages that are lighter in fat and salt, or sausages that are so delicious we don't care what they contain.

Salted and dry-cured meats add flavor to a variety of dishes and may be substituted for each other rather easily: bresaola, made from beef, in place of pork prosciutto; prosciutto for Serrano ham; and so on. While prosciutto and sausages have in recent years become fashionable (and therefore expensive), pastrami and corned beef have remained identified as Jewish deli foods. And it's just as well—they're expensive enough as it is. They are good with sauerkraut, rye bread, and pickles. They may not be fashionable, but they're my kind of soul food.

Sometimes I use pastrami or thinly sliced corned beef in place of prosciutto, with a sliced mango, for example, or in a casserole of shirred eggs.

Cured fish comes in a wide variety as well: with their smoky and/or briny flavor they are often served in small portions as appetizers, or to flavor other dishes, like prosciutto. As with prosciutto, sometimes the occasion demands a large and lavish amount. One of my first memories involves cured fish: a large, crusty roll stuffed with cream cheese and so much smoked salmon it was impossible to get my then tiny mouth around it.

STORAGE TIPS Store sausages according to their type and directions on the package or the butcher's advice. Fresh, smoked, and dried sausages may be successfully frozen. Unopened vacuum packs last about 2 weeks in the refrigerator and up to 6 months in the freezer. Smoked salmon and trout, tightly wrapped, last about a week in the refrigerator and 3 months in the freezer. Dried codfish lasts up to 6 months in a cool, dry place.

Some keeping times (in the refrigerator): bacon and corned beef, 5 to 7 days; salami and other dried sausages, 2 to 3 weeks; fresh sausage, 2 to 3 days; prosciutto or bresaola, 10 to 12 days; canned ham: 6 months unopened, 1 week opened.

Pantry List: Bacon, Cured Meats, Sausages, and Fish

◆◆◆◆◆◆

BACON Thick and thinly sliced, smoked, fresh, pancetta, Canadian, Irish

CURED MEATS Baked or boiled ham, smoked ham (especially West-phalian); salt-cured pork such as prosciutto, Parma, or Serrano ham; bresaola, tasso (spicy pastrami-like cured pork from Louisiana), pastrami, corned beef

FRESH SAUSAGES Italian fennel and hot pepper, American sage, chicken-apple, curry-spiced chicken, Mexican and Central American chorizo, merguez, bratwurst, bangers, seafood

COOKED SAUSAGES Knockwurst, frankfurters, mortadella, kosher salami

AIR-DRIED SAUSAGES San Francisco salami, Spanish chorizo, sausissons d'Arles, Chinese sausages, coppa, soppressata

SMOKED SAUSAGES Turkey and beef, spicy beef, kielbasa (made from pork, beef, or turkey), duck with green peppercorns

SMOKED AND CURED FISH Smoked salmon (lox), herrings, whitefish, dried codfish

Eight Simple Sausage Dishes

◆◆◆◆◆◆

The wide range of sausages available in our markets today is inspiring. Their good strong flavors enrich anything they cook with, giving the cook an opportunity to be creative or to simply sit back and let sausage be the star.

◆◆◆◆◆◆

SPICY SAUSAGE WITH HUMMUS AND CILANTRO Sliced spicy Italian sausages, pan browned, served on a hummus-spread crusty roll, sprinkled with chopped fresh cilantro.

◆◆◆◆◆◆

GRILLED MERGUEZ (or other spicy lamb sausage), cooked over an open fire, served with chopped fresh cilantro and lime, and a shake of hot pepper sauce.

STREETS OF NEW YORK SAUSAGE FEAST SANDWICH Brown fennel-scented Italian sausages; push to side of pan, then brown lots of thinly sliced onions, several chopped garlic cloves, 1 red and 1 green bell pepper, sliced. When all of vegetables are tender, add an optional marinated roasted red pepper or several hot cherry peppers. Open soft French or Italian rolls and grill or brown on skillet. Stuff each roll with a big plump juicy sausage and lots of onions and peppers. Add mustard if you wish.

◆◆◆◆◆◆◆

APPLE-WALNUT-CHICKEN SAUSAGES WITH DICED PUMPKIN Brown diced pumpkin or winter squash in a little olive oil or butter, seasoning with chopped shallots or garlic. Push squash to side of pan and brown sausages, then season whole panful with a little apple juice and cider vinegar. Cover and continue cooking until sausages and squash are both cooked through.

◆◆◆◆◆◆◆

GRAPE LEAF—WRAPPED SAUSAGE Wrap duck or Italian fennel sausages in several layers of grape leaves and pan brown, letting outer leaves brown to a pleasantly crisp exterior, until sausage inside is cooked through and juicy.

◆◆◆◆◆◆◆

BANGERS AND MASH LIKE THEY NEVER ATE IT IN BRITAIN (EXCEPT AT MY HOUSE) Serve a selection of spicy sausages—Spanish chorizo, Italian hot pepper, French garlic, Cajun andouille, etc.—over a bed of garlic mashed potatoes.

◆◆◆◆◆◆◆

SALSICCE AL' ACETO Poach sliced Italian sausages in simmering shallow water until sausages are half cooked and much of their fat has been rendered. Drain and brown, splashing sausages with a bit of wine vinegar and letting it cook down to a reduced essence.

◆◆◆◆◆◆◆

DUCK SAUSAGE WITH RED AND GREEN GRAPES Cook duck-and-peppercorn sausages with red and green seedless grapes pulled off their stems and broken up a bit. Cook down to a flavorful sweet-savory sauce; serve with mustard.

Rustic Kabobs of Italian Sausages, Chicken Livers, and Bacon with Rosemary-Mustard Butter

◆◆ INTERMEDIATE PANTRY

Serves 4 to 6

These brightly flavored kabobs are grilled over an open fire, the sausage and bacon basting the livers with their rich and spicy juices. When they are just lightly browned, they are enlivened with a bit of rosemary-mustard butter spread over them to melt in. Fantastic! Even those who shy away from chicken livers are enticed; first they happily nibble on the sausage and bacon, and by the time they take that first timid bite of the livers, they are devotees.

Serve as an appetizer for a summer grilled menu, or for a main course, the kabobs resting atop creamy golden polenta.

6 ounces bacon, thinly sliced (about 12 slices)
5 Italian fennel sausages, cut into 1-inch chunks
About 10 ounces chicken livers, rinsed and picked over
1 recipe Rosemary-Mustard Butter, page 349

1. Light a charcoal fire in an open grill. Soak wooden skewers in water for 15 to 20 minutes. This will help keep them from burning.

2. Thread bacon, sausages, and chicken livers on skewers, letting bacon weave in and out between livers, so that it acts as a natural basting for kabobs as they cook.

3. Grill over hot white coals until sausage is cooked through, slathering kabobs toward end of cooking with a bit of rosemary-mustard butter. Do not overcook—livers should be still rosy inside.

4. Remove to a platter and spread with more seasoned butter. Serve immediately.

LEFTOVERS Dice and add to **risotto or "dirty rice."** Or toss into a **Bolognese sauce.**

Smoked Duck Sausage with Mesclun, Watercress, Radicchio, and Warm Mustard Vinaigrette

A contemporary interpretation of the warm sausage and frisée so beloved by the French. Vary the mustard according to what is in your pantry—try tarragon or Creole mustard in place of whole-seed mustard.

3 cups mesclun or mixed spring lettuce
1 to 2 cups watercress or frisée
1/4 cup or a small handful of onion sprouts (optional)
1 head radicchio or Belgian endive, cored and cut into bite-sized pieces

(continued)

Serves 4

3 to 4 smoked duck sausages, preferably seasoned with green peppercorns
2 tablespoons whole-seed mustard

2 tablespoons olive oil
1 shallot, chopped
2 tablespoons red wine vinegar

1. Arrange mesclun, watercress, sprouts, and radicchio on plates or in a salad bowl.
2. Cut sausages into bite-sized pieces and pan brown. Drain off excess fat and add mustard, olive oil, shallot, and vinegar to sausages in pan. Warm through and pour quickly over salad. Serve immediately.

Louisiana Gingered Creamed Corn

◆ BASIC PANTRY

Serves 4

Bacon, fresh ginger, and corn combine particularly well. I first tasted this rich, distinctive dish as a bed for soy-and-chili-marinated scallops.

1 onion, chopped
8 bacon slices (preferably thick-cut), diced
2 cups fresh or frozen corn
1-1/2 cups heavy (whipping) cream

1-1/2 teaspoons grated fresh ginger
Salt and hot pepper sauce to taste
2 tablespoons chopped fresh chives or green onions

1. Sauté onion and bacon until onion is softened, then add corn and cream and bring to a boil. Cook a minute or two, letting cream thicken a bit.
2. Whirl in a blender, half-pureeing mixture.
3. Return to pan and reheat with ginger, adding salt and hot pepper sauce.
4. Serve sprinkled with chives or green onions.

◆◆ INTERMEDIATE PANTRY

Yankee Succotash

Sauté **onions, corn, and bacon** as above, then add 1-1/2 cups cooked **cranberry beans,** heat through, then serve seasoned with **salt, pepper,** and 3 to 4 tablespoons chopped **fresh chives.**

Southwestern Chilied Corn

Sauté **onions, corn, and bacon** as previous page, then add 3 tablespoons diced **roasted red peppers,** 1 tablespoon **mild chili powder,** 1 teaspoon ground **cumin,** 1/4 cup **very mild salsa** (or 1/4 cup chopped tomatoes plus hot salsa to taste). Serve topped with 2 chopped **green onions.**

Tropical Red Beans and Rice with Smoked Sausage and Bananas

♦ **BASIC PANTRY**

Serves 4

A full platter of deliciously unruly flavors. If you have unsprayed fresh banana leaves available, serve the meal on them instead of plates, and festoon with edible flowers in the most flamboyant of colors. A large leaf makes a good platter; smaller, cut-up leaves are right for individual plates.

While the dish leans towards the exotic, the ingredients are all pantry foods, and the smoked sausage is easily available in even the smallest of neighborhood grocers. Accompany with lots of iced beer, and offer a hot sauce such as Tabasco on the side, as well as a bowl of chopped green onions to sprinkle over the dish.

1 cup dried red kidney beans	2 cups raw long-grain white rice
4 cups water	
1 onion, coarsely chopped	2 tablespoons chopped fresh cilantro
3 garlic cloves, chopped	
1 tablespoon or more olive oil	2 cups coarsely chopped fresh or canned tomatoes
2 cups chicken broth	
1 medium-large fresh tomato, chopped	1 cup fresh or frozen peas
1/2 teaspoon ground cumin	1 pound smoked beef, turkey, or pork sausage or kielbasa, sliced 1/2 to 3/4 inch thick
1/2 teaspoon curry powder	
1/8 teaspoon or a generous pinch of dried oregano, crumbled	3 to 4 underripe bananas
	2 to 3 tablespoons unsalted butter
1/2 jalapeño, minced, or to taste	Pinch of ground cinnamon

1. Place beans and water in a pot. Bring to a boil, then turn off heat and let sit, covered, for an hour. Return to heat and simmer until beans are tender and some have fallen apart, about 1-1/2 hours.

2. Sauté onion and garlic in 1 tablespoon olive oil until softened; add to beans along with broth, fresh tomato, cumin, curry, oregano, chili, rice, cilantro, and chopped tomatoes. Cover and cook over medium-low heat until rice is barely tender, about 15 minutes.

3. Add peas, cover, and set aside.

4. Brown sausage slices in a skillet, adding a tiny bit of olive oil if sausages do not have enough fat to brown them. Remove from pan and place on top of rice while you sauté bananas.

5. Slice bananas and sauté in butter until lightly browned. Serve rice and beans piled high on a platter, surrounded by browned sausage and bananas. Sprinkle with cinnamon and serve immediately.

Potatoes with Chorizo

◆◆ INTERMEDIATE PANTRY

Serves 4

Anyone who has visited Spain has wonderful memories of evenings spent nibbling tapas, the snacks that accompany chilled dry sherry, excellent beer, or good rough wine. The bars and bodegas scattered throughout the cities, villages, and countryside offer plates of savory foods such as olives and toasted nuts, vegetable and seafood presentations, and always a selection of Spain's superlative cured meats and sausages. Sometimes the dishes are elegant and refined; sometimes they are rugged and rough, with strong primitive flavors. Tapas work best with a group; that way you can order a larger selection and sample a wider variety of tidbits.

This dish is inspired by one I nibbled in Sevilla, after a mad dash through the cobbled hillside streets in a torrential rainstorm. We dried off as we munched on the excellent Serrano ham; the paprika-scented cured pork loin, *lomo;* a dish of potatoes cooked with oxtails; shrimp with garlic; and the following simple dish of potatoes and chorizo, my favorite. The authentic version swam in oil; I've cut down on it considerably, and added a sprinkling of cilantro and a squeeze of lime.

6 large russet potatoes, peeled and cut into eighths lengthwise

Small amount of olive oil for coating

Salt and pepper to taste

2 Spanish chorizos, or, if unavailable, Mexican chorizos, cut into thin slices

4 garlic cloves, chopped coarsely

2 tablespoons chopped fresh cilantro

1 lime, cut into wedges

1. Preheat oven to 375°. Place potato wedges on a baking sheet and toss with a small amount of olive oil to coat. Add salt and pepper.

2. Bake until potatoes are golden and browned in places, and tender inside, about 35–40 minutes.

3. Meanwhile, brown chorizo in a skillet. (You will probably not need extra oil. Add a tablespoonful or so if you do.) When potatoes are cooked, add sausage.

4. Cook together a minute or two with lid on, then serve, sprinkled with cilantro and accompanied with lime wedges.

Dry Soup with Pasta, Mexican Style

[SOPA SECA DE FIDEO]

◆◆ INTERMEDIATE PANTRY

Serves 4

Translating literally from the Spanish as "dry soup," *sopa seca* is the Mexican name given to pasta and rice dishes cooked in broth, enriched with spices and other flavorings. This name was given because rice and pasta dishes are eaten at the beginning of the traditional *comida*, or several-course meal, just after the "wet" soup, or *sopa aguada*.

Note that the pasta is first boiled with a bay leaf before being layered with sauce and baked. The vermicelli takes on the slightly piney aroma of bay leaf and is delicious as is, buttered generously and sprinkled with salt and pepper.

2/3 pound capellini, vermicelli, or other very thin pasta
2 to 3 bay leaves
2 to 3 chorizos, about 3 ounces each
1 onion, chopped
1 green bell pepper or mild green chili such as poblano, chopped

3 garlic cloves, chopped
1 cup tomato sauce
1 cup broth of choice
About 12 ounces (1-1/2 cups) cheese, shredded (jack combined with dry jack is a good combination)

1. Preheat oven to 400°. Boil pasta with bay leaves. When just al dente, after only a few minutes, drain and discard bay leaves.

2. Fry chorizos; when they begin to brown, add onion and pepper and cook together until onion has softened. Add garlic, tomato sauce, and broth.

3. Combine sauce with cooked pasta, then place in a baking dish. Cover with shredded cheese.

4. Bake until top is bubbly and lightly browned, and dish is heated through. Serve immediately.

VEGETARIAN DRY SOUP Omit chorizo and increase onion. Add 1 or 2 tablespoons **mild chili powder** while onion is sautéing.

New England Corned Beef Hash

Serves 4

Corned beef hash is one of my favorite foods. A good one is sublime, but even a bad one isn't really bad. The main criterion seems to be having plenty of corned beef in the hash, and developing a nice brown crust.

Adding a splash of cream to encourage the crust formation and spicing up the corned beef's flavor with a grating of nutmeg at the end were tricks I learned from a class taught by the late James Beard. I was thrilled to find that the culinary legend adored corned beef hash as much as I.

Serve, of course, with poached eggs—the sauce made from the runny yolk becomes part of the hash.

6 to 8 medium cold boiled waxy
   potatoes, peeled and diced
1 medium-large or 2 small
   onions, chopped
8 to 12 ounces (about 2 cups)
   corned beef, diced
Vegetable oil for
   browning hash
2 to 3 tablespoons heavy
   (whipping) cream
Grating of fresh nutmeg
Black pepper to taste
4 to 8 poached eggs
Toasted rye bread

1. Combine potatoes with onions and corned beef. Place in a lightly oiled hot skillet, pancake style, over medium heat.
2. Adding more oil if needed, let brown, turning occasionally with a spatula.
3. When corned beef hash has browned in places, add cream and continue cooking, turning again as bottom gets crusty. Sprinkle with nutmeg and black pepper. Serve immediately, accompanied with poached eggs and rye toast.

Southwestern Chicken Thighs with Smoky Chili Flavors

Serves 4

Marinating chicken thighs and/or legs in a selection of chili spices and citrus juices, then wrapping them in bacon, is a simple technique and produces a shockingly good dish that belies its simplicity.

It's good for a crowd, or for when you want something special that doesn't demand much from the cook.

With its chili spices and the smoky flavors of the bacon, and the tenderizing citrus juices, this chicken emerges from its bake or sauté tasting like particularly delicious barbecue.

8 chicken thighs or legs, or a combination

1 recipe Red Chili-Citrus Paste, page 128
8 thick-cut bacon slices

1. Coat chicken with spice paste.
2. Wrap each coated piece of chicken with a slice of bacon. Let sit at room temperature for up to 2 hours, or longer in refrigerator.
3. Roast in a 375° oven until bacon is crisp and chicken is tender, or pan brown in fat rendered from bacon.

Eggs Cooked with Lamb Sausages, Peppers, and Tomatoes

[CHAKSHOUKA]

Serves 4

Merguez is a lamb sausage of North African origin. It is forcefully spicy, with a rich red color from paprika and other flavorings. Like its distant cousin, Mexican chorizo, merguez comes in a wide array of flavors and heat levels. Some are delicate and fragrant, others hot enough to leave you gasping for water, with tears glistening on your cheeks. The only way to tell is to taste.

When you find a merguez you love, serve it alongside couscous, or cut it into chunks, brown, and add to pasta along with grilled vegetables and tangy yogurt. Or try this dish, a traditional mixture of peppers, tomatoes, merguez, and eggs. Though it's usually eaten as a first course in North Africa or France, it's also an exciting brunch dish, accompanied with garlic-roasted home-fries and a condiment of chopped fresh cilantro, chili, and lime juice (or Cilantro-Lime Paste, page 360), with tropical fruit drinks to cool down the palate.

2 merguez sausages, cut into bite-sized pieces (or substitute Spanish, Mexican, or Central American chorizo)

Olive oil for browning, as needed
4 to 6 garlic cloves, chopped

(continued)

1/2 red bell pepper, thinly sliced	4 medium fresh or canned tomatoes, seeded and diced (don't use winter tomatoes)
1/2 green bell pepper, thinly sliced	4 eggs
1/2 to 1 jalapeño chili, chopped (if merguez is really spicy, omit)	2 tablespoons chopped fresh cilantro

1. Preheat oven to 350°. Brown sausage in a hot skillet, adding a bit of olive oil if necessary.

2. Add garlic, red peppers, green peppers, jalapeño, and tomatoes. Cook for about 5 minutes, or until slightly saucy.

3. Spoon mixture into 4 individual ramekins and break 1 egg into each ramekin.

4. Bake covered until egg white is set, about 15 minutes. (You also can make this in the skillet: With a spoon make 4 indentations in sausage-peppers-tomatoes, then drop 1 egg into each indentation. Simmer over low heat until egg whites have set, basting with sausage-pepper mixture if desired.) Serve immediately, sprinkled with cilantro.

Spaghetti Carbonara with Pancetta and Rosemary

◆◆ INTERMEDIATE PANTRY

Serves 4

Sauté 2 ounces **pancetta,** chopped, in a tablespoon or two of **olive oil,** then toss with 2/3 pound just-cooked al dente **spaghetti,** along with 2 chopped **garlic cloves** and a tablespoon or so of chopped **fresh rosemary.** Beat 1/2 cup freshly grated **Parmesan cheese** with 1 **egg,** then toss into hot pasta and serve immediately. Offer extra cheese and **black pepper** at table.

Sausage Gumbo Ya-ya

◆◆ INTERMEDIATE PANTRY

Serves 4 to 6

Smoked spicy sausage gives its strong flavor to the following gumbo. Any sort of diced poultry such as turkey, duck, or seafood can be added to the gumbo; or use only the spicy sausage.

Along with sausage, good broth and a good roux are important to gumbo. A homemade broth and a carefully prepared roux will make an excellent dish; canned broth and a roux that is either underdone or veering towards burnt will not.

Serve ladled over steamed rice in a bowl, sprinkled with crisp chopped green onions—they contrast nicely with the rich gumbo.

1 onion, chopped
1/2 green bell pepper, chopped
1 celery stalk, chopped
3 garlic cloves, chopped
12 ounces to 1 pound firm
   smoked pork, beef, or duck
   sausages thickly sliced
   (about 1/2–3/4 inches)
2 tablespoons vegetable oil
3 cups rich broth, either duck,
   chicken, turkey, or beef,
   or a combination
1-1/2 tablespoons flour
1/2 teaspoon dried thyme
Dash cayenne or 2 small dried
   red chilies

1/2 red bell pepper, diced
3 medium tomatoes, chopped,
   or 1 cup canned
1/2 cup tomato juice
1 cup cooked chicken, duck,
   turkey, or cooked seafood
   such as shelled shrimp
   or crab
2 teaspoons gumbo filé powder
Salt (if needed) and pepper
   to taste
3 cups freshly cooked
   white rice
6 to 8 green onions,
   thinly sliced

1. Sauté onion, green pepper, celery, garlic, and sausages in 2 teaspoons oil until onions are softened and bits of both onion and sausage are lightly browned. Add broth and let simmer while you prepare roux.

2. To make roux: Heat remaining 4 teaspoons oil over medium-low heat. When hot, sprinkle in flour and stir roux constantly as it gradually takes on color, going from white to beige to caramel, then to a nice nutty brown color. (Stop there. The next color is a not very nice black, and you will have to start all over again.)

3. Add roux to simmering broth mixture, along with thyme, chilies, bell pepper, tomatoes, and tomato juice. Simmer for about 15 minutes, or long enough to meld flavors and thicken somewhat, then add poultry or seafood, and filé powder. Simmer a few minutes longer.

4. Season with salt and pepper, then serve over rice, the whole thing sprinkled with green onions.

Five Things to Do with Cured Fish

◆◆◆◆◆◆◆

◆ Serve bite-sized pieces of smoked trout on cucumber slices, topped with a dab of whipped cream seasoned with horseradish.

◆ Serve madjes (smoked and brined) herring, draped over a large boiled potato, the whole thing sprinkled with chopped fresh parsley and a little olive oil.

◆◆◆◆◆◆◆

◆ LOX AND EGGS Sauté 2 chopped onions in 1–2 tablespoons unsalted butter until they are very soft and browned in bits. Add 4 to 6 ounces smoked salmon, chopped, then pour in 6 beaten eggs and scramble over low heat into soft, creamy curds adding 1–2 more tablespoons of butter. Serve sprinkled with chopped fresh chives or green onions.

◆ Serve a platter of sliced smoked salmon with a selection of garnishes: chopped onion, diced tomato, a nugget of creamy garlic-scented goat cheese, or bowl of sour cream, capers, chopped chives, and buttered thinly sliced rye breads, black breads, and baguettes. A garnish of mesclun and edible flowers would be appropriately lavish and grand.

◆◆◆◆◆◆◆

◆ GRANDMA'S POTATO AND SMOKED SALMON SOUP Cook chunks of potato in an unsalty fish stock, and when potatoes are tender and falling apart add as much chopped smoked salmon as you can afford. Simmer a few minutes, then serve sprinkled generously with chopped fresh dill, chopped green onions, and a dollop of sour cream.

Double-Salmon Rillettes

◆◆ INTERMEDIATE PANTRY

Serves 4

Fresh salmon pairs with smoked salmon in this elegant yet homey spread. I confess to having made this using canned salmon a number of times, and it was very good.

The smoked salmon brings out the essential flavors of the fresh salmon, while the fresh mellows the rather intense salty quality of the smoked.

One 4-ounce salmon steak, about 2/3 cup cooked or canned salmon	1 very thin lemon slice
1 very thin onion slice	1 teaspoon brandy, or 1 very thin tomato slice (optional)
	1 tablespoon olive oil

Salt and pepper to taste

4 ounces smoked salmon (about 2/3 cup), cut into small bits

3 tablespoons unsalted butter

3 tablespoons softened cream cheese

2 tablespoons chopped fresh chives, or 2 green onions, thinly sliced

1. If using cooked or canned salmon, proceed to step 4 and skip steps 1–3. If using fresh, uncooked salmon, place fish on a piece of aluminum foil that is large enough to fold over and enclose the fish. Top fish with onion, lemon, brandy or tomato, olive oil, salt, and pepper. Wrap up to seal edges.

2. Cook by either baking about 6 minutes in a preheated 350° oven, or by steaming until flesh of fish is just firm, about 5 minutes.

3. Let salmon cool in its wrapping. When cool, unwrap, remove onion, lemon, and tomato and save juice to add to rillettes if they need thinning out.

4. Gently sauté smoked salmon in butter for a minute or two. Do not brown. Let cool.

5. Using a blender or food processor, chop the cooked fresh salmon, then add smoked salmon and its butter, cream cheese, and chives or green onions, taking care not to over-process. Add a little salmon cooking liquid if you need it. The mixture should have a coarse texture; use a spoon or fork if you need to instead of a processor. Serve chilled, accompanied with thinly sliced rye bread, baguette, or toasted black bread.

COFFEE, TEA, CHOCOLATE, WINES, AND SPIRITS

Coffee

Coffee drinkers are a passionate lot. I never realized how passionate until I wrote a feature on cappuccino and had to take my phone off the hook for three days as readers called in with suggestions, kudos, complaints, and just to talk. Maybe it was all that caffeine that made them so enthusiastic.

Good coffee's intense, bitter-fragrant taste lends itself to flavoring foods such as chocolate, ice cream, and other sweet dishes. Coffee also is used occasionally in savory dishes: Chinese braised beef, red eye gravy, etc.

Coffee should be bought by the bean and ground fresh each time you make it. Its essential oils are highly fragile, and will begin disappearing as soon as the beans are roasted, and even quicker once they have been ground. For this reason coffee should be purchased in small amounts from a trusted source.

Coffee beans are grown all over the world. While each bean has different characteristics, the main flavor difference is dark roast versus light roast, with dark giving the strong espresso or French-roast flavor.

There are many home methods for making coffee, including machines that grind the beans and brew the pot before you're even awake. There are drip coffee makers where you pour the hot water through the filter yourself, and French-press coffee makers in which you force a plunger down through a carafe of hot water mixed with grounds. Another method is the Middle Eastern ibrik, a tiny pot that produces the foamy thick Turkish coffee beloved throughout the Middle East. There are also inexpensive stove-top espresso makers that produce a very strong little cupful.

Leftover coffee of any sort can be sweetened and frozen into a granita or sorbetto, or it can be made into a syrup for ice cream. It also can be used as part or all of the liquid in making pound cake, or it can be heated and poured over chocolate to melt it for an outrageously deep, dark chocolate dessert.

STORAGE TIPS Store coffee in a cool, dark place. Many people freeze their beans, taking out only as much as they need at a time, while others keep their beans in the refrigerator. I've tried both and decided that I don't like the moisture and freezer/refrigerator flavors that infiltrate the beans. I keep mine on my pantry shelf, in a tightly sealed jar, away from strong light.

Espresso and Cappuccino The original espresso machines were invented simultaneously in Turin and Milano in 1903, and were improved on throughout the decades. The machines shoot a stream of hot steam through the coffee grounds, instantaneously brewing a thick syrupy essence of dark-roasted coffee. Cappuccino and other espresso drinks are made by adding milk and other flavors (see below).

Espresso drinks gained popularity in America in the fifties and sixties with students and artists who had been to Italy and tasted the strong frothy coffee and now wished to drink it at home. Today espresso and specialty coffees are everywhere, and home espresso machines are easy to use and affordable.

A Steamy Affair: A Guide to Espresso Drinks

◆◆◆◆◆◆

ESPRESSO Darkly roasted, specially ground coffee prepared by a rapid infusion of hot water through the grounds. Served in tiny thimble-like cups, often with a twist of lemon, which is frowned on by professionals.

CAPPUCCINO A single shot of espresso combined with hot steamed milk, topped with a frothy head of foam and a shake of cocoa or cinnamon.

CAFFÈ LATTE A shot of espresso topped with a generous amount of steamed milk. Usually served in a tall clear glass rather than a cup.

CAFFÈ MOCHA A shot of espresso topped with frothy hot chocolate.

MACCHIATO A shot of espresso topped with a dollop of foam. It is served in a tiny espresso cup and looks like a mini-cappuccino.

LATTÈ MACCHIATO Reverse the above: a large glass of steamed milk with a small shot of espresso poured on top. Unlike a latte, the espresso does not mix with the milk but floats through it, giving the milk a coffee-colored stain, hence its name, which in Italian means "stained."

CAFÉ AU LAIT A French combination of strong-brewed coffee (not espresso) mixed with steamed milk. It's best served in bowls as it is at breakfast in France and in many contemporary American cafes.

ESPRESSO CON PANNA Whipped cream spooned onto an espresso.

CAFFÈ L'AMORE Espresso topped with a scoop of gelato.

Sacramento Valley Cappuccino Milkshake

◆ BASIC TO
◆◆◆ ADVANCED PANTRY

Serves 2

In California's Sacramento Valley, where I grew up, espresso drinks have caught on with a passion in recent years. But in the excruciating heat of summer, the hot coffee of winter gives way to cooling, icy coffee drinks. Cappuccino milkshakes, sweetly cold and consummately refreshing, are offered at nearly every cafe.

1 cup milk
4 scoops coffee, vanilla, or
  chocolate gelato or other rich
  ice cream

2 shots cooled espresso or
  strong drip coffee

Whirl together into a froth.

Electrified Cappuccino Milkshake

For a hit of indulgence, add a splash of your favorite **firewater** to **above recipe.**

Caffè Chocolatissimo

◆ BASIC TO
◆◆◆ ADVANCED PANTRY

Makes one 4-1/2-by-8-1/2-inch cake

If you're not in love, this is the next best thing. It makes a dense and fudgy slab as redolent of strong coffee as it is of deep dark chocolate. Its brownie-like consistency is more suitable for nibbling in tiny bites than for heartily forking up, so remember that when you cut serving pieces.

Though it smells wonderful as it bakes (and the crust that forms is delicious to pick off and munch on), don't be tempted to eat it warm. It really is better the next day when it has firmed up.

4 tablespoons unsalted butter, at room temperature	Dash of salt
1 cup sugar	3/4 cup unsweetened cocoa
2 eggs	1 tablespoon finely ground
2 teaspoons vanilla extract	espresso or other dark-roast
1/2 cup plus 2 tablespoons flour	coffee (decaffeinated is fine)
Pinch baking soda	1/2 cup chocolate chips

FOR GLAZE

2 ounces semisweet chocolate	2 tablespoons unsalted butter
2 teaspoons dark corn syrup	at room temperature,
2 tablespoons strong-brewed coffee	in 8 pieces

1. Preheat oven to 350°. Cream butter with sugar, eggs, and vanilla. Stir in dry ingredients and mix until well combined, then add chocolate chips.

2. Pour into a buttered 4-1/2-by-8-1/2-inch loaf pan and bake for 20 to 25 minutes, or until cake appears crusty on top and but slightly soupy underneath surface. Do not let it get firm.

3. Remove from oven and let cool completely before glazing.

4. Remove from pan. Some of the bottom will probably stick, but scrape it out and stick it back on. Repairs won't show after glazing.

5. To make glaze: Combine chocolate, corn syrup, and coffee in a saucepan. Heat until melted, stirring constantly, then remove from heat and stir or whisk in butter 2 to 3 pieces at a time. Mixture should be smooth and glossy. Chill for 15 minutes, or until glaze is of spreading consistency, then use it to ice top of cake.

6. Let cool or chill, and serve in tiny pieces.

Tea

No more than fragrant dried leaves steeped in hot water, the range of teas covers as wide a palette as does that of coffee. Whether you choose smoky lapsang souchong or orange bergamot–scented Earl Grey, heart-pumping Irish breakfast or calming camomile, a selection of teas in the pantry gives you an excuse to stop every day at 4 o'clock, put the kettle on, and put your feet up.

Tea should be brewed from loose leaves rather than bags. Always heat the pot by pouring hot water in, letting it sit, then pouring the water off and proceeding to make the brew. Most allow 1 teaspoon per cup, plus "one for the pot." Sugar and lemon or milk are about the only other things you need to consider. But tea also may be spiced, Indian style, or iced, American style. Tea is also a good seasoning, though not as assertive or as versatile as coffee. The Russians classically macerate prunes and other dried fruit in hot tea. Lapsang souchong tea leaves make a fragrant base for sugar-smoking chicken or salmon, and a pinch of camomile is good added to chili powder for a Southwestern accent. And many of the fruit or flower-scented teas make a delightfully refreshing hot-weather ice.

Teas in the Pantry

◆◆◆◆◆◆

Alfalfa	Fruit-flavored teas:	Irish breakfast
Assam	apricot, mango,	Jasmine
Ceylon	orange spice, black	Keemun
Camomile	currant, almond,	Lapsang souchong
Darjeeling	apple, etc.	Mint
Earl Grey	Green tea	Oolong
English breakfast	Herbal mixtures	

Indian Sweet Spiced Tea

[MASALA CHAI]

◆◆ INTERMEDIATE PANTRY

Serves 4

Soothing and warm, this traditional Indian treatment of tea makes a fragrant and satisfying drink. It is delicious prepared with either black tea or an herbal one. With black tea you will get a pleasant caffeine jolt, insulated somewhat by the large amount of milk. Made with herbal tea, this drink comforts on a foggy evening and guarantees a restful sleep; you can give it to kids, too, making them feel rather grown up.

2 cups water
2 cups low-fat milk
1 cinnamon stick
6 to 8 whole cloves
1/2 teaspoon fennel seeds

1 tablespoon honey
2 to 3 teaspoons loose tea
(avoid tea with a tart lemony flavor)

1. Combine water, milk, cinnamon, cloves, fennel, and honey in a saucepan. Bring to a boil.

2. Remove from heat and add tea. Let steep for 5 minutes, then strain and serve.

Apricot Tea Ice

◆◆ **INTERMEDIATE PANTRY**

Makes 3 cups

This makes a particularly endearing summer ice, one of the most refreshing desserts I can think of to end a sophisticated meal or to spoon up on a sun-drenched afternoon.

3 to 4 teaspoons apricot
  tea leaves
3 cups boiling water
2 to 3 tablespoons sugar,
  or to taste

Juice of 1/8 to 1/4 lemon
  for garnish
Fresh edible flowers (optional)

1. Place tea leaves in a heatproof container and pour boiling water over them. Add sugar and let steep for 10 to 15 minutes.

2. Strain and add lemon juice. Let cool completely.

3. Freeze, using an ice cream maker or ice cube tray. (If you use a tray, stir mixture occasionally, scraping up with a fork as the ice crystals form, then whirl in a blender or food processor.)

4. Serve in champagne or wineglasses, garnished with edible flowers if possible.

Chocolate: A Short History

Long before the European settlers set sail for the New World, the Aztecs and Mayans were harvesting the indigenous cocoa beans, crushing them, and serving them brewed into a cold, bitter drink. They often drank this *chocolatl* as part of their ceremonial observances, believing it to be a source of strength and virility.

When the Spanish conquistadors landed they found the drink too bitter and added a bit of sugar and cinnamon. They then brought cocoa back to Europe (though cocoa beans did not flourish there, needing a more tropical climate). The Spanish were the first in Europe to succumb to the charm of chocolate, and sweet hot cocoa was a favorite delicacy of the court. By the beginning of the 17th century, chocolate was becoming the rage in Italy.

The rest of Europe, however, was slow to embrace this strange new concoction, and the drink did not become accepted in France until Louis XIV married Spain's Maria Theresa. Around the same time a Frenchman opened a chocolate shop in London, and from there it spread throughout the rest of Europe.

The American chocolate industry started in the late 1700s, when a certain James Baker opened a chocolate mill (Bakers Chocolate is still one of America's favorites). But chocolate was still consumed primarily as a drink.

"Eating chocolate" as opposed to "drinking chocolate" didn't come about until the mid-1800s, when an Englishman devised a technique to solidify it to an edible consistency; 30 years later a Swiss confectioner began adding milk solids to make milk chocolate.

A Guide to Chocolate Types

Choosing a selection of chocolates for the pantry is easy; keeping them in the pantry is not. Except for bitter unsweetened chocolate, nothing stretches out its beckoning fingers more than does the luscious brown stuff. It can be difficult to keep a chunk of chocolate waiting in the wings for that special cake when the urge to nibble—now—takes over. Let me take this moment to mention that my grandmother still works a full week, doesn't believe in being sick, and has eaten chocolate—sometimes lots of chocolate—nearly every day of her life. My daughter seems to be following in her footsteps.

COCOA The dry powder that remains when the fat and solids are separated. It is essentially chocolate with the fat removed.

COCOA BUTTER is the fat that is removed.

DARK CHOCOLATE Sweetened chocolate without the addition of milk; also known as bittersweet, or semisweet, chocolate.

MILK CHOCOLATE has had milk solids added.

BITTER CHOCOLATE is used only in cooking (its intense bitterness makes you wonder how anyone could have ever drunk it without sugar).

MEXICAN CHOCOLATE has a distinctive whiff of cinnamon.

WHITE CHOCOLATE Sweetened and flavored cocoa butter, without the cocoa solids.

Chocolate Sandwich

◆ BASIC PANTRY

Serves 1

This is plainly one of the tastiest, most satisfying things you could eat. It's delicious dipped languidly into a bowl of café au lait for a lazy Sunday breakfast.

1 thick slice best crusty bread you can find

Unsalted butter, softened
Big slab bittersweet chocolate

Spread bread with butter, then top with chocolate. Eat immediately.

New York Egg Cream

◆ BASIC PANTRY

Serves 1

A legendary drink, evocative of Old New York and the candy store cum soda fountain. The egg cream is sweet, chocolatey, sparkling, and tasting of childhood pleasures. Yet it also is an elegant balance of richness and clarity.

An egg cream, contradicting its name, contains only milk, chocolate syrup, and seltzer: no eggs, no cream. The name, some say, was a witty way of describing richness at a time when no one in his or her right mind could have afforded to put both egg and cream in the same drink.

3 tablespoons really good chocolate syrup
1/4 cup ice-cold milk

3/4 cup ice-cold seltzer (for artistry in egg cream, use a seltzer bottle)

1. Put chocolate syrup in bottom of a 12-ounce glass. Add milk and stir slightly.

2. Slowly add seltzer (add it quickly and you risk painting the kitchen walls with egg cream).

3. Sip off the foam as it forms, then squirt in more seltzer.

VARIATION After you make one egg cream once, you will be a connoisseur, able to adjust the amounts of chocolate, milk, and seltzer you prefer.

Amaretto Hot Chocolate

◆ BASIC PANTRY

Serves 1

Make your favorite **hot chocolate** and add a good shot of **Amaretto** liqueur **or almond flavoring.** Top with **whipped cream** flavored with a bit of sifted **lightly sweetened cocoa.**

Black Magic Cake

◆ BASIC PANTRY

Makes one 8-inch cake

This cake is wickedly chocolate, given a bitter edge by pouring hot coffee over the chocolate and letting it melt rather than heating the chocolate in a double boiler. The result is not only easier to prepare, but the coffee perfumes the chocolate and gives it depth. And when the chocolate is melted and you pour off the coffee, you will have a delicious cup of chocolate-scented coffee to drink.

This cake is a variant of "chocolate decadence," which has been making the rounds in recent years, having originated in France. Cover it in whipped cream, festoon it with fresh fruit, to celebrate something. Highly recommended as a 40th-birthday cake, to help kill the pain.

1 pound chocolate chips	4 large eggs
2 cups very strong, very hot coffee	Pinch salt
1/4 cup sugar	2 teaspoons vanilla extract
1 cup (2 sticks) unsalted butter, at room temperature	Whipped Cream and Fruit Topping, following

1. Preheat oven to 350°.

2. Place 2 cups chocolate chips in a bowl; pour hot coffee over them. Cover and let stand for 5 to 10 minutes, or until chocolate has melted. (*Note:* The coffee will stay separate from melted chocolate and should not be stirred in.) Pour coffee carefully off chocolate and save to drink.

3. Quickly, before chocolate cools and hardens, add sugar, butter,

eggs, salt, and vanilla, and stir until smooth. This may be done easily in a blender or food processor. Stir in remaining chocolate chips.

4. Spray an 8-inch-round and 3- to 4-inch-deep cake pan with non-stick spray, or grease with butter and dust with flour. Pour chocolate mixture into pan and bake 30 to 40 minutes, or until a crust forms on top.

5. Remove from oven and cool. Loosen sides of cake from pan with knife, then carefully invert onto a plate. If any of the bottom falls off—as it always does for me—just press it back on. It will be covered in cream and nobody will see it. Chill until ready to serve.

Whipped Cream and Fruit Topping

1 cup heavy (whipping) cream	6 ripe nectarines
3 tablespoons sifted powdered sugar	1 teaspoon sugar, or to taste
1/2 teaspoon vanilla extract	1 tablespoon brandy
	1/2 cup strawberries

1. Whip cream until just thickened. Add powdered sugar and vanilla and continue whipping until thick and firm, with lovely peaks.

2. Slice nectarines and combine with sugar and brandy.

3. Frost cake with whipped cream, then surround with nectarines and scatter with strawberries.

White Chocolate Fondue with Raspberries

◆◆ INTERMEDIATE PANTRY

Serves 4

White chocolate, melted into a puddle of warm cream and flavored with a wicked dash of fruit brandy, is a delicious amazement, especially spooned over the contrasting flavors and textures of crusty bread and fragile raspberries.

8 ounces good-quality white chocolate	1 loaf fresh crusty French or Italian bread, cut into slices or bite-sized chunks
1/4 cup heavy (whipping) cream	1 cup raspberries
2 tablespoons unsalted butter	
2 tablespoons fruit brandy (eau-de-vie, not liqueur, which is very sweet)	

1. Break or cut white chocolate into small chunks. Process in a blender or food processor until it is in small pieces or coarse grains.

2. Gently heat cream and butter together, stirring until butter is melted. Add chocolate and stir until melted and smooth.

3. Add brandy and serve warm, accompanied with bread and raspberries. Since both fresh bread and raspberries are too delicate and fragile to dip with, simply spoon some warm creamy white chocolate over each bite of bread or spoonful of berries as you eat.

Beers, Wines, and Spirits in the Pantry

Keep a selection of beers, wines, and spirits in your pantry for the wide array of flavors they add to your food. Throughout this book are scattered recipes with a splash of liqueur or a touch of wine.

To expand on the selection of beers, wines, liqueurs, and spirits in your pantry, you may want to build a basic wine cellar or a collection of drinking wines. Put yourself in the hands of a good wine merchant, who can help you put together a cellar that suits your tastes and budget.

With or without a wine cellar, the odd half bottle of wine leftover from a dinner party is a flavorful gift in the kitchen: sprinkle strawberries with Zinfandel or Beaujolais and sugar, add a spoonful or two of red wine to a bowl of rustic vegetable soups, as they do in Southwest France; ditto for green salads. Wine is added to marinades for a reason: it breaks down tough membranes and helps tenderize any meat it's added to while giving flavor to the meat. And wine-simmered stews are what stews are meant to be.

Pantry List: Beers, Wines, and Spirits

Beer, imported and domestic: light lager-type beer, robust dark beer, ale, stout
Bourbon
Brandy, Cognac
Campari
Cassis
Grappa
Liqueurs: Grand Marnier or another orange-flavored one, fraises du bois (wild strawberry), kirsch, framboise (raspberry), poire William (pear), Tia Maria or another coffee-flavored liqueur, Amaretto, Irish Mist, Frangelico, etc.
Marsala or Madeira
Ouzo, Pernod, or Sambuca
Port
Sherry: dry (fino), semi-dry
Tequila
Vermouth, dry
Vodka
Whiskey: Irish, domestic, or Scotch
Wines: white, red, rosé, and sparkling

Red Wine Lamb Ragout with Garlic, Herbs, Peas, and Gnocchi

◆◆ **INTERMEDIATE PANTRY**

Serves 6

Once you've browned the meat and added everything else, the stew will simmer away on its own, emitting a warm fragrant steam throughout the house. This recipe, by the way, works equally well with beef.

Gnocchi adds to the niçoise flavor of the dish. If you've no gnocchi, serve with crusty bread or olive oil–mashed potatoes. Accompany with a salad of mixed greens and herbs, and end the meal with a lovely goat cheese and a plate of whatever fruit is sweetest and freshest in the market.

NOTE Like all long-simmered foods, this is even better the next day.

3 pounds stewing lamb, cut
    into pieces slightly larger
    than bite-sized
1/2 cup flour for dredging,
    or as needed
3 tablespoons olive oil for
    sautéing, or as needed
Salt and black pepper to taste
3 to 4 carrots, diced
2 to 3 leeks, cleaned and cut
    into large dice
3 fresh tomatoes, or 2/3 cup
    canned tomatoes, diced
1/2 teaspoon dried thyme leaves
    (or one sprig fresh thyme)
    or to taste

3 bay leaves
1/4 cup tomato paste
1 cup beef broth
1 bottle robust red wine
    (Merlot, Zinfandel, etc.)
Zest of 1/4 orange, cut
    into thin strips
1 garlic head, separated into
    cloves, peeled, and cut into
    small pieces but not chopped
2 cups fresh or frozen peas
12 ounces vacuum-packed or
    fresh gnocchi (about
    2-1/2 to 3 cups uncooked)

1. Toss lamb with flour. Brown in olive oil and season with salt and pepper. Add carrots and leeks and continue sautéing until vegetables are wilted a bit.

2. Add tomatoes, thyme, bay leaves, tomato paste, beef broth, red wine, orange zest, and garlic. Bring to a boil, then reduce heat and either simmer on top of stove or place in a 325° oven and bake. Either way it will take about 3 hours.

3. Skim off excess fat. If sauce is thin, pour off as much as you can and boil it down to reduce it to a more concentrated, flavorful sauce, then return it to meat. Add peas.

4. Meanwhile, cook gnocchi in boiling salted water until al dente. Drain.

5. Serve gnocchi topped with the long-simmered lamb and peas.

LEFTOVERS Layer the **red wine lamb and pea stew** with al dente **short pasta** for a French casserole called *macaronade*. Add shredded **Parmesan** and **Gruyère** to the layering and bake in a hot oven until browned and bubbly on top.

Seven Things to Do with Red Wine

◆◆◆◆◆◆

When using wine in cooking, as when drinking it, quality counts. Cooking with the same wine you will be drinking adds continuity to a meal.

◆ Prepare a dressing for salad that won't fight with the wine you drink for dinner: Mix 1 tablespoon mustard of choice with 1 tablespoon red wine, then whisk in 3 tablespoons olive oil. Add salt and pepper to taste.

◆ Use red wine as the braising liquid for any sort of meat or poultry dish.

◆ Make a marinade based on red wine: Grate an onion and add it to a chopped garlic clove, 1 cup red wine, 1/2 cup olive oil, and herbs such as oregano or basil. Use for lamb.

◆◆◆◆◆◆

◆ FAIRE CHABROT A tradition from the Southwest of France: pouring a few ounces of red wine into the bottom half of a bowl of robust vegetable soup.

◆ Make Sangría Guadalajara Style, page 335.

◆ Deglaze a pan after sautéing to make a sauce; use for beef, veal, lamb, turkey, duck, or salmon.

◆ Use red wine as half of liquid, along with broth, for cooking a risotto; Italian sausages are good in this, too.

Risotto with Grappa

◆◆ **INTERMEDIATE PANTRY**

Serves 4

Sauté 1 **onion** and 3 chopped **garlic cloves** in 3 tablespoons **olive oil** until softened. Stir in 1 cup **Arborio rice** and let it lightly brown in the onion and olive oil mixture.

Mix 1/3 cup **grappa** with 3 cups hot **broth,** then stir in about a third of this mixture, stirring rice as it absorbs liquid, then adding another third, and repeating until all liquid is absorbed. The rice should be al dente by now.

Stir in 2 tablespoons **unsalted butter,** 1/4 cup grated **Parmesan cheese, salt** (if needed), and **pepper.**

Hot Pepper Tequila–Tomato Cream Pasta

◆◆ INTERMEDIATE PANTRY

Serves 4

A delicious transcontinental sauce pairing the vivid flavors of Italy with the no-less-vivid ones of Mexico. It's an adaptation of the vodka-tomato-cream sauces that were popular in Rome a few years ago, several of which tiptoed around America. The sauce is especially good with pasta topped with seafood such as shrimp, crab, or lobster.

2/3 pound fresh pasta
4 garlic cloves, chopped
2 tablespoons olive oil or butter
1/4 teaspoon red pepper flakes, or to taste
2 tablespoons tequila
8 medium tomatoes, diced (canned may be substituted)

1/3 cup heavy (whipping) cream
Salt and pepper to taste
4 to 6 ounces cooked fresh crab-meat or lobster chunks, or lightly sautéed shrimp (optional)
Grated Parmesan cheese (optional)

1. Bring salted water to a boil and cook pasta until al dente; drain.
2. Meanwhile, warm garlic and pepper flakes in oil, lightly sauté-ing. Remove from heat and add tequila. (Keep your face away from pot, as it may flame up dangerously and dramatically. I redecorated my eye-brows once this way.)
3. Return pan to heat and boil to evaporate alcohol, taking care here, as it is apt to burst into flames if it hasn't already.
4. When flames have died down and liquid is reduced by half, add cream. Cook over medium heat a few more minutes. Season with salt and pepper and serve tossed with hot pasta (and seafood of choice, if desired). Serve immediately, dusting with Parmesan, if desired.

Jalapeño-Tequila Mignonette

This recipe is adapted from Charles Saunders's mignonette at the Sonoma Mission Inn. Chef Saunders serves it with raw oysters on the half shell, but I think the addition of tiny spicy grilled sausages or sliced, grilled merguez or chorizo is a nice contemporary interpretation of a French classic.

1/4 cup white wine vinegar	1 tablespoon chopped
1/4 cup tequila	jalapeño chili
1 tablespoon chopped red	1 tablespoon minced shallot
bell pepper	Salt and pepper to taste

Mix all ingredients.

Sun-drenched Red Pepper and Tomato Soup with Ouzo

This chunky puree of garlic-sautéed peppers and tomatoes with a hit of anise-scented ouzo tastes of the essence of Mediterranean food. Though it's adapted from a recipe I published in another book, the soup is so wonderful it's worth repeating.

Serve as a first course for a celebratory supper when sweet peppers and tomatoes have just come into their own. Begin the meal with the last-of-the-season asparagus, steamed al dente and served cool, with a yogurt-lightened lemony mayonnaise. Proceed to Swordfish Steaks with Sun-dried Tomatoes and Lemons and Artichokes, with olive oil–mashed potatoes on the side. For dessert? Apricot Tea Ice, page 401.

1 medium onion, chopped	2 tablespoons ouzo, or to taste
3 to 5 garlic cloves,	2 teaspoons paprika
chopped coarsely	1/2 teaspoon herbes
2 tablespoons unsalted butter	de Provence
1/2 teaspoon fennel seeds	2 cups chicken or
2 medium red bell peppers,	vegetable broth
coarsely chopped (for a	1/2 cup sour cream
pantry-only soup, use	Sharp Lemon Cream, follow-
roasted red peppers from	ing, for topping
a jar)	1 tablespoon chopped fresh
1 cup chopped fresh or	herbs such as parsley or
canned tomatoes	thyme for garnish

1. Lightly sauté onion and garlic in butter until softened, then add peppers and cook over medium heat until peppers are softened.

2. Add tomatoes, ouzo, paprika, herbes de Provence, and broth, and cook over medium-high heat until mixture comes to a boil.

3. Puree mixture coarsely, leaving a little texture in soup. Stir sour cream to smooth out any lumps, then add several spoonfuls of soup to it. When that is smooth, add it to soup and stir well to mix in.

4. Serve soup immediately, each portion topped with a spoonful of lemon cream.

SHARP LEMON CREAM Mix 1/2 cup **sour cream** with grated **zest** of 1/4 lemon and **juice** of 1/2 lemon, plus a dash of **cayenne pepper**.

Zinfandel Slush with Fruits of the Forest

◆◆ INTERMEDIATE PANTRY

Serves 4

Wine ices are a sophisticated version of a childhood pleasure. I love the phrase "fruits of the forest"; it makes me think of hunting for berries among the trees and bushes. Try to find wild strawberries, fraises du bois, for 1/2 cup of the strawberries.

2/3 cup water
1/2 cup sugar
1-1/2 cups strawberries, cleaned and sliced
1 bottle Zinfandel

1/2 cup *each* fresh blackberries, blueberries, and raspberries
1 tablespoon sugar or fraises du bois liqueur to taste

1. Combine water and sugar and heat gently until sugar has dissolved. Raise heat and bring to a boil, then continue boiling for 5 minutes. Set aside to cool completely.

2. Puree 1 cup strawberries and, once syrup is cooled, combine with pureed berries. Add wine and freeze. Because of alcohol content, sorbet will not freeze solid but remain a bit slushy.

3. Mix whole berries and remaining 1/2 cup sliced strawberries with sugar or liqueur, and serve sorbet-slush with 1 or 2 spoonfuls of berries on top of each serving.

Watermelon-Vodka Slushy

◆ BASIC PANTRY

A suggestion rather than a recipe: Freeze chunks of deseeded **watermelon** on a baking sheet. (You may store these in the freezer, in a plastic bag, for up to 2 weeks.)

Puree watermelon chunks with a hit of **vodka,** a squeeze of **lemon,** and a sprinkling of **sugar.** Whirl until slushy, then enjoy.

Grapefruit Segments with Campari

◆◆ INTERMEDIATE PANTRY

Serves 2

Separate a sweet **grapefruit** into segments, then drizzle with a bit of **Campari** just before serving. Serve as an appetizer rather than a dessert.

Cassis-Cognac Raspberries over Macadamia Brittle Ice Cream

◆◆◆ ADVANCED PANTRY

Serves 4

Macerate, for 10 minutes or so, 1 box (1 cup) **raspberries** in a few spoonfuls of **cassis** and **cognac,** along with a sprinkle of **sugar.** Serve spooned over **macadamia brittle ice cream.** Bliss.

Pineapple with Kirsch, Pistachios, and Orange Zest

◆◆ INTERMEDIATE PANTRY

Serves 4

Peel and slice a sweet **pineapple,** removing as much of central core as you like.

Sprinkle with **powdered sugar, kirsch,** chopped unsalted toasted **pistachio nuts,** and a grating of **orange zest.** Serve immediately.

Fresh Figs in Red Wine

◆ BASIC PANTRY

Serves 4

Allow 4 to 5 **figs** per person. Poach until tender in **red wine** sweetened with a little **sugar;** add a dash of **vanilla extract.** Serve topped with **whipped cream or ice cream.**

Cantaloupe with Port

Serves 2

Slice a ripe, juicy-sweet, just-chilled **cantaloupe** into manageable pieces. Splash lightly with your favorite **port.**

Pomegranate Seeds in Orange Liqueur and Brandy

Serves 4

Remove seeds from 2 large **pomegranates** and toss with a little **powdered sugar** if they are tart. Drizzle with **orange liqueur** and **brandy** and chill before serving.

Oranges with Orange Liqueur and Tequila

Serves 4

Slice 3 ripe sweet peeled **oranges** and toss with a teaspoon or two of **sugar,** a tablespoon or two of **orange liqueur,** and a tablespoon or two of **tequila.** Serve topped with a little grated **lime zest.**

Cherries Poached in Red Wine, Hungarian Style

Serves 4

Simmer 2 cups pitted **ripe red cherries** (preferably pie cherries) in 1-1/2 cups **red wine** with **sugar** to taste and a **cinnamon stick or 1 teaspoon ground cinnamon.**

When cherries are just tender, remove them from wine and boil wine down, reducing volume by one half. Beat 1 cup **sour cream** and stir in, mixing well, then taste for sweetness and season with a dash of **vanilla or almond extract.** Pour sauce over cherries and chill before serving.

Tipsy Milkshakes

◆◆ INTERMEDIATE TO
◆◆◆ ADVANCED PANTRY

Serves 2

Boozy, frothily whipped wonders of ice cream, crushed ice, and fruit. Serve for a lazy summer brunch or as a reviving dog-days dessert. Suggested combinations: Peach ice cream, peaches, Amaretto, brandy; pears, Frangelico, hazelnut ice cream; coffee ice cream and Sambuca (no fruit); black cherry or vanilla ice cream, black cherries, Amaretto, brandy.

2 scoops ice cream
1 cup crushed ice
1/4 cup brandy

1/4 cup liqueur of choice
   (such as almond,
   fraises du bois, etc.)
1 cup fruit to match liqueur
   (peaches, strawberries, etc.)

Whizz all ingredients in a blender until well combined and milkshake-like.

Georgia Peach Wine Bowl

◆ BASIC PANTRY

Serves 6

This wonderfully fragrant, cool mixture of white wine is lightened with the fizz of sparkling water and perfumed with the summer aroma of fresh peaches. Perfect to sip on a Sunday afternoon when the weather is oppressive, enjoying the sounds of summer as the afternoon fades into evening.

4 to 5 ripe sweet peaches or
   nectarines, peeled and
   thinly sliced
2 to 3 tablespoons sugar
   or to taste

2 cups sparkling water
1/4 to 1/2 cup brandy (or peach-
   or apricot-flavored brandy)
1 bottle dry white wine

1. Combine peaches with sugar and let sit for at least 30 minutes.
2. When ready to serve, pour in remaining ingredients and serve over crushed ice.

VARIATION Add a handful of **berries** to the **peach and wine bowl,** along with a dash of **fraises du bois or framboise.**

INDEX